CENTRAL LONDON

LONDONACCESS FOCUS

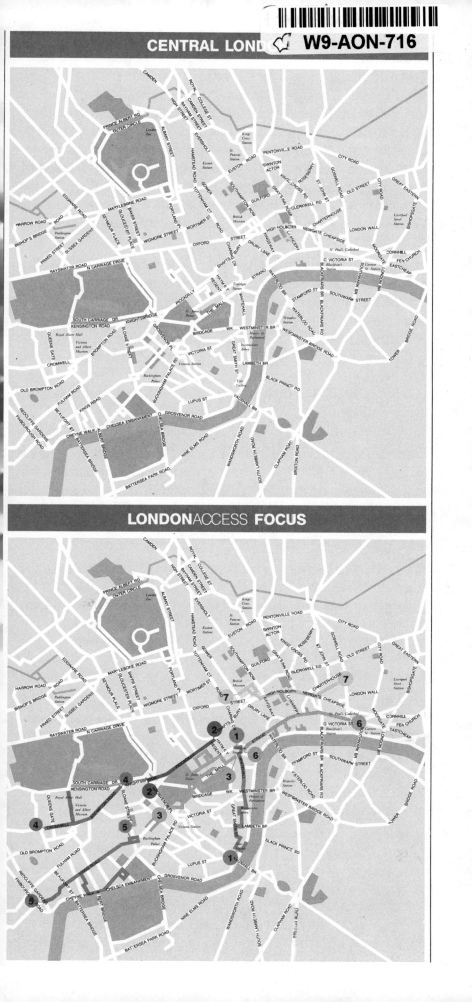

A walk down **Whitehall** from **Trafalgar Square** to **Westminster** is a kind of pilgrimage, a sleeve-shaped journey which echoes the River Thames, covers one-and-a-half acres of land, 900 years of history and thrives as headquarters for history-in-the-making. Kings and queens are still crowned here, democracy is still guaranteed here, and in a rare mood of architectural harmony, power is still juxtaposed here. The **Houses of Parliament**, representing temporal power and the daily democracy of life, serves as a foil for its ancient neighbor, **Westminster Abbey**, seat of spiritual power and the ultimate democracy of death.

Unlike the English, Trafalgar Square is emotional and chaotic. Only partially, accidentally and belatedly did the Square come into its inspired position as gateway to democracy, a pragmatic stretch linking Whitehall with the Houses of Parliament. London's only *grande place* where her citizens can gather to express their joys and concerns, the Square impartially upholds the democratic ideals legislated 500 yards away by Parliament and administered in between by Whitehall. It is design justice that the Square keeps an eye on both.

The walk passes the 3 most prestigious clubs in the land: the **National Portrait Gallery,** the **House of Commons** and **Poet's Corner,** as well as 3 ancient pubs where the distinguished, and those who report on the distinguished, have been quenching their thirsts for centuries. Predictably, the concerns of the great and powerful are primarily greatness and power, so ordinary concerns—shops, banks, hotels—are in rather short supply.

You might stop for lunch on a boat moored to the Thames or for a concert at **St. John's, Smith Square.** You may see the Prime Minister leaving **Downing Street** or entering the House of Commons. You could have a drink in a pub filled with Members of Parliament, only to realize it when the division bell rings and the place empties like a fire drill. Your tour of Westminster Abbey may be delayed by a wedding or a funeral, an encouraging reminder that this magnificent and historical place is not a museum.

The walk ends at the **Tate Gallery,** where you can be restored by tea and scones in the Gallery cafe and be brought to life by the incandescent light in the late paintings by Turner. At the end of the walk, standing on the steps of the Tate and looking out at the Thames, at Millbank and Vauxhall Bridge Road, you may wonder if it is a day by Monet, the pre-Raphaelites or Whistler.

On weekends, Westminster and Whitehall are abandoned to tourists. MPs return to their constituencies, civil servants stay home and many of the restaurants, pubs and shops which exist primarily to serve the governing elite shut as well. The ideal time for this walk is Monday through Thursday when Parliament is in session, even if you have no parliamentarian concerns. On Sunday, the most interesting parts of Westminster Abbey are closed, and the galleries (National Portrait and Tate) don't open till 2PM.

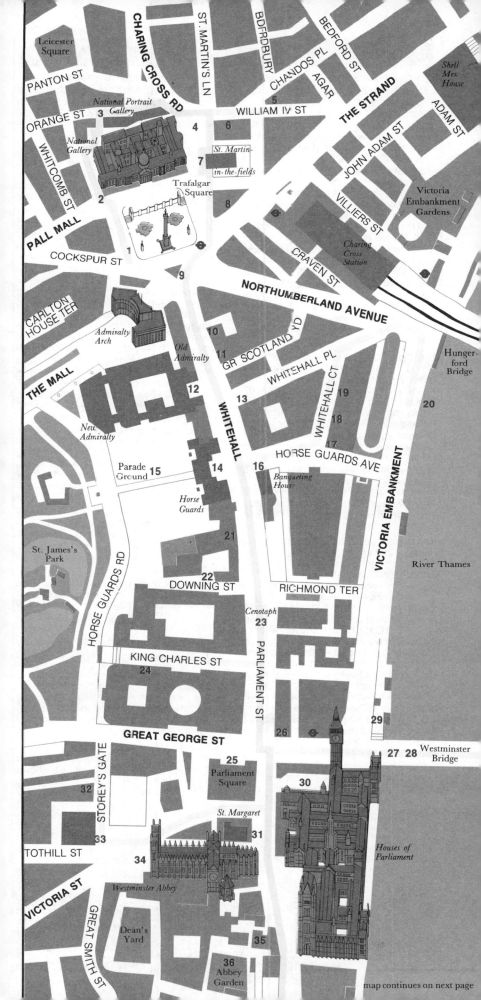

Leicester Square

PANTON ST

CHARING CROSS RD

ST. MARTIN'S LN

BDFDRDBURY

CHANDOS PL

BEDFORD ST

AGAR

Shell Mex House

THE STRAND

ADAM ST

National Portrait Gallery

ORANGE ST

3

WILLIAM IV ST

5

WHITCOMB ST

National Gallery

4

6

John Adam St

Victoria Embankment Gardens

St. Martin-in-the-fields

7

2

Trafalgar Square

8

VILLIERS ST

PALL MALL

1

9

COCKSPUR ST

Charing Cross Station

CRAVEN ST

NORTHUMBERLAND AVENUE

Hungerford Bridge

CARLTON HOUSE TER

Admiralty Arch

10

11

GR SCOTLAND YD

Old Admiralty

WHITEHALL PL

19

THE MALL

12

13

WHITEHALL CT

18

20

New Admiralty

17

HORSE GUARDS AVE

Parade Ground

15

14

16

Banqueting House

VICTORIA EMBANKMENT

HORSE GUARDS RD

Horse Guards

21

St. James's Park

River Thames

22

DOWNING ST

RICHMOND TER

Cenotaph

23

KING CHARLES ST

PARLIAMENT ST

24

29

GREAT GEORGE ST

26

27 28 Westminster Bridge

STOREY'S GATE

25

Parliament Square

30

32

St. Margaret

33

31

TOTHILL ST

34

Houses of Parliament

VICTORIA ST

GREAT SMITH ST

Westminster Abbey

Dean's Yard

35

36

Abbey Garden

map continues on next page

4

4

WHITEHALL

1 Trafalgar Square. (1841) The Square is a testament to England's victory over Napoleon's fleet in the decisive battle off the coast of Spain in 1805, the Battle of Trafalgar. It is even more monumental testimony to the defeat of anything like *Napoleonic* vision in town-planning. Trafalgar Square is London's grandest place. If this was Paris, Haussmann's ruthlessness would have us looking down heart-stopping vistas of Buckingham Palace and Westminster Abbey; broad avenues would connect the Square to Regent Street and the British Museum; and the Square itself, instead of sunken, treeless and confused, would be greenish, elevated and uniform. The triumph of the English at Trafalgar, and 7 years later at Waterloo, was also a triumph of Englishness. Trafalgar Square honestly reflects the victory of democratic style over dictatorial grandeur: the military, architectural and dramatic defeat of what the English dislike most—ostentation.

Until the 1830s, the site was occupied by the Royal Mews, when mews were for mewing—the shedding of old plummage and the growing of new. Edward I (1272-1307) kept his hawks here, and Richard II (1367-1400) kept his falcons and goshawks, a rather distinguished legacy for the famous pigeons and starlings who mew monotonously in the Square today. By the reign of Henry VIII (1491-1547), horses were kept in the Royal Mews. William Kent (1685-1748) built the Royal Stables on this site, then known as Great Mews, Green Mews and Dunghill Mews. The stables stood until 1830, when they were replaced by the National Gallery.

The original designs for the Square were made by **John Nash** (1752-1835), who had already brought elegance and grandeur to London with Regent's Street, Regent's Park and Marble Arch, under the aegis of the Prince Regent, later George IV. With Regent Street, Nash provided the first north-south axis to connect London's 3 main east-west routes (Oxford Street, Piccadilly and the Strand). In his early sketches of Trafalgar Square, Nash saw the site as the medieval turning-point in the road leading from Westminster Abbey to St. Paul's Cathedral. There was no open space, only a widening where the bronze statue of Charles I had stood since 1675, marking the spot where the 3 roads met. Nash designed the Square as a grand axis connecting government (Parliament Square), finance (the City) and aristocracy (St. James's and the Royal Parks). Unfortunately, Parliament accepted Nash's site and rejected his designs. The English may have won the Battle of Trafalgar, but they lost the Battle of Trafalgar Square.

Trafalgar Square as you see it today is the work of **Charles Barry** (1795-1860), the distinguished architect of gentlemen's clubs, including the Reform Club and the Travel-ler's Club in Pall Mall, and the club of clubs, the Houses of Parliament. Barry favored the Italian palazzo style, and he created in Trafalgar Square an economic, Victorian interpretation of the piazza.

Nelson's Column. (1843) Horatio Nelson (1758-1805) entered the service of his country at the age of 12, suffered from seasickness all his life, lost his right eye at the Battle of Calvi, his right arm at Santa Cruz and his life at Trafalgar. The hero whose last words were *Thank God, I have done my duty* is now exiled in perpetuity 170 feet overhead in a grey London sky.

In a city where the sun is no incentive and the past is all-pervasive, there seems to be no need to rush things, and by and large, Londoners do not. From the time of Nelson's funeral at St. Paul's (1805) and the raising of his column in Trafalgar Square (1843), almost 40 years went by. Architect **William Railton's** design of a massive Corinthian column won the competition for the monument in 1837. The capital is of bronze cast from cannons recovered from the wreck of the *Royal George.* On the sides of the pedestal are 4 bronze bas-reliefs cast from the metal of captured French cannons, representing incidents in the battles of St. Vincent, Aboukir, Copenhagen and Trafalgar.

The statue of Lord Nelson is by the sculptor **EH Bailey.** The figure of the naval hero is 17 feet 4 inches high, and his sword measures 7 feet 9 inches. Together with the column, the monument is as tall as an 18-story building, a satisfying reward for a man who was 5 feet 4 inches in real life.

Guarding the column are 4 vast (20 feet by 11 feet) and loveable lions by Queen Victoria's favorite animal painter, **Sir Edwin Landseer.** Late arrivals, it is these magnificent, tender-faced creatures who humanize the Square.

Four octagonal oil lamps which have been converted to electricity occupy the corners of the Square. They are reputedly from Nelson's flagship, *HMS Victory.* One likes to think so.

Every year on 21 October, the anniversary of the Battle of Trafalgar, a parade and service is held in the Square by members of the Royal Navy. Officers from modern ships of the fleet lay wreathes at the bottom of the column, and descendants of those who fought at Trafalgar place an anchor of laurels. Nelson, a genius for naval battle, was a hero with a gift for inspiring devotion.

Statue of George IV. Most noticeable of the many other notables in the Square is George IV (1762-1830), under whose auspices Nash first conceived the Square and who worshipped Nelson (although the feeling was not mutual). After the Battle of Trafalgar had established Britain's command of the seas, George IV commissioned Turner's great battle piece, *The Battle of Trafalgar* (hanging in the National Maritime Museum, London). But George IV's great

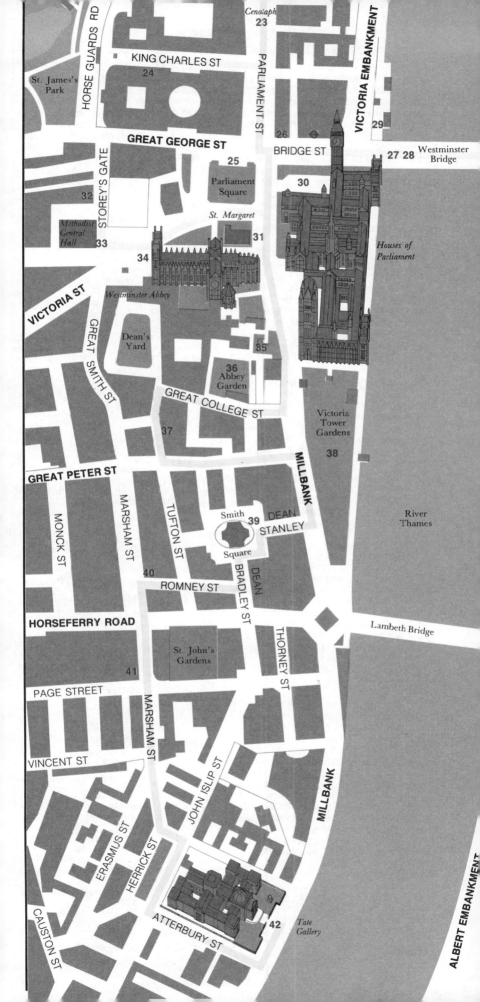

obsession was architecture. As Prince Regent he built the Brighton Pavillion; as King he rebuilt Buckingham Palace and transformed Windsor into the finest of all the palaces of the British monarchy. An expert horseman, he commissioned most of the equestrian paintings by **George Stubbs** in the Royal Collection. Therefore it is baffling that this statue by **Sir Francis Chantray,** commissioned by George IV to surmount Marble Arch, shows the King in Roman dress, riding bareback without stirrups. Completed and placed in the square 12 years after the King's death, *King George IV* had to be added because no one knew who it was.

Statue of James II. Another king in Roman dress, James II (1633-1701), seems less affected, mainly because he had the good luck to have **James Gibbons** (1648-1720) as sculptor. Impulsive and bullheaded, James II annoyed Parliament with his pro-Catholic wife and politics. He was succeeded by his protestant daughter, Queen Mary II, and spent the last 11 years of his life in exile in France.

The naval influence in Trafalgar Square continues with busts of 3 modern heroes: Admirals **Beatty** and **Jellicoe** of the First World War, and Admiral **Cunningham** of the Second. Carved into the stone of the north wall between Jellicoe and Cunningham are the **Imperial Standards** for length, showing you the exact measurements of an imperial inch, foot, yard, rod, chain, pole or perch.

Fountains. In a city blessed with rain, fountains are few. Barry's original fountains and their large pools were part of a design to break up the large, unruly crowds which the government of the day was perceptive enough to realize would congregate. Even with the fountains and their pools, 50,000 people can and do congregate in the Square when the cause of democracy calls. The original fountains designed by Barry now face Parliament in Ottowa, Canada. **Sir Edwin Lutyens** (1869-1944) designed the fountains in the Square to commemorate Admirals Jellico and Beatty. They have first-rate water power, and each morning at 10AM, the earthly mermaids and mermen respond to the repetitive booms of Big Ben in the distance by democratically christening nearby Londoners and visitors, people and pigeon.

The late **Sir John Benjamin,** Poet Laureate and passionate defender of Victorian architecture, saw the weighty stone buildings that surround Trafalgar Square as an historic backdrop. Looking left in the direction of Whitehall are **Herbert Baker's South Africa House** (1935), its somber classical facade indifferent to the opponents of Apartheid who patrol the sidewalk night and day; the rounded **Grand Buildings** (1878) and **Trafalgar Buildings** (1881) designed by the **Francis Brothers** (refurbished instead of demolished); **George Aitchison's Royal Bank of Scotland** (1885); **Reginald Blomfield's Uganda House** (1915); and **Canada House** (1827), the most handsome building on the Square, built by **Robert Smirke.** Originally the Royal College of Physicians, this building of warm Bath stone has suffered from conversion and extension of the upper parts but remains a dignified presence.

2 **National Gallery.** (1838, William Wilkins) The most important building in Trafalgar Square is the National Gallery anchoring the north side. Architects complain that the scale of the neo-classical building is weak in relation to the Square, but the blame should fall on a parsimonious Parliament which compelled Wilkins to use the columns from the demolished Carlton House in the portico. The original building was only one room deep, more a facade than a gallery. But its limited size—now much expanded with an extension in progress—had no effect on its importance. Although relatively small (just over 2,000 pictures), it houses one of the most comprehensive surveys of Western art. (*See the* **St. James's Walk** *for complete details*).

3 **National Portrait Gallery.** (1895, Ewan Christian, JK Colling) After getting your bearings in Trafalgar Square, this is where to begin a day in London, a stay in England or a trip to Europe. It is not an art gallery—eminence of the sitter, not the artist, is what counts. More eloquent than words, the faces in the portraits are the history of England: history as poetry, biography and prophecy. Resist the temptation to wander through the bookshop first or amble up the stairs. Take the slow elevator to the top floor and begin, confusingly, a few steps down on the upper mezzanine. Here you will find the first portrait to break away from the stylized representations of kings: a very natural and touching young **Richard II** (1377-99). Sensitive, cultivated and artisitic, Richard appreciated beauty and was a patron of Chaucer. His talents were for art and beauty and love (he was heartbroken when

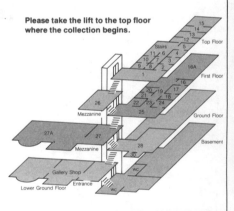

Please take the lift to the top floor where the collection begins.

Top Floor	First Floor
1 The Tudors	16A Special Exhibition Area
2 James I to the Civil War	16 The Young Victoria
3 The Mid-17th Century	17 The Early Victorians
4 The Restoration	18 The 1840s: Poverty
5 William and Mary	and the People
and Queen Anne	19 The Empire
Landing The Jacobites	20 Victorian Technology
6 Early 18th Century	21 Victorian Writers
Arts and Sciences	and Artists
7 The Kit-cat Club	22 Lecture Room
8 George I and George II	23 The Later Victorians
9 The Arts in the	24 The 1880s and 1890s
18th Century	25 The Edwardians
10 Britain Overseas	**Upper Mezzanine**
11 The Struggle	26 The Middle Ages
for America	**Lower Mezzanine**
12 Britain at War	27 The Royal Family
13 The Romantics	27A Special Exhibitions
14 Science and the	**Ground Floor**
Industrial Revolution	28 The Twentieth Century
15 The Regency	30 Special Exhibitions
	(20th Century)

his wife, Anne of Bohemia, died), but the young King had no talent for politics. Deposed by his cousin Henry IV, Richard II was murdered at Pontrefact Castle. This painting of the King is a copy (the original is down the street in Westminster Abbey), but it is an emotional beginning to a royal procession where art, history and British civilization converge.

The great age of portraiture began with the Tudors when **Hans Holbein** (c. 1497-1543) became court painter to **Henry VIII** (1491-1547). Brought to England from Holland by Erasmus, Holbein was the greatest 16th century artist to work in England. His portraits show a profound perception of character, at once powerfully direct and full of nuance. Through Holbein, Henry VIII is indelibly fixed in our minds, although unfortunately for the King, the artist arrived in England after the King was no longer thin, young and handsome.

The most celebrated, acclaimed and painted monarch of all time is **Elizabeth I** (1533-1603), who was virtually an icon during her reign. In many of her portraits, even the decorations on her clothes are emblematic—an ermine on a sleeve symbolizes chastity, pearls represent purity. Elizabeth I's legendary ability to rule was enhanced by being a living idol to her people, a work of living art.

Alongside the kings and queens are the writers who captured the ages for us in words: a portrait of **Shakespeare** (1564-1616) by an unknown artist, the best likeness of the playwright which exists; **Samuel Pepys** (1633-1703) by **John Hayls**; and then a painting of the poet **John Donne** (1572-1631) in *Room 2* which tells us to be dazzled but not blinded. Donne was almost a contemporary of Elizabeth I. While she was proclaiming herself Gloriana, more than mortal, Donne was writing of a heaven *where there shall be no darkness nor dazzling, but one equal light; no noise nor silence, but one equal music; no fears nor hopes, but one equal possession; no ends nor beginnings, but one equal eternity.* As the paintings in the 25 rooms make brilliantly clear, England would not come close to such a heaven on earth for several hundred years. Don't miss:

Holbein cartoon of Henry VIII in black ink and colored washes on paper, part of a wall-painting for Whitehall Palace (now lost). Still visible are the hundreds of tiny pin-pricks which the artist used to transfer his designs to the wall. *Top Floor, Room 1.*

Elizabeth I by Marcus Gheeraets the Younger, done soon after the defeat of the Spanish Armada. The Queen is standing triumphantly on her kingdom of England, stormclouds behind and a brilliant sky before her. *Top Floor, Room 1.*

Charles I and Sir Edward Walker after the campaigns in the West Country in 1644-45. A look of serenity and sadness on the face of the King, as though to presage the tragic future. *Top Floor, Room 2.*

Oliver Cromwell with his son by Walker (c. 1649) **and miniature of Oliver Cromwell by Samuel Cooper (1656).** Both paintings show a man aware of the tragedy around him, and the miniature by Cooper, the finest miniaturist of all, shows a psychological subtlety rare in any painting. *Top Floor, Room 2.*

Admiral Horatio Nelson, Viscount Nelson. Unfinished but brilliant portrait painted from life by **Sir William Beechey** in 1800-01, showing all the passion and fire of the hero who destroyed Napoleon's sea power and of the man, brave, tender and honest. Opposite Nelson is **Emma, Lady Hamilton** (1761-1815) done by **George Romney** in 1785. She was the great love of Nelson's life, the mother of his daughter Horatia, and part of one of the great love stories in British history. *Top Floor, Room 10.*

The Romantics: 3 portraits—**William Blake** (1757-1828) by **Thomas Phillips** in 1807, visionary poet and artist; **John Keats** (1795-1821) by his friend **Joseph Severn** in 1821 one of England's best-loved and finest poets who died in Rome of tuberculosis at the age of 25; and **Lord Byron** (1788-1824) by **Thomas Phillips** in 1814, the Romantic Man-poet, lover and revolutionary. Byron captured the poetic and romantic imagination of the age and died in Greece fighting for Greek independence. *Top Floor, Room 13.*

Jane Austen (1175-1817) by her sister Cassandra. This tiny drawing is the only likeness that exists of the beloved and acute observer of the human heart. *Top Floor, Room 15.*

The Brontë sisters, by their brother Branwell (c.1835). Anne, Emily and Charlotte in a moving portrait of the 3 sisters looking young and serious. The ghost in the background is Branwell, who painted himself out of the portrait. Also by Branwell is the very beautiful, cracked portrait of Emily Brontë. *First Floor, Room 17.*

Charles Darwin (1809-82) by John Collier. A haunting, spiritual portrait of the man who used science to destroy the myth of creation. *First Floor, Room 20.*

Elizabeth Barrett Browning and Robert Browning painted by Gordigian in 1858, in the same room as a portrait by **Ballantyne** of the artist **Landseer** sculpting the lions that are now outside in Trafalgar Square. *First Floor, Room 21.*

Henry James (1843-1916) by John Singer Sargent. The American writer who loved London and settled in England, painted on his 70th birthday by the American artist who lived in London and became the most fashionable portrait painter of his generation. *First Floor, Room 25.*

Beatrix Potter (Mrs. Heelis, 1866-1943) by Delmar Banner in 1938. Peter Rabbit, Jemima Puddle-Duck and Mrs. Tiggy-Winkle were all created by this quintessential Englishwoman who drew animals with great affection, and now draws great, affectionate crowds. *First Floor, Room 25.*

The Twentieth Century on the Ground Floor. Royal portraits including Prince Charles wearing his polo clothes and Princess Diana when she was still plump and girlish; political portraits including Nancy Astor by Sargent and Churchill by Sickert; artist's portraits including Delius by Munch, James Joyce by Blanche, WH Auden, TS Eliot, Dylan Thomas and Virginia Woolf; self-portraits by contemporary British portraitists, including Sickert, Sutherland and David Hockney. Temporary exhibitions are held here and are always worth a look.

The **National Portrait Gallery Bookshop** on

WHITEHALL

the ground floor is one of the best shops for postcards (the best-seller is the melancholy portrait of Virginia Woolf). All the heroes and heroines upstairs are down here in alphabetical order. Like museum shops the world over, this one has cleverly expanded. It stocks all the books you are in the mood to read after gazing at the portraits above.

No admission fee. Occasional charge for special exhibitions. Open M-F 10AM-5PM, Sa 10AM-6PM, Su 2-6PM. Closed national holidays. 2 St. Martin's Place, WC2. 930-1552

There is no cafe within the Portrait Gallery, but next door in the **National Gallery Restaurant** you can have a late second breakfast, lunch or tea. Run by Justin de Blank Ltd., it is a cut above the usual gallery/museum fare. You can order light salads, wine and cheese, tempting cakes and herbal teas. Sit and write postcards from the Portrait Gallery Bookshop. *Open M-Sa 10AM-5PM, Su 2-5PM. Trafalgar Square, WC2. 930-5210*

4 **Statue of Edith Cavell.** In the small island next to the National Portrait Gallery and behind Trafalgar Square is a monument to Edith Cavell (1865-1915), a nurse who was shot by the Germans in 1915 for spying and helping British prisoners escape. The statue by **Sir George Frampton** (1860-1928) was unveiled in 1920 by Queen Alexandra. Four years later, the Labor Government added her famous words, *Patriotism is not enough,* a sentiment which would have shocked Nelson, who thought patriotism was everything.

5 **The Chandos.** ★ ★ $ A cooked English breakfast is served from 8 to 10:30AM in *The Opera Room* on the first floor of this handsome pub across the street from the Post Office. *Open daily 8AM-12PM. William IV St.*

6 **Post Office.** One of the liveliest buildings around Trafalgar Square is the Post Office, built in the 1960s. It used to be open 24 hours a day, and is still London's only post office with late hours. *Open M-Sa 8AM-8PM, Su 10AM-5PM. 24 William IV St., WC2. 930-9580*

7 **St. Martin-in-the-Fields.** (1726 James Gibbs) John Nash's design for Trafalgar Square was never realized. But his role in it endures because it was his idea to open up the vista which brings St. Martin-in-the-Fields into the Square. The church is not actually part of the Square, but it is doubtless its single source of pure loveliness. Built by **James Gibbs** (1682-1754), its Wren-like steeple rises 185 feet from the ground, almost the same height as Nelson's Column. The steeple atop the portico of Corinthian columns has been an inspiration for many American churches. The porch offers shelter to passers-by on rainy days, and the steps are a resting place for tired tourists. On Monday and Tuesday at 1:05PM, you can enjoy the famous lunchtime concerts of chamber and choral music in the light and airy church where Charles II was christened and his mistress Nell Gwynn was buried. *Concerts free. St. Martin-in-the-Fields, Trafalgar Square, WC2. 930-0089*

8 **Lyon's Corner House.** ★ $ Although you can't imagine Virginia Woolf, Bertrand Russell or TS Elliot here, this restaurant was once part of a chain of eating palaces that are documented in the London novels and memoirs of a whole era. Now they have all been replaced by hamburger chains, except for this newly resurrected one just off Trafalgar Square. You can sit down for an English breakfast between 8 and 10AM or get a quick cup of hot chocolate, coffee or tea if you need warming up. *Open daily 8AM-8PM. 450 The Strand, WC2. 930-9381*

Whitehall: A Royal residence for 160 years, from the reign of Henry VIII to James II; a street connecting Trafalgar Square to Parliament Square; a concept—more synonym than euphemism—for civil service, bureaucracy and government administration. However confusing the concept of Whitehall is for the average citizen, for the visitor to London it is hopeless. You can *go* to Whitehall, *be* Whitehall, *represent* Whitehall, and be told that sooner or later in this country, all roads lead to Whitehall—and none more hazardous than those which actually lead to Whitehall from Trafalgar Square. The royal palace which gave the area its name was destroyed by fire in 1698, and the name, White Hall, was simply a term for a grand hall used for banquets and festivities. Now it is a half-mile of stone buildings from Trafalgar Square to Westminster Abbey with high, impenatrable facades, tall cupolas and serious names: the Foreign Office, the Commonwealth, the Admiralty, the Ministry of Defense, the Civil Service Department, the Cabinet Office, the Treasury and, down a side street, the official residence of the Prime Minister.

9 **Statue of Charles I.** (1633) Whitehall physically begins at the statue of Charles I (1600-1649) on his horse, gazing onto the scene of his tragic execution at Banqueting House on 30 January 1649, with Parliament looming in the distance. It was his quarrel with Parliament that led to his downfall. In 1642 civil war erupted between the Parliamentarians (the Roundheads, led by Oliver Cromwell) and the Royalists (known as the Cavaliers) over Parliament's demand to approve the King's choice of ministers. Charles was tried for treason to the realm and died on the scaffold.

Now stranded in an islet, unreachable except by the most intrepid pedestrian, Charles I is the oldest, finest and most poignant statue in London. The horse's left foot bears the date *1633* and the signature of the sculptor, Frenchman **Hubert Le Sueur.** When the Civil War broke out in 1642, the statue was hidden in the churchyard of St. Paul's, Covent Garden. After the King's execution, Cromwell sold the statue for scrap to a resourceful brazier named John Rivett. A brisk trade in candlesticks, thimbles, spoons and knifehandles, a kind of *Charles I Souvenir Shop,* thrived until the Restoration, when the statue miraculously reappeared. Charles II rewarded the Royalist brazier with £1,600. The statue finally found its home on Whitehall in 1675.

The King, whose last word was *Remember,* is remembered every year at 11AM on 30 January, the anniversary of his execution, by a solemn procession from St. Martin-in-the-Fields to his statue. Wreaths of flowers are placed at his monument by members of the Royal Stuart Society.

10 **Silver Cross.** ★ ★ $ Charles I licensed this as a brothel and pub in 1643. The facade is Victorian, but the building is 13th century, with a wagon-vaulted ceiling, ancient walls sheathed in lead and, in the bar, a plaster ceiling embossed with vine leaves, grapes and hops made while Charles I was still living down the street. For the past 250 years, it has been the *local* for the Old Admiralty next door, and for nearly as long it has been the pub of journalists who report on Whitehall. It opens early and serves English breakfasts, home-cooked lunches, afternoon teas and excellent evening buffets. A warm and special pub. *Open M-F 8AM-11PM, Sa-Su 9AM-10:30PM. 33 Whitehall, SW1. 930-8350*

11 **Clarence.** ★ ★ $ A Whitehall institution, this 18th century pub has gaslights inside and out, oak beams overhead, sawdust on the floor and wooden tables and pews. The old farm equipment on the beams may be in deference to the regulars from the Ministry of Agriculture next door, but this is also a pub for connoissieurs of real ale: a choice of 7 served with full bar meals twice daily. *Open M-Sa 11AM-3PM, 5:30-11PM; Su 12-2PM, 7-10:30PM. 53 Whitehall, SW1. 930-4808*

12 **Old Admiralty.** (1725, Thomas Ripley) The stone screen adorned with sea horses is by **Robert Adams** and leads into the cobbled courtyard. For 200 years the world was run from this building, and while the world has changed, the Old Admiralty has not. In the Board Room upstairs, a wind dial (1708) over the fireplace still records each gust of wind over the roof, even though no one waits here for a sign that the wind will carry the French across the Channel. The present Admiralty still meets in the building. Smoking has never been allowed, a rule that even Churchill humbly obeyed.

In Trafalgar Square you feel Nelson's presence; here you feel his heart. It is possible to imagine him warming himself by the fire and checking the time by the clock which has stood in the room since the Admiralty was built. The room has changed little since Nelson took his orders here, or from when he returned 5 years later to lay in state, awaiting his funeral at St. Paul's. In the vestibule stands Bailey's original model for Nelson's statue in Trafalgar Square. *Open by appointment and for groups only. Apply in writing to Old Admiralty, Spring Gardens, London, SW1.*

13 **Ministry of Defense.** (1898, William Young and Son) In this more pacific age, the Old War Office is called the Ministry of Defense. Inevitably, it lacks the romance of the Old Admiralty across the street, but the Baroque domes above its corner towers, visible from Trafalgar and Parliament Squares as well as St. James's Park, have a lingering Imperial grandeur. *Whitehall, SW1.*

14 **Horse Guards.** (1750-60, William Kent) The 2 troopers are magnificent and impassive on their horses, elegant concoctions of tunics and plumes under archway and clock tower. Even the twin sentry boxes are pure Gilbert and Sullivan. The **Mounting of the Guard** takes places at 11AM each morning (don't confuse this with the **Changing of the Guard** which happens at 11:30AM at Buckingham Palace). Londoners under the age of 12, the best judges of these things, prefer the daily calvary show at Horse Guards to the infantry performance outside Buckingham Palace. The real experts race through St. James's Park and see both. Young would-be soldiers will also explain that the red tunics and white plumes are the Life Guards, blue tunics and red plumes are the Blues and Royals, the soldiers are not allowed to talk, and if you don't touch their swords or the velvet-soft muzzles of the horses, you can photograph or be photographed with them.

The Horse Guards have been guarding since the days of Charles II (1630-85) when they guarded Whitehall Palace. The Palace burned down in 1698, but the guarding has continued. Horse Guards itself was rebuilt in 1760. It was designed by **William Kent** but built after his death by **John Vardy.** So what do they guard now? Less palatial concepts—like history, tradition and magic. *Mounting the Guard: M-Sa at 11AM, Su at 10AM. Mounted guardsmen are on duty around the clock. Whitehall, SW1.*

15 **Horse Guards Parade.** Go through the arch at Horse Guards and you will be in Horse Guards Parade. Ignore, if you can, the cars and dwell on the white stone and splendid Palladian building with arches, pediments and wings, architecturally one of the finest buildings in London. The Parade ground, now so ingloriously used as a parking lot for Whitehall's high and mighty, used to be the Whitehall Palace tiltyard. In 1540, Henry VIII invited knights from all over Europe to compete in a tournament on this site.

Every year on the second Saturday in June, the Queen leaves Buckingham Palace on her horse Burmese and rides to Horse Guards Parade for the **Ceremony of Trooping of the Color.** This is the most spectacular military display of the year in a country that has no rival in matters of pomp. An annual event dating back to medieval times, it was originally an exercise to teach soldiers to recognize their regimental flags. Now it is the sovereign's official birthday, ceremonial acceptance that English weather does not guarantee a successful outdoor occasion before June. Crowds line the Mall to watch the Queen, an accomplished horsewoman, seated sidesaddle, ride with instinctive dignity into Horse Guards Parade. The Queen on a horse is incomparably majestic. *Behind Horse Guards, Whitehall, SW1.*

Opposite the Horse Guards, at Banqueting House, is the site of the **old Whitehall Palace,** once the largest palace in all of Europe. It began in 1245 as the London residence of the Archbishops of York, called **York Place,** and acquired dimensions of grandeur in 1514 when Cardinal Wolsey moved in. The Cardinal had already begun the incomparably splendid Hampton Court, the palace outside London which rivaled Versailles in size and sumptuous splendor. Thus it was an experienced hand that created the palatial proportions in York Place, building magnificent gardens, a wine cellar, a chapel and lavish accommodations for the lords, knights and ambassadors of Europe. Wolsey presided over a miniature Renaissance Court that included 23 acres, 800 servants and *folie* and audacity, as Henry VIII, his neighbor and King, lived a few yards down the road in very second-rate accommodations at the Palace of Westminster. After the Cardinal's fall in 1530 (he failed to obtain papal consent for the King's divorce from Catherine of Aragon), Henry VIII lost no time in making York Place his. He changed the name to Whitehall, acquired the land to the west from the Abbot of Westminster and created St. James's Park, built 3 tennis courts, a tiltyard (now Horse Guards Parade) and a bowling alley. Henry VIII married Anne Boleyn here, and he died here in 1547. Elizabeth I was taken from the Palace of Whitehall to be prisoner in the Tower, then returned in triumph as Queen. The first performance of *Othello* was performed at Whitehall. After the execution of Charles I in 1649, Oliver Cromwell moved into the Palace, with John Milton as his secretary. Cromwell died here in 1658, and Charles II succeeded him to the throne here. It remained the royal residence until the reign of William III, when on 4 January 1698, a fire started by a laundrymaid burned the Palace to the ground. All that remains today is the name, the wine cellar, a riverside terrace, the walls of the tennis courts and Banqueting House.

16 **Banqueting House.** (1622, Inigo Jones) On a bitter winter's day in January 1649, a small procession left St. James's Palace and walked through the park to Whitehall. A King of England was going to his execution. Crossing Whitehall, Charles I may have gotten his first glimpse of the scaffold built outside the central windows of Banqueting House and his last look at the perfectly proportioned Palladian building commissioned by his father James I.

Inigo Jones

Banqueting House and the fate of Charles I are inextricably bound. The proportions of the hall, one of the grandest rooms in England, create a perfect double cube at 110 feet long and 55 feet high. This design represents the harmony of the universe, peace, order and power—the virtues of divine kingship instilled in Charles I by his father. The magnificent ceiling, which Charles commissioned from **Peter Paul Rubens,** represents the apotheosis of James I, a visual statement of James's belief in the absolute right and God-given power of kings. If you follow the panels from the far end of the room, you see James rising up to heaven, having created peace on earth by his divine authority as King: peace reigns, the arts flourish and the King is defender of his realm, the faith and the Church.

When Charles I tried to impeach 5 members of Parliament, Civil War broke out between the Parliamentarians and the Royalists. Seven years later, the King was tried in Westminster Hall and convicted of treason to the realm.

On the day of the execution, Charles I wore a second shirt so that he would not shiver in the cold and have his people believe he was afraid. He was a king in life and a sad and courageous king in Death: *I go from a corruptible to an incorruptible crown where no disturbances can be.*

With one blow, England was without a king, and severed with Charles's head was the belief in the divine right of kings. Until this moment, kings were the chosen representatives of God on earth. Now men would choose princes.

Three centuries later England still has her kings and queens, and Banqueting House still stands. In spite of being one of the most important buildings in all of English architecture, it is almost always empty. Empty but not haunted: there is no feeling that the ghost of Charles I lingers under the newly cleaned ceiling. A bust of Charles I over the staircase entrance (added by **Wyatt** in 1798) marks the site of the window through which he stepped onto the scaffold. *Small admission fee. Open Tu - Sa 10 AM - 5PM, Su 2 -5PM. Whitehall, SW1. 930-4179*

17 **New Ministry of Defense Building.**
(1959, Vincent Harris) These vast
buildings were placed behind Whitehall on
Horse Guards Avenue out of respect to the
scale and proportion of Inigo Jones's Banqueting House. Started just before the First
World War (1913) and completed after the
Second (1959), this is where the real prob-
lems of war and peace are handled—with a
few exceptions. In the basement is all that
survives of the original Whitehall Palace:
Henry VIII's wine cellar. The Tudor brick-
vaulted roof is 70 feet long, 30 feet wide and
weighs 800 tons. Because the wine cellar in-
terfered with the line of the new building, it
was moved 40 feet to one side, lowered 20
feet and then pushed back to its original site.
A huge excavation was made, a mausoleum
of concrete and steel built around the cellar
to protect it, and a system of rollers devised
which shifted the cellar a quarter of an inch
at a time until it had completed its journey
of 43 feet. The whole operation was finished in May 1949, two-and-a-half years after
it began, and cost £100,000 when that was
a vast sum. All the same, you can only see
it on Saturday afternoons by appointment.
*Apply in writing to the Department of the
Environment. Horseguards Ave., Whitehall,
SW1.*

18 **Whitehall Court.** (1884, Archer and
Green) This massive Victorian attempt
at a French château was a grand apartment
building—both HG Wells and George Bernard Shaw had flats—and home of several
clubs, including the Farmers' and the Liberal
Club. *Whitehall Court, SW1.*

19 **Royal Horse Guards Hotel.** *Moderate.*
Once the apartments of the influential,
the 284 rooms and suites overlooking the
Thames are now for the affluent. The reception rooms and the restaurant, the **Granby,**
have the feel of a gentlemen's club, but the
guest rooms are light and spacious and
more feminine. At lunchtime the hotel bar
fills with civil servants from the Ministry of
Defense, a quieter breed than that which fills
the pubs nearby. *2 Whitehall Ct., SW1. 839-
3400*

20 **RS Hispaniola.** ★ ★ $$ Walk down
Whitehall Place or through the gardens
behind Whitehall Court to reach Victoria Em-
bankment on the Thames and have lunch or
dinner in this *restaurant ship* floating on the
river. The boat doesn't actually go any-
where, but watching other boats sailing up
and down the river makes you feel maritime.
When the sun is out, sit on the upper deck
and eat fresh Colchester oysters. The fish
is excellent and the menu features game in
season. *Spanish. Reservations recom-
mended. Open M-F 12-2PM, 7-10:30PM; Sa
7-10:30PM. Victoria Embankment, West-
minster Pier, WC2. 839-3011*

21 **Cabinet Office.** (1733-36, formerly the
Treasury) Several great architects had
their hands in the design, including **William
Kent, Sir John Soane** and **Sir Charles
Barry** (1846). The building exudes Victorian
self-confidence and weightiness. At the
north end is the office of the Privy Council,
the Queen's private council comprising
princes of the blood, high officers of the state
and Members of Parliament appointed by
the Crown. It seems fitting that Sir Walter
Raleigh, once a member of Elizabeth I's
Privy Council, stands opposite. (Raleigh ex-
hibited a very stiff upper lip on the scaffold.

Testing the ax for its sharpness he re-
marked, *This is a sharp medicine, but it will
cure all diseases.) Whitehall, SW1.*

Drawing courtesy of David Gentleman

22 **Downing Street.** History and television
have made the street one of the most
famous and familiar in the world. But modern
politics and terrorism have shut it off from the
public. Named after its builder, **Sir George
Downing** (Harvard, class of 1642), the street
lost its quiet, residential air when **No. 10**
became the official residence of the first
prime minister, Sir Robert Walpole, in 1735.
The facade is modest, but inside there is
considerable grandeur. Some of the women
who have lived in the house have com-
plained about the lack of space and light. But
Margaret Thatcher, the first female occu-
pant to be Prime Minister, makes few com-
plaints and shows no signs of preferring to
live elsewhere.
No. 11 Downing Street is the official resi-
dence of the Chancellor of the Exchequer.
No. 12 is the office of the Chief Government
Whip, the title for the Member of Parliament
responsible for organizing and maintaining
discipline in the party ranks in the House of
Commons.

23 **Cenotaph.** (1919, Sir Edwin Lutyens)
Rising in the center of Whitehall is this
austere memorial to the dead of the First and
Second World Wars. The simple structure
of Portland stone shows no sign of imperial
glory or national pride or religious symbol:
it is not a monument to victory but a monu-
ment to loss. Between the wars, men would
take off their hats whenever they passed.
Now hats have gone out of style and
memories have faded, but once a year, on
Remembrance Sunday (second Sunday in
November), a service is held to remember
the dead of these wars. It is attended by the
Queen, the royal family, representatives of
the Army and Navy, the Prime Minister and
leading statesmen. Wreaths are placed at
the monument while bands play the haunt-
ing music of Elgar's *Nimrod.* At 11AM, a 2
minute silence is observed in memory of
the dead.

24 **Cabinet War Rooms.** Churchill
masterminded the British war effort
from this complex 17 feet underground, and
now six of the rooms are open to the
public. You will find the room where the War
Cabinet met and the control room crammed
with phones and maps covered with marker
pins showing the positions of military

defenses. Churchill made his stirring wartime broadcasts from the room behind the door marked *Prime Minister*. You can almost hear that steadfast, bear-like growl: *Let us therefore brace ourselves to our duties and so bear ourselves that if the British Empire and its Commonwealth last for a thousand years men will still say, this was their finest hour.* It is amazing to think that from these poky little rooms Churchill brilliantly conducted a global war. *Admission fee. Open Tu-Su 10AM-5:50PM. Clive Steps, King Charles St., Whitehall, SW1.*

The Battle of London

At tea time on a gloriously fine Saturday afternoon—7 September 1940—400 German planes came over London and bombed a virtually undefended city. After dark another armada of 250 bombers followed, helped to their targets by fires already blazing every mile along both sides of the Thames. By dawn, 430 civilians had been killed, and 1,600 carried wounded from the debris of their homes...This was the start of the Battle of London--Goering's blow right into the enemy's heart...

For 57 nights without let-up the Luftwaffe attack continued. Every night during that September and October, bombers were over, at least 200 strong. London was caught off-balance. Defense was impossible, devastation enormous. The death toll: 9,500... By this, the first mass civilian attack in history, the Germans hoped to force a surrender. It failed.

London: 2000 Years of a City and its People, by **Felix Barker** and **Peter Jackson**. MacMillan Publishers Ltd., London, 1974

25 **Parliament Square.** (1850, Sir Charles Barry) Barry conceived the Square as a kind of garden foreground to his new Houses of Parliament. The first monument you see is **Winston Churchill** standing on the corner looking obstinate, determined and onto the House of Commons, which he loved with all his heart and all his life. This 12 foot bronze statue by **Ivor Robert-Johns,** unveiled in 1973, has not transformed the landscape or led to the renaming of Parliament Square. But it is the memory of Churchill more than Nelson or King Charles I that dominates Whitehall. Among the many other brooding statesmen in the Square are **Disraeli** (Lord Beaconsfield) by **Raggi** (1833); and **Abraham Lincoln,** tall and rumpled and looking like the man who knew too much. His statue is a copy of the **St. Gaudens'** in Chicago.

26 **St. Stephen's Tavern.** ★ ★ ★ $ This is Parliament's pub, complete with a division bell which rings to warn the MPs to go back across the street and vote. Even though it looks a little seedy on the outside, wedged between junky souvenir shops, inside it has a sense of importance. The **Dive Bar** serves good seafood and English cheeses, and the restaurant upstairs features good English food (game, Scottish beef, spring lamb). MPs and political journalists are serious drinkers, so this place is usually full. Cartoons of MPs who have won, lost and died cover the walls. *Pub open M-Sa 11AM-3PM, Su 12-2PM. 10 Bridge St., SW1. 830-3230*

Earth has not anything to show more fair:
Dull would he be of sould who could pass by
A sight so touching in its majesty:
This City now doth, like a garment, wear
The beauty of the morning; silent, bare,

Ships, towers, domes, theatres, and temples lie
Open unto the fields, and to the sky;
All bright and glittering in the smokeless aire.
Never did sun more beautifully steep
In his first splendour, valley, rock or hill;
N'er saw I, never felt, a calm so deep!
The river glideth at his own sweet will:
Dear God! The very houses seem asleep;
All all that mighty heart is lying still!

William Wordsworth (1770-1850)
Composed upon Westminster Bridge, 3 September 1803

27 **Westminster Bridge.** (1862, Thomas Page) Once you get this close to the Houses of Parliament, you really have to walk onto Westminster Bridge. The Gothic buildings, rising almost vertically from the Thames, are one of the most famous views in the world and an inspiration for poets and painters and believers in democracy. The 810 foot cast iron bridge is not the one that inspired Wordsworth to write his sonnet. But the view surpasses by far what Wordsworth saw that early morning in 1803. He would not have seen the highly-wrought Houses of Parliament with the imposing Victoria Tower. He could not have set his watch by the clock lovingly, if wrongly, called Big Ben. Looking down the river, he would not have seen Whitehall Court, the Shell-Mex House, the Savoy or Somerset House in the background. Standing on the new Westminster Bridge stirs up poetic feelings and the magnificence of Westminster and Whitehall reveals itself.

28 **Boadicia.** (1902, Thomas Thorneycroft) Queen Boadicea, a symbol of liberty, is well-placed at the Westminster end of the bridge, looking out onto the Houses of Parliament from her chariot. Under the rule of the Emperor Nero, a savage revolt broke out in the newly conquered province of Britain when Roman soldiers forced their way into the palace of the widowed Queen Boadicia. They flogged the Queen for refusing to surrender the lands of the Iceni and raped her 2 daughters. In her fury, Boadicea led a savage rebellion, massacring the inhabitants of the Roman capital at Colchester, then turning south to the undefended port of Londinium. No mercy was shown, and the flourishing town was quickly destroyed. 70,000 lost their lives. But the revenge of the Queen of Iceni was short-lived. The Romans, led by Paulinus, met the Britains in a formal battle and annihilated them. Boadicea and her daughters took poison, ending the rebellion. In the bronze statue, Boadicea has her 2 half-naked daughters at her side, but the cause of freedom is made more difficult in a chariot that lacks reigns.

29 **Westminster Pier.** Perhaps the only thing better than walking in London is floating along the Thames. Westminster Pier is the main starting point for boat trips downstream to the **Tower of London** and upstream to **Kew** and **Hampton Court.** *From April to October, boats going upstream leave about every 20 minutes starting at 10AM and boats going downstream leave every 30 minutes from 10:30AM. From March to November, services to the Tower and Greenwich leave every half hour. Full information is available from the River Boat Information Service, Westminster Pier, 730-4812*

30 **Houses of Parliament.** (1840-60, Sir Charles Barry and Augustus Pugin) To the modern world, no single view so powerfully symbolizes democracy as this assemblage of Gothic buildings that look as though they have been here throughout the 900 years this has been the site of English government. In fact, these buildings have been standing just over 100 years, but their Gothic style powerfully represents the aspirations and traditions of those 9 centuries. The *Symbol of Democracy*, the *Mother of Parliaments*, remains a royal palace. It is officially called the New Palace of Westminster, a name which goes back in history to the 11th century when this was the site of the old Palace of Westminster. First occupied by Edward the Confessor (1042-66), the building was the principal London residence of the monarch until 1529, when Henry VIII moved down the street to Whitehall Palace. Parliament continued to sit here until the Palace was burned to the ground in the disastrous fire of 1834. All that is left of the ancient Palace of Westminster is the undercroft and cloisters of **St. Stephen's Chapel** and **Westminster Hall.**

After the fire of 1834, it was decided to build new and enlarged Houses of Parliament on the same site. A competition was held for a building in either the Gothic or Tudor style. The winners were **Sir Charles Barry** and **Auguste Pugin.** Barry gave the buildings an almost classic body. Pugin, with his unrivaled knowledge of Gothic style, created a meticulous and exuberant Gothic design. The Houses of Parliament is built on an axial plan which reflects almost ladder-like the hierarchical nature of British society: House of Commons, Commons Lobby, Central Lobby, Lords Lobby, House of Lords, Princes Chamber and Royal Gallery. The building covers an area of 8 acres and has 11 courtyards, 100 staircases, 1,100 rooms and 2 miles of passages. The House of Commons is in the northern end (MPs enter from New Palace Yard on the corner of Bridge Street and Parliament Square) and the House of Lords is in the southern end.(The Peers entrance is in Old Palace Yard, where **Guy Fawkes** was hanged, drawn and quartered in 1606 for trying to blow up Parliament and where Sir Walter Raleigh was beheaded in 1618.)

Within the Houses of Parliament are:

Westminster Hall. (1097) Built by **William Rufus,** son of William the Conqueror, this vast, barn-like room is where Parliament began and where Simon de Montfort marched in and enforced it. At the end of the 14th century, Richard II had the hall rebuilt (c. 1320-1400, **Henry Yevele**), adding the massive buttresses which support 600 tons of oak roof. The Hall contains the earliest surviving example of a hammerbeam roof, which was a miracle of engineering in its day—it marked the end of supporting piers. The austere and venerable room has witnessed earth-shaking moments of history almost since its beginning. Under the benevolent eyes of the carved angels in the arches of the beams, the King who built the Hall was deposed the year the work was completed and successor Henry IV was declared King. In 1535, Sir Thomas More, former speaker of the House of Commons, stood trial here for treason against his former friend and tennis partner, Henry VIII, and was beheaded on Tower Hill. Seventy years later, on 5 November 1605, England's most famous terrorist, Guy Fawkes, was accused of trying to blow up King James I and Parliament. Charles I, King of England, stood trial in his own Hall in 1649 and was convicted of treason. Oliver Cromwell, the most formidable parliamentarian who ever lived, signed the King's death warrant and had himself named Lord Protector here. After the restoration of Charles II to the throne, Cromwell was brought back to the Hall, or rather his skull cut from his skeleton was brought back, and stuck on a spike on one of the oak beams, where it rattled in the wind for 25 years until it finally blew down in a storm. And it was here, in Westminster Hall, that Churchill lay in state for a fortnight while a grateful nation paid its last respects.

Crypt Church. Though once abused and desecrated, and even used as the Speaker's coal cellar, the chapel was richly restored by **EM Barry,** and has a wonderful pre-Raphaelite feeling. The main walls, vaulting and bosses have withstood at least 5 fires. Members of both Houses of Parliament use the chapel for weddings and christenings.

St. Stephen's Porch. The public enters the Houses of Parliament through the porch and hall. Now there is a security check with metal-detecting arches, airport-style, right next to Westminster Hall.

Central Lobby. The security check is an understandable but inglorious entrance to the Lobby, the crossroads of the Palace of Westminster, connecting the House of Commons with the House of Lords. Citizens meet their MPs in this octagonal vestibule. The ceiling, 75 feet above the floor, contains 250 carved bosses with Venitian mosaics which include the emblems of England, Scotland and Ireland. Above the ceiling is the central spire of the Palace, a feature that was not in Barry's original plans, but imposed by a ventilating expert who insisted it be built as a

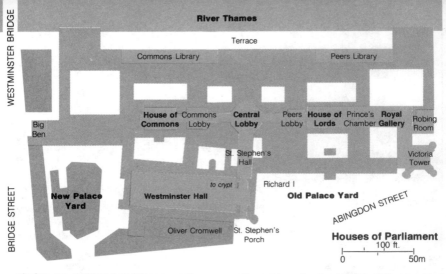

House of Commons · Commons Lobby · Central Lobby · Peers Lobby · House of Lords · Prince's Chamber · Royal Gallery · Robing Room · Big Ben · Victoria Tower · St. Stephen's Hall · to crypt · Richard I · New Palace Yard · Westminster Hall · Old Palace Yard · ABINGDON STREET · Oliver Cromwell · St. Stephen's Porch

River Thames · Terrace · Commons Library · Peers Library · WESTMINSTER BRIDGE · BRIDGE STREET

Houses of Parliament

100 ft.

0   50m

shaft to expel *vitiated air.* It has never been needed or used for anything. In the floor of encaustic tiles, Pugin inscribed the Latin text from Psalm 127: *Except the Lord keep the house, they labour in vain that build it.*

Members' Lobby. Off the Central Lobby is the Members' or Commons Lobby, the Piccadilly Circus of Commons life where Members gossip and talk to the Lobby journalists. It is architecturally rather bleak, referred to as *neo-Gothic,* and was never quite restored after the wartime German bombing in 1941 which left it in ruins. A more moving reminder of the destruction is the **Churchill Arch,** made from stones damaged in the fire of 1941. Churchill proposed that it be erected in the Lobby in memory of those who *kept the bridge* during the dark days of the war. Above the main door of the Commons Chamber is the family crest of **Airey Neave,** placed here after he was assassinated in New Palace Yard by terrorists in 1979.

House of Commons. The House was completely destroyed in the air raid of 10 December 1941, and it was rebuilt after the war in 1950 by **Gilbert Scott,** simply and without decoration and, under Churchill's influence, in the exact proportions of the prewar House. It is impressively small: only 346 of the 650 Members can actually sit down at any one time, the rest crowding around the door and the Speaker's chair. The smallness is believed to be fundamental to the sense of intimacy and conversational form of debate which characterize the House. Equally important is the layout of the Chamber, with the party in office (called *the government*) and the opposition facing each other, their green leather benches 2 swordlengths apart and separated by 2 red lines on the floor which no Member is allowed to cross. The **Press Gallery** and the **Public Gallery** are at opposite ends of the Chamber.

Each day the House opens with a procession in which the Speaker (wearing a wig, knee breeches and a long black gown) enters, preceded by the Serjeant-at-Arms, who carries a mace (the symbol of authority), and followed by the train-bearer, chaplain and secretary. The day begins with prayers, and no strangers (journalists or visitors) are ever admitted. MPs face the seats behind them—an extraordinary sight—because in the days when they wore swords it was impossible to kneel on the floor. Therefore they turned to kneel on the benches behind them. Every member has to swear loyalty to the Crown (a problem for Irish MPs for the past 100 years), although no monarch has been

allowed to enter the House of Commons since 1642 when Charles I burst in to arrest his parliamentary opponents. *Open to the public only by prior appointment with a member of Parliament or by waiting in line, starting at about 5PM. Sessions are held M-Th from 2:30PM, often until late; F 9:30AM-3PM. Prime Minister's question time is Tu and Th at 3:15 PM. 219-4272*

Queen Elizabeth comes to the Houses of Parliament once a year for the **State Opening of Parliament,** and she delivers her speech (a policy statement written by the party in office) in the **House of Lords.** She enters through the **Royal Entrance,** a gate beneath the **Victoria Tower** which she alone uses. She proceeds to the **Norman Porch** and into the **Robing Room,** where she puts on the Imperial State Crown amidst the astonishing splendor of Pugin's decoration. Every inch of the room is covered in gem-like Gothic and Tudor motifs and hung with pictures depicting the legend of King Arthur. The procession continues into the **Royal Gallery,** which is 110 feet long, 45 feet wide and lined with paintings, including *The Death of Nelson* and *The Meeting of Wellington and Blucher at Waterloo.* Both paintings are 45 feet long and 12 feet high. They took the artist, **Daniel Maclise,** 6 years to complete, an appropriate recognition of 2 events without which this grand, Gothic and democratic place would not exist. Finally, the Queen passes through the **Prince's Chamber,** which is the anteroom to the House of Lords and a celebration of Tudor, with dark paneling and full-length portraits of Henry VIII, 5 of his 6 wives and his mother.

House of Lords. This is the most elaborate part of Barry's design and Pugin's ultimate masterpiece: Victorian, romantic and stunning. At 80 feet long, it is not grand in size, but it is extravagantly ornate. Stained glass windows shed a dark, red light, and statues of the barons of Magna Carta stare down from the walls. They look like saints, emphasizing the sacred look of the room, but the long red leather sofas on either side suggest a chapel not really consecrated. Between the 2 sofas is a huge red pouff, the *Woolsack* (the traditional seat of the Lord Chancellor), stuffed with bits of wool from all over the Commonwealth. At the far end of the room under a gilded canopy is the ornate throne of the Queen. *For hours see* **House of Commons.** *Sessions M-W 2:30 PM, Th 3PM, occasionally on F. 219-4272*

Outside the Houses of Parliament are:

Big Ben. The most beloved image in all of London is Big Ben, towering 320 feet over the Thames, telling time and lighting up the London sky. Every guidebook will tell you that Big Ben is not the clock, but the bell. However, in people's hearts, the clock tower is, and always will be, Big Ben. Its 4 dials are 23 feet wide. The minute hands are each as tall as a red London double-decker bus. The pendulum, which beats once every 2 seconds, is 13 feet long and weighs 685 pounds. Besides being endearing, the clock is a near-perfect timekeeper. After spending 3 years under scaffolding, the clock tower has emerged several shades lighter and glistening—4,000 books of gold leaf were used to reguild the gold surfaces. The hours are struck on the 13-and-a-half-ton bell, named *Big Ben* after the First Commissioner of Works when the bell was hung. Since 1885, a light shines in the tower at night when Parliament is sitting.

Victoria Tower. When it was built, the 336 foot tower was the tallest in the world—taller than early American skyscrapers—and it is still the world's highest square masonry tower. Barry saw the Palace of Westminster as a legislative castle and this was to be its keep, its great ceremonial entrance. The Victoria Tower, technologically far ahead of its time, later had to be massively reconstructed to save it from collapse. It is now an archive of over 3 million parliamentary documents dating back to 1497 and including the death warrant of Charles I. During the day, the Royal Standard flies when the Queen is present and the Union Jack when Parliament is sitting. On a clear day, the flag can be seen by the naval men in Greenwich.

The Houses of Parliament was an inspired collaboration between 2 men of vastly different talents and visions, **Sir Charles Barry** and **Augustus Pugin.** They worked together in the fertile harmony of mutual respect, each expanding the realm of possibility for the other. Barry was a man of classical ideas and temperament. His Traveller's Club in Pall Mall shows his neo-classicism at its best. Pugin was a Gothic genius, in love with tracery, foliage, bays, emblems, oriels, turrets and paneling, a medieval world of tapestries and trumpets. Pugin's drawings won Barry the competition; Barry's solid experience and talent provided Pugin his Camelot. The 2 men combined romanticism with logic. But Pugin, under constant attack from the Parliamentary Commissions who decried his efforts and cut his salary in half, died at the age of 40 in Bedlam madhouse; Barry died of worry and overwork within months after the work was finished.

31 St. Margaret's Church. (1504-23, Robert Stowell; the original church was founded in the 12th century) Sir Walter Raleigh was beheaded out front and is buried beneath the altar; Samuel Pepys married a vivacious 15 year old in the church in 1655; John Milton married here a year later and Winston Churchill in 1908. It has been the parish church of the House of Commons since 1614. The magnificent Flemish glass window was commissioned by Ferdinand and Isabella of Spain to celebrate the engagement of their daughter, Catherine of Aragon, to Prince Arthur, the older brother of Henry VIII. By the time the window arrived, Henry had become King and married Catherine—by then his brother's widow. On an ordinary day, this would be quite enough to get one's attention, but St. Margaret's has the bad luck of being wedged in between the Houses of Parliament and Westminster Abbey. Most people go past thinking it is an extension of the latter. Treasures in the church include stained glass windows in the south aisle, done by artist **John Piper** in 1967; the west windows, given to the church by Americans; the **Milton** window, with the blind poet dictating to his daughter; a memorial to **Sir Walter Raleigh,** the colonizer of Virginia, with lines from the American poet **John Greenleaf Whittier:** *The New World honours him whose lofty plea for England's freedom made her own more sure;* and a tablet near the altar where Raleigh is buried that urges, *Reader—Should you reflect on his errors Remember his many virtues and that he was a mortal.* St. Margaret's Street, Westminster, SW1.

32 Westminster Arms. ★ ★ $ Home-cooked steak, kidney pie and real ale make this a popular pub with MPs, journalists and young clerics in the neighborhood who are summoned by bells—the division bell in the pub and the church bells next door. A nice atmosphere. *Open M-Sa 11AM-3PM, 5:30-11PM; Su 12-2PM. 9 Storey's Gate, SW1. 222-8520*

33 Central Hall. The **Imperial Collection of Crown Jewels of the World** is on display in a replica of Napoleon's Throne Room at Fontaineblue. The collection contains fascimiles, with 9K gold and real and semi-precious stones, of the Crown Jewels of Britain, Russia, Iran, Germany, Bavaria, Prussia, the Vatican and France. They were created by European artisans over the last 205 years. Many of the originals were lost in wars and revolutions. *Admission fee. Open daily Apr-Sept 10AM-6PM, Oct-Mar 11AM-5PM. Central Hall, Westminster, SW1. 222-1333*

34 Westminster Abbey. (1245, Henry of Reims) One of the finest Gothic buildings in the world, it is officially called the Collegiate Church of St. Peter, and it is the most faithful and intimate witness of English history. Westminster Abbey has survived the Reformation, the Blitz and, requiring even more miraculous tenacity, 9 centuries of visitors, pilgrims, worshippers, wanderers and tourists. Today the Abbey is like a medieval Heathrow, with windows, buttresses and vaulting all heavenward, taking flight; and the traffic below earthbound, in awe.

Courtesy Walter Annenberg, from *Westminster Abbey*, published by the Annenberg School of Communications, 1972

0 10 20 30 40 50   100 *feet*

It is almost impossible to see the Abbey without being surrounded by thousands of tourists, either moving aimlessly down the aisles or purposefully following a raised umbrella that is reeling off Abbey Highlights. If possible, come here for a service, when the Abbey empties of tourists and regains some of its serenity. In any case, try to avoid the Abbey in the mornings when all the guided bus tours in London combine Westminster Abbey with the Changing of the Guard (likewise, avoid St. Paul's in the afternoon before 3PM, when the afternoon tours combine St. Paul's and the Tower of London).

Once upon a time, this really was an abbey, a monastic community designed for the monkish life of self-suffcent contemplation, with cloisters, refectory, abbot's residence, orchards, workshops and kitchen gardens. A Benedictine Abbey founded before 750, it was called Westminster (*west monastery*) because it was west of the City of London. The existence of the Abbey today is due to the inspired determination of Edward the Confessor, who set to work on a great monastery to promote the glory of God in 1050. In order to supervise the progress of the abbey and efficiently preside over his Kingdom of England, he moved his palace next door—hence, the Palace of Westminster—and established the bond between Church and State which has endured for more than 900 years.

Edward the Confessor was brought up in Normandy and built his Abbey in a Norman style, advanced and unlike anything which had ever been seen in England. The King, ill and unable to attend the consecration of his church, died a week later on 6 January 1066. No one knows if his successor, Harold, was crowned here or at St. Paul's, but after Harold's death at the Battle of Hastings, William the Conqueror was crowned here on Christmas day in 1066. Since then, the kings and queens of England have all been crowned at Westminster Abbey.

In 1245, Henry III decided to rebuild the now canonized St. Edward's church in a style more maginficent. Influenced by the French Gothic style of the cathedrals of Amiens and Reims (Sainte Chapelle in Paris was being built at the same time), Henry started to build, at his own expense, the soaring and graceful church that is here today. The King's architect, **Henry of Reims,** worked with great speed in cathedral terms. By 1259, the chancel, transepts, part of the nave and the chapter house were complete, giving the medieval church remarkable unity of style. The nave, continued in the late 14th century by **Henry Yevele** (master mason who built Westminster Hall), was built in the style originally planned by Henry of Reims.

The only important additions to Henry III's church have been the **Henry VII Chapel,** begun in 1503 and believed by many to be the most beautiful and most perfect building in England, and the towers on the west front, built in the 18th century from the designs of **Wren** and **Hawksmoor.**

The best way to enter the Abbey is under the towers by the **West Door,** where you can take in the majestic height of the roof: 102 feet to the exalted vault, the pale stone touched with gold and tinted by the colored glass of the aisle windows. The eye is pulled upward in prophetic astonishment at the sheer beauty of it all, then immediately distracted groundward by the chaos of the white marble figures. You understand at once that any tour of Westminster Abbey will have to be 2 tours, even if taken simultaneously: one a tour of the plan and beauty of the building, serene and coherent; the other a survey of the haphazard and wonderful confusion of the once great and now dead. It requires great presence of mind to deal with both at the same time.

Standing at the entrance, you see the impressive length of the stone-flagged nave, the decorated choir screen in front of the nave (too gold, too gaudy, too late) and above, the Waterford chandeliers, 16 in all, presented by the Guinness family in 1655 to mark the 900th anniversary of the consecration of the Abbey. Criticized for being more Mayfair than Gothic, they have come under the spell of the Abbey and now look superbly right.

Immediately in front of you, beyond the stone honoring Winston Churchill, is the grave of the **Unknown Warrior,** a nameless British soldier brought to the Abbey from France on 11 November 1920. The flag which covered the coffin hangs nearby, alongside the Congressional Medal of Honor. The poppy-filled slab contains earth and clay from France, a terrible and moving reminder of a whole generation lost.

To your right is **St. George's Chapel,** the Warrior's Chapel, with an altar by **Comper** and a tablet on the west wall commemorating the one million men from the

Empire and the Commonwealth who died in the First World War. A memorial to Franklin D. Roosevelt hangs here. Just outside the Chapel is a haunting portrait of the young **Richard II**. It is the first genuine portrait of a king painted in his lifetime. The sad brevity of Richard's life seems to show in his face. The **choir screen**, designed by **Blore** in 1828, jolts a bit. Its bright goldness drains the color from Lord Standhope and Sir Isaac Newton, who are framed within the arches. Near Newton, a Nobel bevy of scientists are gathered, including Charles Darwin, who used science to destroy the myth of creation, and Ernest Rutherford, who unsettled creation by his discovery of the atomic nucleus.

Behind the screen is the **choir**. The choir stalls are Victorian. but the choir itself has been in this position since Edward the Confessor's own abbey stood on the site. The organ was installed in 1730, but it has been uplifted, rebuilt and enlarged. Organists at the Abbey have been quite distinguished, including Orlando Gibbons, John Blow and his pupil, Henry Purcell.

Because the **North Transept** has one of the main entrances to the Abbey (**Solomon's Porch**), it is thick with people coming and going, adding confusion to the mixed bag of the distinguished who are here permanently. Still, persevere until you reach **St. Michael's Chapel** in the east aisle and **Roulbiliac's** monument to **Lady Nightingale**. The poor woman was frightened by lightning and died of a miscarriage. She collapses into her husband's arms, while he, frantic and helpless with fear, watches Death, a wretched skeleton, aim its spear at his wife. Maddeningly, this aisle is frequently used for storing chairs. Ask an attendant for permission to visit.

The Sanctuary. Kings and queens have been crowned in coronation services in the Sanctuary since the time of Richard II in 1377. A platform is created under the central space (the lantern) between the Choir and the Sanctuary. The **Coronation Chair** is brought from the **Confessor's Chapel** and placed in front of the high altar. Since the coronation of Charles I. the anthem *I was glad when they said unto me, We will go into the House of the Lord* is begun as soon as the sovereign enters the West Door. When Queen Elizabeth entered the Choir for her coronation in 1952 under the eyes of God and the television cameras, a chorus of *Vivat, vivat, vivat regina Elizabetha* rang out from the voices of Westminster School's scholars. At the Sanctuary, she was presented by the Archbishop of Cantebury to the people 4 times, in turn on all sides, who then acclaimed her with loud cries of *God Save the Queen*. After an elaborate ceremony of oaths, a service of holy communion, and annointing with special oil, robed in gold and delivered of ring, sceptor and orb, the archbishop performed the act of crowning.

To the north are the 3 finest medieval tombs in the Abbey: **Aveline of Lancaster**, rich, pretty and the first bride to be married in the new Abbey in 1269; **Edmond Crouchback**, the Earl of Lancaster and the youngest son of Henry III; and **Amyer de Valence**, Earl of Pembroke.

Behind the Altar is the **Shrine of Edward the Confessor**. This is the most sacred part of the Abbey, the destination of pilgrims. The Purbreck marble tomb contains the body of the saint. Beside the saint are Henry III, who built the church in homage to the Confessor; Henry's son Edward I, the first king to be crowned in the present Abbey; and his beloved Queen Eleanor, for whom he set up the Eleanor Crosses all the way from Lincoln to the tomb where she is buried.

The **Coronation Chair**, when not in use for coronations, stands behind the High Altar. Built in 1300, the chair was designed to incorporate the **Stone of Scone**. The Stone, part of the Scottish throne since the 9th century, was captured and brought back from Scotland by Edward I in 1297. The Stone in the Throne represents the union of the 2 countries, a union which, 600 years later, is not without resistance. The Stone has been stolen from the Abbey by Scottish nationalists several times, most recently in the 1950s, but it has always been recovered. The grafitti on the back of the chair was done by 18th century schoolboys at Westminster School.

Henry VII Chapel. If you are able to look at one and only one part of the Abbey, this must be it. Because you pay a small admission fee, the Abbey suddenly becomes quieter and emptier, a blessing as this is one of the most beautiful places you may ever see. Notice the exquisite tracery of the fan vaulting, miraculous intricacies and ecstasies of stone, Matisse-like in their exuberance; the high wooded choir stalls which line the nave—and their misericordes; the carvings beneath the seats, including a woman beating her husband, and mermaids, mermen and monkeys; the black and white marble floor; and throughout, the royal badges, a kind of illustrated Shakespeare of Tudor roses, leopards of England, the *fleur-de-lys* of France, the porticullis of the Beauforts, greyhounds and falcons and daisy roots. This is the Renaissance in England, and Heaven is on Earth in a world alive with confidence and harmony, beauty and art. The Chapel is the grand farewell to the great Gothic style and the perfect setting for the **Order of the Bath**, the chivalrous knights who were installed in the 18th century and still exist today (the most recent installation of a Knight of the Bath was in 1982). In the aisles on both sides of the Chapel are a few unforgettable tombs. In the south aisle rests **Lady Margaret Beaufort** by **Torrigiani**. She was the mother of Henry VII, and was a remarkable Renaissance woman devoted to education, the arts and the journey of her soul. Her effigy, one of the finest in the Abbey, shows a delicately lined face with the gentle sensitivity which in time becomes beauty.

Having restored religion to its original sincerity, established peace, restored money to its proper value, etc... Most world leaders would die for an epitaph like that, but it seems rather an understatement for **Queen Elizabeth I**. Her 4-poster tomb in the north aisle relects Gloriana more gloriously, although how she feels about being buried with her half-sister, **Queen Mary I**, whom she had beheaded, God only knows.

At the end of the aisle are the 2 infant daughters of James I: **Sophia**, under her velvet coverlet, died at birth; and **Mary**, leaning on one elbow, died at age 2. Both, look-

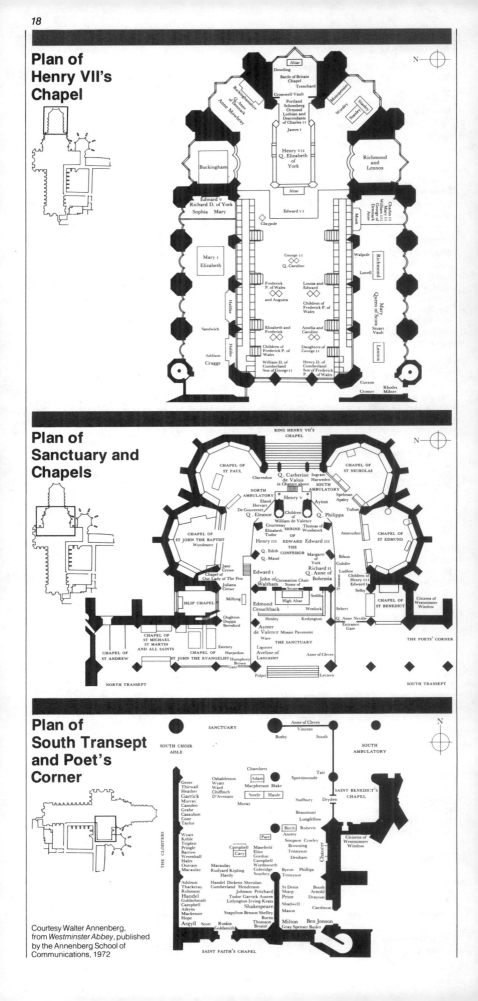

Plan of Henry VII's Chapel

Plan of Sanctuary and Chapels

Plan of South Transept and Poet's Corner

Courtesy Walter Annenberg, from *Westminster Abbey*, published by the Annenberg School of Communications, 1972

ing like small dolls, bring tears to mothers' eyes and fascinate small children.

Poet's Corner. In 1889, Henry James came to Westminster Abbey for the memorial service of Robert Browning whose ashes were being consigned to Poet's Corner. Afterwards he wrote that Browning stood for *the thing that, as a race, we like best — the fascination of faith, the acceptance of life, the respect for its mysteries, the endurance of its charges, the vitality of will, the validity of character, the beauty of action, the seriousness, above all, of the great human passion.* James's testimony to Browning seems a perfect testimony to Anglo-Saxon England, the Abbey, and above all, to its corner of poets, where the honors are the *greatest that a generous nation has to confer.* All those honored here are not buried here, but among those honored are Chaucer, Spenser, Jonson, Shakespeare, Milton, Dryden, Dr. Johnson, Thomas Gray, Sheridan, Goldsmith, Blake, Wordsworth, Coleridge, Shelley, Keats, Jane Austen, the Brontë sisters, Walter Scott, Macaulay, Thackeray, Dickens, Longfellow, Ruskin, Kipling, Byron, Dylan Thomas, George Eliot, WH Auden, DH Lawrence, Lewis Carroll, Gerard Manley Hopkins, TS Eliot and, since 1976, Henry James. One of the newest stones was unveiled on 11 November 1985. It is a memorial to the poets of the First World War. Among those mentioned are Rupert Brooke, Robert Graves, Herbert Read, Siegried Sasson and Wilfred Owen. Above the dates *1914-1918* is the statement from Owen: *My subject is War, and the pity of war. The poetry is in the pity.*

Westminster Abbey is open daily 9AM-4PM, unless attending a service. Holy Communion daily at 8AM and 5PM. You cannot walk around the Abbey during services. Guided Super Tours lasting 90 minutes are given M at 9:45AM, 10:15AM, 11AM, 2:15PM and 3:30PM; Sa 10AM, 10:45AM and 12:30PM. The Jericho, Parlous and Jerusalam Chambers can only be seen on a Super Tour. Reservations in the South Aisle of the Nave. 222-5152

Chapter House. (1250) From 1257 until Henry VIII's reign, this exquisite octagon with Purbeck marble roof served as the Parliament House for the Commons. *Open daily Oct-Feb 9:30AM-3:30PM. Mar-Sept 9:30AM-6PM.*

Chapel of the Pyx. (c. 1090) Once the monastery treasury, it passed to the Crown during the Dissolution. *Open on application to the Chapter House.*

Dean's Yard. You can only gaze through the iron gate at the charming, tree-shaded yard behind the Abbey. The yard and the buildings of Westminster School arranged around it are not open to visitors.

Great Cloisters. The courtyard offers a breathtaking view of the buttresses and flying buttresses on the south side of the Henry VII Chapel. The large brass-rubbing center in the Cloisters is open M-Sa 9AM-5:30PM; closed Su.

Abbey Treasures Museum. This holy **Madame Tussaud's** is the highlight of the day for children, who definitely prefer the macabre to the historical. The wax effigies were used for lyings-in-state and funerals, and the clothes are not costumes but the real thing, including Nelson's hat with its green eye-patch. The Abbey represents the divine harmony of immortal man with God; the Museum is an unnerving reminder of the mortal in us all. *Admission fee. Open daily 10:30AM-4:30PM.*

35 **Jewel Tower.** (1366, Henry Yevele) Edward III built the Tower to hold his jewels and silver. There are no jewels (not of the ruby and diamond variety, that is) in this last surviving domestic part of the royal Palace of Westminster. But you can see the drawings submitted in the competition for the Houses of Parliament. These fascinating architectural documents make you even more certain that Barry and Pugin were the right men at the right time. *Admission fee. Open M-Sa 10:30AM-4PM, closed 1-2PM. Abingdon St., Westminster, SW1.*

36 **Abbey Garden.** The 900 year old garden (the oldest cultivated garden in England) is open to the public on Thursdays. Its main attraction is lavender, which you can have shipped to the US. *Open Th 10AM-6PM (4PM Oct-Mar). Band concerts 12:30-2PM Aug-mid-Sept.*

37 **Whippel's.** The shop is the supplier to the religious trade. Bishop's purple socks are out of stock at the moment (*they're on order but hard to get nowadays*), but this is a great source for church candles. They will make beeswax candles in any size you want. *Open M-F 9:30AM-5:30PM. 11 Tufton St., SW1 222-4528*

38 **Victoria Tower Gardens.** These gardens are a tranquil oasis overlapping the Thames, ideal for a picnic lunch or an afternoon nap. Two varying principles of heroism can be found in the sculpture: **AG Walker's** statue of **Emmeline Pankhurst** (1858-1928), the leader of the woman's suffrage movement who was often imprisoned for her beliefs; and a replica (1915) of **Rodin's Burghers of Calais** (1895), who surrendered to Edward III in 1347 rather than see their town destroyed. *Westminster, SW1.*

39 **St. John's, Smith Square.** (1728, Thomas Archer) Itzak Perlman and YoYo Ma have given lunchtime concerts in the Church, along with the Allegri, Endymion and Amadeus Quartets. The musical reputation is high indeed, in part because each Monday the concerts are broadcast live on BBC Radio 3. You won't find this church unless you are looking for it, but it is a treasure—original, idiosyncratic and personal. After almost being destroyed by bombs in 1941, St. John's was rebuilt but not reconsecrated. *Westminster, SW1.*

40 **Wilkens.** ★ $ There are not many like this around: a healthfood *caf* with delicious salads, thick homemade soups and granary bread. Self-service, cheap, cheerful, fast. *Open daily 8AM-6PM. 61 Marsham St., SW1. 222-4038*

41 **Lockets.** ★ ★ $/$$ MPs dine here regularly on the kind of food you find in English novels: roast beef, pheasant and grouse in season and jugged hare. It is like eating in the Stranger's Dining Room at the House of Commons, only the food is better and the wine list is vastly superior. *Open M-F 12:15-2:30PM, 6:30-11PM. Marsham Ct., Marsham St., SW1. 834-9552*

Tate Gallery

42 **Tate Gallery.** (1897, Sidney JR Smith; 1979, northwest extension, Michael Huskstepp; 1987, Clore Gallery, James Stirling) If you can only handle one major museum and if you like paintings, the Tate is where you will find true happiness. It houses 2 great national collections comprised of more than 10,000 works, yet it is accessible and welcoming.

The collections are an interesting mix of mid-sixteenth century and modern international art, including the works of living artists which are, naturally, controversial. Arguments to house the collections separately come up from time to time. But it is a singular pleasure to be able to look at Turners and Blakes, Duncan Grants and Gwen Johns, Whistlers and Seargents, and Rothkos and Giacomettis, all hanging happily within minutes of each other.

The Gallery began life through the generosity of **Sir Henry Tate** (of the sugar manufacturer Tate & Lyle) who donated his collection of 70 *modern* British paintings and sculptures and offered to pay for a building to house it. A vacant lot on the River Thames at Millbank, previously occupied by Jeremy Bentham's Model Prison (from which less than mode! prisoners were sent down the Thames to the Colonies) was acquired, and the wedding cake building with its majestic entrance was opened in 1897. Its formative years were spent as a kind of annex of the National Gallery. But in 1955 a formal, albeit friendly, divorce took place, and the Tate was finally independent. You will recognize and revel in the lively good-nature of this

museum, a spirit which sets it apart in the world of cultural institutions, and makes cultural fatigue wonderfully impossible.

The Tate Gallery issues free plans of the gallery at the entrance. Because the vast collection is changed regularly, this is an invaluable way to locate what you want to see.

The **Turner Bequest** is one of the great treasures London offers to its citizens and its visitors, and one of the truly remarkable collections of the work of one artist. At his death in 1851, the artist **JMW Turner** left his personal collection of nearly 300 paintings and 19,000 watercolors and drawings to the nation, with the request that his finished paintings (some 100) be seen all together, under one roof. In spite of his staggering generosity, his wish was ignored for more than 125 years. Finally, Turner's one hope has been realized with the **Clore Gallery** extension. Designed by **James Stirling, Michael Wilford and Associates,** the Clore Gallery for the Turner Collection makes up in concept and design for the long neglect of Turner's wish. The paintings are top-lit with daylight, the kind of light, with all its varied and changeable qualities, in which the artist expected his pictures to be exhibited. Works on paper (watercolors and drawings) are in galleries where daylight is kept out in order to prevent the fading of the images. Not only has the architect taken great care to see that the art is sympathetically displayed and scientifically preserved, he has also made it possible for visitors to glimpse the River Thames as they stroll past the pictures. The River played a prominent part in Turner's life and art—he painted it, and he lived and died on its banks in Chelsea. Don't miss Turner's *Views of Petworth House, Sussex,* the home of his great patron and benefactor, George Wyndham, 3rd Earl of Egremont; *Peace: Burial at Sea,* a memorial to his friend, the painter Wilder, who died at sea off Gibralter; and the pictures of Venice.

Other works in the Tate that must be seen are **Gainsborough's** portraits of *Sir Benjamin Truman, Suffolk Landscape* and the Italian dancer *Giovannae Baccelli;* **George Stubbs's** *Mares and Foals, The Haymakers* and *The Reapers;* the polite paintings by **Sir Joshua Reynolds, Romney** and **Lawrence,** which give you a glimpse into the serene world of the 18th century; the **William Blake** collection, the richest and most comprehensive in the world, now brilliantly housed together in Room 7; the Pre-

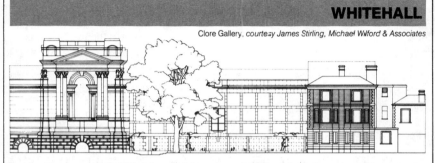

Clore Gallery, courtesy James Stirling, Michael Wilford & Associates

Raphaelites, especially **Millais's** exquisite *Ophelia* and **Rosetti's** paintings of his wife as *Beata Beatrix;* the irresistible portraits of **John Singer Sargent,** especially *Carnation, Lily, Lily, Rose;* and **Whistler's** *Old Battersea Bridge, Miss Cicely Alexander: Harmony in Grey and Green; Little White Girl: Symphony in White No. II* and *Hammersmith Bridge on Boat Race Day.* Hanging nearby are the newly appreciated paintings of **Tissot.**

The French Impressionist collection marks the beginning of the Tate's modern collection, and it includes **Manet's** *Woman with a Cat,* which once belonged to Degas; **Berthe Mirosot's** *Girl on a Divan,* **Bonnard's** *La Table* and *Place de la Concorde;* the brilliant Provencial landscapes of **Cézanne; Van Gogh's** *Yellow Chair;* and **Vuillard's** *Seated Woman.*

Cubism is represented with some outstanding pictures by **Braque, Picasso** and **Juan Gris.** An exciting and remarkably comprehensible outline of 20th century art includes works by **Kokoschka, Leger, Masson, Matisse, Edward Munch** (*The Sick Child),* **Kandinsky, Mondrian** and **Malevich. Rodin's** large marble carving, *The Kiss,* made a few years after the version in the Musée Rodin, is one of the most popular pieces in the Gallery.

The figures in the Bloomsbury world of 1920s and 1930s London, including writers Virginia Woolf, Vita Sackville-West, Lytton Stratchey, John Meynard Keynes, and on its fringe, TS Eliot, and painters Duncan Grant, Vanessa Bell (sister of Virginia Woolf), Augustus John and Gwen John now hang together and are fascinating viewing for anyone caught up in the Bloomsbury period. *No admission fee, except for certain major exhibitions. Open M-Sa 10AM-5:50PM, Su 2-5:30PM. Millbank, SW1. 821-1313; recorded information, 821-7128*

Tate Gallery Shop. Superbly printed post cards, most at 10p, excellent books, T-shirts with masterpieces from the Tate, the ubiquitous Tate Gallery canvas bags, prints, posters, framing facilities, and a few special *made for the Tate* items which change frequently. *Open M-Sa 10AM-5:30PM, Su 2-5:30PM.*

Coffee Shop. ★★$ Self-service and excellent, with good game pies, pâtés, salads, hot dishes and wine. The cakes and pastries and coffee and tea make this a popular afternoon meeting place. It seems like a great place to meet people as well, as everyone sits at long crescent-shaped tables. *Open M-Sa 10:30AM-5:30PM, Su 4-5:15PM.*

Tate Gallery Restaurant. ★★★$$ The Tate Gallery Restaurant is known for 2 things: the romantic and beautiful **Rex Whistler** mural, *Expedition in Pursuit of Rare Meats,* painted in 1926-27; and the wine list, which is unquestionably the best in town, due to the sheer number of superb bottles

and the amazingly low prices. The recently refurbished restaurant, called the **Rex Whistler Room,** is frightfully chic and comfortable. A lunch here is hard to beat, surrounded by the wit and elegance of the mural. Order a 1978 *5eme cru classe* Chateau Lynch-Bages to go with your thoroughly English and delicious lunch. Your neighbors will be astute members of the wine trade, distinguished patrons of the arts, and sometimes couples who have come up from the country to compare their Joseph Derbys, Turners and Stubbs's with the Tates. Enjoy the most charming lunchtime rendezvous in the whole of London. *Book far in advance. Lunch only, M-Sa 12-3PM. 834-6754*

Tate Gallery Bests
Alan Bowness
Director, Tate Gallery

David des Granges, *Saltonstall Family*
William Hogarth, *Calais Gate*
George Stubbs, *Haymakers*
William Turner, *Snowstorm*
Dante Gabriel Rossetti, *Annuciation*
Pierre Bonnard, *The Bath*
Pablo Picasso, *The Three Dancers*
Henri Matisse, *The Snail*
Max Ernst, *Pieta*
Henry Moore, *Falling Warrior*
Ben Nicholson, *White Relief*
Mark Rothko, *The Rothko Room*
David Hockney, *A Bigger Splash*

When US State Department employees travel to London on business, they must get by on a $138 per day allowance.

BESTS
John Gorham
Designer, London

Pasticceria Cappuccetto has smashing creamy cakes and fresh fruit pastries. *8-9 Moor St., W1. 437-9472*

Try **Gaby's** (next door to Wyndham's Theatre) for lovely hot Salt Beef sandwiches and other Mediterranean specialties. My favorite is chicken liver on rye. The chicken liver comes about 2 inches thick, a meal in itself. *30 Charing Cross Rd., WC2. 379-5777*

Rock and Sole Plaice is a good, old-fashioned, traditional English fish and chippy. They also do a very tasty banana or pineapple fritter. Yummy! *47 Endell St., Covent Garden, WC2. 836-3785*

Patisserie Valerie is a good place for tea and overhearing *pseuds* gossip. It gets very crowded and you may have to wait awhile. *44 Old Comptor St., W1. 437-3466*

In this mile long street called **Piccadilly** London wears her heart on her sleeve. Like a love affair, the street begins in an atmosphere of gesture and respect at **Hyde Park Corner**, then gently eases into the intimate tranquility of **Green Park**, the *lovers only* mystique of the Ritz, the champagne and caviar indulgence of Fortnum and Mason and the exuberant vows of Wren's own favorite church, **St. James's,** Piccadilly. But as **Eros** gets closer, something happens. The grandeur begins to diminish and the street loses its dignity. Instead of coziness, it is all confusion and traffic. Everything becomes familiar and *louche*. By the time the God of Love is in sight, poised on one foot and aiming his arrow, there are unmistakable signs of ordinariness and doubt. This is Piccadilly Circus? This is Eros?

Piccadilly Circus will probably always baffle the attempts to render it worthy of a great city. Yet it remains surprisingly loved by Londoners and visitors who are irresistably drawn to the area by its one feature of distinction, the statue of Eros. A journey to Eros offers all the joys of traveling, with a perfect miniature version of the essence of London *en route*.

The walk ends at the God of Love in a pedestrian precinct, and begins at the **Goddess of Peace** in a quadriga. Along the way, you pass the last house in Piccadilly, known as No. 1, London (**Apsley House**); an oasis of green (Green Park); the longest wait for the best hamburger in London (Hard Rock Cafe); the headquarters for London's cafe society (Langan's Brasserie); the most beautiful dining room in the world (the Ritz); a Regency shopping center (the **Burlington Arcade**); a bank by Lutyens; a hotel by Norman Shaw and a church by Wren. Piccadilly is the home of one of London's favorite galleries, (the **Royal Academy**) and was the home of Lord Byron (**Albany**). If it is raining, you can stay dry under the Rolls-Royce of umbrellas (Swaine, Adeney, Brigg), and in lieu of an umbrella, you can have tea at the most luxurious grocery store in London (Fortnum and Mason).

ROTTEN ROW

CARRIAGE RD

KNIGHTSBRIDGE

WILTON PL

KINNERTON ST

WILLIAM MEWS

WILTON CRESCENT

RAPHAEL ST

HARRIET WALK

SLOANE ST

Lowndes
Square

LOWNDES ST

BROMPTON RD

BASIL ST

PAVILION ROAD

HANS CRESCENT

MOTCOMB ST   BELGRAVE MEWS

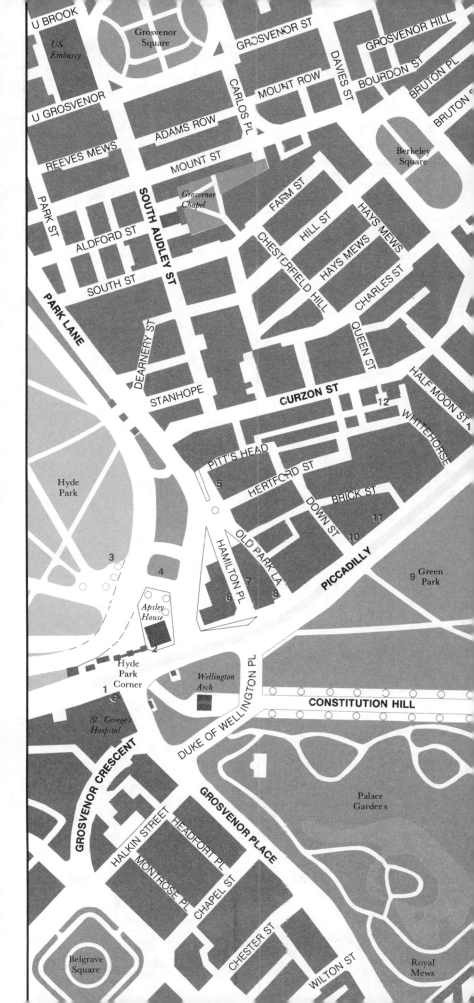

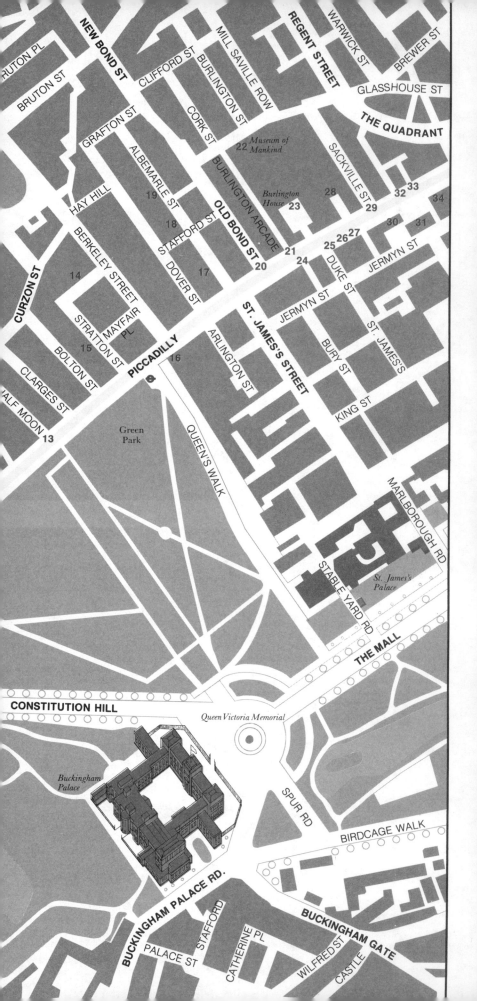

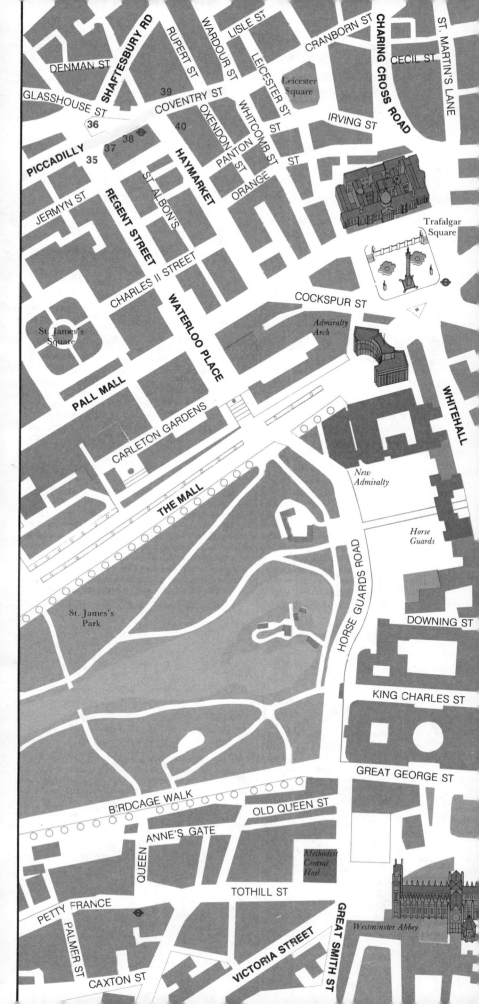

PICCADILLY

The best time to be in Piccadilly is on a weekday when every foot of the mile long stretch is luxuriously and romantically alive. On Saturdays, many shops close at 1PM, and some shops and restaurants don't open at all. The **Wellington Museum** at Apsley House is open Tuesday through Thursday from 10AM to 6PM, so ideally your walk will fall on one of those days. Piccadilly goes past 1 of London's oldest West End theatres, the **Criterion,** and ends in the heart of the West End theatreland, so you could end this walk the way Londoners do, in the company of George Bernard Shaw, Noel Coward or Tom Stoppard.

1 **Hyde Park Corner**. *It is doubtless a signal proof of being a London-lover* quand même *that one should undertake an apology for so bungled an attempt at a great public place as Hyde Park Corner,* Henry James wrote at the turn of this century. Many decades, improvements and embellishments later, Hyde Park Corner is still being bungled, and now suffers the ultimate indignity: it is a traffic island, albeit a grand one. In order to reach this pivotal triangular patch, you must go beneath it into a warren of underpasses, where you will best make your way by following the sounds of a forlorn harmonica and the clinks of 10-pence pieces being tossed into the player's hat by grateful pedestrians.

In a battlefield of automobiles, the **Goddess of Peace** reins in the Horses of War, the beautiful and dramatic statue placed on the corner in 1912 after the Boer War. She is one of the finest silhouettes in the London sky and uniquely presents an almost identical profile from either side. Looking at the Goddess of Peace, you almost forget that 200 cars a minute are circling the Corner and that with the tyranny of the automobile, cities have no hope of peace. The sculptor, **Captain Adrian Jones,** created the Goddess of Peace after a career of 23 years as a calvary officer. He combined his unique equestrian knowledge with a true artistic gift to make the statue a stunning monument to peace. Tragically, the First World War broke out 2 years after it was placed at Hyde Park Corner, and the monuments that surround the Goddess of Peace are memorials to the many thousands who would die in a world-wide stampede of the Horses of War.

The Goddess dominates sky and square from her position on top of the arch designed by **Decimus Burton,** which was placed on the Corner in 1828. Few arches have been pushed around as much as this otherwise impressive structure. It was originally built as a northern gate to the grounds of Buckingham Palace and surmounted with a statue of the Duke of Wellington. But it now leads nowhere, with the Goddess of Peace on top. It was initially called **Wellington Arch,** but the name was changed to **Green Park Arch,** and now is mostly known as **Constitution Arch.** Its triumphant decline seems endless: after some years as a police station, it is now a skyward funnel for exhaust fumes from the underpass below.

A **statue of David** with his back to the motorized world stands as memorial to the Machine Gun Corps. It was designed by sculptor **Francis Derwent Wood** in 1925, and it bears a muscular resemblance to Rupert Brook. You almost see his haunting words written on the battlefields of France, where he dreamt of *hearts at peace, under an English heaven.* Instead, we read that *Saul hath slain his thousands but David his tens of thousands.*

The massive monument facing St. Georges Hospital is the splendid **Royal Artillery Monument,** designed by **CS Jaeger** in 1920. It bears the sadder, more prosaic inscription: *Here was a royal fellowship of death.* Four bronze figures weighed down with the knowledge of death surround a huge gun aimed at the Somme, the battlefield in France where so many men in the Royal Artillary died in the First World War.

The huge equestrian statue of the **Duke of Wellington** that formerly surmounted the Arch was sent to Aldershot in 1883, where it still stands. The statue in Hyde Park Corner facing Apsley House is the work of **Sir JE Boehm** (1888). It shows the Duke on his beloved horse, **Copenhagen,** who bore his master nobly for 16 hours on that fateful day at the Battle of Waterloo. When Copenhagen died in 1836, he was buried with full military honors. The inscription on his headstone reads: *God's humble instrument, though meaner clay, should share the glory of that glorious day.*

Art long ago ceased to be monumental. To be monumental, as the art of Michelangelo or Rubens was monumental, the age must have a sense of glory. The artist must have some faith in his fellow men, and some confidence in the civilization to which he belongs. Such an attitude is not possible in the modern world—at least not in our Western European world. We have lived through the greatest war in history (1914-18), but we find it celebrated in thousands of mean, false and essentially unheroic monuments. Ten million men killed, but no breath of inspiration from their dead bodies. Just a scramble for contracts and fees, and an unconcealed desire to make the most utilitarian use of the fruits of heroism. **Herbert Read,** English essayist, in *A Coat of Many Colours,* 1945

2 **Apsley House.** (Wellington Museum; c.1770, Robert Adam) The honey-colored stone and grand proportions provide solid dignity to Hyde Park Corner, and although it never looks open and requires subterranean tenacity to reach, the effort is well worth it. Known as **No.1, London,** this was the home of the man who finally defeated Napoleon, the Duke of Wellington.

The house is a mix of flawless Adam proportions and added-on grandeur made possible by a generous gift of £200,000 from Parliament as gratitude for the defeat of that little man Napoleon. Inside the house, the loser at Waterloo looms considerably larger than life in a statue by **Canova** which augments Napoleon to an idealized 11 feet, covered not in medals but with the ubiquitous fig leaf. Napoleon commissioned the statue, then rejected it because it failed to express his calm dignity—and because the winged figure of victory was turning away from him. It stayed packed away in the attic of the Louvre until 1816, when it was bought by the British government and presented by George IV to the Duke of Wellington, for whom victory had been perfectly placed.

The museum contains a touchingly idiosyncratic collection of victorious loot, stupendous services of Sèvres and Meissen, silver and gold plate, glorious batons, swords and daggers (including Napoleon's court sword taken from his carriage after the Battle of Waterloo), flags, medals and snuff boxes.

The **Piccadilly Drawing Room** on the first floor is a jewel of a room, with wall-hangings, curtains in butter yellow, windows that frame Hyde Park Corner and excellent paintings, including *Chelsea Pensioners Reading the Waterloo Despatch* by **Sir David Wilkie.**

The **Waterloo Gallery,** designed by **Benjamin Wyatt** in 1828, is the big draw in Apsley House. The vast 90-foot corridor is called the Waterloo Gallery because banquets were held in it each year on the anniversary of the great victory over the French. The room was designed to display the Duke's magnificent collection, particularly the Spanish pictures captured at the Battle of Victoria and subsequently presented to the Duke by King Ferdinand. The collection includes paintings by **Ribera, Murillo** (the beautiful *Isaac Blessing Jacob*), **Correggio** (*The Agony in the Garden*—the Duke's personal favorite) and 3 outstanding pictures by **Velasquez,** including the early *Water Carrier of Seville.* Also in the room are 2 notable **Van Dycks:** *King Charles I* and *St. Rosalie Crowned with Roses by Two Angels.* The windows fascinate almost as much as the pictures. They are fitted with sliding mirrors which transform the room, at night, into an evocation of Louis XIV's *Galerie des Glaces* at Versailles.

At the far end of the Waterloo Gallery is **Goya's** *Equestrian Portrait of Wellington.* Don't worry if you find this a disappointing Goya. X-rays show the picture was originally of Joseph Bonapart. Last-minute political alterations called for the head to be replaced with Wellington's, who never liked it and kept it in storage in his country house at Stratfield Saye, Berkshire. *Admission fee. Open Tu-Th & Sa 10AM-6PM, Su 2-6PM. Apsley House, 149 Piccadilly, W1. 499-5676*

PICCADILLY

3 **Statue of Achilles.** (1822, Sir Richard Westmacott) Behind Apsley House in Hyde Park is the memorial to the Duke of Wellington from the Ladies of England, paid for by a women's subscription. It is cast from cannons captured at Salamanca, Vitoria and Waterloo. The statue's flagrant nudity was once a shock, but now is a fascination.

4 **Statue of Lord Byron and his Dog.** (1880, Richard Belt) The feeble and boring statue of the poet is separated from Achilles by Park Lane. It is all the more annoying because it was chosen by sentimental Victorians who rejected the one artist most suited to recreate Byron: Rodin.

5 **Hilton Hotel.** *Deluxe.* The Queen was not at all pleased with the view from the 28 story modern hotel when it was first built in the 1960s—guests could catch a glimpse of royal life, right over the Buckingham Palace garden wall. (She has since landscaped for privacy.) But the view of the city and Hyde Park from the high-rising hotel is marvelous. This is the archetypal Hilton, with 509 simply decorated rooms and all the American-style comforts. **Trader Vic's** is within the complex, as is the **British Harvest** and the **Rooftop Restaurant** (with dancing). *22 Park Lane, W1. 493-8000*

6 **Inter-Continental.** *Deluxe.* The English like to stay here and pretend they are in America. They are dazzled by the telephones, clotheslines and scales in the bathrooms, as well as the oversized everything: rooms, beds, towels and closets. They watch in amazement as people discuss business over breakfast in the **Coffee House,** shop in the **Aquascutum** and **Cartier** boutiques and book Rolls-Royces to take them on shopping trips further afield. The elegant women in the elegant lobby are more likely to be company presidents than the wives of company presidents. The Inter-Continental may lack English charm, but you can be certain that nothing will go wrong. *1 Hamilton Place, Hyde Park Corner, W1. 409-3131*

Within the Hotel are:

Coffee House. ★ ★ ★ $$ These are the breakfasts of champions, with a choice of 3: the basic Continental, the breakfast buffet or the classic English breakfast with kippers, kedgeree, kidneys et al. You can also go *à la carte. Open daily 7-12AM. 409-3131*

Hamilton's Supper Club. ★ ★ $$ Such a club is rare in London: you can order whatever you want until 1AM and dance until 3AM. Try the *salade frisée aux lardons* (curly endive salad with bacon and poached egg) or *steak frites,* or come after the theatre and eat scrambled eggs with smoked salmon. *Open Tu-Sa 7PM-1AM. 409-3131*

Le Soufflé. ★ ★ ★ $$$ *Luxe luxe luxe* with a *Michelin* star, caviar and cool Art Deco. The diners sip their champagne (a choice of 25 on the wine list) with the nonchalance of film stars and tuck into their stuffed quail with the expertise of brain surgeons. There is nothing amateur on either side of the kitchen. Chef **Peter Kromberg,** wedged in between such considerable reputations as Anton Mosimann (100 yards away at the Dorchester) and Michael Quinn (100 yards away at the Ritz), has made an inspired rise to the occasion. Try the hot and frothy smoked salmon souffle with chives, the *feuilleté of asparagus* and *jambon de canard* (a ham of duck) to begin, then consider *petite nage de sole et homard aux concombres* and *paupiettes de turbots aux langoustine,* served with a sauce of red and black caviar and chives. The vegetables are Mozartian: tiny leeks, baby onions, crisp beans, carrots and *courgettes.* End with the figs, filled with cream, floating in a sea of raspberry *coulis.* The wine list is a labor of love even though the prices are the kind usually associated with things which are forever. Have a look at the special *sommelier's choice* and the 6-course menu. The service is impeccable. *Open daily except Sa lunch 12:30-3PM, 7-11:30PM. Sunday brunch 12-4PM. 409-3131*

7 **Inn On The Park.** *Deluxe.* The hotel was built in 1970, but it is suffused with the elegance of other eras—1930s ocean liner, first class, with fabulous antiques thrown in. Howard Hughes stayed here in his declining and difficult years, so this hotel has a pretty good track record of perfect service. Afternoon tea is served in the Queen Anne-style lounge, all sweetness and light, against a background of harp or piano music. The Inn offers the largest choice of teas in London, as well as a lethal sequence of sandwiches, scones and pastries. *Hamiliton Pl., Park Lane, W1. 499-0888*

Within the hotel are:

Lanes. ★ ★ $$ The set lunches deserve their popularity. This isn't imaginative food, just very good and honest food—English roasts, Scottish salmon, game in season. *Open daily 12-3PM, 6-12PM. 499-0888*

Four Seasons. ★ ★ $$$ The hotel's French restaurant overlooking a private garden has an extensive wine list and specializes in lunches under 600 calories, including salad of pigeon and sauteed monkfish in a light saffron sauce. *Open daily 12-3PM, 7-11PM. 499-0888*

8 **Hard Rock Cafe.** ★ ★ ★ $ People have been waiting in line to eat here for almost 2 decades, undeterred by rain, sleet or snow. The Hard Rock has the best hamburgers in town, and until the Los Angeles and New York branches opened, possibly the best hamburgers in the world. For Americans, it is a round trip ticket to home in the 1960s: Budweiser beer, Chicago Bears, hamburgers the size of catcher's mitts, waitresses with name tags (*Dixie, Cookie*) and hot fudge sundaes. The best time to go (dare I say?) is late afternoon, when it is neither lunch nor dinner. The music isn't brain-damaging loud and you don't have to wait. *No beer between 2:30 and 6PM. Open daily 12PM to 12:15AM. 150 Old Park Lane, W1. 629-0382*

9 **Green Park.** Greener than emeralds from Asprey, the 60 acres of sable-soft grass is the kind of luxury money can't buy in a city. There are no flowerbeds in the park. Instead ancient beech, lime, and plane trees spread their limbs like maps of the world. In spring, a tapestry of daffodils and crocuses appears. The sloping canvas chairs cost a few pence—don't worry, the chair collector will come to you, and he will give you a little sticker as proof that you have paid. Sit down and read *English Hours* by Henry James, the morning newspaper or just observe the perfect Englishness all around you. The noble mansions around Green Park that established the atmosphere of wealth, luxury and society have nearly all disappeared, replaced by their 20th century equivalent—*hotels deluxes*. Still, the flavor of grandeur is continuous, undefeated and immediately perceptible.

10 Athenaeum. *Deluxe.* This hotel is small compared to its modern neighbors and offers the kind of service that feels more like a private house than a hotel. The old-fashioned feel is in ways that count—plumbing, towels the size of tents, monogrammed linen sheets and telephone and switchboard services—but it is totally modern. If you like to begin the day with a jog, Green Park and Hyde Park are on the doorstep. The restaurant is excellent and is especially popular at lunchtime. If you are planning a longer stay, there is an adjoining apartment house. The hotel makes special effort for women traveling on their own. *116 Piccadilly, W1. 499-3463*

11 Park Lane Hotel. *Deluxe.* For starters, it isn't on Park Lane; it's on Piccadilly overlooking Green Park. It sounds anonymous and modern, but it is old, lovely and full of character. The rooms are personal, the suites have their original 1920s decor and dreamy Art Deco bathrooms and the clientele is fiercely loyal. *Piccadilly, W1. 499-6321*

Within the hotel are:

Brasserie on the Park. ★ ★ $ Real brasserie classics—mussels marinieré, onion soup—with health-conscious salads, hamburgers, steaks and English grills. Simple, easy food at easy-going prices. *Open daily 10:30AM-12:30PM. 499-6321*

Bracewells. ★ ★ ★ $$ This oak-paneled restaurant feels like a gentlemen's club,and the excellent wine list has the kind of wines and prices that are usually found only in those privileged places. But the food is definitely superior to clubland. Think about the English oysters, the poached halibut with saffron and shredded leeks, the chicken cooked with fresh ginger and lime and the lavish trolley of desserts. This is a bargain, with set menus available at lunch and dinner. *Open M-Sa 12:30-2:30PM, 7-11:30PM; Su 12:30-2:00PM, 7:00-10:30PM. 499-6321*

12 Shepherd's Market. The best way to reach this tiny and exclusive square, filled with small white houses, boutiques, restaurants and pubs, is from Curzon Street, through the covered passage at No. 47. This was the site of the May fairs of the 17th century, and now it is home to 2 of London's best pubs: **Shepherd's Tavern** (50 Hertford St.) and **Bunch of Grapes**, with its tiny restaurant **Ted's Pantry** (Shepherd's Market). Both serve excellent pub lunches and refreshingly cold beer and ale. *Mayfair, W1.*

13 Half Moon Street. Poke around the street a few minutes—it is home to some very distinguished ghosts. **Boswell** (1740-95) lived here, recording his walks with Johnson and taking endless cures for his gonnorhea, which he then wrote about in graphic detail in his London journal. **Fanny Burney** (1752-1840) also lived on the street, as did the essayist **Hazlitt** and the poet **Shelley**. More recently, Half Moon Street was the address of **PG Wodehouse's Bertie Wooster** and his faithful **Jeeves**.

14 Langan's Brasserie. ★ ★ $$ Like the Café Royal and the Closerie des Lilas, Langan's Brasserie will eventually be in the literature of the age, even though the genius recalled will be of the deal-making Hollywood genre, not *The Sun Also Rises*. The beautiful, clever, rich and promising come here to see and be seen, and it is good luck for everybody that the food is as good as it is, thanks to **Richard Shepherd,** chef and one-third owner. **Michael Caine** also owns a part. But the most visible member of this triumverate is **Peter Langan,** an outrageous Irishman whose capacious head, linen suits and intransigent behavior have made him an institution. Dress glamorously and have a look at the pictures. Langan's eye for 20th century British art will outlive his palate. Start your meal with the spinach soufflé with anchovy sauce, order a plainish main course and end with *crème brûlée*. Avoid Langan's on Saturday nights when *tout-Londres* is nowhere near London and the restaurant fills with couples from the suburbs. *Open M-F 12:30-2:45PM, 7-11:45PM; Sa 7-12PM. Stratton St., WI. 491-6437, 491-8822*

15 May Fair. *Deluxe.* This is an appropriate hotel to be next to Langan's. It has its own cinema and built-in theatre and a Polynesian restaurant with garrulous parrots and blue lagoons. The hotel manages to combine idiosyncrasy with polished competence making it the perfect haunt for theatre, film and media folk who all think it is their own discovery. *Stratton St, W1. 629-7777*

16 The Ritz. *Deluxe.* Two more evocative words are hard to imagine. Such is the power of the Ritz that the name can be spelled in light bulbs and still be glamourous. The hotel was built in the style of a French château with a Parisian arcade from the designs of **Mewès** and **Davis** in 1906. For everyday,ordinary, aspiring folk, this is a kind of *Brideshead Revisited,* a world of elegance, beauty and perfection that is rooted in the past and maintained with fastidious dedication. The champagne era had little in common with the Perrier age. Men and women danced cheek to cheek to strˌnged orchestras, waiters were anonymous and moved like members of the *corps de ballet,* and hotels were an art, one of the civilizing forces in any capital city. The Ritz is dedicated to the memory of that bygone age, applying politeness and gallantry to modern hotel tactics.

A wonderful way to begin any day is with breakfast at the Ritz, more appropriate after a stroll in Green Park. The menu offers such English treats as Cumberland sausage, Lancashire black pudding, haddock kedgeree and Scotch kippers. But lunch may well be the Ritz's finest hour: the delicate pastel colors of the world's most beautiful dining room, subtly lit by dim London daylight; a table by the windows overlooking Green Park; a grilled Dover sole washed down with *Krug Grande Cuvée.*

Pity about the tea at the Ritz. It is so popular that you must book ages in advance, and it is about as special as tea at Paddington Station. Forego this disappointing pleasure and have a better tea somewhere else, returning here for a glass of champagne after the tea hoardes have gone. *The Ritz Restaurant is open daily 12:30-2:30PM, 6:30-11PM. Palm Court is open for coffee from 10-11:30AM and tea (2 sittings) at 3:15 and 4:30PM. Piccadilly, W1.* 493-8181

17 John Murray. The publisher opened his office on Albemarle Street in 1812, and went on to publish the works of Byron, Jane Austen, George Crabbe and a host of other literary greats. This is the place that Byron's autobiography was burned after his death because the poet's friends thought it was too shocking. The seventh John Murray runs the firm today.*No. 50 Albermarle St., W1.*

18 Granary. ★★$ Simple English national dishes such as lamb with mint sauce and summer pudding, set out on a self-service counter. *Open M-F 11AM-7PM, Sa 11AM-2:30PM. 39 Albemarle St., SW1.* 493-2978

19 Brown's Hotel.*Deluxe.* There is no discreet plaque saying that Henry James stayed here, and he probably didn't, but there is something perfectly Jamesian about this hotel just off Piccadilly. It is very popular with the kind of Anglophile Americans who come to England once a year to look at pictures, visit their tailor, see a few plays and visit friends they have known since the war. Theodore Roosevelt spent his honeymoon with Edith here in 1886 (they got married a few blocks away at St. George's, Hanover Square), and Franklin D. Roosevelt spent his honeymoon with Eleanor here in 1905. You feel that it is just as intimate and democratic and English country house now as it was then. The restaurant is worthy of a presidential palate, and this is one of the best places for tea in London. The rooms are intimate and lamplit, the sofas and chairs solid and comfy and the sandwiches, scones and cakes plentiful and superb. Naturally it gets crowded, so book if possible. *Restaurant open M-Sa 12:15-2:30PM, 6-10PM; Su until 9PM. 22-24 Dover St., W1.* 493-6020

The sequence of events in **English afternoon hotel tea** is: small sandwiches (the famous cucumber as well as salmon, tomato and egg); followed by scones (on which you put a layer of butter, a layer of jam, and a layer of clotted cream—whipped cream is cheating); then toasted teacakes; and finally, pastries. It requires a certain stamina, and if all you want is a cup of tea, you will have some difficulty.

20 Bond Street. This is Fifth Avenue, Rodeo Drive, the Faubourg-St. Honore, Old and New Bond Street and the most expensive property on the Monopoly board. Imperturbably chic Bond Street leads from Piccadilly to Oxford Street and is paved with Gold American Express Cards all the way. The legendary shopping street just celebrated its 300th birthday, cheating only a little bit: *Old* Bond Street was built in 1686, but *New* Bond Street, which begins at Clifford Street, only dates back to 1721. You can blame the confusing street numbering system on a Parliament, which in 1762 forbade the use of hanging signs to identify shops (too many customers were being decapitated in high winds), and numbered the streets separately, first up the east side toward Oxford Street and then down again on the west.

Art galleries flourish on Bond. You can buy a Turner at **Thomas Agnew & Son,** a Francis Bacon at **Marlborough Fine Arts,** a Vanessa Bell at **Anthony d'Offay** or an Unknown at **Sotheby's,** the world's largest auctioneer. You can shop at the almost endless number of chic shops—**Gucci, Hermes, Yves St. Laurent, Cartier, Louis Vuitton, Ralph Lauren, Chanel, Kurt Geiger, Magli.** The real challenge is to find what is uniquely English, but it is worth the effort.

More Bond Street Bests:

Asprey & Co. This luxurious gift shop specializes in the finest and the rarest, from crocodile suitcases to Faberge frames. More wedding presents for the Prince and Princess of Wales came from here than any other single source, including the engagement ring He gave to Her.*Open M-F 9AM-5:30PM, Sa 9AM-1PM. 165 New Bond St., W1.* 493-6767

Charbonnel et Walker. The fabulous chocolates come in boxes that are equally sweet treasures. *Open M-F 9AM-5:30PM, Sa 10AM-2PM. 31 Old Bond St., W1.* 629-4396

Folio Books. Located in the Royal Arcade, this bookshop makes handsome editions of all the favorite English writers—is there anything nicer than a beautifully bound and printed set of Jane Austens? *M-F 9:30AM-6PM, Sa 9:30AM-1PM. 5 Royal Arcade, W1.* 629-6517

W. Bill. Pleasantly cluttered and un-Bond Street, with heavy sweaters, cashmere and tartans. *Open M-F 9AM-5:30PM, Sa 9:30AM-4PM. 93 New Bond St., W1.* 629-2837.

Smythson's. Very Bond Street and very English. Their invitations feel like diplomas and are the most desired in town. The leather address books and diaries are equally coveted, and even though it's *un peu prétentious,* their address book divided into 3 sections and simply inscribed *London New York Paris* is extremely useful for fortunate vagabonds. *Open M-F 9:30AM-5:30PM, Sa 9:15AM-12:30PM. 54 New Bond St., W1.* 629-8558

21 Burlington Arcade. (1819, Samuel Hare) The Regency promenade of exclusive shops may be considered a forerunner to the shopping malls that bear so little resemblance to it. The Arcade was built in the years after Waterloo for Lord George Cavendish and was inspired by Continental models. Its purpose was to provide the Regency gentry with a shopping precinct

OXFORD STREET

shoes **R. Cartier**

woollens **W. Bill**
restaurant **Old Vienna**

BLENHEIM STREET

shoes **K. Geiger**
Royal Bank of Scotland
linen and lingerie **Frette**
cashmere **Brainin of Bond St.**
shoes **Alan McAfee**
jewelry **Nawbar & Co.**
clothing **Daniel Hechter**
women's clothing **Lucy's**
men's designer clothing **Lanvin**
shoes **Russell & Bromley**

BROOK STREET

Barclays Bank
Bond St. Silver Galleries
clothing **Saint Laurent**
shoes **Kurt Geiger**
shoes **Bally**
jewelry **Crombie**
works of art **Christopher Gibbs**
men's silk clothing **Cecil Gee**

LANCASHIRE COURT

44 shops **Bond St. Antique Centre**
men's clothing **Herbie Frogg**

Midland Bank

GROSVENOR COURT

Chinacraft

men's clothing **Beale & Inman**
women's clothing **Beale & Inman**
men's clothing **St. Laurent**
women's clothing **Robina**

BLOOMFIELD PLACE

women's jewelry **Marie Clair**
antique jewelry **SJ Philips**
men's clothing **Zilli**
clothing **Polo/Ralph Lauren**
antiques **Partridge**
fine art **Wildensein & Co.**
The Fine Art Society
leather travel goods **Louis Vuitton**
Irish Tourist Board **Ireland House**

BRUTON STREET

clothing **Hermes**

clothing **Emanuel Ungar**
jewelry **Van Cleef & Arpels**

Air France

National Westminster Bank

women's clothing **Valentino**

Church's Shoes

London Savoy Taylors Guild

GRAFTON STREET

NEW BOND STREET

Francisce M. clothing

CW Andrew chemist
Bambino children's clothing

DERING STREET

Mira women's clothing
Pratesi Italian bed linens

Milton's patisserie
Please Mum children's clothing
Escada women's clothing
Rayne shoes
Bentley & Co. goldsmith

BROOK STREET

Fenwicks dept. store

Smythson's fine stationery

Jason fabrics
White House linen and clothing
Chappell pianos
Magli shoes
F. Pinet women's shoes

MADDOX STREET

Regine clothing

Frost & Reed Art Gallery

Mallet antique
Gerald Austin men's clothing

Sotheby's auctioneer

Bond St. Carpets

Cesar shoes

Celine accessories

Tessiers antique jewelry
Russell & Bromley shoes

CONDUIT STREET

Air India

CLIFFORD STREET

Watches of Switzerland
Patek Philippe watches
George Jensen silver and porcelain
Piaget watches
Adler jewelry
Hennel jewelry

GRAFTON STREET

Asprey & Co

jewelry Collingwood

women's clothing Karl Lagerfeld

Cartier
shoes Rossetti
jewelry Chaumet
jewelry Boucheron
leather accessories Loewe
women's clothing Chanel
accessories Gucci
woollens W. Bill

THE ROYAL ARCADE

chocolates Charbonnel et Walker
silversmith Holmes
shoes Bally
facial salon Yardley

STAFFORD STREET

Midland Bank
leather goods Andrew Soo's

Marlborough Graphics Gallery
Lloyds Bank
fine art Thos. Agnew & Sons
amber specialities Sac Freres

pearls Ciro

PICCADILLY

OLD BOND STREET

Philip Antrobus jewelry
Adele Davis women's clothing
Anne Bloom jewelry
Booty jewelry
Etienne Aigner accessories
Rolex watches
Richard Green art gallery
National Westminster Bank

BURLINGTON GARDENS

Salvatore Ferragmo shoes

Pierre Cardin clothing
Sulka men's shirts

Rayne women's clothing

Colnaghi Art Gallery
The Leger Art Galleries
Benson and Hedges
Brainin cashmere
Jindo Fur Salon
WR Harvey & Co. antiques
Fenzi men's clothing
Ackermann Gallery sport prints
ADC Heritage antique silver
Tyme watches

PICCADILLY

free from the mud splashed by carriages and carts on Piccadilly. The top-hatted Beadles who still patrol the Arcade today were originally installed to protect the prosperous shoppers from pickpockets and beggars. Now they supposedly ask you not to whistle or run, and they lock the gates at 5:30PM each afternoon. Burlington Arcade was badly damaged in the Blitz, but it recovered and rebuilt, and today exudes an atmosphere of intimate but not inconceivable luxury, with 38 shops that offer lasting treasures. Admire the glass roof and the small, delicately detailed shop fronts. The ostentatious facades were added in 1911.

Burlington Arcade Bests:

N. Peal. The 3 shops in the Arcade, 2 for men and one for women, have the best cashmere in London, from the addictive socks (it is the only place you can find cashmere knee socks for women) to the cashmere capes. Wise Englishwomen would rather be draped in cashmere than diamonds, preferably in men's 2-ply cashmere cardigans. The best is never cheap and N. Peal is no exception. *Open M-F 9AM-11PM. Men's Shop: No. 54, 493-5378. Women's Shop: No.37-40, 493-0714*

BURLINGTON GARDENS

Irish Linen Company
tobaconist Sullivan Powell
cashmere & woollens S. Fisher
small antiques Demas
fashion jewelry Ken Lane
The Pen Shop
animal bronzes Christie
small antiques Gerald Sattin
antique and modern silver Holmes
cashmere S. Fisher
coats Berk
jewelry Simeon
antique and modern The Pewter Shop
dolls and lead soldiers Hummel
fine art MacConnal-Mason
woollens Noble Jones
Chinacraft

hairbrushes Clements
clothing James Drew
coats Wetherall

BURLINGTON ARCADE

N. Peal woollens

DL Lord fine leather
Donaldson, Williams & G. Ward tailors
Armour-Winston Ltd fine jewelry
Goldsmiths and Silversmiths Assoc. jewelry
Berk women's cashmere

Tricker Shoes

C Barrett & Co. Oriental antiques
SJ Rood & Co. silver and jewelry
N. Peal men's cashmere
Penhaligon's perfumers
Scott men's ties and woollens
Church's English Shoes/A. Jones boots
Dunhill tobacconist
Zelli fine porcelain
Clements accessories
Johnson Walker-Tolhurst antique jewelry
Lord men's shirts and woollens
Lord women's woollens
B. Barnett Ltd. jewelry

PICCADILLY

James Drew. Silk shirts, mostly with high necks, each one a work of seamstress's art. *Open M-F 9AM-5:30PM, Sa 9AM-1PM. No.3, 493-0144.*

Clements. One of the best shops for very English presents that you can fit in your suitcase: silver wine coasters (real silver, Georgian reproduction, very handsome); silver peppermills (with initials and date, a nice wedding present); and a large selection of corkscrews and quality knives. *Open M-F 9AM-5:30PM, Sa 9AM-1PM. No.4-5, 493-3923; No.63, 493-0997*

B. Barnett Ltd. This shop facing Piccadilly has pearls worthy of the Queen Mum— creamy, pinkish pearls in Edwardian sizes at prices more Edwardian than you'll find anywhere. *Open M-F 9AM-4PM. Closed Sa, Su. No.71-72, 493-0144*

The Pewter Shop
18 Burlington Arcade
London, W.1.
TELEPHONE: 01-493 1730.
Orders sent to all parts of the world

The Pewter Shop. Museums and private collectors come here first. *Open M-F 9AM-5:30PM, Sa 9AM-4:30PM. No.18, 493-1730*

S. FISHER

S. Fisher. The 10-ply cable-knit cashmere sweater will set you back a bit, but it will keep you warm for life. The shop has a beautiful choice of shetlands, cashmeres and Irish sweaters. *Open M-F 9AM-5:30PM, Sa 9:30AM-5PM. No.22-23, 493-4180*

Richard Ogden. Antique jewelry, with museum-quality pieces of Art Nouveau. *Open M-F 9:30AM-5:30PM, Sa 9:30AM-4PM. No.28-29, 493-9136*

Irish Linen Company. Linen napkins that could sail a small ship, sheets that assume you have a laundry service which collects and delivers, and special cloths for drying the Waterford crystal wine glasses which grace the linen tablecloth can be found in this classic shop. It is all from another era and very nice. *Open M-F 9AM-5:30PM, Sa 9AM-4:30PM. No.35-36, 493-8949*

Sullivan Powell. Havana cigars, briar pipes, Turkish and Virginia cigarettes in cedar boxes. *Open M-F 9AM-5:30PM, Sa 9AM-1PM. No.34, 629-0433*

Penhaligon. Very English and very special perfumes, all with the scent of an English country garden. Try *Bluebell.* The bottles and labels are enchanting, with a collection of antique silver and perfume bottles that are truly tokens of love. *Open M-F 10AM-6PM, Sa 10AM-5PM. No.55, 629-1416*

22 **Museum of Mankind.** (1869, Sir James Pennethorne) If you leave the Burlington Arcade on the northern end at Burlington Gardens and turn right, you may find you are in a Bengal village or with a primitive mountain tribe in Peru. Take your chances and go to the Museum of Mankind, a department of the British Museum and one of London's least known and most imaginative museums. Children love the skulls, sculpture, masks, weapons, pottery, textiles and puppets from tribes all over the world, especially the American Indian war bonnets, bows and arrows and peace pipes. The permanent collection (in *Room 8*) includes a life-sized skull carved from a piece of solid crystal from Mexico and a stunning Benin ivory mask from Africa. A very realistic exhibition is staged once a year (for example, a reconstruction of a village in Gujerat in northern India, with real huts and Gujerat artisans weaving and carving). All this is in the heart of, but light-years away from, Piccadilly. The exterior of the Museum is an example of High Victorian architecture, with statues of leaders in science and philosophy punctuating the sky, and a confusion of styles—classic versus Italian Gothic—in a kind of architectural détente. The bookshop in the Museum has replicas of art and artifacts. *Open M-Sa 10AM-6PM, Su 2:30-6:00PM. 6 Burlington Gardens, Piccadilly, W1. 437-2224*

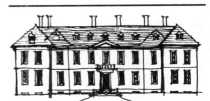

From an engraving by Jan Kip after Leonard Knyff, 1707

After the changes made c. 1717

The present front as developed by Sydney Smirke, 1872-74

Courtesy Royal Academy of Arts

23 **Royal Academy of Arts, Burlington House.** The last surviving palace of 18th century Piccadilly. The core is still 17th century, but the pure Palladian facade, built by **Colen Campbell** around 1717 and immortalized by **Hogarth** and **Gay,** was replaced with the Victorian neo-Renaissance front by **Banks** and **Barry** in 1873. The Pic-

PICCADILLY

cadilly frontage has an imposing grandeur which is enlightened by colorful banners that herald the exhibitions inside. These—as well as the Royal Academy itself—are always worth seeing.

In the courtyard stands **Sir Joshua Reynolds,** often draped irreverently with posters or flags connected with the exhibition, a spirited inclusion he would not have objected to as the first president of the Royal Academy.

In the rooms along the quadrangle, learned societies have their headquarters: the **Geological Society**, the **Royal Society of Chemistry**, the **Society of Antiquaries**, the **Royal Astronomical Society** and until recently, the most prestigious society of all, the **Royal Society**, which has the most outstanding scientists in Britain. Their headquarters are now in Carlton House Gardens.

The Royal Academy, founded in 1769, marked the recognition of the importance of art and artists in this country and, for better or worse, made artists members of the Establishment. Artistic temperament what it is, many balked and refused to exhibit at this official marketplace for art—Romney, Blake, Rossetti and Whistler refused, while Gainsborough initially exhibited. The division has not really healed with time—you can be certain that Francis Bacon and David Hockney are not part of the Academy. The initials *RA* after an artist's name (meaning he is or was one of the 50 honored Academicians) may add to the price of an artist's work in the salesrooms, but they do not significantly affect his reputation in the art world. In the last 10 years, the Royal Academy has entered a new phase that is livelier and more innovative.

In the center of the entrance hall are ceiling paintings by **Benjamin West** —*The Graces Unveiling Nature* and *The Four Elements.* Four paintings by **Angelica Kaufmann** (1741-1807) hang at each end—*Genuis* and *Painting* near the door to the Library on the east and *Composition* and *Design* on the west. The central staircase is surmounted by a roundel by **William Kent** of *Architecture Contemplating the Portrait of Inigo Jones.* On the first floor is the **Saloon,** the only surviving part of Burlington House by Campbell, with the ceiling by William Kent.

Exhibitions take place in the rooms on the first and second floors. The **Summer Exhibition** is the big event of the year at the Academy, and one of London's important social occasions. 10,000 works by 4,000 artists are submitted, with 1,300 finally selected. The gala opening in June looks like a Royal garden party with pictures. The Academy's reputation now rests on its loan exhibitions (this is where the enormous *Venice* show originated), but its permanent collection ought to be on show more frequently. Splendid pictures by Reynolds, Gainsborough, Constable, Turner, Wilkie, Raeburn, Munnings and Sickert comprise a collection which is both personal and interesting. The collection contains the works of past members who, upon election, deposited a work, known as a *Diploma piece.* They are exhibited periodically on the top floor in the **Diploma Galleries,** which can be reached by an unnervingly slow freight elevator.

The Academy's greatest treasure is a Carrara marble relief of *Madonna and Child with the Infant St. John* by **Michelangelo,** carved in 1505. It is one of only 4 major sculptures by the artist outside of Italy and it is on display in the **Annex Gallery.** *Admission fee for special exhibitions. Open daily 10AM-6PM. Royal Academy, Burlington House, Piccadilly, W1. 734-9052*

Within the Academy are:

Royal Academy Shop . Jam - packed with wonderful items. You will find a vast range of artist's materials, including a superb anatomical lion, a framing service, easels, brushes and paints. The shop has jigsaw puzzles of favorite paintings, a large collection of art books, catalogues from exhibitions abroad, silk scarves designed by famous artists and the obligatory canvas Museum bags. *Open daily 10AM-6PM, 734-9052*

Royal Academy Restaurant. ★ ★ $ Big and cafeterial, but a welcome refuge from the non-stop glamour of Piccadilly. Women in tweed suits and sensible shoes, in town for the day, sit in the attractive paneled room, peacefully drinking tea and eating cakes. Hot and cold lunches are served between 11:30AM and 2:30PM. There is also a good salad bar. *Open daily 10:30AM-5PM. 734-9052*

24 **Piccadilly Arcade.** (1910, Thrale Jell) Built as an extension of the Burlington Arcade a century later, this charming, relaxed collection of shops connects Piccadilly to Jermyn Street.

Within the Arcade are:

Gered. The China specialists have a complete and very tempting collection of Wedgwood and Spode. All their price lists include the import price and the amount in dollars. *Open M-F 9AM-5:30PM, Sa 9AM-1PM. No.173-174 Piccadilly Arcade. 629-2614*

Armory of St. James's. Decorations and medals for the otherwise unrewarded. *Open M-F 10AM-6PM. Closed Sa. No. 17 Piccadilly Arcade. 493-5082*

Benson & Clegg. The tailors to George VI will make you a suit or provide you with a set of dazzling buttons and hand embroidered crests for your own blazer. *Open M-F 8AM-5PM, Sa 8AM-12PM. No. 9 Piccadilly Arcade. 491-1454*

New and Lingwood. This is one of the best, and somehow least known, shops in the Arcade, located on the Jermyn Street side. It started as the London branch of the Eton shop, where New and Lingwood has outfitted Etonians for many decades. The shop has beautiful ready-made shirts and a small but choice selection of sweaters, including a forest-green cable-knit cashmere sweater that is a lifetime commitment but worth every pound and pence. You can also have shirts made to order. Upstairs, incorporated within the shop, is **Poulsen and Skone,** makers of fine shoes which require another serious commitment, but in this instance they share the burden, providing care and service for your shoes for life. The ready-made shoes are pretty wonderful too. *Open M-F 9AM-5:30PM, Sa 10AM-3PM. No. 53 Jermyn St. 493-9621*

Sims and Reed. Booksellers who specialize in rare books on art and architecture. *Open M-F 10AM-6PM. Closed Sa. No. 58 Jermyn St. 493-5660*

25 **Fortnum & Mason.** On the hour, the clock chimes sweetly, and 2 mechanical figures emerge from the miniature doors. Dressed in livery of 18th century servants, Mr. Fortnum and Mr. Mason turn and bow to each other while the bells chime the Eton school song. The clock is a recent addition to the wonderful store, placed here in 1964, but it says everything: this 18th century treasure house is ready to serve you most excellently, as it has been serving the privileged since 1707.

Fortnum & Mason

Inside, the crystal chandeliers reflect in the polished mahogany, highlighting temptations of caviar, truffles, marrons glaces, hand-dipped chocolates, Stilton cheeses, teas, honeys, champagnes and *foie gras*. This is one of the world's most magnificent grocers and oldest carry-out stores. The luxurious hampers which are such a feature of Ascot and Glyndebourne began in 1788 as packed lunches (known as *Concentrated Lunches*) for hunting and shooting parties and Members of Parliament *who may be detained*. Game pies and boned chickens and lobster and prawns would be dispatched for these privileged folk. During the Napoleonic Wars, officers in the Duke of Wellington's army ordered hams and cheeses. Baskets were sent to Florence Nightingale in the Crimea, to Mr. Stanley while he was looking for Mr. Livingston and to suffragettes imprisoned in London's Holloway Jail, who shared their hampers from Fortnum and Mason with fellow prisoners. If you are lucky enough to have tickets for Glyndebourn, Wimbledon or Ascot, or if you just feel like a luxurious picnic in St. James's Park, Green Park, Kensington Park Gardens or Regents Park, indulge in a hamper worthy of the occasion. The *Executive Hamper for 2* includes Parma ham and melon, smoked salmon cornettes, fresh roasted poussin, ox-tongue, salad, profiteroles, cheeses, champagne and chocolate truffles. Add a thermos of coffee, and have a lordly repas under an English sky for less than you would pay in most terrace restaurants. You are attended by gentlemen in morning coats who write down your choices and requests, accompany you from department to department and advise with knowledge, patience and charm.

The teas are famous and their blue-green tins are as much a sign as a guarantee of good taste. Try the *Finest Broken Orange Pekoe*, a delicious everyday tea. (You will be encouraged to put less tea in the pot and drink it without milk in order to appreciate the true flavor.) Also try the Paulliac of tea: *Formosa Oolong Peach Blossom*. If you provide a sample of your local water, the store will carefully match it with one of their 68 varieties of tea. There is even a New York blend. After you have wisely invested a fortune in English honeys, Fortnum's own marmalades, teas, a game pie or 2, a tin of English biscuits, a couple of pottery crocks of Stilton, and a jar of Gentlemen's Relish (a very special anchovy paste) decorated with pheasants, consider lunch at Fortnum's. *Open M-F 9AM-5:30PM, Sa 9AM-1PM. 181 Piccadilly, W1. 734-8040*

Within the store are:

Fountain Restaurant. ★ ★ ★ $$ Sadly, the interior was recently redecorated, and although it looks terribly elegant, all the neutral dove greys and recessed lights look anonymously like New York. One misses the 1950s aqua-blue room with its seaside mural behind the counter. Still, the food is the same, and there is a new counter for those who pop in alone and want a delicious and uncomplicated meal. Surprisingly, this restaurant is also open in the evening (until 11:30), so besides breakfast, lunch and tea, you can come here for dinner, before and after the theatre. The grills are first-class, the pies (game, steak and kidney) are excellent, and if you just want something light, the sandwiches are fit for Ascot. The ice cream sundaes are famous, and this is one of the only restaurants in London where you can get fabulous coffee, espresso or cappuccino—again, at the counter. The Fountain is a favorite place for tea, and a number of writers, artists and London figures use this as their club (that's JP Donleavy sitting in the corner). It is without a doubt the best place in the area for breakfast. But if you have already eaten, come for what the English call *elevenses*—coffee and a Danish. *Open M-Sa 9.30AM-11:30PM. 734-4938*

St. James's Restaurant. ★ ★ ★ $$ This fourth floor restaurant is far less known, hence quieter and ideal for exchanging confidences over roast beef and Yorkshire pudding. Your neighbors look like they have come to London to bid on a little something at Christie's or Sotheby's, very tweed suit and proper *Open for coffee M-Sa 9-11:30AM, lunch 12-2:30PM, tea 3-5PM. 734-8040*

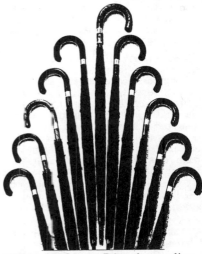

26 **Swaine Adeney Brigg.** As one of London's oldest and most traditional family run businesses, it is graced with 2 Royal warrants (Whip and Glove Makers to the Queen, Umbrella Makers to the Queen Mother). In a country where rain is a national characteristic, umbrellas are serious business, and Swaine Adeney Brigg makes the Rolls-Royce of umbrellas. Go in and look around. Upstairs you will find the finest in country clothing, including the whole range of the dark green waxy raincoats (Barbours) worn by the landed gentry, and everything to do with the sartorial side of riding horses and hunting. Ask one of the salesmen to explain the difference between the traditional and the classic umbrella, examine the runners, opera caps and ferrules and the hand and top springs. You will be given a wide choice of handles—crooks steamed and

PICCADILLY

bent by hand; woods including malacca, whangee, congo, chestnut, cherry, hickory, ash and maple; or if you prefer a leather handle, choose from handsewn calf, Morocco, pigskin, ostrich, lizard or crocodile. Then there's the choice of fabrics, including a wide selection of nylons or the best English silk. If in the end you choose the classic Brigg umbrella with the best English black silk cover, Malacca crook and gold collar engraved with your name and address, be assured that waiters will understand when you say you wish to keep your umbrella. There are also walking sticks, some sinister, but all remarkable. *Open M-F 9AM-5:30PM, Sa 9AM-4:30PM. 185 Piccadilly, W1. 734-4227*

27 Hatchards. The 18th century bookshop still has the charm of that age, but it has moved into the paperback era with considerable booksmart. Now it is a book emporium, with an excellent selection of children's books (*2nd floor*), art books (*1st floor*) and reference books, including dictionaries, Bibles and the Oxford Companions to Music, Literature, etc. (*ground floor*). In the literature department on the second floor you can buy all 12 volumes of Byron's *Letters and Journals,* edited by Leslie Marchand, or you can settle for the single volume of Byron's biography (all published by John Murray a few yards down the street). You'll find the complete works of just about all of your favorite English writers as well as second-hand and rare books. As you enter from Piccadilly, have a look at the recent hardcover fiction. In the modern annex, a travel section with guides, literary and otherwise, will keep you going for years. If books are your thing, this is paradise. *Open M-F 9AM-5:30PM, Sa 9AM-1PM. 187 Piccadilly, W1. 439-9921*

28 Albany. (1770-74, Sir William Chambers and Henry Holland; 1804) The building looks across Piccadilly at Fortnum from its little courtyard and is more like a Parisian *hotel particulier* done in English Palladianism. Originally built for Lord Melbourne, it was converted to *chambers* for bachelor gentlemen in 1803. The Albany has been home to Byron, Macaulay, Gladstone and more recently, JB Priestley and Graham Greene. *Albany Courtyard, W1.*

29 Sackville Street. Take a quick look at this almost (almost) pure Georgian street, with a confident modesty that evokes sense and sensibility, pride and prejudice.

30 Midland Bank. (1922, Sir Edwin Lutyens) This charming neighbor of St. James's Church is worth a glance. The architect kindly deferred to St. James's by creating a bank in domestic scale in brick and Portland stone. *196A Piccadilly, W1.*

31 St. James's, Piccadilly. (1676-84, Sir Christopher Wren) The church is the favorite of the man who gave us St. Paul's Cathedral and some 50 other London churches, but you have to go inside to fully understand why. The newly-pointed brick, the replaced and restored spire and crafts market in the courtyard give no idea what miracle is inside. But miracle it is: the wide-open spaciousness, the barrel-vaulted roof, the rows of 5 two-tiered windows, the Corinthian columns, the brass, the gilt, the paint. It has always been a fashionable church, especially created for large congregations of the wedding kind. The organ was built for James II, and the wonderful white marble font with figures of Adam and Eve and the Tree of Life, carved by **Grinling Gibbons,** christened, amongst many others, William Blake in 1757. Of his church Wren said: *There are no walls of a second order, nor lanterns, nor buttresses, but the whole rests upon pillars, as do also the galleries, and I think it may be found beautiful and convenient; it is the cheapest form of any I could invent.* Ah, the economy of genius. The church is also a moving tribute to its congregation. Almost completely destroyed in the bombing of 1940, it was restored with determination and dedication. The spire was completed in 1968 by **Sir Albert Richardson.** *Open M-Sa 10AM-6PM, Su 12-6PM. Lunchtime concerts Th-F 1:10PM. 197 Piccadilly, W1. 743-4511*

Within the Church Yard are:

Wren Cafe. ★ ★ $ A cheerful place to come for homemade soups (thick vegetable soups served with thick slices of whole meal bread), herbal teas and healthy, delicious salads, as well as cakes, fruit tarts and coffee. *Open M-Sa 10:30AM-6PM, Su 11AM-4PM. 734-7449*

Piccadilly Market. This lively crafts market in the courtyard of St James's Church always attracts large crowds on Fridays and Saturdays. There is usually a good selection of pottery, hand-knit sweaters, carved wood children's toys, enameled jewelry and boxes, all at very modest prices. *Open F-Sa 10AM-4PM.*

London Brass-Rubbing Center. You can rub effigies of medieval brasses (mostly fascimiles), creating your own knight in shining armor. If you feel pressed for time, buy a ready-made knight. This is a nice place to spend time with children who love creating copies of tiny effigies. *Open M-Sa 10AM-6PM, Su 12-6PM. St. James's Church Hall. 437-6023*

32 New Piccadilly Hotel. *Deluxe.* In 1908, this was London's newest and most elegant hotel, built by one of the leading Edwardian architects, **Norman Shaw.** He combined dazzling opulence (telephones in every room, 150 bathrooms and turkish baths) with architectural perfection. Throughout the 1920s and 30s, the hotel's reputation held fast. But after WWII, it began a major decline. In 1983, Gleneagles of Scotland bought the hotel. £16 million later, it is one of the showcases of Piccadilly and is a generous and sorely needed physical and psychological facelift to Piccadilly Circus. What Norman Shaw created has been preserved (by a protection order as well as by good sense). But late 20th century notions of essential luxury are found in the health club, with squash courts, solarium, swimming pool, gym, turkish baths, Jacuzzi, hairdressing and beauty salon, sauna and *fitness cuisine* brasserie. The glamour is in the facilities; the rooms are comfortable and pleasant, but not remarkably grand. *Piccadilly, W1. 734-8000*

Within the hotel are:

Oak Room Restaurant. ★★$$$ The original pale oak-paneled elegance looks like a set from *Edward VIII and Mrs. Simpson. Cuisinier* **David Chambers** prepares such lunch and dinner creations as *Mignons de Chevreuil aux Myrtilles, Croquette de Poine Willams* (venison in a blueberry sauce with a pear and cinnamon croquette) and *Oefs de Cailles a la Crème de Fines Herbes, au vin Rouge* (quail eggs, poached in red and white wine, served with a creamy chive sauce). *Open daily 12-10PM. 734-8000*

Terrace Garden Restaurant. ★★$$$ This stunning brasserie in a conservatory still feels undiscovered, and it is a very nice way to begin or end a theatre evening. The crab soup served with Roville, Gruyere and croutons is delicious. There is also a daily 3-course *table d'hôte*. Afternoon tea is served from 3-5:30PM. *Open daily 3-5:30PM, 7-10PM. 734-8000*

The grand Baroque facade of the **Piccadilly Hotel** is without a doubt the most handsome part of the present quadrant around Piccadilly Circus. The tragedy is that it was built here, and that it was done at the terrible expense of **John Nash's** original quadrant, which was destroyed to make way for the hotel. Nash's elegant and ceremonial conception was shattered, for once not out of the greed of businessmen and the indifference of the public, but due to the architectural citadel itself, which purposely and purposefully ignored Nash's grand and remarkably fine plan. The guilt does not rest on **Sir Norman Shaw,** who genuinely attempted to restore the graciousness of this area and produced magnificent plans that respected the genius of Nash. But Shaw was defeated and withdrew his name from the Piccadilly development of 1912, and died soon after. The ghost of Nash has haunted this site ever since, making it almost impossible to successfully resurrect and restore the dignity that would make Piccadilly Circus worthy of a great city.

33 **Cording's.** If London wasn't a Dickensian tangle of ground leases, this shop would have been abolished and the grandeur of the Piccadilly Hotel extended. Only the web of London's property laws would enable the ceremonial designs of Nash to be destroyed and this little shop to remain. Cording's has been here since 1839, and has kept its character in an ever-changing world. You can get terrific raincoats, waterproof boots, country wools and tweeds, all of high quality and costing somewhat less than next door at Burberry's and Simpson's. *Open M-F 9AM-5:30PM, Sa 9:30AM-1PM. 19 Piccadilly, W1. 734-0830* .

34 **Simpson's.** The ultra-modern building by **Joseph Emberton** is a case of *if you wait long enough you'll get used to it.* It was one of the great pioneering *rational* store designs, with lavish use of materials, including glass lifts, travertine floors, space and light. But does it belong to Piccadilly? Fifty years later, Londoners completely accept the store (and its very high-quality clothing under the Daks label). Visitors complain that it is an eyesore. But architects admire what they see, especially when lit at night, and what they don't see—the welded steel structure (the second in England), with massive girders on the first floor. Simpson's now has an impressive women's department, with 3 floors of very tweedy country suits and the latest from French, English and American designers. But it is mainly known for its men's clothes, with the highest quality suits, tweed jackets, overcoats and raincoats. The service is slow, courteous and intelligent. *Open M-Sa 9AM-5:30PM, Th until 7PM. 203 Piccadilly, W1. 734-2002*

Within the store are:

Simpson's Wine Bar. ★★$ This light, airy slip of a wine bar overlooks Jermyn Street. It is pretty basic—coffee, croissants and Danish pastries in the morning, and quiche and salad at lunch, when it gets crowded with well-dressed people who want to eat simply and quickly. *Open M-Sa 9AM-5:15PM, Th until 6:45PM. 734-2002*

Simpson's Restaurant. ★★$$ Diners wear the kind of clothes sold in the store (smart, traditional, English) and eat the kind of food that they have in their own country houses, or so it seems. The restaurant serves proper English breakfasts (not the croissant lark, but eggs, bacon, sausage, kidneys and kippers). At lunch, choose from roast joints—beef and lamb—carved from the trolley, English cheeses and trifles and syllabubs for pudding. Then top it off with a proper English tea. Quite agreeable all 'round. *Open M-Sa 9AM-5:15PM. 734-2002*

35 **Regent Street.** Signs of the grand designs of **John Nash** are quite apparent, with Regent Street (in fact this is Lower Regent Street) at your right, running southward to Waterloo Place and the Mall, and northward to Oxford Street and Regent's Park; and Shaftesbury Avenue on the northeast, leading to Soho and the heart of theatreland. But what you see and what Nash actually created are two sadly different things. Nash planned Piccadilly Circus as an elegant square with a long arcade, very much like the Rue de Rivoli running alongside the Tuilleries in Paris. The Quadrant, an even larger version of the crescent at Regent's Park, was the very essence of the scheme, and so crucial that Nash financed its construction out of his own pocket, persuading his builders to take leases instead of payment when his own money ran out. Completed in 1819, it must have been very handsome indeed. Destruction of the Quadrant began in 1848, with serious obliteration in 1905. Since then, planners have tried with monotonous regularity to restore and re-create Piccadilly Circus. The latest attempt is the 1986 effort you see today: a pedestrian precinct that one can only hope won't succumb to the shabbiness to which the area is prone.

To the right of Regent Street is **Waterloo**

OXFORD STREET

Oxford Circus Tube

clothing **Benetton**

Oxford Circus Tube
Wedgewood Gift Centre

Bally shoes
Laura Ashley women's clothing

National Westminster Bank

PRINCES STREET

patisserie **Lindy's**

HANOVER STREET

LITTLE ARGYLE STREET

Dickins and Jones dept. store

Aer Lingus

GREAT MARLBOROUGH STREET

MADDOX STREET

Liberty and Co. clothing

Barclays Bank

hairdressers **R. Fielding**
Linguaphone
Furs For All

Laura Ashley women's clothing

FOUBERT'S PLACE

Jaeger clothing
Chinacraft
Hamleys toys

CONDUIT STREET

fine leather **Henry's**
Scotch House

Ciro pearls
Berk The Scottish Shop

NEW BURLINGTON PLACE

Noble Furs
Royal Jordanian Airline
Saudi Airline
Qantas

TENISON COURT

Mappin and Webb jewelry

NEW BURLINGTON STREET

Next clothing and interiors

Burberrys
wine merchants **Hedges & Butler**

Gered china and Wedgwood

NEW BURLINGTON MEWS

BEAK STREET

REGENT STREET

Woollen Centre

Lawleys china and glass
Bally shoes
Jaegar Man clothing
Country Casuals clothing
Air Canada
Delta
Reject China Shop
Lloyds Bank

HEDDON STREET

Singapore Airlines
Scottish Woollens

porcelain and glass **Wilson & Gill**
Midland Bank

HEDDON STREET

REGENT PLACE

T & J Perry jewelry
Burtons men's clothing
Garrard & Co. Ltd. jewelry

pen specialists **Pencraft Ltd.**

VIGO STREET

GLASSHOUSE STREET

men's clothing **Austin Reed**

Aquascutum
Mitsukiku Japanese gifts

Scotch House woollens and tartans

SWALLOW STREET

The Cloth House

QUADRANT ARCADE

MAN IN THE MOON PASSAGE

AIR STREET

British Airways
Chinacraft

British Airways

Cafe Royal

Barclays Bank

AIR STREET

Piccadilly Circus Tube

Piccadilly Circus Tube

PICCADILLY

Place, presided over by the **Duke of York Column** (1834, Benjamin Wyatt). The street was supposed to mark the southern end of Nash's triumphal way from Carlton House Terrace to Regent's Park. In the distance, you can see the Victoria Tower at the Houses of Parliament.

36 **Eros.** After a rest-cure of almost 2 years during which he was treated for a near-century of exposure to the elements, the **God of Love** has returned and once more reigns over Piccadilly Circus. London's best-loved statue rises lovingly to the occasion, symbolizing London itself to millions of people all over the world. The statue is a memorial to **Lord Shaftesbury** (1801-85), a man of great virtue and a tireless reformer and educator. The sculptor, **Alfred Gilbert**, was no less idealistic. He believed that Shaftesbury deserved something which would represent generosity of spirit and love of mankind and would symbolize, according to the sculptor, *the work of Lord Shaftesbury, the blindfolded Love sending forth indiscriminately, yet with purpose, his missile of kindness, always with the swiftness the bird has from its wings, never ceasing to breathe or reflect critically, but ever soaring onwards, regardless of its own perils and dangers.* A prophetic statement of an artist's intent.

Gilbert created his statue in aluminium, the first time the material had been used for such a structure. As a result, the 8 foot figure is so light that it sways in the wind. Gilbert was paid £3,000 for his work, even though it had cost him £7,000 to build it. His eventual and inevitable bankruptcy left him with little alternative but to leave the country, living first in Bruge, Brussels and then in Italy. Lord Shaftesbury himself died lamenting, *I cannot bear to leave this world with all the misery in it.* One cannot but feel he would have been sadder still to know what misery had afflicted the artist who tried to honor him. The creator of Eros was rejected, but the statue found an enduring place in the hearts of Londoners. *Piccadilly Circus, W1.*

37 **Criterion Theatre.** (1870, Thomas Verity) Tawdry signs have long buried the French chateau facade of this theatre. It is London's only *underground* theatre in the physical sense of the word—you go down a series of steps even for the upper circle. The lobby is decorated with Victorian tiles. *Piccadilly Circus, W1. Tickets and reservations: 930-3216*

38 **Criterion Brasserie.** ★ ★ $$ The restaurant was designed by **Thomas Verity** in 1870, along with the Criterion Theatre, when Piccadilly was the hub of the empire. As Piccadilly's fate declined and the area became full of junkies, derelicts, boarded up buildings, sex cinemas and takeaway kebab houses, the Criterion sunk to a new low as the fastest cafeteria in London, serving 20 meals a minute. In 1983, thanks to the kiss of life the GLC and the refurbished Eros were bringing to the area, Trusthouse Forte decided to rehabilitate the Criterion. Behind decades of plywood and formica and grease and smoke, they found pure gold, or at least the closest thing: shimmering, dazzling gold mosaic Byzantine vaulted ceilings and marble walls. Now elegantly restored to its former Victorian splendor, it is the prettiest brasserie/café outside of Vienna. The food is French brasserie with English flavoring and American portions. Stick to the simple dishes—salads, steaks, lamb chops. *Open M-Sa 12-3PM, 6-11PM. 222 Piccadilly, W1. 839-7133*

39 **Trocadero.** The *Troc* has a long history on this site, going back to the 1740s, when it was a tennis court. In the 19th century, it went from circus to theatre to music hall to restaurant. In the 1920s and 30s, the *Troc* flourished under Charles Cochran's *Supper Time Revues.* Now it is what is apparently called an *entertainment* complex, filled with shops and restaurants; the first **Guinness World of Records Exhibition;** a 40-minute film with dramatic effects called *The London Experience*—(you can smell the smoke of the Great Fire of London); the **World Center of Holography,** featuring the world's largest hologram; a brass rubbing center; a terrific record shop (**HMS**); a large bookstore (**Athena Books**); a nightclub (**Shaftesbury on the Avenue**); and the **Golden Nugget Casino,** with 14 Roulette wheels, 10 Black Jack tables and one punto banco. (All casinos in England require membership—apply in person, produce your passport, then wait 48 hours.) This 200,000 square foot mixed bag of shops, restaurants and entertainments is made for tourists and is especially popular with English visitors from the provinces, families and young people. The Holography Center, Guinness Book of Records and London Film Exhibitions are the *best* of the Trocadero. The restaurants rarely rise above roadside cafe. *Restaurants and shops are open daily until late; Golden Nugget Casino open daily 2PM-4AM; Holograms and Guinness Exhibit open daily 10AM-10PM; Brass Rubbing Center open M-Sa 10AM-10PM, Su 12-8PM. Coventry St., Piccadilly Circus, W1. 439-4938*

40 **Design Center.** A fabulous showplace for the best of British design, from toys to tackle, cars to cards, and woolies to wellies. The government sponsored Design Council, originally the Council for Industrial Design, has been providing changing exhibitions of the latest innovations in British domestic design since 1956. If you have any questions about where to find what you are looking for, the experts in the Center offer free and helpful advice, and the selective *Design Index* lists approximately 7,000

PICCADILLY

manufacturers of well-designed goods. After looking at what is on display, you can browse in the Center bookstore or refresh yourself at the coffee bar. *Open M-Sa 9:30AM-6PM (W-Th until 8PM); Su 1-6PM. 28 Haymarket, SW1. 839-8000*

BESTS

R E Huber
General Manager, London Hilton

Capital Hotel for the intimacy.
London Hilton on Park Lane for the view.
The Ritz for tea.
The restaurant at the **British Harvest**.
The **Connaught** for the luxury.

Sheila Hicks
Fabric Designer

Camden Lock Market and all the small and large markets on the edge of Regents Canal. They are filled with crafts, second-hand clothes, jewelry and foods from all over the world. The kids can watch puppet shows on an old barge turned into a small theatre.

Eating **lunch at Le Routier** at Camden Lock and watching the boats along the canal as well as the crowds. The restaurant is medium priced and serves standard, old-style French cooking, but excellent fish.

Walking along the canal path at Camden Lock to Little Venice and passing 19th century industrial buildings, 18th century houses and Regent's Park. There are no cars along this quiet quarter of the busy city. If you are lazy, try the same journey by canal boat and watch the scene in comfort.

Eating **lunch** at a funky restaurant, like **Diwani Bhel Poori** on Drummond St., NW1. It is frequented by middle class intellectuals and students who enjoy excellent food at amazingly low prices. The stuffed *dosa* is wonderful. How do they manage that thin, firm, crispy pancake?

Lunch or dinner at Nontas on 16 Camden High St., NW1. It has a pleasant atmosphere, good service and reasonable prices. Try the fish kebab or humus! They don't hurry you out when you are finished except on Fridays and Saturdays.

English breakfast at the Savoy on the Strand, WC2. It is maddeningly expensive, but it has a great atmosphere. The service is superb, if clearly *snotty*. Gaze at the amazing views of the South Bank, the Thames and the Art Deco decor. Then pay the bill with the aplomb of one used to such indulgences!

J P Donleavy
Writer

It was always my unfailing custom to perambulate to at least one of London's mainline stations every day. These included in order of their attraction: **Paddington, Victoria, Charing Cross** and **Liverpool Street**. In such places, I usually spent one-and-a-half hours around peek arrival time meeting trains off which no one ever came that I knew. But it is astonishing at how excited I could get in such hope. Next, I would snatch a taxi from in front of some intending, weary traveller and rush to tea time, usually at **Fortnum's** for their China Lapsang Souchong tea and Sacher torte chocolate cake. Over the years, as the Jermyn Street part of Fortnum's would get thronged, I also repaired to the emptier 5th floor venue. **Christie's** on King Street was also a nice place to stop off to use the gents' convenience and to take pleasure in other people's possessions, as well as to partake in the sad atmosphere of mature ladies depositing their pearls for appraisal.

Sometimes, on a variation of a theme of friendship, I would take tea with one William Donaldson (aka Henry Root) in either of 2 places: **Basil Street Hotel** or **Browns**. These discreetly sedate places were chosen because there were often indiscreet matters to discuss. Mr. Donaldson was always a marvellous pleasure to see, and he was always as prompt to the split second as I was, which meant we would confront each other 2 minutes early. On occasions when our conversation was extremely indiscreet, the venue was changed to a suite at the **Grosvenor House**.

However, my most stable stand by, following a walk through Mayfair after tea, was champagne at **Claridges**, followed by either a stroll under the massive plane trees in **Berkeley Square** or a visit to **Farm Street Church**. Then, with absolutely nowhere to go or no one to see, I would repair back to Victoria Station, meet the trains for a couple of hours, and then either take an apple out of my pocket to eat or go dine on game pie and beer at one of the **Pall Mall clubs**.

Peter Jackson
President, British Topographical Society

The **Wallace Collection** in Manchester Square because it seems like a privilege to be able to visit a grand townhouse to see the owners' private art collection rather than walking around a museum.

The **Black Friar Pub** on Queen Victoria Street because it is unlike any other pub in London, covered outside and in with carvings and mosaics of jolly monks being anything but monkish.

Sir John Soane's House in Lincoln's Inn Fields because it has the most unexpected interior, with visual suprises around every corner—a labyrinth of curiously shaped rooms crowded with works of art.

The **view of St. Paul's from Cardinal Cap Alley, Bankside** because this was my favorite view 30 years ago and in spite of all the rebuilding since then, it hasn't changed much.

St. Bartholomew the Great church in Smithfield because, although the centuries have played about with it, you still get a feeling of Medieval London among its massive Norman masonry.

The **Burlington Arcade** in Piccadilly because each little shop has a personalized intimacy which is fast vanishing.

Wenceslaus Hollar (1607-1677) is my favorite artist because he was a superbly accurate draughtsman without whom we would have almost no idea of what pre-fire London looked like.

A Picturesque Tour Through the Cities of London and Westminster by **Thomas Malton** (1792) is my **favorite book** because it is, quite simply, the most beautiful London book ever published, and because I have never been able to afford a copy.

The statue of **Sir Sydney Waterlow** in Waterlow Park, Highgate because he is the only London statue sensible enough to carry an umbrella.

Rosamind Julius
Julius International Design Consultants

A walk in **Regents Park** at any time of year.

Lunch at the **Connaught Hotel.**

Standing on **Westminster Bridge** in the evening, looking at the daggers of light reflecting onto the Thames.

Theatres—the old and the new.

The **cosmopolitan mixture** of people one sees and meets.

Dinner at **Langan's Brasserie,** *Stratton St., Piccadilly, W1.*

The **book shops.**

Leslie Julius
Julius International Design Consultants

The **trees**—everywhere.

A walk on **Hampstead Heath** on Sunday morning.

Drinks at the **Spaniards** on Hamstead Heath.

A **concert** at the **Royal Festival Hall.**
English pubs.

Always exciting **exhibitions.**

The **view** from a **Nash terrace** looking north over Regent's Park.

Polly Hope
Sculptor, London

Cheshire Street Market, part of the Sunday morning Petticoat Lane complex, is perhaps the last remaining view of Dickensian London and going fast. You will find excellent values in second-hand light bulbs, single used boots, old tail-coats, rusty fork-lift trucks and occasionally such designer delights as second-hand Eames chairs, Deco crockery and light fittings. Plenty of forties and fifties furniture. The Market starts around 4AM. Bring a flashlight for finding things in the back of lorries. They pack up soon after midday. The terms are strictly cash, so keep your plastic cards well away in your inside pocket. Take the Aldgate or Aldgate East tube station, then walk up Brick Lane. The chaos starts under the railway bridge.

Peter Harrison
Designer, New York

Kew Bridge pumping station is an astounding and beautifully preserved example of Victorian high technology. Three truly huge steam engines used for over 100 years to pump water into London's water mains are on display. Amazingly, they run them on weekends, so you can see these colossal machines in action. There is also a museum with several smaller steam engines which they also run. *Open Sa-Su 11AM-5PM. Kew Bridge Rd., Brentford. 568-4757*

For Filofax nuts, try **Chisholm's** on Kingsway. They have more Filofax items than I have ever seen in the world. An absolute must if you have the disease. *103 Kingsway, WC2. 405-0992*

Richard Williams
Animator, London

Parma Snack Bar just off Soho Square has the best fried eggs in London. *Sutton Row, W1.*

Best Restaurants
Gerry Rosentswieg
The Graphics Studio, Los Angeles

Alastair Little. High-tech decor. *California cuisine* prepared by owner/chef Alastair Little. *49 Frith St., Soho. 734-5183*

Langan's Brasserie. Very chic. Reservations essential. *Stratton St., W1. 493-6437*

Le Suquet. French seafood. *104 Draycott Ave., SW3. 581-1785*

Sea Shell. Fish and chips. Take-away in front, restaurant behind. *Closed Su & M. 49-51 Lisson Grove, NW1*

Sweetings. Perhaps the oldest fish restaurant. Fish in a sea of pinstriped suits for lunch in the City. *Open M-F 11:30AM-3PM. 39 Queen Victoria St., EC4. 248-3063*

Geales. Fish and chips in Nottinghill Gate. Located behind the Gate Cinema. *2 Farmer St., W8. 727-7969*

Arlecchino. Very good Italian food in Nottinghill Gate. *Open M-Sa until 1AM, Su until 11PM. 8 Hillgate, W8. 229-2027*

Red Fort. Indian food in elegant surroundings. *77 Dean St., Soho. 437-2525*

Khyber. Indian food. *45 Westbourne Grove, W2. 727-4385*

La Brasseria. French brasserie which also serves English breakfast from 8AM. *272 Brompton Rd., SW3. 584-1668/581-3089*

Le Caprice. Theatre people chic, behind the Ritz. *Arlington House, Arlington St., SW1. 629-2239*

Simpson's-in-the-Strand. Traditional English carvery. Frock coat elegance—ties necessary—but worth it. *100 Strand, WC2. 836-9112*

Peter's Restaurant. Taxi drivers cafe. Great English breakfast. *59 Pimlico Rd., SW1. 730-5991*

St. James's is about mystery and magic; royalty and aristocracy; pomp and civilized circumstances; and kings, queens and gentlemen.

In this elegant, heart-shaped enclave, gentlemen's London has long been a tightly knit purlieu of royal London, an anachronistic neighborhood of refinement where time has stood still. Gentlemen still go to their clubs, that unchallenged English invention with its air of infinite mystery; shoes are still made with painstaking care for royal feet; hats are still sewn seamlessly for aristocratic heads; and when the Queen is home at **Buckingham Palace,** the Royal Standard flies.

This is one of the most agreeable walks in London, a cameo portrait of England and Englishness utterly unchanged by time, wars, developers, mass production, pollution, the weak pound or the Common Market. Here daylight—if daylight be reality—has been kept at bay, preserving for us the England we secretly yearn for: the England of history books and literature, heros and heroines, Meredith and Oscar Wilde, *Ravenshoe, Can You Forgive Her* and *Vivien Grey.* St. James's is history and address book, champagne and syllabub. It is also—feminists and egalitarians be warned— what remains of two ancient British ideas: the segregation of classes and the segregation of sexes.

You can begin the journey in the presence of Nelson at **Trafalgar Square** and in the company of Turner and Constable, among 2,000 others, at the **National Gallery,** one of the richest and most extensive collections of paintings in the world. After regarding aesthetic perfection, you can contemplate the material arts on **Jermyn Street,** where window shopping is museum-like and the prices can reach old master figures.

In an area no larger than a football field, you can have a pair of shoes made to fit your own feet; design your own family crest; and be measured for shirts (with a minimum order of 6 and a minimum wait of 6 weeks). You can buy Stiltons, Cheddars, Wensleydales and Caerphilys in a shop that may convince you that the French are the second-best cheese producers in the world (Paxton and Whitfield). You can choose wild hyacinth bath oil from a famous perfumer (Floris), or Ajaccio Violet from a regal barbershop (Ivan's and Trumper's); find refuge in a Victorian pub (the Red Lion), or surrender for a couple of hours in one of the best English restaurants in London (Wilton's). You will see where kings and queens lived before they moved to Buckingham Palace, and where She lives now, although like 99 percent of Her subjects, you will have to be satisfied with gazing at facades. You can have a look at some of the treasures from the Royal Collection, check out the royal horses and coaches and end the day in London's most romantic park, where Charles I walked to his death at Banqueting House and his son Charles II walked with his spaniels (**St. James's Park**).

St. James's on a Saturday feels like a Sunday. The streets are empty, few gentlemen can be seen going into their clubs, and while quite a few shops are open, you never know which ones. The National Gallery is always best on weekday mornings. If you want to see the **Changing of the Guard** at **Buckingham Palace** (11:30AM daily, alternate days in winter), do the second half of the walk

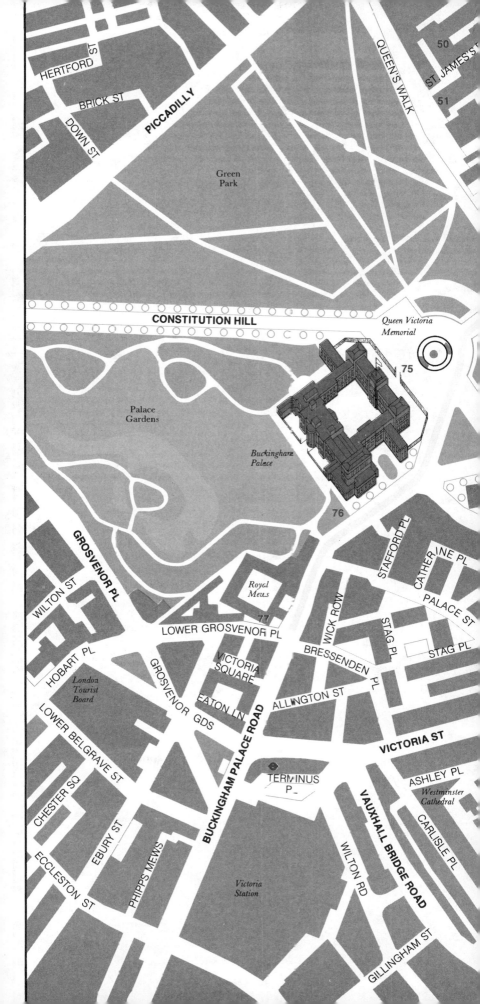

HERTFORD ST

BRICK ST

DOWN ST

PICCADILLY

50

ST JAMES'S

51

QUEEN'S WALK

Green
Park

CONSTITUTION HILL

Queen Victoria
Memorial

75

Palace
Gardens

Buckingham
Palace

76

GROSVENOR PL

WILTON ST

Royal
Mews

77

STAFFORD PL

CATHERINE PL

PALACE ST

HOBART PL

London
Tourist
Board

LOWER GROSVENOR PL

GROSVENOR GDS

VICTORIA
SQUARE

EATON LN

BRESSENDEN PL

WICK ROW

STAG PL

STAG PL

LOWER BELGRAVE ST

CHESTER SQ

ALLINGTON ST

VICTORIA ST

BUCKINGHAM PALACE ROAD

TERMINUS
P

ASHLEY PL

Westminster
Cathedral

ECCLESTON ST

EBURY ST

PHIPPS MEWS

Victoria
Station

WILTON RD

VAUXHALL BRIDGE ROAD

CARLISLE PL

GILLINGHAM ST

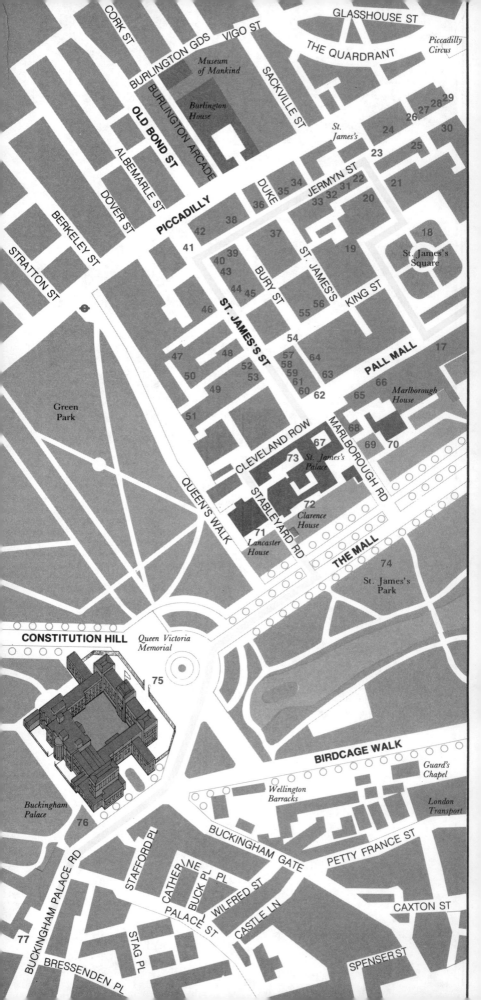

GLASSHOUSE ST

Piccadilly
Circus

CORK ST

BURLINGTON GDS

VIGO ST

THE QUARDRANT

Museum
of Mankind

SACKVILLE ST

BURLINGTON ARCADE

Burlington
House

St.
James's

26 27 28 29

24

30

23

25

OLD BOND ST

ALBEMARLE ST

DOVER ST

DUKE

JERMYN ST

22

35 34

21

33 32 31

36

PICCADILLY

BERKELEY ST

38

37

20

42

19

18

41

39

40

ST. JAMES'S

St. James's
Square

43

STRATTON ST

44 45

BURY ST

56

46

55

ST. JAMES'S ST

KING ST

54

47

48

57

64

17

52

58

Green
Park

50

53

59

63

PALL MALL

51

49

61

62

66

60

65

Marlborough
House

CLEVELAND ROW

68

67

69

70

MARLBOROUGH RD

73

St. James's
Palace

QUEEN'S WALK

STABLEYARD RD

72

Clarence
House

71

Lancaster
House

THE MALL

74

St. James's
Park

CONSTITUTION HILL

Queen Victoria
Memorial

75

BIRDCAGE WALK

Guard's
Chapel

Wellington
Barracks

London
Transport

Buckingham
Palace

76

STAFFORD PL

CATHERINE PL

BUCK PL

BUCKINGHAM GATE

WILFRED ST

PETTY FRANCE ST

BUCKINGHAM PALACE RD

PALACE ST

CASTLE LN

CAXTON ST

77

STAG PL

SPENSER ST

BRESSENDEN PL

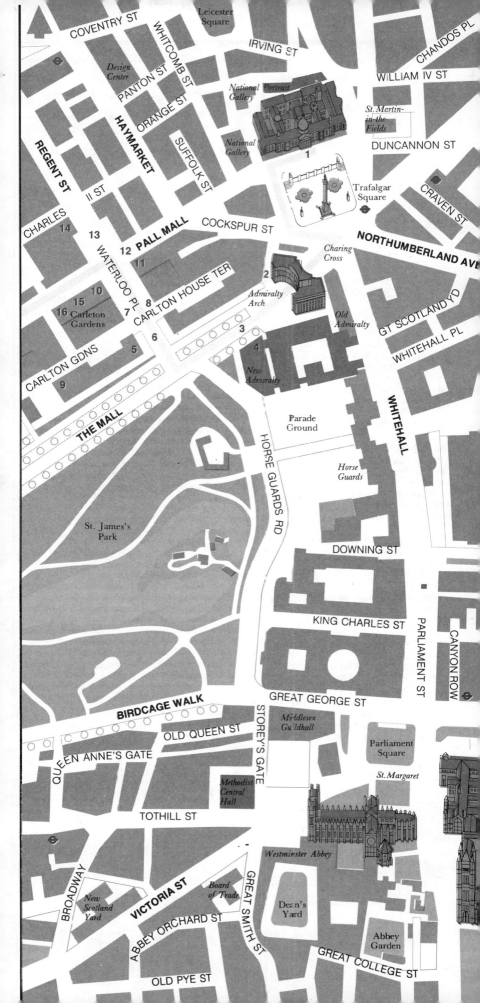

first. Few of the interiors of the royal palaces are open, so good weather is desirable for the part of the walk from the bottom of St. James's Street (Marlborough Row) to Buckingham Palace and St. James's Park. Otherwise, an umbrella is essential. The **Queen's Gallery** is open Tuesday through Saturday; and the **Royal Mews** is open Wednesday and Thursday afternoons. Services are held in the **Queen's Chapel** on Sunday mornings in the summer and in the **Chapel Royal** on Sunday mornings in the winter. At 10AM each morning in St. James's Park, the pelicans emerge stiffly from their sanctuary by the lake and have an English breakfast of kippers and other whole fish.

1 **National Gallery.** (1838, William Wilkins) In fact, there are 3 national galleries in London—the National Gallery, the National Portrait Gallery and the Tate Gallery. Together they contain some of the finest art treasures in the world. The National Gallery is one of the very smallest picture galleries, with no vast collection of any one school or any single painter and no vast cellar of pictures in storage. Almost all of the 2,050 pictures are on view, and virtually all of them are worth seeing.

Unlike most of the great national galleries of Europe, the National Gallery is not built upon the foundations of a former royal collection, nor did it inherit a nationally-based collection. Its beginnings were late (1824) and modest: 38 paintings from the collection of Russian émigré and marine insurance underwriter **John Julius Angerstein.** The government paid £57,000 for the pictures, which included 5 paintings by Claude and Hogarth's *Marriage à la Mode* series, and opened the Gallery to the public in the Angerstein's former townhouse at 100 Pall Mall.

Two other collectors, **Sir George Beaumont** and the **Rev. William Howel Carr**, promised important collections of paintings to the nation if a suitable building was provided to house them. In 1838, the National Gallery opened. The Beaumont and Howel Carr paintings, along with Angerstein's, formed the nucleus of the national collection.

The building must certainly have influenced the early character of the collection. It was built on the site of the former Royal Mews, but the stables with barracks to the rear of the site could not be built upon, so the design could only be one room deep. This resulted in a stage-set of a museum with a long, drawn-out facade. But the restrictions on the architect weren't limited to size: Wilkins was also forced to incorporate into the portico the 8 columns salvaged from the demolished Carlton House, a precedence of compromise which has dogged extensions and additions to the National Gallery ever since.

The limited size of the Gallery led to a purchasing policy which now makes it the envy of museums throughout the world: buy the best works of the greatest masters. For 150 years, the National Gallery had one invaluable resource for its purchasing: the English aristocracy who had been shopping on the Continent for masterpieces to add to their private collections for 400 years.

As the collection grew, so did the National Gallery. The dome and additional rooms were added in the 1870s, followed by the central staircase and further additions in 1911. In 1975, the excellent northern extension was opened, providing space for temporary exhibitions.

The pictures in the National Gallery are predominately and supremely by the old masters. They present one of the finest histories of Western European painting in existence, from Duccio in Italy (c.1300) up to Cèzanne and Klimt in the early 20th century. Even in their native countries, painters such as Holbein, Van Dyke and Velazquez are not represented with masterpieces of such greatness.

When the Tate Gallery opened in 1897, it took on the dual role of modern art museum and home of British art. Many of the British

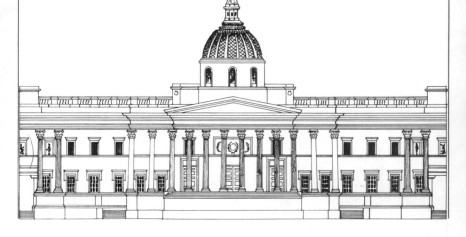

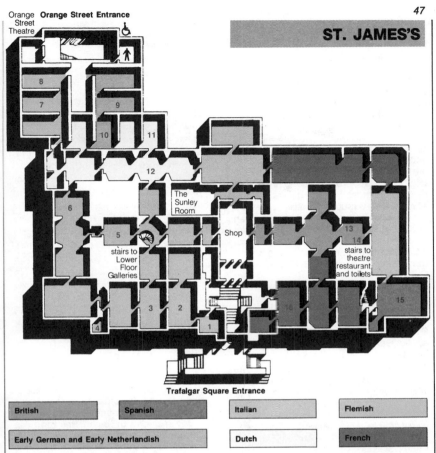

Orange Street Theatre · **Orange Street Entrance**

ST. JAMES'S

The Sunley Room

Shop

stairs to Lower Floor Galleries

stairs to theatre restaurant, and toilets

Trafalgar Square Entrance

British	Spanish	Italian	Flemish

Early German and Early Netherlandish	Dutch	French

paintings in the National Gallery were transferred to the Tate, leaving the National with a small but choice **British collection.** It consists of 2 paintings by **Stubbs,** including *The Milbanke* and *Melbourne Families;* 6 by **Reynolds,** including the portrait of young *General Banastre Tarleton* during the American War of Independance; 5 by **Constable,** including *The Haywain;* 10 by **Gainsborough,** including *Mr. and Mrs. Andrews* and *The Morning Walk;* 7 by **Hogarth,** 6 of which are part of the *Marriage à la Mode* series about a marriage based on money and vanity; and 8 **Turners,** including *Rain, Steam and Speed—the Great Western Railway.*

There is no substitute for looking at the pictures, and one of the bonuses of a free museum is being able to look at only a few at a time guiltlessly. No one has to see it all in one go, and no one should. A lifetime spent looking at these paintings seems about right, starting with old favorites - and acquiring new loves along the way. If you are daunted by the size of the collection or pressed for time, the National Gallery has made a kind of *Top of the Pops* of the 16 most famous pictures. The leaflet describing them costs a few pence, and is well worth it. The 16 masterpieces are:

1. **The Wilton Diptych** (c.1395). Room 1

2. **Paola Uccello** (c.1397-1475), *The Battle of San Romano.* Room 2

3. **Piero Della Francesca,** (active 1439, died 1492), *The Baptism of Christ.* Room 4

4. **Leonardo Da Vinci** (1452-1519), *Cartoon: The Virgin and Child with Saint Anne and Saint John the Baptist.* Room 7

5. **Giovanni Bellini** (active c.1459, died 1516), *The Doge Leonardo Loredan.* Room 10

6. **Titian** (active before 1511, died 1576), *Bacchus and Ariadne.* Room 9

7. **Anthony Van Dyck** (1599-1641), *Equestrian Portrait of Charles I.* Room 21

8. **Peter Paul Rubens (1577-1640),** *Le Chapeau de Paille (The Straw Hat).* Room 22

9. **Jan Van Eyck** (active 1422, died 1441), *Giovanni Arnolfini and his Wife.* Room 24

10. **Hans Holbein the Younger** (1497-1543), *The Ambassadors.* Room 25

11. **Rembrandt** (1606-1669), *Self Portrait at Age 63.* Room 27

12. **Jan (Johannes) Vermeer** (1632-1675), *A Young Woman Standing at a Virginal.* Room 28

13. **John Constable** (1776-1837), *The Haywain.* Room 35

14. **JMW Turner** (1775-1851), *The Fighting Temeraire.* Room 35

15. **Diego Velazquez** (1599-1660), *The Toilet of Venus (The Rokeby Venus).* Room 41

16. **Georges Seurat** (1859-1891), *Bathers, Asnières.* Room 45

The **Reserve Collection** on the lower floor of the Gallery is an art lovers dream attic, with stacks of minor masterpieces, damaged paintings by great artists and good fakes. It is fun to try and figure out what's what.

The National Gallery Mosaics by Russian-born artist **Boris Anrep** on the floors of the vestibules and half-way landing are works of art which usually go unnoticed. In the west vestibule, the theme is *The Labors of Life,* with 12 mosaics, completed in 1928, including *Art,* which shows a sculptor at work; *Sacred Love,* depicting a father, mother, child and dog; and *Letters,* showing a child's slate with 2 favorite children's books, *Robinson Crusoe* and *Alice in Wonderland.* In the north vestibule, the theme is *The Modern Virtues,* with 15 mosaics completed in 1952.

Compassion shows the Russian poet Anna Akhmatova saved by an angel from the horrors of war; *Compromise* has the actress Loretta Young filling a cup with wine, symbolizing American and British friendship; *Defiance* shows Winston Churchill on the white cliffs of Dover, defying an Apocalyptic beast in the shape of a swastika; *Leisure* is TS Eliot contemplating the kindly Loch Ness monster and Einstein's formula. In the east vestibule are 11 mosaics completed in 1929 representing *The Pleasures of Life:* a Christmas pudding; a conversation with 2 girls gossiping; *Mudpie* with 3 mud pies, a bucket and a spade; and *Profane Love,* showing a man and two girls with a dog. In the half-way landing is *The Awakening of the Muses,* an illustrative archive of London's beau-monde in the thirties. It shows the Hon. Mrs. Bryan Guinness (one of the Mitford girls and later Lady Diana Mosley) as Polyhymnia, Muse of Sacred Song; Christabel, Lady Aberconway as Euterpe, Muse of Music; Clive Bell as Bacchus, God of Wine; Virginia Woolf as Clio, Muse of History; Sir Osbert Sitwell as Apollo, God of Music; and Greta Garbo as Melpomene, Muse of Tragedy.

Special exhibitions at the National Gallery include the **Artist's Eye,** an annual event in which a well-known artist selects a number of pictures from the Gallery and displays them in a setting of his own design, along with a couple of his own works. Artists who have acted as *Eye* include Anthony Caro, RB Kitaj, David Hockney and Francis Bacon. The **Art in Focus** exhibition provides an in-depth analysis and presentation of a major work, usually a new acquisition. **Artist in Residence** is a new scheme in which an artist works in a studio at the Gallery for 6 months, displaying finished works and spending one day a week discussing the work with visitors. *No admission fee. Guided tours leave the vestibule M-F at 11:30AM. Open M-Sa 10AM-6PM, Su 2-6PM. Trafalgar Square, WC2. 839-3321*

Within the Gallery are:

National Gallery Shop. It isn't as with it as some museum shops—you can't buy objects or T-shirts with the *Arnolfini Marriage.* But the Gallery publications are outstanding and you won't find them in bookshops. For a general survey of the collection, *The National Gallery* by **Homan Potterton** is excellent. It contains a chapter on conservation techniques, a brief history of the collection, a complete list of all 2,050 pictures and fresh and lively discussions of the major paintings. The shop carries a good range of art history books, Christmas cards and postcards, as well as color slides and black and white photographs of every picture in the collection. *Open M-Sa 10AM-5:40PM, Su 2-5PM. 839-3321*

National Gallery Restaurant. ★ ★ $ Cheerful, cafeteria-style service, with healthy soups and salads, hot meals at lunchtime, wine and cheese, coffee, tarts and cakes and Indian, Chinese and herbal teas. *Open M-Sa 10AM-5PM, Su 2-5PM. 839-3321*

At long last, the empty space to the left of the **National Gallery** is going to have its much-debated **extension**. Considerable controversy has surrounded the extension, especially when gallery trustees decided that they could get the new space free by offering the site to a developer who would incorporate the extension into an office complex. The developer was found, and 79 architects submitted designs, but then Prince Charles stepped in. He called the intended design a *carbuncle on the face of Trafalgar Square* and criticized the shameful scheme of getting a building for the nation's art treasures for free. The Prince of Wales's protests resulted in the rejection of the office block extension and ultimately led to the present plan. The Sainsbury family, owner of the Sainsbury supermarkets, is making a gift of the building to the nation, and the Philadelphia firm of **Robert Venturi, John Rauch and Denise Scott Brown** will design it. The new building will house the Early Renaissance, Italian and Northern collections, provide space for temporary exhibitions, replace the exisiting National Gallery Shop and provide 2 additional restaurants. The architects plan to maintain the height-line of the William Wilkins National Gallery and to match its Portland stone.

2 Admiralty Arch. (1911, Sir Aston Webb) Somehow the inglorious race of traffic around Trafalgar Square doesn't prepare you for this magnificent arch which is really a screen with 5 arches: the iron gates of the center arch that open for ceremonial processions, 2 side arches for traffic and 2 smaller arches for pedestrians. Its very monumentality is a surprise because it is so un-London. The grand Corinthian structure in Portland stone marks the first part of the royal processional route from Buckingham Palace to St. Paul's Cathedral. Admiralty Arch isn't very old and isn't even Victorian. It is Edwardian, part of Edward VII's tribute to his mother, although the King himself was dead before the memorial was completed. *Trafalgar Square, WC2.*

3 The Mall. Two double rows of plane trees line this royal processional road, which is London's only planned avenue, sweeping rhetorically to a splendid, monumental climax. The regal stretch from Trafalgar Square to Buckingham Palace was originally an enclosed alleyway for playing the game *paille maille* (similar to croquet) during the days of Charles II. It was transformed into a formal vista of Buckingham Palace by **Aston Webb** in 1910 as part of a memorial to Queen Victoria. On Sundays, the Mall is closed to traffic and becomes a promenade.

4 Citadel. The curious historical monument has an air of mystery because it is completely covered in climbing ivy. It is actually a bomb shelter which was built in 1940 for members of the Admiralty and was never demolished. Perhaps it is kept (and scrupulously maintained by the Parks Department, which mows the acre of grass lawn on top) as a reminder of better times, when shelters like this could conceivably provide protection from bombs. *The Mall, SW1.*

5 Carlton House Terrace. (1827-32, John Nash) These high-gloss, creamy white buildings with their formal facades facing the Mall are the last contribution Nash made to London before his death in 1835. The 1,000 foot long Terrace is a stately confection of Doric columns and human-scale

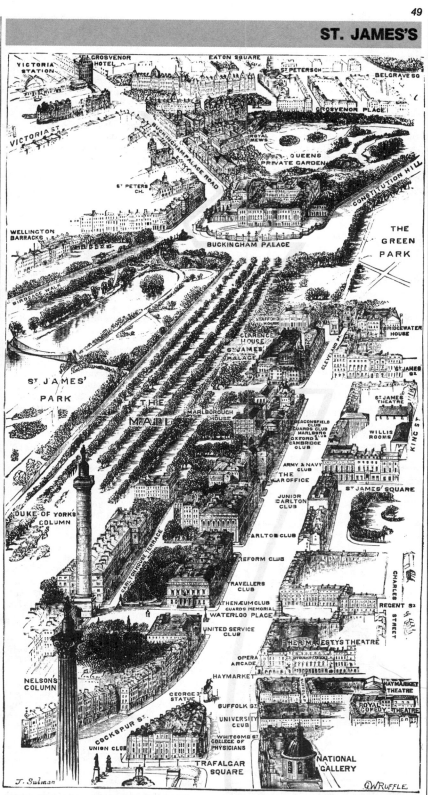

arches. The upkeep is considerable, but the clean, warm outline, intercepted by the **Duke of York Steps,** is a splendid contribution to the Mall: an impressive backdrop for royal processions by day, a royal wedding cake when floodlit at night.

Carlton House Terrace replaced **Carlton House,** the palatial home of Frederick, Prince of Wales (later the Prince Regent and finally George III). The Prince purchased Carlton House in 1732 and transformed it at staggering expense into what was considered the most beautiful mansion in England. But he grew bored with his treasure and demolished it in 1829. The columns were saved and recycled into the portico of the National Gallery, and Nash was asked to build Carlton House Terrace. Originally the Terrace was to line both sides of the Mall in the style of Regent's Park, providing grand townhouses for the aristocracy, but only one side was built. *The Mall, SW1.*

Within the Terrace are:

Mall Galleries. Traditional paintings by members of the **Royal Society of Portrait Painters** and the **Federation of British Ar-**

tists, as well as occasional degree shows from the various art schools, are exhibited in the Galleries. It is a good place to find English landscapes, watercolors and oils that are Turner-ish, Constable-ish and affordable, the kind of pictures that look wonderful when you get them all the way back home. *Small admission fee. Open daily 10AM-5PM. The Mall, SW1. 930-6844*

Institute of Contemporary Arts. The ICA is a lively arts center, with 3 exhibitions running at any one time in its 3 galleries. Photography, architectural drawings, paintings, happenings and event-art all take place in an atmosphere of industrious punk-avant-garde. In the evenings the cinema shows good foreign and cult films and excellent film series. Experimental films, videos and films by new filmmakers are screened in the cinémathèque. There is also a video library where films may be viewed; a theatre where experimental drama is performed; and a bookshop which has all the latest art books, as well as magazines, postcards and Virago novels. The restaurant serves healthy, filling food—vegetarian mousakas, whole-meal lasagne, thick mushroom soups, brown bread and salads, followed by a selection of luscious cheesecakes, apple pies, chocolate cakes, tea and coffee.

In order to see the exhibitions or even have a cup of coffee, you must take out a day membership, which is a good value if there is a lunchtime event that appeals to you. The events are worth checking into, as they sometimes have well-known writers interviewing other well-known writers and artists interviewing artists with questions from the public. *For recorded information, call 930-6393. Open Tu-Su 12-11PM. 12 Carlton House Terrace, SW1 (now known as Nash House). 930-0493*

Sir Issac Newton

The Royal Society. Founded by King Charles II in 1660, the Royal Society is one of the most distinguished scientific bodies in the world. In the 17th century, the Society was the hub of scientific discovery. Newton, Halley, Dryden and Pepys chatted about inventions, although Pepys, then president, never understood Newton's *Principia*. Past presidents include Wren, Newton, Davy, Huxley, Thomson, Rutherford and Fleming. The Society moved to Carlton House Terrace in 1966 after nearly 300 years in Burlington House on Piccadilly. *Carlton House Terrace, SW1. Not open to the public.*

6 Duke of York Steps and the Duke of York Monument. (1834, column by Benjamin Wyatt, statue by Sir Richard Westmacott) This dramatic column in front of the steps of Carlton House Terrace dominates Waterloo Place and seems pretty serious for a man immortalized in a nursery rhyme. The Duke of York was the second son of George III. His 7 ton statue was financed by withholding one day's pay from all soldiers. The Duke's impressive distance from it all (137 feet in the sky) was necessitated by his debts—he died owing £2 million, the pink granite column reputedly the only means of keeping him out of reach of his creditors.

O, the Grand Old Duke of York, he had ten thousand men. He marched them up to the top of the hill and he marched them down again. And when they were up, they were up, and when they were down, they were down, And when they were only halfway up they were neither up nor down!

Popular during the Duke's lifetime but first published in **Arthur Rackham's** *Mother Goose* in 1913

7 Waterloo Place. One of the few and most impressive pieces of town planning in London, Waterloo Place marks the beginning of John Nash's triumphal route from Carlton House Terrace to Regent's Park. Carlton House Terrace frames Waterloo Place, which intersects Pall Mall on its way north into lower Regent Street and Piccadilly Circus.

8 Statue of Edward VII. (1921, Sir Bertram Mackennal) In front of the Duke of York Steps and facing Waterloo Place is Edward VII, looking beefy and well. The King gave us the Edwardian age: a secure, elegant world for the rich and aristocratic, where to amuse and to be amused were *raisons d'etre*. Because of the long life of his mother Queen Victoria, he only reigned for 9 of his 69 years. He brought color and pageantry to the monarchy, but also a sense of serious commitment toward such issues as the quality of worker's lives and the treatment of Indians by English officials. Edward was aware that beyond Europe lay his empire, the largest the world had ever known. As King, he created the *Entente Cordiale* with France and used all of his considerable diplomatic skill and charm to ease the conflicts between Germany and England, conflicts that were tragically too deep for any monarch to bridge. But it is his voracious appetite for which he is remembered: at his last formal dinner at Buckingham Palace on 5 March 1910, he made his way through 9 dishes, including salmon steak, grilled chicken, saddle of mutton and several snipe stuffed with *foie gras*. His death 2 months later signaled the end of the Edwardian Age, although souvenirs of that elegant way of life can be found tucked away in the small streets behind the statue.

9 Carlton House Gardens. During the Second World War, the Free French occupied No. 4, where de Gaulle's message to his countrymen is recorded in the plaque on the wall. *Behind Carlton House Terrace, The Mall, SW1.*

10 Athenaeum Club. (1830, Decimus Burton) This is the most august of the gentlemen's clubs and one of the most distinguished buildings in London, designed by the man who gave London the Screen at the entrance to Hyde Park and Constitution

Arch. The elegant cream stuccoed facade is pure architectural dignity. A Wedgewood-like frieze wraps around the building above the first floor windows, while a large gilded figure of Pallas Athena, goddess of wisdom, practical skills and prudent warfare, graces the porch and accurately sets the requirements for those who enter: bishops, scientists and the top brains of the Civil Service and Foreign Office.

Inside, the atmosphere is one of intimidating wisdom. Darwin broods over the living eminent and distinguished. The **Royal Society Dining Society**, an elite group within the formidably elite Royal Society, meets here, and members of that clever and select circle are de facto members of the Athenaeum. If you meet an Englishman who is a member, you can be suitably impressed. *107 Waterloo Place, SW1.*

11 **Institute of Directors.** (1828, John Nash) For 150 years, the building was the home of the **United Service Club**, known as the **Senior**, which was founded in 1815 for the triumphant officers of the Napoleonic wars. The building, the first commissioned by a club, was originally built by **John Nash.** But what you notice most are the alterations by **Decimus Burton**: the Doric columns and the Corinthian portico. While it is not as unforgettably beautiful as the Athenaeum, opposite, it is still handsome. The granite mounting block outside on Waterloo Place was put there by Wellington to help short men get on their horses.

Lifestyles, incomes and Labor Governments do not lend themselves to a world of expensive exclusiveness, and in 1974, when most clubs were enjoying a comeback, the Senior collapsed. Now it is a business center for the the **Institute of Directors**. By appointment, you can go inside and see the original 19th century furniture designed for the club, including the 15-foot chandelier presented by George IV to commemorate the Battle of Waterloo, and the inimitable masculine tonality of mahogany and leather that is a gentleman's club. *116-119 Pall Mall, SW1. 839-1233*

12 **Pall Mall.** Americans pronounce it *Paul Maul*, like the cigarettes, but the upper-class English who have their clubs here say *Pel Mel*. Named after the ball game imported from France that is played in the Mall which runs parallel, this is the ancient road from the City to St. James's. Pall Mall is lined with gentlemen's clubs and a few appropriately exclusive shops. It is a stately boulevard by day, but a windy, monumental wasteland by night. A word of warning: traffic tears down this broad one-way avenue with terrifying speed, so cross carefully.

13 **Crimean War Memorial.** (1862) **Florence Nightingale** (by **Walker**), one of the few women represented in this masculine part of London, holds her famous lamp. Standing next to her is **Sidney Herbert** (by **Foley**), Secretary for War during her days of devotion to her country. **Honour** on the other side, cast from captured Russian cannon, seems to have her eye on the bear-skinned guardsmen below. *Located at the foot of Lower Regent St., SW1.*

14 **Crafts Council.** This is an oasis and palace for British craftsmen and a showcase for architectural design. See the crafts on display in the 2 galleries, then consider the good taste in the coffee bar, with

its yellow, stained wood bar counter, z-shaped wood stools with blue covers by **Bair**, milky glass conical lamps by **Arteluce**, and craft objects adroitly installed behind the bar that you can gaze at and purchase after you finish your cappuccino. If there was more British design like this, the Italians would be given a run for their money. *Open Tu, W, F and Sa 10AM-5PM, Th 10AM-7PM, Su 2-5PM. 12 Waterloo Place, SW1. 930-4811*

At lunchtime, taxis and modest chauffeur-driven Rovers draw up in front of the palazzi of Pall Mall and the 18th-century houses on St. James's Street. Men wearing pin striped suits enter buildings with no names which are distinguished by large first floor windows that look onto the street below. These are **gentlemen's clubs,** an invention and all-pervasive image of the English. **Parliament** is a club, and the **Army** (officers only, of course) is a club. **Whitehall** is a club, and a man's college at **Oxford** and **Cambridge** has always had the mystique of a club. St. James's is clubland, a chain of palaces where like minds and like interests can meet—or not meet, as the clubs are as much for the reclusive as the gregarious. They began in the 18th century as coffee houses and chocolate houses, then became exclusive casinos, where whole estates were often gambled away in a night. After the Second World War, the clubs went into a serious decline, and like so many institutions, seemed on the verge of collapse. A number sold off their palatial premises and split the money amongst their members. But in the new Conservative climate, the clubs are thriving again, with waiting lists of 8 to 10 years for the more popular ones. Women are now allowed in as guests in certain dining rooms (rarely the nicest rooms), although die-hard misogynists say this is the beginning of the end of a club's reputation. Whether or not major policy decisions are still made over the port and Stilton is hard to say, but when the pin stripes emerge an hour and a half later it certainly looks as though an important vote has been taken.

15 **Travellers' Club.** (1832, Charles Barry) The Travellers was founded in 1819 by the Duke of Wellington, whose portraits loom throughout the club. One of the requirements for membership is to have traveled at least 500 miles from London, although the candidates' book shows that the present membership has gone somewhat farther afield. The special handrail on the staircase was put there to assist Napoleon's Foreign Minister, the lame Talleyrand, up the stairs. The neo-classical, plain stuccoed facade shows the architect **Charles Barry** (Trafalgar Square and the Houses of Parliament) doing what he loved best. *106 Pall Mall, SW1.*

16 **Reform Club.** (1839, Charles Barry) Members must subscribe to the Reform Bill of 1832 in order to be accepted into this absolutely stunning club. It looks like a film set and apparently a few films have been made here, but so great is the discretion or indifference that no one who belongs knows just which films. The design is classicism without bounds: a huge indoor courtyard with marble pillars and balconies, a vast library with leather chairs, library tables and real fires in the enormous fireplaces—and not a sound. The kitchen is the size of a ballroom and has a good reputation. This is the club of economists, members of the Treasury and, increasingly, writers and television executives. Reform does not seem a major concern here. *104 Pall Mall, SW1.*

17 **Royal Automobile Club.** (1911, Mewes and Davis, with E. Keynes) Here is a club that takes members rather more readily than most. The opulent Edwardian building with rooms in grand Louis XVI style was designed by the Frenchman whose earlier contribution to London was the Ritz. But more enticing are the squash courts, Turkish baths, solarium and the marble swimming pool, which is the most beautiful in London, with Doric columns covered in fish-scale mosaics. George Bernard Shaw swam in it in the past and JP Donleavy swims in it today after games of *de Alfonse* when he is in London. Many of the 12,000 members live abroad and use this as their London address. Unlike other clubs, no one seems to know anyone else. There are 3 dining rooms, a bar and bedrooms which are modest, comfortable and considerably cheaper than a hotel. In spite of its democratic outlook, the only women you see are wives and daughters of members. *89 Pall Mall, SW1. 930-2345*

18 **St. James's Square.** The fine 17th century square was laid out in the 1660s by **Henry Jermyn,** first Earl of St. Albans and friend of the widow of Charles I, Henrietta Maria and her son Charles II. The King gave the land to the Earl in gratitude for his faithful devotion while the King was in exile in France. The Square was designed with mansions on all sides for the nobility who wanted or needed to be near the palace. Sir Christopher Wren, who designed the church for this noble suburb (St. James's, Piccadilly), probably had a say in the elegant and dignified shape of the Square.

The gardens in the center of the Square are open to the public, which is unusual in leafy, residential London squares where residents have keys to carefully locked gates. The handsome bronze statue of **William III** on horseback (1808, John Bacon the Younger) includes the molehill on which the horse stumbled, throwing the King and causing his death. During the First World War, a rustic building resembling a country inn was erected in the center of the Square for American officers. Called the Washington Inn, it stood until 1921. At **No. 32,** in the south east corner, the allied commanders under General Eisenhower launched the invasions of North Africa (1942) and North-West Europe (1944). On the north side of the Square at **No.10** is **Chatham House,** the residence of 3 Prime Ministers: the Earl of Chatham (1759-61), the Earl of Derby (1837-54) and WE Gladstone (1890). At **No. 16,** Wellington's dispatch announcing his victory at Waterloo was delivered by the blood-stained Major Percy to the Prince Regent, who was dining with his Foreign Secretary, Lord Castlereagh. Included with the dispatch were the captured French eagle standards, which can be seen in the Wellington Museum at Hyde Park Corner.

St. James's Square became known worldwide overnight when the **Libyan People's Bureau** at **No. 5** was besieged on 17 April 1984. Gunmen within the building fired on demonstrators outside, killing young policewoman Yvonne Fletcher. Because diplomatic immunity made it impossible for the police to enter the building, the siege went on for 10 days, and the suspects were deported instead of arrested. Fresh flowers are placed on a memorial in the Square opposite No. 5 year round in honor of Yvonne Fletcher. The building is still empty, with iron gates in the windows, a grim reminder and further disgrace to the peaceful and beautiful Square.

19 **London Library.** (c. 1760s, James Stuart) *It is not typically English. It is typically civilized,* wrote EM Forster in an essay devoted to this private subscription library, founded in 1841 by **Thomas Carlyle.** Inside, the London Library looks like a down-at-heel club, with worn leather chairs in the reading room, Victorian portraits on the walls and high windows looking over the Square. Past members include Tennyson, Gladstone, Henry James, Thomas Hardy, HG Wells, EM Forster, Aldous Huxley, Virginia Woolf and Edith Sitwell. Present members are historians, biographers, critics, novelists, philosophers, playwrights and scriptwriters.

Unlike clubs in the neighboring precincts, the London Library does not suffer from undaunted misogyny, although the equal numbers of men and women you are likely to see in the reading room are fairly recent, and the carpet on the stairs stops one flight before the ladies' loo. Annual membership is around $125, life membership is several thousand and special, shorter memberships are available for visiting academics, writers and literary Anglophiles. *14 St. James's Square, SW1. 930-8873*

20 **Colombina.** ★ ★ $ A refreshingly simple, delicious and inexpensive trattoria with a Neapolitan chef. The deep-fried mozzarella in bread-crumbs served with a sauce is a favorite, along with the excellent fish dishes and grills. It is popular with writers doing all day stints in the London Library. *Open M-Sa 12-3PM, 6-11PM. 4-6 Duke of York St., SW1. 930-8279*

21 **Wheelers in Appletree Yard.** ★ ★ $$ It is easy to miss this tiny restaurant tucked in between St. James's Square and Duke of York Street. Wheelers is the smallest member of a 125-year-old chain of restaurants. The menu offers 3 kinds of oysters: No. 1 and No. 2, from different beds in different parts of the country, and their famous Colchester specials, available around November. Try the grilled Dover sole or poached Scottish salmon, washed down with the house white wine. They have never figured out vegetables. *Open M-Sa 12:15-2:30PM, 6:15-10:45PM. Duke of York St., SW1.930-2460*

22 **Red Lion Pub.** ★ ★ ★ $ A Victorian jewel with mahogany paneling and beautiful old mirrors, each engraved with a different British flower. Come early and have a sandwich and a beer. Later it becomes crowded and smoky. *Open daily 11AM-3PM, 5:30-11PM. 2 Duke of York St., SW1. 930-2030*

23 **Jermyn Street.** Named after the Earl of St. Albans, **Henry Jermyn,** the narrow street runs parallel to Piccadilly and connects the Haymarket with St. James's Street. It is only a few blocks long and the architecture isn't remarkable (the west end of Jermyn Street was badly damaged during the October raids in 1940 when all but one of the buildings between Duke Street and Bury Street were destroyed). But Jermyn Street is the essence of St. James's, an exclusive shopping club for traditional well-to-do Englishmen who dress like the Duke of Edinburgh and Prince Charles. The shops rely on quality and specialized knowledge. Shopping here—browsing and buying—is educational and sensual, expensive and worth it.

24 Simpson's. The main entrance of the department store is on Piccadilly, but there are 2 entrances on Jermyn, and the steps of the store offer a good view of this once-and-now neo-Georgian street. Also on the Jermyn Street side of Simpson's, within the store, is a **Burberry** boutique with a small but good selection of high quality raincoats, wool suits and jackets. Burberry's knows that their raincoats are an investment, and for a small sum you can insure your new Burberry against theft and loss for one year. *Open M-Sa 9AM-5:30PM, Th until 7PM. Main entrance at 203 Piccadilly, W1. 734-2002. (See Piccadilly Walk for complete description.)*

25 L'Ecu de France. ★ ★ ★ $$$ The *doyenne* of French restaurants in London, with a setting and style that is classic and very *haute,* and a menu that is nouvelle and imaginative. The restaurant has a set menu for lunch and dinner which includes a main course, dessert and coffee. The veal cooked in pastry leaves and the orange pancakes are sublime. *Open M-Sa 12-2PM, 6:30-11:30PM; Su 7-11:30PM. 111 Jermyn St., SW1. 930-2837*

26 Hawes and Curtis. The shiny green and white shop is a branch of the bespoke tailors on Savile Row, and is owned by Turnbull & Asser. Check the shop out if you are looking for a bargain on Jermyn Street (almost a contradiction in terms) because there is usually a selection of items on sale, including shirts from Turnbull & Asser and cashmere sweaters at the turn of the season. *Open M-F 9AM-5:30PM, Sa 9AM-1PM. No. 3 Jermyn St., SW1. 493-3808*

27 Bates. The tiny gentlemen's hat shop looks undaunted by the 20th century, and time seems to be on its side. Hats are reappearing, with felt, *low crown fedoras* selling more briskly than in the 1940s. You will pay less here than at the famous Lock's on St. James's Street. Be sure and look at **Binks,** the huge tabby cat who lived here between 1921 and 1926. He was so beloved that a taxidermist was enlisted after his death...*Open M-F 9AM-5:30PM; Sa 9:30AM-1PM, 2-5PM. 21A Jermyn St., SW1. 734-2722*

28 Ivan's and Trumper's. Ivan's, barbers to very distinguished heads (with royal warrants from Edward VII, George V and George VI), was recently taken over by Trumper's, who still has a shop in Mayfair. Trumper's hair brushes, shaving brushes and soaps, hair tonics and aftershaves are irresistible. Their *Ajaccio Violet* smells like violets, comes in old fashioned bottles and is appreciated by women as well as men. *Open M-F 9AM-6PM, Sa 9AM-1PM. No. 20, Jermyn St, SW1. 734-1370*

29 Alfred Snooker. Although Jermyn Street goes up to the Haymarket, the worthwhile shopping begins at Regent Street, and one of the first shops is a newcomer to the area. Snooker's has nothing to do with the billiards game which is the most popular sport on English television. It has to do with Scottish woolens, handsome heathery shetlands in good designs and plain cashmeres at popular prices, which the owners claim are lower than at **Marks and Spencer.** *Open M-Sa 9:30AM-6PM. 18 Jermyn St., SW1. 439-2512*

30 Rowley's. ★ ★ $$ This small and special steak house serves only charcoal-grilled steaks with rosemary butter. The set lunch and dinner menu is reasonably priced and very good. *Open daily 12-2:30PM, 6-11:30PM. 113 Jermyn St., SW1. 930-2707*

31 Harvie and Hudson. The fabrics used by these third generation shirtmakers are of the finest quality cotton poplin, designed, colored and woven just for them. The Windsor collars are slightly wider spread and the prices for their tweed jackets and overcoats are extremely reasonable. *Open M-F 9AM-5:30PM, Sa 9AM-5PM. No. 77, 96, 97 Jermyn St., SW1. 930-3949*

32 Paxton and Whitfield. Mr. Paxton became the partner of Mr. Whitfield 150 years ago. Their shop is in a house built in 1674, and at any one time you can find 300 cheeses from 11 countries in it. English cheeses are finally being acknowledged for the outstanding cheeses they are, and for being ideal partners with wine. When you taste the golden Cheddars, the peach- and ivory-colored Cheshires, the russet Leicesters, the marbled green Sage Derby and the blue-veined Stilton, you will never think about French cheeses in quite the same way. The shop also has fabulous game pies, hams, pâtés and every kind of cheese biscuit and bread. This is a perfect place to put together a picnic to take to St. James's Park. Stop at one of the St. James's wine merchants nearby to find the perfect young claret to go with it. They are very nice about giving tastes of the cheeses. *Open M-F 8:30AM-6PM, Sa 9AM-4PM. 93 Jermyn St., SW1. 930-0250*

33 Floris. Since 1730, the Floris family has been creating delicious scents, bath oils and soaps from the flowers of the English garden. Jasmine, rose, gardenia, lily of the valley and, one of the newest, wild hyacinth,

REGENT STREET

Barclays Bank
restaurant **Smiles**
Scottish sweaters **Alfred Snooker**
hairdresser and perfumer **Trumper**
men's clothing **Herbie Frogg**
hatters **Bates**
shirtmakers **Hawes & Curtis**

Plaza Cinema

Rowley's English restaurant
Van Heusen men's shirts

Church's men's shoes

EAGLE PLACE

**National Westminster Bank
Simpsons**

BABMAES STREET

A L'Ecu de France restaurant

Astleys Briar pipes

Racsons handknits

Gold-Pfeil leather luggage

TM Lewin shirtmakers

Cesar women's shoes

Francesco Smalto men's clothing

David Hicks interior design

Oggetti designer accessories

Kensington Carpets

CHURCH PLACE

St. James's Church

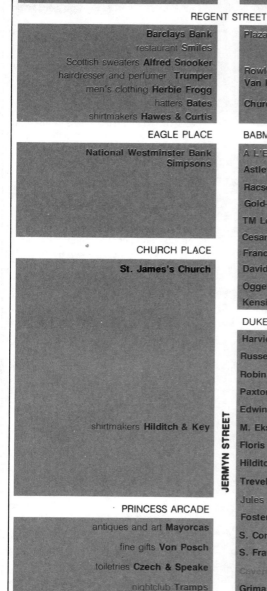

JERMYN STREET

DUKE OF YORK STREET

Harvie & Hudson shirtmakers

Russell & Bromley men's shoes

Robin Symes antiquities

Paxton & Whitfield cheesemongers

Edwin R. Cooper chemist

M. Ekstein Ltd antiques

Floris perfumers

Hilditch & Key shirtmakers

Trevelyan shirtmakers

Jules Bar & Restaurant

Foster & Son bootmakers

S. Conway shirtmakers

S. Franses antique textiles

Cavendish Hotel

Grima designer jewelry

shirtmakers **Hilditch & Key**

PRINCESS ARCADE

antiques and art **Mayorcas**
fine gifts **Von Posch**
toiletries **Czech & Speake**
nightclub **Tramps**
restaurant **Fortnum & Mason**

DUKE STREET

tobacco **Dunhill**

jewelry **Charles De Temple**

Arthur Davidson European art

Harvie & Hudson shirtmakers

Ultimo men's clothing

Francesco men's clothing

Taylor of Old Bond St hairdressers

Hilditch & Key shirtmakers

PICCADILLY ARCADE

men's clothing **New & Lingwood**
men's clothing **Uno**
restaurant **Wiltons**
Victor Frances Gallery
Fry Gallery
old master paintings **Heim**
men's clothing **Vincci**
Italian restaurant **Franco's**
National Westminster Bank

BURY STREET

Turnbull & Asser hosiers and glovers

Vincci men's clothing
RE Tricker shoes
Vincci women's clothing

Davidoff tobacco

ST. JAME'S STREET

all smell fresh and clean and as close to the real thing as you can imagine. Jacqueline Onassis favors their Sandlewood fragrance, and Nancy Reagan started ordering their bath soaps after her last visit to Buckingham Palace. You will also find large natural sponges, bone and ivory combs, fine English brushes, antique objects for *la toilette,* and a line of scents for men. The perfumer is the *manufacturer of toilet preparations to His Royal Highness the Prince of Wales,* who has given the shop the seal of excellence called the royal warrant. *Open M-F 9:30AM-5:30PM, Sa 9:30AM-4PM. 89 Jermyn St., SW1. 930-2885*

34 **Hilditch and Key.** Made-to-measure shirts for men and women, including such discriminating women as the Princess of Wales. The shirts are all cut by hand: the bodies with shears, the collars with a knife. The collars, always considered the most important part of a shirt, are turned by hand and have removable stiffeners which you must take out for laundering. The buttons are real shells, never synthethic. Besides the fine English cotton poplins, H & K carries a good selection of Viyella, a soft and warm half cotton-half wool mixture. The women's shirts come in many of the same colors and fabrics as the men's, but with an additional choice of bright, clear colors. The nightshirts (for men and women) and pajamas are quite wonderful. *Open M-F 9:30AM-6PM, Sa 9:30AM-4:30PM. 73 and 37 Jermyn St., SW1. 734-4707*

35 **Fortnum and Mason.** The rear entrance of the store, known fondly as the **Queen's Grocer,** is located on Jermyn Street. It is the best place in St. James's for breakfast, and one of the best places in London for things epicurean. The quickest route to the ice-cream concoctions at the **Fountain** is also from this side of the store. *Open M-F 9AM-5:30PM, Sa 9AM-1PM. Main entrance 181 Piccadilly, W1. Rear entrance on Jermyn St. 734-8040 (See **Piccadilly Walk** for complete description.)*

36 **Dunhill's.** It was on this very site in 1907 that Alfred Dunhill opened his small tobacconist shop. The philosophy that made his lighters, watches, fountain pens and pipes famous throughout the wealthy world, *It must be useful, it must work dependably, it must be beautiful, it must last, it must be the best of its kind,* is the motto of a new generation of ambitious consumers. Dunhill has expanded to meet their every need, having dropped only the *It must be useful* as a strict requirement. *Open M-F 9:30AM-5:30PM, Sa 9:30AM-4:30PM. 30 Duke St., SW1. 499-9566*

37 **Green's Champagne and Oyster Bar.** ★ ★ ★ $$$ Green's is a gentlemen's club that is open to the public and filled with Berter Wooster look-a-likes, although the waiters aren't as deferential as Jeeves. The food, though very English, is better than you will find in any club. By all means, have

champage, then choose from a mountain of lobsters, crabs, oysters and salmon, all fresh, simply prepared and outstanding; or try the excellent game (when in season) because you can get grouse, pheasant, wild duck and partridge, hung properly and roasted perfectly. The puddings are all English favorites—treacle tart, gooseberry fool. Crowded at lunchtime, less so at night. *Open M-F 11:30AM-3PM, 5:30-10:45PM. Closed Sa, Su. 36 Duke St., SW1. 930-4566*

38 **Wilton's.** ★ ★ $$$ During Johnny Apple's long reign as *New York Times* bureau chief in London, he wrote with care and affection about food and wine, nourishing along the concept of good English cuisine as surely as the English scene nourished him. One of his favorites was Wilton's. It changed locations during his stay, but took its glass screens, polished mahogany and clublike atmosphere with it, so you would never know you aren't still on Bury Street. The fish is innocently swimming in sea or stream only hours before it is placed in front of you. The smoked salmon and oysters are excellent. The ingredients are prime, English and wisely and simply prepared. In fact, it is considerably better than it was during the Bury Street days. *Open M-F 12:30-2:30PM, 6:30-10:30PM, Sa 6:30-10:30PM. 55 Jermyn St., SW1. 629-9955*

BY APPOINTMENT
TO H.R.H. THE PRINCE OF WALES
SHIRTMAKERS

Turnbull & Asser LTD

39 **Turnbull & Asser.** The name is very familiar to Americans who wear English custom-made shirts, especially now that there is a Turnbull & Asser club in New York and appointment weeks in department stores throughout the country. But it isn't the same as coming into the solemnity of this dark wood-paneled shop where you can't be certain if the man next to you is a Duke or the salesman. The store's made-to-measure service takes 6 weeks, with a minimum of 6 shirts after you approve the first. There is a lot to think about when you embark on made-to-measure shirts: the shape of the collar, the length of the points, pockets, monograms, the shape and color of buttons, a 2 or 3 button cuff. You must also be patient. First you are measured and a sample shirt is made, which Turnbull will send to you. Then you must make a set of fastidious and obsessive notes and return the shirt. This routine can go on for quite some time before you get a shirt that is perfect, and Mr. Williams cheerfully acknowledges that *Turnbull & Asser shirts know their own way across the Atlantic.* If you can't be bothered, choose from their large selection of ready-mades. The clients are not all male and include Candice Bergen and Jacqueline Bisset. Turnbull & Asser reflects Jermyn Street's Beau Brummel legacy rather more faithfully than the other shirtmakers on the street, with daring colors and stripes that the Regency dandy would have found impossible to resist. It is worth noting that the fine craftsmanship, simple, elegant lines and exquisite colors appealed to Beau Brummel, who emptied his pockets on many a stroll down the street, and died penniless and in impoverished exile in France. *Open M-F 9AM-5:30PM, Sa 9AM-1PM. 71 and 72 Jermyn St., SW1. 930-0502*

40 **James Drew.** The firm hands that create luxurious menswear at **Turnbull & Asser** do the same for the ladies next door under the name **James Drew.** The styles are usually flirtatious translations of menswear, served up in lavish silk blouses, dresses, pajamas and skirts, as well as heavy crepe de chines and jacquards in rich Gainsborough colors. *Open M-F 9AM-5:30PM, Sa 9AM-1PM. No. 70 Jermyn St., SW1.*

41 **St. James's Street.** The elegant street connecting Pall Mall with Piccadilly serves as compass for this royal and aristocratic quartier. At the bottom of the street is Henry VIII's gatehouse to St. James's Palace, with a sentry on duty. Pall Mall enters the street just in front of the Palace, continuing its tradition of gentlemen's clubs, although the 18th century clubs here are considered more social and arrogant than the clubs a minute away on Pall Mall. There are no signs to indicate which club is what—if you are a member, you know, and if you aren't, you don't need to know. If you are meeting someone for lunch at his club, you could cross the street several times before getting it right.

42 **White's.** (1788, James Wyatt) No. 37, St. James's Street is London's oldest, most famous and still most fashionable club. This is where the late Evelyn Waugh sought *refuge from the hounds of modernity,* and where **Prince Charles** had his stag party the night before he married **Princess Diana.** If you are sufficiently well-connected to be proposed and accepted for membership, there is a waiting list of 8 years. *No. 37, St. James's St., SW1.*

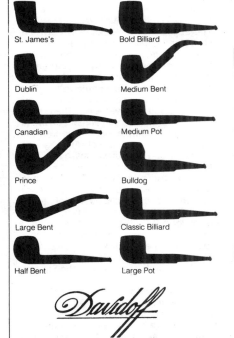

St. James's	Bold Billiard
Dublin	Medium Bent
Canadian	Medium Pot
Prince	Bulldog
Large Bent	Classic Billiard
Half Bent	Large Pot

Davidoff

43 **Davidoff.** Using 3 recipes for flavor, **Zino Davidoff** has created a cigar and pipe smoker's heaven, with the finest Havana cigars, presumably even more plentiful now that Castro has given them up per-

sonally. The shop has an ineffable masculine pull—the handmade wooden humidors, the matchboxes, the cigar cases in leather and crocodile, the cigar holders. The sweet, leathery smell of unsmoked cigars evokes a sense of order, prosperity and calm masculinity which, for the non-smoker, vanishes with the first puff of smoke. But this is a new era. *Open M-Sa 9AM-6PM. 35 St. James's St., SW1. 930-3079*

44 **Boodle's.** (1775, John Crunden) This is one of the best examples of *club* design with the central arched Venetian window in the upper room of the club. Two Rolls-Royces ferry the members back and forth from their offices at lunch, a recent development which some members believe bodes badly for the future. Until recently, Boodle's was the club for fashionable men about town and the kitchen was reputedly the best in clubland. *No. 28, St. James's St., SW1.*

45 **Economist Building.** (1964, Alison and Peter Smithson) The Economist complex is considered one of the few examples of successful modern architecture in London. The architects designed a group of buildings which are compatible with the 18th century scale of St. James's Street, but maintain their 20th century integrity. The complex provides a public open space, offices for *The Economist* magazine, a bank and apartments. The tower is taller than ideal, but one wishes that more architects in this sensitive part of London had behaved so honorably. In the forecourt are **Henry Moore's** *Reclining Figure* (1969) and **Michael Sandle's** *Der Trommler* (1985). *25 St. James's St., SW1.*

46 **Brook's.** (1778, Henry Holland) The inveterate gambler Charles James Fox was a famous member of this club, founded in 1762, and Beau Brummel won £20,000 in one night when this was a great gambling club for Whig aristocrats. Now its members are far less reckless country gentlemen who wouldn't consider gambling away their land. *No. 61 St. James's St., SW1.*

47 **St. James's Club.** Here is a club unlike any other in the neighborhood. You can stay once during the off season before applying for membership (August and November through April). When Hollywood comes to London—Steven Spielberg, Cher, Natassja Kinski, Angelica Houston, Chevy Chase, Liza Minelli and Dudley Moore—it stays here. The inside has tented ceilings, Jacuzzis (well, 2 Jacuzzis) lots of mirrored walls to augment the rather small sizes of the rooms, Art Deco furnishings, towels as thick as sable pelts and a piano bar that feels straight out of Casablanca, with mirrors. If luxury without the language barrier has a certain appeal, St. James's is the club for you. *7 Park Place, SW1. 629-7688*

48 **St. James's Sandwich Company.** ★★$ Blue Ball Yard was built in 1742 as stables for the mansions on St. James's Square. Now it is the home of this sandwich shop, where you can stop for delicious and uncomplicated picnic meals on your way to St. James's Park. All the sandwiches are served in granary baps, which are flat, brown rolls made with whole grains. Try the smoked salmon and cream cheese, smoked salmon pâté, avocado and prawns, turkey and blue Brie or smoked mackerel pâté with tuna. *Open M-F 9:30AM-3PM. 23 Blue Ball Yard, St. James's, SW1. 499-1516*

49 **Dukes Hotel.** *Deluxe.* This hotel in a gaslit courtyard on St. James's Place is a kind of miniature palace, with 53 rooms, 14 suites, an elevator that descends with the stateliness of a dowager duchess and a loyal clientele who relish the location, tucked away in the heart of St. James's, and the extreme courtesy of the staff. It seems churlish to mention that late at night you can hear taxis turning around in the cul-de-sac courtyard, but if noise is your problem, simply ask for a room in the back. The dining room is small and produces excellent English food. The clublike atmosphere is fitting for the neighborhood. *St. James's Place, SW1. 491-4840; reservations, 492-3090*

50 **Stafford Hotel.** *Deluxe.* A few steps beyond the Dukes in a quieter cul-de-sac is a hotel that is virtually a club for its loyal guests—the Marquess of Bath stays here when he is in London, not at his clubs. The feeling that this is an English hotel run for the English is a relief after the anonymous international luxury hotels. The rooms are large and comfortable and are being redecorated. The Stafford dining room has a winelist that resembles a fine club (200 labels which are housed in the cellars that once belonged to St. James's Palace). Tea at the Stafford ranks high on the list of London's best teas, served in a large room filled with antiques, silver teapots, Wedgewood china and real fires in the fireplaces at each end of the room. It's the next best thing to staying in the hotel. *St. James's Place, SW1. 493-0111*

51 **Spencer House.** (1752-54, John Vardy) The entrance to this beautiful Palladian mansion faces St. James's Place, with its finest facade facing Green Park. The house was built for the **Earl of Spencer**, ancestor of **Princess Diana**, and has stayed in the family, although it is no longer used as their town residence. The interior of the house has been well preserved, including a painted room by **James Stuart**, and the exterior has changed little since Vardy built it. *No. 28 St. James's Place, SW1.*

52 **The Carlton.** (1827, Hopper) This club of Conservative politicians is for men only, but of course **Prime Minister Margaret Thatcher** is allowed in, and a larger-than-life portrait of her hangs at the top of the double staircase inside. The large drawing room overlooking St. James's Street is filled with ambitious young men dressed like Sir Anthony Eden. *No. 69 St. James's St., SW1.*

Popular consensus maintains that the Carlton Club *thinks* it runs the country, Boodle's runs the country, and White's owns the country.

53 **Suntory.** ★ ★ $$$ The restaurant is one of 10 in the world owned by the Suntory Japanese Whiskey Company and the standards are as high as the prices (well, almost). In the *teppan yaki* room, you can watch the chefs dissect pieces of beef and seafood with mesmerizing skill. Everything gleams and sizzles and startles with freshness, but unfortunately, there is no sushi bar. *Open M-Sa 12-2:30PM, 7-10:20PM. 72-73 St. James's St., SW1. 409-0201*

54 **King Street.** King Street connects St. James's Square with St. James's Street. Once its greatest claim to fame was the St. James's Theatre, which premiered Oscar Wilde's *Lady Windermere's Fan*, The *Importance of Being Earnest*, Pinero's *The Second Mrs. Tanqueray*, and later, Terence Rattigan's *Separate Tables*. Unfortunately, the theatre was demolished, even though Vivien Leigh interrupted a Parliamentary session in an attempt to save it, but a few old residents remain.

55 **Christie, Manson and Woods Ltd.** Better known simply as Christie's, one of the world's leading auction houses. In the art and antiques trade, Sotheby's, the largest auction house, is said to be run by businessmen trying to be gentlemen, while Christie's is run by gentlemen trying to be businessmen. You can safely count on both houses being composed of gentlemen and businessmen and knowledgeable experts too. Founded in 1766, Christie's has occupied this address on King Street since 1823, except for a period during and after the war when the building was being repaired from damage it suffered during the Blitz. (There is a charming Rowlandson print of Christie's Auction Room, c.1808, from the series *A Microcosm of London* by **Rowlandson** and **Pugin**.) If you come here in the morning when the sales are generally held, you may see millionaires in battle over a painting by Tissot or an emerald necklace. If it is a very important sale of paintings, representatives from the world's museums will be here enigmatic and determined, the atmosphere a cross between a Broadway opening and an operating theatre, with the auctioneer both surgeon and leading actor. Have a look in the various rooms and galleries around the auction room where items to be sold are on view. This is like being in an informal museum, with the added bonus that if you lose your head over the 17th century carpet or the sentimental Victorian watercolor of the girl and the rabbit, you can attend the sale and bid on it. Art and antiques aren't the only items to come under the hammer: since 1766, Christie's has been selling wine at auction. The auction houses now have premises that specialize in non-Masterpieces, such as ordinary paintings, furniture and carpets, which can be great fun. *Open M-F 9AM-4:45PM. 8 King St., SW1. 839-9060. (Also in South Kensington at 85 Brompton Rd., SW7. 581-7611)*

The Antique Trade
by Lennox Money
President: Lennox Money Antiques Ltd.

The **3 principle auction rooms** in London are in easy walking distance of each other, with **Phillips** at the Oxford Street end of Bond Street. **Sotheby's,** midway down Bond and **Christie's,** across Piccadilly on King Street near St. James's Palace.

All the salesrooms compete with each other through a network of local agents and roadshows to attract a constant flow of antiques. The auction houses divide the goods into specialty sales groups, cooperating with each other to ensure that similar items are on sale at all the houses during the same period to attract overseas buyers. Catalogues are available weeks in advance and monthly lists of sale dates are available on request.

Most of the goods on sale are bought by antique dealers, unlike in New York, where private buyers predominate. The salesrooms try to attract their private buyers through lush cataloguing in order to bid up the dealers. But dealers seldom look at the catologues, preferring to use their own judgment. Sotheby's and Phillips charge a 10 percent premium plus VAT on the premium on top of the price at which an object is knocked down in the sale, while Christie's charges 8 percent.

Another house which attracts a fashionable crowd of pedestrian shoppers is **Bonham's** on Montpelier Street, within 200 yards of Harrods. The theme of the sales usually coincide with the current social events, such as Cruft's Dog Week, Valentine's Day, the Oxford and Cambridge Boat Race, Derby Day and the Chelsea Flower Show.

Next door to Bonham's is the **Lots Road Galleries Auction Room**, a favorite with young people, more because of the personality of the auctioneer and the hours (sales start after work, at 6:30PM on Monday evenings) than the offerings.

Christie's, Phillips and Bonham's have **secondary salesrooms** in London, while Sotheby's has moved one to Billingshurst in Sussex, a 90-minute drive from London. Collectors' items and a wide variety of less important furniture and pictures are offered in the secondary rooms. They are useful for those trying to furnish their homes or for those with a specialist's interest trying to collect on a budget.

Christie's secondary salesroom at 85 Old Brompton Road has a particularly wide range of specialist sales. Phillips has a general sale at the Salem Road room in Bayswater every Thursday, and Bonhams's room on Lots Road has one on Tuesdays. Even the wives of Sotheby's directors can be found here looking for furniture for their country cottages. Because the salesroom *experts* have not sorted the goods into categories, those with eclectic tastes may find them more fun than the auctions in the West End. They are full of surprises, often depending on the taste of those who have just died. Catalogues are only available a few days before the sales. Christie's doesn't charge a buyer's premium, but Phillips and Bonham's still charge 10 percent. Salesroom goods are seldom in fit condition, and with the difficulty of finding restorers, you may want to buy from dealers who offer goods in presentable order, but those who over-slick things up should be avoided.

---

56 **Spink and Co.** These art dealers are reputed to be the largest in the world, specializing in coins, medals and Oriental and English art. The rooms have the atmosphere of a museum, but many of the treasures are affordable. The exhibitions by living English artists held in the gallery are worth a look. *Open M-F 9:30AM-5:30PM. 7 King St., SW1. 930-7888*

57 **Lobb's.** Four generations of Lobbs have shod the rich and famous since

John Lobb walked from Cornwall to London to set himself up as a shoemaker. The list of distinguished feet is considerable: the royal feet of Queen Victoria, Mountbatten, King George VI and of course, Her Majesty the Queen; the less royal feet of Cecil Beaton, Winston Churchill, Frank Sinatra, Cole Porter and Katherine Hepburn; and the less loyal feet of spy Guy Burgess. In the basement of the shop, the wooden lasts of customers are kept until they die—and some for long after that. The method of making the shoes is almost the same as in Queen Victoria's day. They draw an outline of your foot in their book, look at it from every angle in search of fallen arches or other flaws, and then, on a long slip of paper folded in the middle, take a series of measurements, which are marked by snips in the paper. The drawing is converted into wooden models of your feet, around which the leather is molded. After a few days of walking the streets of London, the $600 price tag may seem reasonable for shoes that fit perfectly. *Open M-F 9AM-5:30PM, Sa 9AM-1PM. 9 St. James's St., SW1. 930-366*

BESTS
Edward Sexton
Savile Row Tailor

Bespoke Tailors:
Edward Sexton. *37 Savile Row, London, W1. 437-2368*

Anderson & Sheppard Ltd. *30 Savile Row, W1. 734-1420*

Malcom Plews. *33 Savile Row, W1. 434-1290*

Shirts & Hosiery:
Woods & Brown. *Sackville St., W1. 734-3821*

Hilditch & Key. *73 Jermyn St., SW1. 930-5336*

Turnbull & Asser Ltd. *71 Jermyn St., SW1. 930-0502*

Gentlemen's Hatters:
Herbert Johnson. *13 Old Burlington St., W1. 439-7397*

James Lock & Co. Ltd. *6 St. James's St., W1 930-5849*

Bates. *21 Jermyn St., SW1. 734-2722*

Umbrellas:
Swain, Adeney, Briggs & Sons Ltd. *185 Piccadilly, W1. 734-4277*

Smith, James & Sons. *53 New Oxford St., WC1. 729-4731*

Shoes:
Alan McAfee. *17-18 Old Bond St., W1 499-7343*

J. Lobb. *9 St. James's St., SW1. 930-3664*

H. Maxwell. *11 Savile Row, W1. 734-9714*

Hairdressers:
Michael John. *23a Albemarle St., W1. 629-6969*

Ivans. *20 Jermyn St. SW1. 734-1370*

---

58 **Lock & Co.** The house of Lock has been covering the heads of the good and the great since 1700, and moved to this building in 1764. Lord Nelson's famous cocked hats were made here, and the Duke of Wellington, Beau Brummel and all the American ambassadors to the Court of St. James's also covered their heads with hats from Lock & Co. The first bowler hat was made here in 1850 for the gameskeepers of a Mr. William Coke, and the shop still refers to the style as a *Coke*. There are about 16,000 hats in stock, but you can have one made-to-measure with the French *conformateur* that has been used for getting head measurements for 150 years. In England, only the vicar carries an umbrella in the countryside, so the flat, tweed caps are a best seller for country-lovers—JP Donleavy, the Royal Princes and all Sloanes buy their tweed caps here. *Open M-F 9AM-5PM, Sa 9:30AM-12:30PM. No. 6 St. James's St., SW1. 930-8874*

When It's Warranted: Suppliers to the Royal Household

Only the **Queen**, the **Queen Mother**, the **Duke of Edinburgh** and the **Prince of Wales** can grant the elegant and coveted **Royal Warrant**. To qualify, a business has to supply the Royal household directly with services or goods for a minimum of 3 years. The list of Royal Warrant holders is published on the first day of January in the *London Gazette*. The **Princess of Wales**, the most famous Royal shopper, apparently hasn't been supplying the Royal household long enough to issue her own warrant. If you want to consume royally, here are some of the choices of the Royal Family:

The General Trading Company, where the Prince and Princess of Wales had their wedding list, holds all 4 Royal Warrants. *Sloan St., W1. 730-0411*

Hatchards Ltd. Books on the Royal family are only outsold by books on roses. What the Royals read is a mystery (although Charles read Jung). *Piccadilly, W1. 437-3924*

Stephens Brothers Ltd. Shirtmakers and hosiers to the Duke of Edinburgh. You can only buy their shirts; the Duke and his boys get socks too. *16 Sackville St., W1. 734-2424*

R. Twining and Company Ltd. Suppliers of tea and coffee to the Queen, although rumor has it that weak *Ty-phoo* is used at the Palace Garden parties. *216 Strand, WC2. 353-3511*

Truefitt & Hill. Provided George IV with wigs and now cuts what still grows for the Duke of Edinburgh. The cutting is slow; shoes are cleaned free. *23 Old Bond St., W1. 493-2961*

John Lobb. The library of lasts in the basement represents some of the most illustrious feet in the world: Cecil Beaton, Winston Churchill, Cole Porter, Katherine Hepburn, Guy Burgess and of course, the Queen (and Queen Victoria before her). Nowadays a pair of Lobb shoes will set you back about $750, and you'll have to wait 6 months. *9 St. James's St., SW1. 930-3664*

Hardy Brothers Ltd. Fishing tackle shop. Queen Victoria had a Hardy rod, as has every Prince of Wales this century. It was Hardy who developed a big game reel for Zane Grey. A *Zane Grey* reel for catching marlin or swordfish now goes for $4,000. You can buy a pair of Hunter green wellies for $25. *61 Pall Mall, SW1. 839-5515*

59 Overton's. ★ ★ $$ This old-fashioned, bow-windowed restaurant and oyster bar appeals to an affection for Englishness and a fondness for fish. It serves the English classics: smoked Scotch salmon, whitebait and potted shrimps to begin, followed by Dover sole, turbot, halibut, salmon trout and Scotch salmon. Stick to the grilled or poached dishes. The restaurant serves theatre dinners and suppers from 6-11PM. *Open M-Sa 12-2:30PM, 6-11:30PM. No. 5 St. James's St., SW1. 839-3774*

60 Berry Bros. and Rudd. The shop looks much as it did in the 18th century, with its ivy-covered frontage and its austere interior, containing a long, dark room, a large oval table, a few chairs, antique prints, a few bottles of wine and a pair of enormous scales embossed with *The Coffee Mill*, acquired from the grocer who originally occupied the site. Since the 1760s, clients have been weighing themselves on the scales, and their weights are recorded carefully in the shop's ledgers. Weight-watching was serious business even in the days when corpulence signified prosperity. The **Duke of York**, who led his men up the hill and down again, weighed 14-and-a-half stones (a stone is 14 lbs.), but the weight of his brother, **King George IV**, famous for his large girth, is not recorded. The life-loving poet **Byron** was obsessed with his weight, periodically depriving himself of all but a biscuit a day to try and scale down. Records show him at 159 pounds with boots in 1824 and at 180 pounds without them in 1846. But it is the wine which marks Berry Bros. and Rudd for prosperity. The distinctive black and white labels have been appearing on bottles of claret for over 200 years, and the cellars contain bottles that many a Frenchman would be in awe of. Consider a Julienas or a Moulin-a-Vent for the picnic in St. James's Park. *Open M-F 9:30AM-5:00PM. No. 3 St. James's St., SW1. 930-1888*

61 Pickering Place. (1731) The 18th century alleyway still has timber wainscoting for the first 6 feet from the ground. Halfway along the alley on the right is a plaque, *The Republic of Texas Legation 1842-45*, which commemorates the days when Texas was an independent republic and this was its legation. It was rented to the Texans by Berry Bros. during a time when the wine business was in a serious slump. At the end of the alley is a court surrounded by houses that looks more like a cul-de-sac in a cathedral town than the center of London. *St. James's St., SW1.*

62 The House of Hardy. Queen Victoria and every Prince of Wales this century has had a Hardy fishing rod. Hardy developed the special big game reel for Zane Grey for catching marlin or swordfish which now costs $4,000. All Hardy rods are manufactured at Alnwick in Northumberland, and each takes about a month to make. In the shop on Pall Mall, you can choose from 20 types of rods and just as many reels, trying a few casts in the special high-ceilinged room just to be sure. The shop is a good place to buy green Hunter *wellies* (tall rubber boots). *Open M-F 9AM-5PM. 61 Pall Mall, SW1. 839-5515*

63 Crown Passage. A little haven of ordinariness, an escape from elegance. The sandwich bars serve ordinary sandwiches and awful coffee, and there are a few antique and coin dealers. *Between Pall Mall and King St., SW1.*

64 **Red Lion.** ★★$ A popular pub, with the same name as the pub on Duke of York Street on the other side of St. James's Square. It has good home-cooked food for lunch and dinner—shepherd's pie, steak and kidney pie—and a lunchtime winebar upstairs. *Open M-Sa 11AM-3PM, 5:30-11PM. Crown Passage between Pall Mall and King St., SW1. 930-8067*

65 **Oxford and Cambridge Club.** This is the last club in Pall Mall and more democratic and less misogynistic than the others, although women aren't entirely equal: out of a total membership of 4,000, there are only 500 women. They are called *women associate members,* and cannot have lunch in the coffee room or read in the upstairs library or morning room bar. It is as though the Club hasn't been in touch with the goings on at Oxford and Cambridge, where distinctions of this kind have long been obliterated. Still, there is a lot to be said for the club. It offers reciprocal membership with numerous clubs in America, including the University Club, and you can stay here for a fraction of the price of hotels. The dining rooms are not High Table, but the wine lists really are. *71 Pall Mall, SW1. 930-5151*

66 **Schomberg House.** (c. 1698) This house at the St. James's Street end of Pall Mall is a rare example of Queen Anne architecture. Its warm brown-red brick, tall Dutch windows and human scale are a relief after the imposing Italianate stones and stucco. **Gainsborough** lived here in his later years and died here in 1788, after finally reconciling with his old friend and enemy Joshua Reynolds. His parting words were, *We are all going to Heaven and Van Dyck is of the company.* After World War II, the house was completely gutted and filled with modern offices. *80-82 Pall Mall, SW1.*

Next door to **Schomberg House** is the house of the famous and pretty orange seller **Nell Gwynn.** All the property on Pall Mall belongs to the Crown, with the exception of **No. 79,** because Nell Gwynn refused to live in a house that she did not own.

67 **St. James's Palace.** The whole area of London we call St. James's (pronounced by Londoners with 2 syllables as *Jameses*) owes its genesis to the Palace of St. James's. The name comes from the hospital that sheltered leprous women on the site in the 13th century. **Henry VIII** purchased the land in 1532 to build a small royal palace for Anne Boleyn. He had made Whitehall Palace the chief royal residence after the fall of Cardinal Wolsey, pouring his great energy and Renaissance imagination into enlarging it even further. But he regarded the rambling brick mansion called St. James's Palace with affection. The feminine nature of the Palace is seen in its history of Royal births—**Charles II** (1630), **James II** (1633), **Mary II** (1662) and **Queen Anne** (1665) were all born at St. James's. Charles

The gatehouse, St. James's Palace

Drawing courtesy of David Gentleman

II never liked Whitehall, so he spent time, energy and money building up St. James's. But it did not become the official residence of the sovereign until 1698 when Whitehall Palace burned down. It remained the monarch's London residence until **Queen Victoria** ascended to the throne in 1837 and moved the court, under strong pressure from her Prime Minister, to Buckingham Palace. Its presence in modern British life has never completely vanished. To this day, all foreign ambassadors present their credentials to the Court of St. James's.

The Palace had four courts, but fire, rebuilding and time have cut the number in half. The state rooms, which can be seen over the wall towards the Mall, were rebuilt by **Sir Christopher Wren** in 1703. Not a lot remains of the Tudor palace, but the most charming surviving part is the **Gatehouse** and **Clock Tower,** which face St. James's Street. The tower of worn red brick has four stories and sits astride a pair of vast and worn gates. The turrets crowned with battlements and the sentry box manned by a handsome soldier from the Guards seem too Gilbert and Sullivan to be true, but their anachronistic presence is a heartening reminder that this is why St. James's exists. *Pall Mall, SW1.*

68 **Queen's Chapel.** (1627, Inigo Jones) This architectural gem was the first church built in the classical style, and like Banqueting House in Whitehall, also by Inigo Jones, the interior is a perfect cube. The Chapel was originally built for the **Spanish Infanta,** intended bride of Charles I, and then became the Chapel of his wife Henrietta Maria, also a Roman Catholic. Now it is a part of the Chapel Royal. Services are held every Sunday from Easter until the end of July. The gold and white coffered ceiling is original. On summer Sundays the Chapel is marvelously lit by light from the wide Venetian window. *Open for services Su at 10:45AM from Easter to end of July. Marlborough Rd., SW1.*

69 **Friary Court.** The changing of the rather small guard at St. James's Palace takes place here daily at 11AM, and afterwards you can usually enter the courtyard and look around. Every new sovereign is proclaimed from the balcony in this courtyard and it was from here that 18-year-old Queen Victoria wept when she heard the cheers of her subjects. The **State Apartments,** through the door in the north east corner, are only open on special occasions, usually when royal gifts are on display, and the wait can be considerable. Inside is the **Amoury Room,** lined with ancient weapons, and the **Tapestry Room,** with tapestries woven for Charles II. The last hand at decorating these rooms was **William Morris's** in the 1860s, an inspired choice for someone in the Queen's household. The Morris genius was perfectly suited to the Tudor proportions. *St. James's Palace, Pall Mall, SW1.*

70 **Marlborough House.** (1710, Sir Christopher Wren) The house was built for **John Churchill,** first Duke of Marlborough, but more for the Duchess than the Duke. Formidable, turbulent, brilliant and beautiful, **Sarah Churchill,** first Duchess of Marlborough (pronouced Mawlborough) laid the foundation stone which survives within the house and reads *Laid by Her Grace The Dutches of Marlborough May ye 24th/June ye 4 1709.* The Duchess hated the monumental palace of Blenheim which was built for the Duke by Queen Anne after his victory at the Battle of Blenheim. So she chose **Sir Christopher Wren** to build her London mansion, instructing him to make it *strong, plain and convenient,* which he did. The Crown acquired the house in 1817. Unfortunately, the pure perfection created by Wren has been much disguised by the additions and enlargements made in 1861-63 by **James Pennethorne.** Edward VII lived here while he was Prince of Wales. George V was born in the house, and his consort, Queen Mary, lived here during her widowhood. In 1959, Queen Elizabeth presented the house to the nation so that it could become the Commonwealth Center in London. *Marlborough will be closed for repairs in late 1986. Tours, by appointment only, M-F at 11AM or 3PM, depending on availability. Adjacent to St. James's Palace on the south side of Pall Mall, SW1. 930-9249*

71 **Lancaster House.** (1827, Benjamin Wyatt) Originally called York House and later called Stafford House, Lancaster House was built for the **Duke of York,** of the column and the nursery rhyme, who extravagantly commissioned it but died before paying for it, whereupon it was sold to the Duke of Sutherland. Chopin played for Queen Victoria in the Music Room and the Duke of Windsor lived here when he was the Prince of Wales (1919-30). Since being restored from war damage, the building has been the setting for State banquets and conferences. The Louis XV interiors are among the most sumptuous in London. *Admission fee. Open Sa and Su 2-6PM from Easter to November. Stable Yard, The Mall, SW1. 839-3988*

72 **Clarence House.** (1829, John Nash) Until Queen Elizabeth's accession to the throne in 1952, she and Prince Philip lived here. Now it is the home of the **Queen Mother.** When she is in residence, a lone piper plays his bagpipes in the garden at 9AM, a gentle Scottish alarm clock for one of the best loved members of the Royal Family. *Attached to the west side of St. James's Palace, Pall Mall, SW1.*

73 **Chapel Royal.** (1532) This Chapel west of the gatehouse at St. James's Palace was built by **Henry VIII.** It is one of the great gems of Tudor London and a treasure of any epoch. The beautiful coffered ceiling was painted by **Hans Holbein.** Married beneath it were William III and Mary II (1677), Queen Anne (1683), George IV (1795), Queen Victoria (1840) and George V (1893). But what stirs the memory most is not the royal weddings, but **Charles I,** the sad, brave king who took Holy Communion in the Chapel on the morning of his execution, 30 January 1649. You can attend services in the chapel every Sunday until the Sunday before Easter. *Ambassadors' Court, St. James's Palace, Pall Mall, SW1. The courtyard and Chapel are only open on Sundays at 10:45 AM for services from Oct. to Good Friday.*

ST. JAMES'S

74 **St. James's Park.** Henry VIII created this oldest and most perfect of royal parks, with 93 acres and an enchantment of water, birds, views, gaslights and Englishness, even though the French landscape gardener, **Le Nôtre**, played a part in creating the formality and flower beds. It is a royal park in the best sense of the word: monarchs have lavished all that monarchs have to lavish in expense and ingenuity to make it the graceful, contemplative place it is today. **Henry VIII** drained the marshland between the 2 palaces at St. James's and Whitehall to make a deer forest. **Charles I** created the formal walks, and walked formally and bravely across the park to his execution. His son **Charles II** created what you see today, an exotic oasis of trees, flowers, ducks, geese and pelicans. It was Charles II who, soon after the Restoration, opened the park to the public. **George IV** got Nash to reshape the canal and create the meandering lake, crossed by the bridge which grants magical views of Whitehall and Buckingham Palace. At 10AM each morning, the pelicans stretch their wiry limbs and emerge for a breakfast of kippers, as though they are aware of their distinguished lineage—they are direct descendants of the pair given to Charles II by a Russian ambassador.

A family on the throne is an interesting idea also. It brings down the pride of sovereignty to the level of petty life. No feeling could seem more childish than the enthusiasm of the English at the marriage of the Prince of Wales. They treated as a great political event, what, looked at as a matter of pure business, was very small indeed. But no feeling could be more like common human nature as it is, and as it is likely to be.

Walter Bagehot: *The English Constitution,* 1867.

---

75 **Buckingham Palace.** (1913, Sir Aston Webb) The Royal Palace is the most gazed at building in London, not because of its magnificence, because it is not very magnificent, or its great age, because what one is gazing at is a somber facade of Portland stone and French pilasters that dates from 1913. The gazes are inspired by the magic and the mystique of the monarchy—and like Maude informed her young lover in *Harold and Maude,* we may not believe in monarchy but *we miss the kings and queens.*

This is the oldest monarchy of all, and it is in the last country in the world where monarchy exists on a grand and sanctified scale, with religious processions, a titled and healthy aristocracy and, as the Prince and Princess of Wales prove, hysterical adulation from the country's—and worlds'—people that transcends nationalities, classes and parties.

Her Most Excellent Majesty Elizabeth the Second, by the Grace of God, of the United Kingdom of Great Britain and Northern Ireland and of her Realms and Territories Queen, Head of the Commonwealth, Defender of the Faith, Sovereign of the British Orders of Knighthood, is the 40th monarch since the Norman Conquest, descended from Charlemagne and King Canute. Her accession in 1952 coincided with the beginning of the end of the Empire, and she has presided over its dissolution with noble Queenship. She is probably one of the best informed diplomats in the world today, having had continuous access for 35 years to the leaders of the world. She has known Churchill, Khrushchev and Eisenhower, and knows every major head of state in the world today. Every Tuesday night when the Queen is in London, the Prime Minister goes to Buckingham Palace for a talk with the Queen. Her concerned involvement, excellent memory and sharp insight have been appreciated by almost all the Prime Ministers of her reign. (The relationship between the Queen and Mrs. Thatcher is said to be one of mutual admiration but not great warmth or intimacy.)

Will she *retire,* step down and turn the monarchy business over to her eldest son? The answer is no. The Queen is Queen for life, and the monarchy's continuity and survival depends on adherence to the spiritual laws of the monarchy: under the hereditary system, the last intake of breath by the dying sovereign coincides absolutely with the next intake by the living sovereign, hence the ancient cry *The King is dead—Long live the King.*

When the Queen is in residence at Buckingham Palace, the Royal Standard waves above. The visitor's viewpoint is the rather dour eastern facade, completely rebuilt by **Sir Aston Webb** in 1913. The front western facade, visible only from a helicopter, is by **John Nash.** The main building is flanked with 2 classical pavillions and overlooks an immense sweep of lawn, 43 acres of private gardens, expanses of woodlands, giant trees, over 200 species of wild plants, a lake graced with pink flamingos, an herbaceous border and tennis courts. This is where the **Queen's Garden Parties** are held each summer.

Buckingham Palace

The original house, built for the Duke and Duchess of Buckingham in 1703, was bought by George III some 60 years later for his beloved Queen Charlotte, who filled it with children and made it into a family house, then known as **Queen's House.** George IV commissioned Nash to make it into a home more worthy of a monarch, but the plans became grander and more difficult to execute with time. The transformation process had many of the elements of a Laurel and Hardy film, not the least being the scheme to surround the Palace with scaffolding to disguise the fact that a new Palace was being constructed, whilst the permission had been granted only for renovations and repairs. When the King died, Nash, who had transformed London into a royal and elegant city, was dismissed by an angry Parliament. An investigation into the Palace's spiraling costs revealed financial irregularities. Publicly disgraced, Nash died in 1835.

William IV was not pleased with the achievements of Nash's successor, Blore, and offered the Palace to Parliament as a permanent home following the fire which destroyed Westminster in 1834, but the government refused. William IV, claiming the air was better for his asthma, stayed at Kensington Palace until his death.

Buckingham Palace became the official residence of the sovereign when Queen Victoria moved in. The Royal Standard flew here for the first time, and the dance-loving Queen and her Consort Prince Albert extended the Palace, building the State Supper Room and the Ball Room. The Queen also removed the Marble Arch from the front of the Palace and had it placed at its present site on the north side of Hyde Park.

Sir Aston Webb, architect for George V and his popular wife Mary of Teck, transformed the facade of Buckingham Palace, replacing the faking Caen stone with Portland stone and adding the French-inspired pilasters. George V also saw the unveiling of the **Victoria Memorial** in front of the Palace, a sentimental wedding cake of a sculpture by **Sir Thomas Brock** (1911), with a seated Queen Victoria (13 feet high) facing the Mall, surrounded by the figures of Truth, Justice and Motherhood—all dear to the Queen's heart. At the top, glistening in gold, is Victory attended by Constancy and Courage. It may suffer from the defects of Victorian sentimentality and excess, but it is hard to imagine Buckingham Palace without it. *The Palace is not open to the public. Changing of the Guard, in the forecourt, April to August, daily at 11:30AM; September to March, alternate days only.*

76 **Queen's Gallery.** (1830, John Nash) This royal treasure chest was originally a conservatory and then a chapel. In 1963, it was established as an art gallery by Her Majesty. There are continuous exhibitions, imaginative and scholarly, of the royal treasures of the British monarchy, a collection unparalled in magnificence and variety. The exhibitions change every 6 months. *Admission fee. Open Tu-Sa 11AM-5PM, Su 2-5PM. Buckingham Gate, Buckingham Palace Rd., SW1.*

77 **Royal Mews.** (1825, John Nash) The state coaches from all periods are on display, including the state coach acquired by George III in 1762 that is still in use today. The coach is a Cinderella design, with elaborate carvings representing 8 palm trees, branching at the top and supporting the roof, and 3 cherubs, representing England, Scotland and Ireland. It is 24 feet long, 8 feet wide and 12 feet high, and weighs 4 tons. *Open W-Th 2-4PM. Buckingham Palace Rd., SW1.*

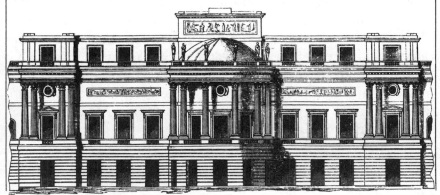

Buckingham Palace, Garden Front

Cromwell and Brompton

Roads gently embrace in front of the flamboyant Baroque **Brompton Oratory,** uniting at that almost imperceptible angle two roads, two villages (Kensington and Knightsbridge) and two different worlds. It seems an unlikely union. **South Kensington,** with its nexus of museums, is Victorian and high-minded, evidence of one man's grandiose vision of the educational and moral value of art, while luxe and high-spirited **Knightsbridge** is home ground for the chic, sophisticated and fashionable. But like all successful unions, the two bring out the best in one another, and a day spent in the company of both is unimaginably satisfying.

This walk includes dinosaurs and their living relatives; an earthquake; a launch pad—and the actual Apollo 10 capsule; an 11 foot bed for weary travelers mentioned in *Twelfth Night*; the art of China, Islam and the Italian Renaissance; a quarter of a million butterflies; 10 acres of the greatest collection of antique furniture and decorative art in the world (not for sale); and 15 acres of fabulous furniture, decorative art and just about everything you could conceivably desire (all for sale).

The walk begins at the **Natural History Museum,** a building which exudes Victorian confidence, worthiness and grandeur, and looks more like an ecclesiastical railway station than a museum which houses more than 50 million items from the natural world. The walk culminates at **Harrods,** whose motto is no less modest: *Omnia, Omnibus, Ubique—All Things, For All People, Everywhere.* And if the sheer magnitude of what's on sale leaves you feeling muddled and breathless, a perfect detour into **Hyde Park** and **Kensington Gardens** will help you recover from the pursuit of knowledge and culture, and prepare your mind for the material matters available nearby. The Hyde Park Hotel, at the end of the walk, is a worthy shrine for any Anglophile pilgrim who thinks tea in late afternoon is as necessary as it is civilized. Nearby is one of London's best winebars, Le Metro, for displaced Francophiles, and a special pub, the Grenadier, which was once the Officer's Mess for the Duke of Wellington's soldiers.

This is a Monday-through-Saturday walk if you want to include shopping at Harrods. But if you are primarily a museum-trotter, this could be your perfect Sunday in London, beginning with lunch at an excellent French restaurant (St. Quentin is practically across the street) and finishing in time for the opening of the museum at 2:30PM. Because much of the walk is spent indoors, it is ideal for a rainy day, except for the detour into Hyde Park and Kensington Gardens.

Map labels

The Orangery

Round Pond

Kensington Gardens

L

Kensington Palace

Bandstand

PALACE AVENUE

GARDENS

BROAD WALK

THE FLOWER WALK

KENSINGTON ROAD

Queen's Gate

CROMWELL ROAD

ASHBURN

ASHBURN MEWS

GLOUCESTER

STANHOPE M

Stanhope Gardens

COLL

The mathematicians worked out that the **Crystal Palace** must collapse after the first strong wind; the engineers claimed that the galleries would break up and crush the visitors; the economists predicted that prices would rise drastically as a result of the vast influx of people, while doctors warned of a reappearance of the black death of the Middle Ages as a result of these crowds, which reminded them of the crusades. The moralists predicted that England would become impregnated with all the evils of the civilized and uncivilized worlds, while the theologians argued that this second Tower of Babel would also incur the vengeance of an insulted God. —**Prince Albert**, in a letter to Frederick William IV of Prussia.

On a perfect spring day, 1 May 1851, at 12 noon, the **Great Exhibition on the Works of Industry of All Nations** was opened by Queen Victoria and Prince Albert. The name that people took to their hearts was the **Crystal Palace,** the gigantic and revolutionary greenhouse designed by **Sir Joseph Paxton.** It covered 19 acres and was a marvel of delicate cast iron ribbing with 300,000 panes of glass. The length was 1,848 feet, 3 times the length of **St. Paul's,** and the height of 108 feet was so high that 3 elm trees on the site could be in-

corporated into it. Paxton was not an architect, but a creative and brilliant gardener who worked for the Duke of Devonshire. His building was as futuristic in concept as it was revolutionary in design, with pre-fabricated, standardized and interchangeable units which were erected by 2,000 men in just 22 weeks. The building was taken down in 1852 and re-erected in Sydenham. Only the gates remain.

The main impetus of the Exhibition was to raise the standard of the industrial design of goods which were being mass-produced by machines. Some 14,000 exhibitors from 40 countries demonstrated the latest developments in technology and the arts. Six million people attended, many traveling on the railway for the first time. The popular and innovative Exhibition made a profit of nearly £200,000, which the Prince wanted spent on a permanent center for education, museums and learned societies. By 1856, a total of 87 acres had been purchased and roads were being built—the new Cromwell Road, a westward extension of Brompton Road, joined with Kensington Road via Exhibition Road and Prince Albert Road (now Queen's Gate), forming a complex of museums and colleges, a monument to Victorian curiosity and industry.

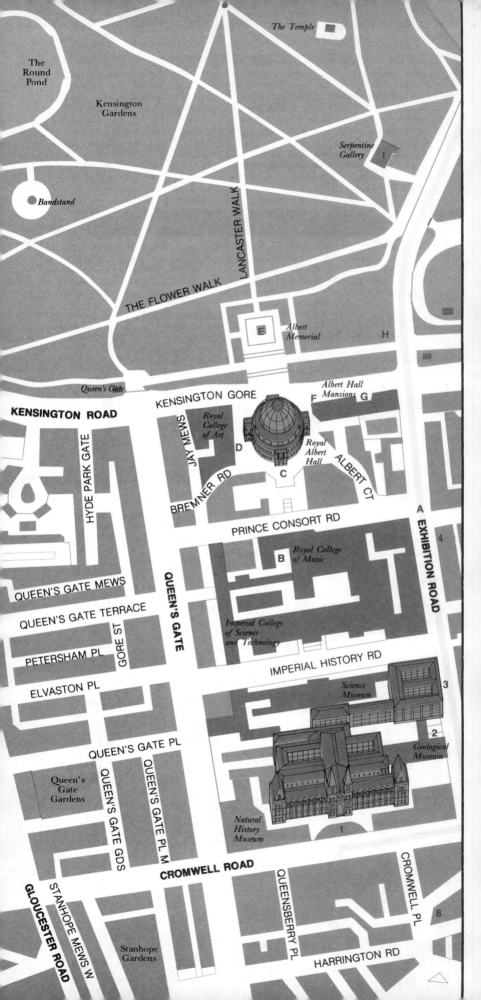

The Round Pond

Kensington Gardens

The Temple

Serpentine Gallery

I

Bandstand

THE FLOWER WALK

LANCASTER WALK

E

Albert Memorial

H

Queen's Gate

KENSINGTON GORE

Albert Hall Mansions

F

G

KENSINGTON ROAD

HYDE PARK GATE

JAY MEWS

Royal College of Art

D

BREMNER RD

Royal Albert Hall

C

ALBERT CT

A

EXHIBITION ROAD

4

PRINCE CONSORT RD

Royal College of Music

B

QUEEN'S GATE MEWS

QUEEN'S GATE TERRACE

GORE ST

QUEEN'S GATE

Imperial College of Science and Technology

PETERSHAM PL

ELVASTON PL

IMPERIAL HISTORY RD

Science Museum

3

2

Geological Museum

QUEEN'S GATE PL

Queen's Gate Gardens

QUEEN'S GATE GDS

QUEEN'S GATE PL M

Natural History Museum

1

CROMWELL ROAD

CROMWELL PL

STANHOPE MEWS W

GLOUCESTER ROAD

QUEENSBERRY PL

8

Stanhope Gardens

HARRINGTON RD

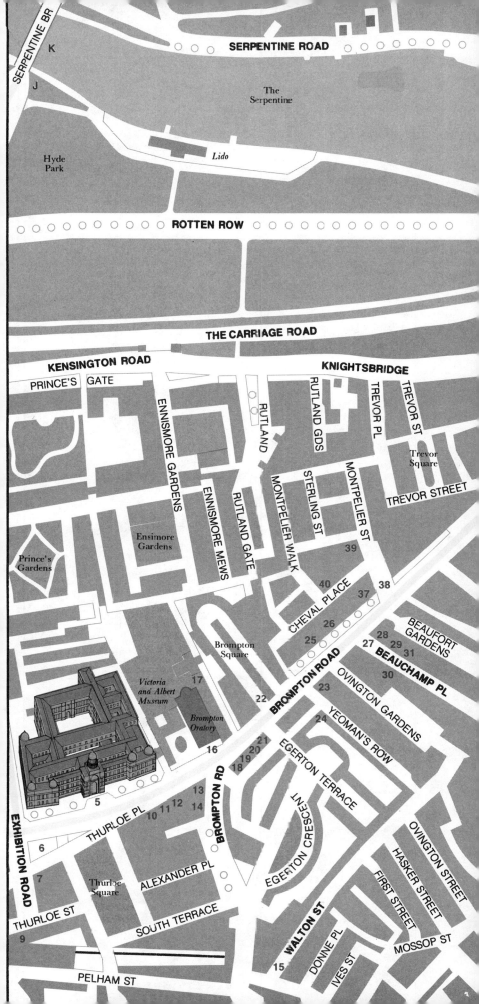

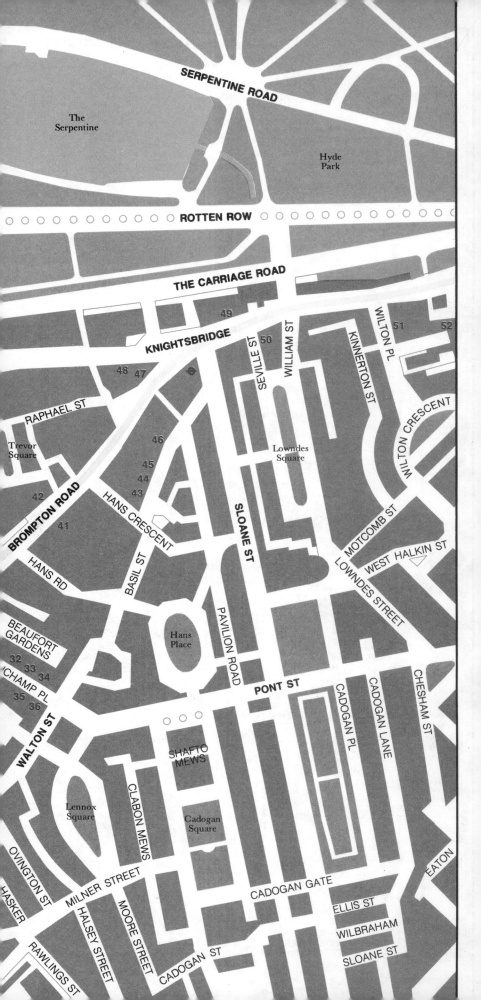

1 **Natural History Museum.** (1873-80, Alfred Waterhouse) If you take a taxi into London from Heathrow, the twin-towered, Byzantine, terra cotta and slate blue museum is the first real feast for the eye. It looks superb in sunlight and breathtaking when lit up against a night sky. Animal figures grace the outside of the building, and inside, painted panels of wild flowers decorate the high curved ceiling. As you enter the nave-like central hall, you expect to see a high altar (or a diesel engine). But in this holy terminus dedicated to the wonders of Creation, rising high above the ordinary human figures below, is the 85-foot-long skeleton of **Diplodocus Carnegii,** the 150-million-year-old dinosaur believed to be the largest flesh-eating land animal to have ever existed. Off to the left side of the hall are push button computer games where you can trace the evolution and extinction of the species, which dominated the earth for about 140 million years and died about 65 million years ago.

The Natural History Museum is part of the **British Museum,** which was founded by an Act of Parliament in 1753. It houses the national collections of zoology, entomology, paleontology, minerology and botany. With 4 acres to cover and some 50 million possible items to see, you may have to choose between dinosaurs, humans, whales, birds and mammals. But be sure to see the excellent display on the origin of the human species on the first floor, including specimens from **Darwin's** historic voyage on the *HMS Beagle.* Also stop by the **Whale Hall** to gaze at the overwhelming model and skeleton of a Blue Whale. In the **bird** display in the west wing, parents linger in front of the extinct dodos, those giant pigeons who couldn't fly, and flightless emus and ostriches, while children race ahead to the penguins. The **mammals** exhibition shouldn't be missed, especially the rare giant panda **Chi-Chi**, who died of old age at the London Zoo in 1972 and now permanently munches bamboo in the north mammal hall. The **Human Biology** exhibition features the story of fertilization and birth and the story of hormones and cells, an encouraging follow-up to **Man's Place in Evolution**. *No admission charge. Open M-Sa 10AM-6PM, Su 2:30-6PM. Cromwell Rd., SW7. 589-6323*

Within the museum are:

The Natural History Museum Shops. These are terrific! The post cards in the first shop are the best bargain in town, with gentle gorillas, gory bugs, lavish butterflys and fleas in costume, all for 5p. The shop next door carries plastic dinosaurs, while the gift shop has more deluxe items—fossils, replicas of skulls and crystal goblets etched with endangered species. But the best shop is the bookshop, which has an excellent collection of gardening books, beautifully illustrated guides to wildflowers, and more specifically, Hugh Johnson's *Encyclopaedia of Trees*, the *Catalogue of the Rothschild Collection of Fleas* in 5 weighty volumes and a replica of Darwin's journal of the *Beagle*, all well worth the detour. *Open M-Sa 10AM-6PM, Su 2:30-6PM. 589-6323*

Snack Bar. The menu consists of basic English school food: fish fingers and chips, beans on toast, sausage and chips, Cornish pasties, a diet pretty low on the evolutionary scale. But the place is worth a sociological survey and very appealing to young children. *Open M-Sa 10AM-6PM, Su 2:30-6PM. 589-6323*

**Museum Bests
RH Hedley**
Director, Natural History Museum

As soon as visitors enter the Museum, they are confronted by the large **Diplodocus skeleton** which seems to stand for much that people expect and enjoy in a natural history museum.

It is a strange sensation seeing the model of the **Australopithecus woman** in *Man's Place in Evolution*. She is slight and tough; almost human, but not quite.

Children get particular pleasure in running their hands over the model of the **Swanscombe man's skull** in *Man's Place in Evolution*. Using that extra sense beyond sight makes the experience more meaningful and memorable.

Children gaze at the **giant redwood tree section** with a sense of wonder; they marvel at its size, and as they count the rings, it gradually dawns on them just how long it has lived.

There is such satisfaction in a really clear and well thought out comparison, like the **analogy between the rolled-up newspaper and the brain cortex** in *Human Biology*.

The computers in the *Human Biology* exhibition have tremendous attracting power; it is hard to resist having a go at the **Imposters** game, which is an important educational tool.

The suspended flotilla of **dolphins** in the *Whale exhibition* always attracts people as they pass; it brings home the range of adaptions that natural selection has brought about in response to different habitats.

The **diorama** in *Introducing Ecology* beautifully captures the atmosphere of the countryside. The artistry that has gone into its construction makes it easy for your imagination to see nature at work in dozens of energy transforming food chains.

2 **Geological Museum** (1935, John Markham) This museum is often overlooked because it is wedged in between the two giants, the Natural History and Science Museums. Even on a Saturday, you can gaze peacefully at rubies, emeralds, sapphires and diamonds, including a model of the *Koh-i-noor* diamond, cut under the supervision of Prince Albert and first shown at the Great Exhibition of 1851. Don't miss **The Story of the Earth** display, which is entered by way of a 25-foot-high *cliff* from the Highlands of Scotland. You will be taken on a journey through the first billion years on earth, complete with erupting volcano and earthshaking earthquake.

The exhibits get more didactic as you go up, culminating in the world's largest display of metalliferous ores and a model of **Stonehenge** on the second floor. *No admission charge. Open M-Sa 10AM-6PM, Su 2:30-6PM. Exhibition Rd., SW7. 589-3444*

3 **Science Museum.** (1913, Sir Richard Allison) This inspired tribute to science couldn't be more appropriately located than in the nation that gave us Newton, Darwin, Davy, Huxley, Thomson, Rutherford and Fleming. A visit here leaves you with the inevitable realization of just how many fundamental scientific discoveries have been British. The museum is especially enjoyable for the young, who can push, pull and test the countless knobs, buttons and gadgets. Exhibits change regularly, so pick up a map from the museum shop.

The lower ground floor is heaven for the small and curious. It is filled with such items as a burglar alarm to test, a model lift to operate, a take-off and landing simulator for would-be aviators, a periscope for spying on the floor above and many more gadgets, all to be tried and tested. For the more domestic, there is an authentic Victorian kitchen and a large collection of appliances.

The emphasis on the ground floor is on power, transport and exploration, with the **Foucault Pendulum** demonstrating the rotation of the earth on its own axis. Also on display are **Puffing Billy** (1813), the oldest locomotive in the world; the **Boulton and Watt** pumping engine (1777); the first diesel engine made in England; 8 fire engines; full scale models of a submarine and a moon lander; and most popular of all, the actual **Apollo 10 capsule.**

A star dome in the astronomy section dominates the first floor. But you will also find everything you ever wanted to know about map-making, time measurement, iron, steel and glass-making, agriculture, meteorology and telecommunications. Don't miss the new display on computer technology called *The Challenge of the Chip.*

The second floor deals with the more didactic subjects of chemistry, atomic physics, nuclear power and computers. Be sure to see the models of sailing ships and warships and the equipment from *Gipsy Moth IV*.

The art of flight is explored on the third floor, from the hot-air balloon to the Concord. Of special interest is the **De Havilland Gipsy Moth**, used by **Amy Johnson** on her flight to Australia in 1930; a replica of the craft built by **Orville** and **Wilbur Wright** in 1903; and WWII aircraft. The aeronautics section shares the floor with a history of photography and cinematography from 1835.

The new **Wellcome Medical Museum** on the fourth and fifth floors contains 40 tableaux and dioramas depicting medical history, from trepanning in neolithic times to open heart surgery in the 1980s. Clever, often spine-chilling displays cover tribal, oriental, classical Greek, Roman, medieval and Renaissance medicine. The vast collection of curiosities include **Florence Nightingale's** moccasins, a microscope made for **Lister**, **Dr. Livingston's** medicine chest, and **Napoleon's** beautiful silver toothbrush.

The **museum shop** offers a few booklets and postcards and the **snack bar** on the third floor is only for the hungry. *No admission charge. Open M-Sa 10AM-6PM, Su 2:30-6PM. Exhibition Rd., SW7. 589-3456*

Museum Bests
Neil Cossons
Director, Science Museum

The great sequence of **steam engines** in the East Hall, the first thing visitors see when entering the museum. Here are the pioneer contributions of Newcomen, Watt, Trevithick and Parsons.

Puffing Billy, built in 1813, and the oldest surviving steam locomotive in the world.

Philip de Loutherbourg's dramatic painting *Coalbrookdale by Night* in the Iron and Steel Gallery.

The engine of **Henry Bell's steamer Comet** and the collection of **marine steam engine models.**

The **Orrery,** named after the Earl of Orrery, for whom it was made in 1716.

The Vickers **Vimy aircraft** in which Alcock and Brown made the first non-stop crossing of the Atlantic in 1919.

The **Portsmouth blockmaking** machinery built by Henry Maudslay to the designs of Sir Marc Brunel.

The **George III Collection** of scientific apparatus.

Launchpad, a hall full of interactive exhibits demonstrating principles of science and technology.

The ingenious **automatic teamaker** of 1904.

4 **Ognisko Polski.** ★ ★ ★ $ In fact, this is a Polish club, but non-members are welcome. It is a favorite, and supposedly secret, haunt of many of the museum and South Kensington Bohemians and intellectuals. The bar and restaurant are sort of elegant, the food very *zrazy, kasza* and *kolduny,* and the atmosphere unbeatable. It

is a kind of poor man's Russian Tea Room, with a set lunch and dinner which often includes *bigos* (chopped beef or pork, cabbage, sauerkraut and onions simmered in a spicy sauce). *Open M-Sa 12:30-2:30PM, 6:30-11PM; Su 1:30-3:30PM, 6:30-11PM. 55 Exhibition Rd., SW7. 589-4670*

A **Exhibition Road.** If a morning of museum-going has filled your mind with things cultural but left you craving the out of doors, continue up Exhibition Road into the refreshing greenery of Hyde Park and Kensington Park Gardens. The route is lined with monuments to the purposeful Prince Albert, including the new Paleontology Building of the Natural History Museum (1975), the Geological Museum, the Science Museum, and the Henry Cole Wing of the V&A. The road culminates in the gargantuan Albert Hall, which, along with Kensington Park Gardens, is presided over by the Albert Memorial.

B **Royal College of Music.** (1894, Sir Arthur Blomfield) Inside the elaborate building is a remarkable collection of more than 500 musical instruments, ranging from the earliest known stringed keyboard instruments to some wonderfully bizarre concoctions of the 19th and 20th centuries. There is also a portrait collection with more than 100 paintings and several thousand engravings and photographs, including **Burne-Jones's** portrait of **Paderewski** (1890) and **Epstein's** bust of **Vaughn Williams.** *Admission charge. Music collection open M&W from Oct-June, 11AM-4:30PM. Portrait collection open M-F by appt. Prince Consort Rd., SW7. 589-3643*

C **Albert Hall.** (1871, Fowke) This stupendous piece of Victoriana is a memorial to Prince Albert, ordained and encouraged by Queen Victoria. The vast 735-foot red-brick elliptical hall, with its glass and iron dome, can hold 8,000 people. Apparently the Prince approved of the design (although he wanted this site to be for another National Gallery), and it is a fitting climax to the cultural complex honoring the education of the mind and spirit which he believed in so strongly.

Albert Hall still operates under a Royal Charter, and is the venue for sporting events, beauty contests, pop concerts, military tatoos and, most famous of all, the **Henry Wood Promenade Concerts,** performed daily between mid-July and mid-September. Known as the *Proms,* these performances of classical music have an informal atmosphere and are packed with sincere lovers of music. The last night of the Proms are famously emotional and tickets are by lottery. *Kensington Gore, SW7. Information: 589-3202. Tickets: 589-8212.*

D **Royal College of Organists** (1875, HH Cole) This eccentric 4 story building was designed by a soldier in the Royal Engineers, a policy consistent with Prince Albert's preference for engineers and artists over architects. It delights passers-by with its euphoria of decoration and colors—blues, reds and yellows—and its frieze of musicians. What's missing from this picture? Well, there is no organist…and no organ. *Kensington Gore, SW7.*

E **Albert Memorial.** (1872, Sir Gilbert Scott) A little to the west of where the Crystal Palace once stood sits Prince Albert, holding the catalogue of the Great Exhibition of 1851 and gazing down on the museums, colleges and institutes which his vision, energy and endeavor inspired. His *throne,* crowned by a spire of gilt and enameled metal which ends in a cross rising 180 feet high, is an imposing piece of Victorian art made loveable by its sheer excess. The monument was commissioned by the Prince's mournful widow, Queen Victoria, and unveiled by her in 1876. Below the bronze statue of the Prince Regent are marble statues of animals representing the 4 continents, while allegorical figures representing Agriculture, Commerce, Manufacture and Engineering stand at the 4 angles. On the pedestal is a magnificent procession of reliefs of the greatest artists, writers and philosophers of the Victorian era. The Memorial is a gift to Londoners and London-lovers, but it was never a gift to the Prince, who pleaded against such a rememberance. *It would disturb my quiet rides in Rotten Row to see my face staring at me, and if (as is very likely) it became an artistic monstrosity like most of our monuments, it would upset my equanimity to be permanently ridiculed and laughed at in effigy,* wrote the Prince prophetically. Indeed, for many years the monument was denounced as an example of the worst of Victorian sentimentality and ugly excess. But time, on our side and the Prince's, has brought the Memorial and the Prince into deserved veneration. *Kensington Gore, SW7.*

F **Albert Hall Mansions** (1879-86, Norman Shaw) The warm brick mansions were one of the earliest blocks of flats in London. If they weren't so utterly English—the style is Queen Anne Revival with oriels, gables, dormers and arches—they would seem almost European in their scale and grandeur. The flats are extremely desirable because of their superb location and palatial-size rooms. They are occupied by an appreciative elite, including the English designer Jean Muir, whose flat is decorated entirely in white. *Kensington Gore, SW7.*

G **Royal Geographical Society.** (1873-75, Norman Shaw; formerly Lowther Lodge) The statues outside of the informal Dutch-style building are of **Sir Ernest Shackleton,** who commanded 3 expeditions to the Antartic and discovered the location of the south magnetic pole in 1909, and **David Livingstone,** who discovered the Zambezi River, the Victoria Falls and the source of the Nile, and was famously rescued by the journalist HM Stanley. Inside is an outstanding map room with a collection of more than half a million maps and a model of Mount Everest. The Society sponsors monthly exhibitions (mainly photographic) of travel and travelers throughout the world. *No admission charge. Open M-F 10AM-5PM. 1 Kensington Gore, SW7. 589-0648*

H **Kensington Park Gardens and Hyde Park.** Of all the features which make London the most liveable city in the world—the innate courtesy of the English, the civilized lay of the land with its squares and humane, domestic architecture, the thick layers of sympathetic history—it is the parks, the vast oases of green, that give the city an almost unique supply of urban oxygen and humanity.

It is inconceivable to know London without spending time in the parks, and for many Londoners and visitors, the vast, natural wonderland of Hyde Park and Kensington Park Gardens in the heart of the city is not only a favorite part of London, but a compulsory stop-over.

Even a half hour here is like a day in the country, walking across grass, sheltered by trees, with a soundtrack of birds and a cast of exuberant dogs, placid dog owners, joggers, pin-striped businessmen, nannies with prams the size of economy cars, children briefly angelic in their school uniforms and lovers who stroll in their own pool of private peace. The English, unlike the French and the Italians, don't look very impressive walking along city streets. But in their parks, they become distinguished, their features enhanced by the blue of the sky, the green of the grass. They thrive in natural settings, even ones which are surrounded on every side by busy roads and the relentless noise and movement of city life.

Kensington Gardens is the *My Fair Lady* of London parks, elegant, charming, and romantic, merging as seamlessley as a silk dress into the vaster green of Hyde Park. The difference between the 2 parks and just where they do merge is a mystery to many. But true lovers of London earth and sky can define perfectly the area which begins at Kensington Palace and extends to Alexander Gate on the south and Victoria Gate on the north, with the connecting Ring Road as boundary.

The gardens, which were laid out by Queen Anne, were originally the private property of Kensington Palace, and they still have a regal air, enhanced by the presence of the Royal home. They were opened to the public in the 19th century on Saturdays only, and became a fashionable venue for promenades. Many English writers, among them Thackeray, Matthew and Arnold, have praised their *sublime sylvan solitude,* as Disraeli put it. The **Round Pond**, constructed in the 18th century, was originally octagonal, and the **Broad Walk** leading from the pond to the Palace was once lined with magnificent elm trees.

I **Serpentine Gallery.** Once the Kensington Gardens Tea House, the beautiful building is now the ideal art gallery, which ambitiously provides a setting for monthly exhibitions of contemporary art. *No admission fee. Open summer, daily 10AM-6PM; winter, 10AM-dusk. Kensington Gardens, W8. 402-6075*

J **Serpentine Restaurant. ★ $$** The street between the Serpentine Gallery and Restaurant is the dividing line for Kensington and Hyde Park, and this falls in the latter. The location overlooking the Serpentine and the park is hard to beat and the food can be refreshingly simple: charcoal grills, Dover sole, trout. *Open M-Sa 12-3PM, 6-10:30PM; Su 12-3PM, 7-10PM. Hyde Park, W8. 723-8784*

K **The Serpentine.** This 40 acre artificial lake was formed by damming the West Bourne, a stream which no longer exists. The river-like lake is London residence to a vast range of waterfowl. But the swimming hole, the **Lido**, was recently closed due to a health hazard. In 1816, Harriet Westbrook, first wife of the poet Shelley, committed suicide by drowning in the Serpentine. Nearby is the Boathouse, where rowboats may be hired by the hour for a perfect afternoon by Renoir.

The **Long Water**, an extension of the Serpentine, leads to **Peter Pan** (1912, Sir George Frampton), the most popular figure in Kensington Park Gardens. The statue is almost rubbed smooth by adoring little hands. *Hyde Park, W8.*

L **Kensington Palace.** It looks more like a grand English country house than a palace, and that is the essence of its charm. Known in royal circles as *KP*, it is very much a living palace. Present residents include the **Prince and Princess of Wales** and the 2 little princes, who occupy the largest apartment, with 3 floors on the north side; **Prince and Princess Michael of Kent;** the **Duke and Duchess of Gloucester,** their 3 children and his mother, **Princess Alice,** who have 35 rooms at their disposal; and **Princess Margaret,** who has a mere 20 rooms but the best views. The Queen decides who lives in the Palace, and no one

pays rent. But the residents are responsible for all alterations and decorating, as well as their own electricity, telephone and heating bills.

The Palace's historical claims are quite considerable, dating back to 1689 when **William III** commissioned **Sir Christopher Wren** to build a palace out of the existing **Nottingham House**, away from the damp conditions of Whitehall Palace which aggravated his asthma. Past residents include 5 monarchs: **William and Mary, Anne, George I** and **George II. Queen Victoria** was born here and stayed until she became Queen and moved into Buckingham Palace. But it was in this non-palatial palace, then known as Kensington House, that she was awakened with the news that she was Queen, and it is here that the present Queen occasionally comes to visit her grandchildren.

In 1899, on Queen Victoria's 80th birthday, the **State Rooms** were opened to the public and in 1975 more rooms were opened.

A visit to the Palace starts at the small entrance in front of the **Queen's Staircase,** where you buy tickets, guides and cards. The steps lead to the **Queen's Apartments,** looking much as they did when Sir Christopher Wren decorated them for William and Mary. Next door to the **Queen's Gallery,** with fine carvings by **Grinling Gibbons,** is the **Queen's Closet,** which is anything but a closet. It was the setting for the famous and final quarrel between Queen Anne and the Duchess of Marlborough. After you pass the **Queen's Bedchamber,** with its tempting four-poster bed, the rooms become grander. The **Privy Chamber** has Mortlake tapestries by **William Kent** on the ceiling and overlooks the state apartments of Princess Margaret. Beyond is the **Presence Chamber** and the **King's Staircase.** One of the most stunning rooms is **King William's Gallery,** designed by Wren with wood carvings by Gibbons and an Etruscan ceiling painted by Kent. This room leads into the Duchess of Kent's drawing room and its ante room, which contains Queen Victoria's Georgian doll house and her toys. But perhaps the favorite room is **Queen Victoria's Bedroom,** where the young Princess received the news of her accession. It is now filled with mementos of the long-reigning queen, including the curtained cradle where her babies, and those of Queens Alexandra and Mary, slept.

The **Council Chamber** contains souvenirs and artifacts from the Great Exhibition, including the painting over the mantelpiece of Prince Albert holding the plans of the Crystal Palace. Also look for the extraordinary ivory throne from India, the lavish silver-gilt table pieces, some of which were designed by Prince Albert, and the centerpiece with 4 of Queen Victoria's dogs. There is an excellent exhibition of **Court Dress** on the ground floor. *Admission charge. Open M-Sa 10AM-5PM (last admission 4:15PM), Su 1-5PM (same as above). Kensington Gardens, W8. 937-9561*

5 **Victoria and Albert Museum.** (Main quadrangle, 1856-84, Fowke, Sykes and others; Cromwell Road entrance, 1909, Sir Aston Webb) If you have a curious mind and a receptive heart and if you like *stuff,* the Victoria and Albert Museum will become one of your favorite places on earth. It is one of the most addictive and rewarding museums in the world, covering 10 acres of enchantment and delight. The museum is the prodigious offspring of the Great Exhibition of 1851, opening a year later as the Museum of Manufactures, with a collection of objects purchased from the Exhibition. The initial intent was to display *manufactured* art, but when great works of art were bequeathed to the museum (including the permanent loan of the Raphael Cartoons and the largest collection of Constables), the scope expanded, and the intention and name were changed to the Museum of Ornamental Art. In her last major engagement, **Queen Victoria** laid the foundation stone for the buildings that face Cromwell Road, and at her request, the museum was renamed once again. The **Victoria and Albert Museum**, affectionately known as the **V&A,** is eclectic, idiosyncratic and immense, yet accessible and humane, a museum that is worthy of the vision and original energy of its founders.

If there is such a thing as the *South Kensington style,* the V&A is its finest example. The massive building is a concoction of red brick, terra cotta and mosaic, with assertions of Victorian confidence towering beside Victorian gloom. **Henry Cole,** the museum's first director, preferred engineers and artists to architects. The resulting cast-iron structure with corrugated iron facings built by **William Cubitt** in 1855 looked more like a decorated factory and quickly became known as the **Brompton Boilers.** The building was removed in 1867 to form the Bethnal Green Museum. **Sir Aston Webb's** Cromwell Road facade, begun in 1891 and completed in 1909, evokes the Victorian ethos of pomp and Imperial importance. It is flanked by statues of Queen Victoria and Prince Albert by **Alfred Drury** and Edward VII and Queen Alexandra by **Goscomb John.** On top of the great central tower is the figure of *Fame,* resting upon a lantern shaped like an imperial crown.

Entering the museum is like embarking on a great, extravagant and wonderful expedition. You will get lost in the more than 150 rooms, but the V&A is the best place in town to be lost, every cul-de-sac a treasure trove of discovery. The museum was recently reorganized under the exuberant direction of **Sir Roy Strong,** and is now lighter, cleaner and slightly less chaotic. But even the best-laid plans of museum curators are no substitute for a little aimless wandering. The maze of galleries and labyrinthine passages is still a wonderland, where masterpieces hide behind idiosyncrasies.

There are 2 types of galleries within the museum. The **Primary Galleries** contain masterpieces grouped around a style, nationality or period, while the **Study Collections** are geared more toward connoisseurs,

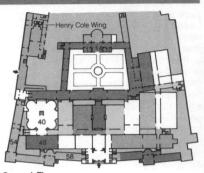

Ground Floor
Upper Ground Floor

Lower Ground Floor

Second Floor

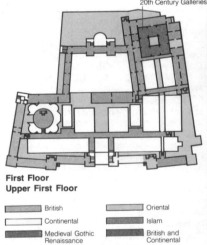

20th Century Galleries

First Floor
Upper First Floor

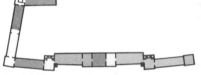

	British		Oriental
	Continental		Islam
	Medieval Gothic Renaissance		British and Continental
	Closed		Special Collections

scholars, dealers and collectors who are interested in studying a subject in detail.

The V&A publishes a useful booklet which lists a hundred objects that present the essence of the museum in terms of quality and content. It also gives interesting bits of trivia about the objects on display. *The position of jade in traditional China was roughly the equivalent to that of gold in the West ...Jade is so hard that it cannot be scratched even by steel...The huge Elizabethan Bed of Ware was said to have been occupied by 26 butchers and their wives on 13 February 1689...In the 1830s, Charles Dickens tried to purchase the bed.* If you are suffering from museum-lag and want to narrow down your looking, here is a list of some of the *must sees* in the V&A:

CROMWELL & BROMPTON ROADS

Great Bed of Ware. (c. 1590, English) The bed is easily the most famous in the world, mentioned by Shakespeare in *Twelfth Night* and by countless writers and historians. It is nearly 9 feet high, 11 feet long and 10½ feet wide, a size that sometimes distracts from the beauty of the carved, painted and inlaid decoration. *Room 54.*

Paul Pindar House Front. (Early 17th century, English) The front of the house, with its carved oak and leaded glass windows, was built by Sir Paul Pindar in Bishopsgate and was presented to the Museum in 1890 by the Great Eastern Railway Company. One guide to London wrote that in the V&A, the house *finds a home safe from the destructive hands of the modern builder.* Room 48.

Raphael Cartoons. The cartoons were drawn with chalk on paper and colored with distemper by Raphael and his scholars in 1513 as designs for tapestry work for Pope Leo X. The tapestries are still at the Vatican. Three of the original cartoons are now lost; the others are here because Rubens advised Charles I to buy them for the newly opened tapestry factory at Mortlake. After Charles's death, Cromwell bought them for £300, and they remained at Whitehall until William III moved them to Hampton Court. They have been on permanent loan at the V&A since Queen Victoria ruled Britain. *Room 48.*

Norfolk House Music Room. (c. 1753, English) This Baroque gold and white room was once in a grand London house on St. James's Square. Note the overmantel, carved and gilded with a cluster of musical instruments. *Room 58.*

Morris, Gamble and Poynter Rooms. The original tea room, cafe and restaurants in the museum occupied this space until 1939, and they almost knock you sideways with longing for those aesthetically elaborate and civilized days. The **Green Dining Room,** decorated for the museum by **William Morris** and **Philip Webb,** features Burne-Jones stained glass and painted panels representing the months of the year. The wallpaper and furniture are by William Morris. The chimney piece in the **Gamble Room** came from Dorchester House on Park Lane. It is surrounded by pillared and mirrored ceramic work and a ceiling of enameled iron plates which incorporates a quotation from *Ecclesiastes.* The **Grill Room,** designed by **Sir Edward Poynter,** still has the original grill, set in a Dutch dream of Minton blue and white tiles representing the seasons and the months. The 3 rooms form a first-class example of Victorian design. *Rooms 13, 14 and 15.*

Costume Court. The recently enlarged and expanded room houses a collection of fashion dating from around 1580 to the present and draws more crowds than any other exhibit in the V&A. The English and Continental fashions, with outfits from the 1960s and early 70s, are strangely exotic. *Room 40.*

Twentieth Century Galleries. (Entitled **British Art and Design, 1900-1960**) Huge, sealed glass *rooms* have been built to house the objects which trace British design from the Arts and Crafts movement started by **William Morris** in the 19th century to the new functionalism of the 20th. You will find sculpture by **Eric Gill** and **Henry Moore;**

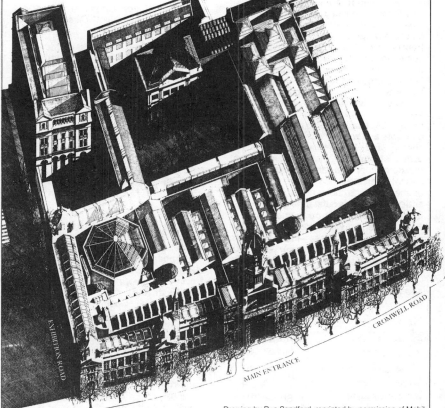

Drawing by Ron Sandford, reprinted by permission of Mobil.

stained-glass windows by **John Piper**; and almost everything from the **Omega Workshops** (the decorative arts movement of Bloomsbury from 1913-1919), including a screen of swimmers painted by **Vanessa Bell** and an inlaid tray called *The Wrestlers* by **Henri Gaudier-Brzesca**. New galleries that will include Continental and British design up to the present will open in the next few years.

Henry Cole Wing. This splendid addition opened in 1984 and houses the **Constable Collection,** which was presented to the museum by the artist's daughter. It provides a trip to the English countryside through the eyes and genuis of one of England's most beloved painters. Especially appealing are the small canvases and sketches on the 6th floor. Also have a look at the watercolor and photography exhibits on the 3rd floor and the 16th to 19th century European paintings, including some superb Turners, on the 4th floor. *No admission charge, but a £2 donation is strongly appreciated. Open M-Th&Sa 10AM-6PM, Su 2:30-6PM. Closed F. Cromwell Rd. SW1. 589-6371*

Within the museum are:

V&A Restaurant. ★ ★ ★ $$ The new restaurant on the ground floor of the Henry Cole Wing is one of the best museum restaurants in town, with imaginative salads, first-class hot foods like steak and kidney pies, old-fashioned English desserts like bread-and-butter pudding and rhubarb crumble, and excellent ordinary wines, including an English white wine. The restaurant is good for lunch, snacks or afternoon tea. *Open M-Th&Sa 10AM-5:30PM, Su 2:30-5:30PM. Closed F. 589-6371*

V&A Shop. Now located to the left of the entrance, the shop is a tempting example of Sir Roy Strong's belief in *consumer oriented museums* and *quality products.* The shop stocks a range of items taken or adapted from pieces in the V&A collections. Special items include a handsome portfolio bound in marbled paper with 12 facsimilies of hand-colored engravings of English country houses, among them Burghley, Longleat, Chiswick House and Fonthill Abbey, taken from 2 volumes in the National Art Library in the V&A. Also available is a beautiful set of 8 *pots à creme;* a facsimile of an 18th-century silver box; William Morris needlepoint cushions; and for the more extravagant museum shopper, a hand-carved copy of an intricate Grinling Gibbons lace cravat made of limewood. The choice of postcards, books and publications is outstanding. Just inside is the **V&A Crafts Shop,** a showcase for British craftsmen, with original objects in pottery, silver, gold and glass—future treasures for the museum itself. *Open M-Th&Sa 10AM-5:30PM, Su 2:30-5:30PM. Closed F. 589-6371*

Museum Bests
Sir Roy Strong
Director, Victoria and Albert Museum

Founded out of the profits of the Great Exhibition of 1851 to raise the level of design in an industrialized society, the **V&A is an exhibit in its own right.** The historic building is now being restored, so enjoy the magnificent marble entrance hall, the Italianate terra cotta facade of the quadrangle and the suite of rooms which made up the first museum cafeteria in the world, including one by William Morris.

Do not miss the **Victorian Cast Court,** plastercasts of the world's greatest sculpture from Trajan's column to the facade of St. James of Compostella—all arranged in one breathtaking tableau.

Wander through the **Dress Collection,** a vivid panorama of the fashions and foibles of 4 centuries of clothes from ruffs and farthingales to Dior and Saint Laurent.

Relax on the top floor of the new **Henry Cole Wing** and look at the greatest collection of paintings by John Constable. View London's sky and skyline through the windows.

The **Medieval Tapestry Court** contains a delight: the *Hardwick Hunting Tapestries* —a potent evocation of the hunt in which lads and ladies engage in courtly dalliance. Not far away is a masterpiece in tenderness: Donatello's *Chellini Madonna,* whilst in the **Carlton Court** hang the greatest work of art in the V&A—Raphael's designs for tapestries depicting the *Acts of the Apostles.*

And a final favorite, our **New Restaurant,** a showplace for inventive food in the British tradition and an ideal place in which to pause for refreshment before looking at more of our 8 miles of galleries!

---

6 **Ismaili Center.** (1983, Casson, Conder & Partners) The controversial modern building opposite the **V&A** is a religious and cultural center for the Islamic community. Within the building is the **Zamana Gallery,** with an entrance on Cromwell Gardens. *No admission charge. Open M-Th&Sa 10AM-5:30PM, Su 1:30-5:30PM. Closed F. Thurloe Pl., SW7. 730-4830*

7 **Paper Tiger.** ★ ★ ★ $$ London's first Szechuan Chinese restaurant has remained popular for years simply because the spicy and hot food is good. The 9 course feasts are recommended nourishment for a weekend afternoon of serious museuming. The setting, even though in a basement, is pretty and un-Chinese, with pale pinks and wicker. *Open M-F 6-12PM, Sa-Su 12-2PM only. 10 Exhibition Rd., SW7. 584-3737*

⊷ Hoop & Toy ⊷

8 **Hoop & Toy.** ★ $ The name of the pub refers to the game of metal hoop and wooden stick, which is now only featured in illustrated children's books. The pub has the atmosphere of days gone by, with gaslights inside and out, dark wood, polished brass, Edwardian drawings on the walls and a menu with 18th century dishes like beef & ale pie. A *Free House* which offers a large choice of beers and ales. *Open M-Sa 11AM-3PM, 5:30-11PM; Su 12-2PM, 7-10:30PM. Thurloe Pl., SW7. 589-8360*

9 **The Dacquise.** ★ ★ $ For **V&A** regulars, the routine often includes lemon tea and apple strudel at this Polish cafe. Nothing has changed since WWII— the look of the Polish waitresses, young, pretty and efficient; the menu of *kasza* (boiled buckwheat), and *zrazy* (beef rolls stuffed with cucumber and bacon and mushrooms). Polish émigrées meet here for morning coffee, lunch, afternoon tea or dinner. *Open daily 10AM-11:30PM. 20 Thurloe St., SW7. 589-6117*

10 **Rembrandt Hotel.** *Moderate.* This appropriately named hotel facing the V&A has welcomed guests since the turn-of-the-century. It is now part of the **Sarova** group and offers the kinds of facilities that some travelers find very reassuring: telex, direct dial telephones, 24-hour food and porterage service. The real jewel in the hotel's crown is access (at extra cost) to the incredibly posh **Aquilla** health club, now located within the hotel. The club is a conscious attempt to recreate a Roman spa. It is a marbled world of tiles, pillars, arches and murals, complete with a gymnasium, a 50 by 20 foot pool with a jacuzzi, a fountain, music and grotto, sauna, separate jacuzzi, solarium and salad bar. The hotel itself is more down-to-earth and present day, with 2 restaurants. **Masters** serves a buffet lunch and *à la carte* dinner (with hotel classics like Tournedos and scampi). The **Conservatory** offers light meals and sandwiches throughout the day and afternoon tea. You can get a traditional English breakfast here, including grilled kidneys, kippers and smoked haddock. *Thurloe Pl., SW7. 589-8100*

Best Homesick Diner Meals
(American food in London, based on a consensus of 12 American gourmets under age 12 and a couple of Yankeephiles who know a good hamburger when they eat one)

Smollensky's Baloon. Two floors full of art deco treasures, trompe l'oeil murals, girls in pink Swatch watches and yuppie men drinking Perrier. *1 Dover St., W1. 491-1191*

Joe Allen's. Baked potato skins, great hamburgers, salads, brownies, actors and opera singers. This is where everyone comes after the theatre, opera and concerts. Conveniently located in Covent Garden and open late. *13 Exeter St., WC2. 836-0651*

Texas Lone Star. A roomful of fruit machines keeps children mesmerized while parents eat the spicy Mexican (well, Mexicanish) food. Great value, especially for large families. *154 Gloucester Rd., SW7. 370-5625*

Steamboat Charley's. Crabcakes, clams, tuna melts and very popular with the age 12 contingent. *205 Kensington Church St., W8. 727-3184*

Chicago Rib Shack. French-fried onions, barbequed spareribs and chicken, cornbread, iced tea and large families who look happy to be here. *1 Raphael St., Knightsbridge, SW1. 581-5595*

Henry J. Bean. Very popular in summer with the vast garden lined with picnic tables. Tacos, hot dogs and all the American classics. Owned by **Bob Paton** (Chicago Rib Shack, Chicago Deep Dish Pizza) who really has transformed the palates of Londoners. *195-197 King's Rd., SW3. 352-9255*

Britannia Hotel. They call their menu *The Best of Both Worlds*—the old world and the new world, presumably. No gimmicks, just good food—tropical fruit salads, lean delicious burgers and an atmosphere that appeals to grownups. *Grosvenor Sq., W1. 629-9400*

11 **Period Brass Lights.** The antique shop specializes in Ormulu wall lights and English cut glass lead crystal. *Open M-F 10AM-5:30PM, Sa 10AM-1PM. 9A Thurloe Pl. SW7. 589-8305*

M. P. Levene Ltd

12 **MP Levene Ltd.** This much respected silver shop is a favorite with the diplomatic community in London. It carries a beautiful selection of silver frames and objects that are the epitome of English country house and an impressive choice of old Sheffield plates and silverware. If you ask, the sales people will patiently explain the markings on the English silver. *5 Thurloe Pl., SW7. 589-3755*

13 **Felton & Sons Ltd.** One of the many joys of life in London is that flowers don't cost the earth. This florist has been here since 1900, and is known for its sumptuous and rare blossoms. *Interflora. Open M-F 8:30AM-5:30PM, Sa 8:30AM-12PM. 220-224 Brompton Rd., SW3. 589-4433*

The Wine Gallery

14 **The Wine Gallery.** ★ ★ $ The vast majority of wine bars in London sell substandard wine, slabs of defrosted quiche and salads straight from plastic tubs, delivered (one hopes) daily. But the Wine Gallery—or Galleries, as there are now 3 in London—serves good, honest wines and fresh food prepared with care and imagination. Try the salads, homemade pâtés, steamed mussels in season, fish soup and grills. Licensing hours for wine bars are generally the same as those for pubs, but the Wine Gallery is more generous in its timekeeping. *Open M-Sa 12-3PM for lunch, 3-6PM for coffee and tea, 6-12PM for dinner; Su 7-11PM for dinner. 232 Brompton Rd., SW3. 584-3493. (Also 294 Westbourne Grove, W11 and 49 Hollywood Rd., SW10.)*

15 **Walton Street.** Fashionable shops are moving next to neighborhood hardware stores on this quiet street just steps away from the bustle of Brompton Road. Walton Street is a street in transition. Only the elegant window displays on the rather bare facades of the buildings at the lower end of the street reveal the array of goods inside: antique Rolex watches at **Van Peterson**; Lalique crystal vases at **Saville-Edells**; hand-knit sweaters by Moussie Sayer at **Moussie**. Members of the Royal family decorate their nurseries with furniture made by the carpenters at **Dragon's** and their heads with hats from **John Boyd**. Two 19th century brick ovens turn out cookies, cakes, croissants and even pizza at **Justin de Blanc Hygienic Bakery**. Restaurants such as **Ma Cuisine**, **San Martino** and **Waltons** have loyal followings, and the only pub, **The Enterprise**, is a Walton Street institution. As you wander toward Beauchamp Place, the street's domestic side becomes apparent. The shops are less frequent and the facades grow brighter, turning into noble townhouses guarded by iron gates at the more affluent top end of the street.

DRAYCOTT AVENUE

English restaurant **Waltons**
contemporary art **Oliver Swann**
jewelry **Van Peterson**
French restaurant **Ma Cuisine**
handknit sweaters **Moussie**
realtor **Maskells**
Italian restaurant **San Martino**
shoes **Footloose**
Walton St. Stationery Co.
dress agency **Pamela**
hatter **John Boyd**

**Knightsbridge Hand Laundry &
Dry Cleaning**
children's int. des. **Nursery Window**
wool and sweaters **Filpucci**
Brotherton Gallery
maternity and kidswear **Balloon**
hairdressers **Ellis/Helen**
fine art **Walter Bagshawe**
estate agent **Janet Osband**
estate agent **Michael Kalmar**

Oasis artificial flora

Percy Bass interior design

Malcolm Innes paintings
Oliver Swann paintings
Monogrammed Linen Shop
Chesterfield estate agents
John Cambell framing and restoration
Maria Andipa Icon Gallery
Clarges Gallery
Ktori lingerie
Pomme D'Api kid's clothing
Section hairdresser
Violy women's clothing
Susanne Gary interior design
Ridley & Co. estate agents
Danielle interior design

FIRST STREET

public house **The Enterprise**
Fine gifts **Saville-Edells**

HASKER STREET

kid's furniture **Dragons 1**

furniture **Dragons II**

antique prints **Stephanie Hoppen**

antiques **HW Newby**

furniture **Kingcome**

OVINGTON STREET

WALTON STREET

wine merchants **Threshers**

interior design **Nina Campbell**

hairdressers **Mignon & Michael**

deli **La Picena**

French restaurant **La Popote**

LENNOX GARDENS MEWS

GYNDE MEWS

Italian restaurant **Totos**

La Reserve wine merchants

Wm. Hawkes & Sons silversmith and jeweler

Forty Eight Walton Street antiques

Justin De Blanc Hygienic Bakery

LENNOX GARDENS

OVINGTON SQUARE

PONT STREET

BEAUCHAMP PLACE

St. Columba's Church

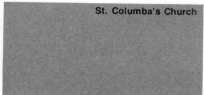

16 **London Oratory of St. Philip Neri.** (1880-93, Herbert Gribble) Better known as the **Brompton Oratory**, it is the first important Roman Catholic church to be built in London after the Reformation. The smell of incense greets you upon entering the high Roman Oratory, with domes and vaults, a domed nave and Italian ornaments and statues, including the gigantic Carrara marble statue of the **Apostles,** carved by **Mazzuoli,** a disciple of Bernini, which stood for 200 years in Siena Cathedral, and the altar in the **Lady Chapel,** constructed by **Corbarelli** and sons in 1693, which came from Brescia in northern Italy. In ecclesiastical and liturgical terms, an Oratory is a congregation of secular priests living together without vows. The Fathers of the Oratory are not monks, and thus are not bound together by the 3 religious vows, but by the internal bond of charity and the external bond of a common life and rule. The

Oratorian movement in England came about as the result of the conversion of John Henry Newman, a Victorian whose conversion to Catholicism shook the Anglican establishment. Don't miss the paintings of **Saints Thomas More** and **John Fisher** by **Rex Whistler** in **St. Wilfred's Chapel,** and the **dome,** designed by **G. Sherrin,** with wooden ribs faced with 60 tons of lead standing an emotional 200 feet high. The marble statue of **Cardinal John Henry Newman** (1896, Bodley and Garner) on the grounds of the Brompton Oratory shows the Cardinal in the High Roman style he espoused. He was the founder of the Oxford movement and also wrote the hymn *Lead, Kindly Light.* Cardinal Newman died in 1890 at the age of 80. *Brompton Rd., SW3.*

17 **Holy Trinity.** (1829, Donaldson) In marked and very English contrast to its neighbor, the Brompton Oratory, Holy Trinity, Brompton is Victorian Gothic. There is no smell of incense here. Holy Trinity is an Anglican Church with an active congregation involved in healing, movements for peace and the Alternative Service. If women are ever ordained as priests in Britain, this church will be one of the first at which they can serve The choir is exceptionally good. *Cottage Pl., SW7.*

18 **St. Quentin.** ★ ★ ★ $$$ *The Good Food Guide,* England's *Michelin,* wrote its 1986 entry for the Brasserie St. Quentin entirely in French, the first and only time the Guide has done so. Even though this Frenchest of restaurants is owned by an Irishman, you are probably better off if you are unperturbed by Gallic manners. The food is extremely good *nouvelle cuisine,* with fish dishes deserving every star available, lots of *poivre rose,* and juliennes of this and medallions of that. You also won't find better cheeses or French bread. (Their new delicatessen at 256 Brompton Road has the best croissants, *pain aux raisins* and other French treasures in town.) The decor is traditional brasserie, with a long zinc bar, mirrors, brass, glass and waiters dressed the part. The tables along the banquette are uncomfortably close together, and you can't help but wish this was a real brasserie open all day long. At least it offers *café complet* on weekends, an ideal start to a Saturday morning dedicated to the V&A. *Open daily 12-3PM, 7PM-12AM. 243 Brompton Rd., SW3. 589-8005*

19 **Shura Leathergoods Ltd.** These shops, dotted throughout London, are a good source for leather handbags, sensible, well-made shoes, and luggage ranging from luxurious to cheap, including old-fashioned carpet bags. *Open M-Sa 9AM-6PM. 239 Brompton Rd., SW3. 589-7222*

20 **James Hardy and Co.** Knock on the door first, and you will be warmly welcomed by these silversmiths who have been here since 1853. The shop carries silver frames, jewelry, antiques and silverware. *Open M-Sa 9:30AM-5:30PM. 235 Brompton Rd., SW3. 589-5050*

21 **Sun and Snow.** A smart (in the English sense) sportswear shop, with the latest in fashionable ski gear, including a good selection for kids. In summer, it carries everything you need for squash, tennis, swimming and running. *Open M-Sa 9:30AM-5:30PM. 229 Brompton Rd., SW3. 581-2039*

22 **Brompton Square.** London excels at creating pretty squares, and it is hard to imagine a more humane design for urban planning. This early 19th century square, which is not square or even rectangular but horse-shoe shaped, is home for prosperous, house-proud Londoners whose only concessions to the 20th century are the burglar alarms mounted on the perfectly maintained houses and the BMWs which line the Square. A plaque at No. 6 honors the French poet Stephane Mallarme, who came to London to learn English and lived here in 1863. A chronically impoverished poet, however great his talent, would be unlikely to reside in this handsome Square today.

23 **Bunch of Grapes.** ★ $ Once upon a time, the glass snobscreen separated the upstairs and downstairs bars in this authentic Victorian pub. Now all is convivial and democratic, with tourists and locals alike welcomed and served delicious homemade food at lunchtime, snacks in the evening and 4 real ales. *Open M-Sa 11AM-3PM, 5:30-11PM; Su 12-2PM, 7-10:30PM. 207 Brompton Rd., SW3. 589-6944*

24 **Luba's Bistro.** ★ ★ $ A fixture in the neighborhood since before WWII. Nothing has changed in the last 30 years, including the menu and, truly, the prices. Russian classics such as *borscht, kapoostniak* (braised cabbage with prunes and sour cream), *blinis, vereniki* and *piroshki* all make good beginnings. Follow them up with *kooliebiaka* (salmon trout pie) buckwheat *piroshki* or *chicken kiev*. Bring your own wine for a tremendous savings. If you are watching your budget, the bistro might become a regular haunt. *Open M-Sa 12-3PM, 6-12AM. 6 Yeoman's Row, SW3. 589-2950*

25 **Crane Kalman Gallery.** Good 20th century British and European paintings, with works by **Degas, Dufy, Nicholson, Moore** and **Sutherland,** to name a distinguished few, are exhibited in the Gallery. *Open M-F 10AM-6PM, Sa 10AM-4PM. 178 Brompton Rd., SW3. 584-7566*

26 **Alistair Sampson.** Go to the vast room in the back of this small antique shop to find early English pottery, oak furniture, brass, primitive paintings and unusual decorative pieces. *Open M-F 9:30AM-5:30PM. 156 Brompton Rd., SW3. 589-5272*

27 **Beauchamp Place.** (Pronounced Beecham Place) Treat jostles with treat on this Regency street, where you can easily spend a whole day or a whole week shopping in the boutiques and smart shops. You will find the best of British designer clothes, old maps and prints, reject (not that you will ever find the flaw) china and crystal, antique silver, made-to-measure shoes and lingerie fit for the Princess (who buys it here). While struggling to resist or not to resist the many covetables on the street, you can eat in restaurants which are equally smart, fun and delicious.

28 **Reject China Shop.** These are dotted along the street now and carry the finest porcelain, crystal and stoneware. A certain energy and dedication is required to find the real bargains; there is a lot of truly awful stuff and the prices seem far from rejected. But if you have the stamina, you might be eating off the finest English, French or Italian din-

---

BROMPTON ROAD

	Reject China Shop
	Pasta Prego Italian restaurant
leather goods **Henry's**	**Chinacraft**
Knightsbridge Furniture Co.	**Janet Reger** lingerie
women's clothing **Cannibal**	**Chinacraft**
Maltese knitwear **Crochetta**	**Adele Davis** women's clothing
shirtmakers **Valbridge**	**Sava** women's clothing
	Shahzada Indian restaurant
Reject China Shop	
women's clothing **Beauchamp Place Shop**	**Kanga** women's clothing
antique prints **The Map House**	**Dumpling House** Chinese restaurant
women's clothing **Monsoon**	**Break of Day** fine gifts
jewelry **Annabel Jones**	Ports Portuguese restaurant
Pizza **Pomodoro**	**Caroline Charles** women's clothing
women's clothing **Footlights**	**Tan Giudicelli**
jewelry **Ken Lane**	13 ½ Italian restaurant
Portuguese restaurant **Ofado**	**Eyecompany** optician
	Whistles women's clothing
Russian restaurant **Borscht n'Tears**	
jewelry **Folli Follie**	**Stanley Leslie** antique silver
The Grove Tavern	**Bianca Furs**
women's clothing **Ashley & Blake**	**Paddy Campbell** women's clothing
shoes **Deliss**	**Old England** woollens
hairdresser **Edmonds**	**Delia Collins** beauty salon
restaurant **Sonny's Gourmet Place**	**Sarah Spencer** women's clothing
Portuguese restaurant **Caravela**	
Lebanese restaurant **Maroush II**	**Selecta Video**
women's clothing **Beauchamp Place Shop**	**Maison Panache** women's clothing
tapestries **Luxury Needlepoint**	**Sylvia's** novelty gifts
	Scruples women's clothing
Reject China Shop	**Bruce Oldfield** women's clothing
women's clothing **Spaghetti**	**Hallidays** carved pine mantelpieces
oyster bar **Bill Bentley**	**San Lorenzo** Italian restaurant
	Verbanella Italian restaurant

BEAUCHAMP PLACE

WALTON ROAD

nerware the rest of your days, toasting with Baccarat or Waterford crystal, and gloating besides. *Beauchamp Place Corner carries bone china; 34-35 Beauchamp Place carries pottery and gifts; 56-57 Beauchamp Place carries crystal and glass. 581-5190 or 581-0737*

29 Janet Reger. If you are looking for *crepe de chine* pajamas and the kind of silk lingerie that the finest fantasies are made of, this is the only address you'll ever need. The brassieres are brilliantly designed, amplifying or diminishing with seductive perfection, as required. *Open M-F 10AM-6PM, Sa 10AM-5PM. 2 Beauchamp Pl., SW3. 584-9360*

30 The Map House. Antiques, rare and decorative maps, botanical prints and aquatints line every inch of this small townhouse with honest prices. *Open M-Sa 9:45AM-5:45PM. 54 Beauchamp Pl., SW3. 589-9821*

31 Caroline Charles. Only the finest silks and linens are used by this top English designer. Caroline Charles's style is very English, but never without her own brand of sophisticated elegance. She creates clothes that you will want to wear for a lifetime. *Open M-F 10AM-5:30PM, Sa 11AM-4:30PM. 11 Beauchamp Pl., SW3.*

32 Menage à Trois. ★★$$$ Popular with the Princess of Wales, whose eating habits once obsessed the press. The concept here is to serve first courses and desserts, but no main courses, so you can have a series of luxury dishes and a selection of desserts, yet still feel virtuous. The ingredients are truly palatial—salmon, scallops, langoustine, lobster and caviar, all served with artistic verve. Even the matches are well designed. You might walk past several times without seeing this basement restaurant, but it is worth finding, a perfect place to celebrate an extravagant commitment at Caroline Charles, Janet Reger or Bruce Oldfield, with the added bonus that whatever you bought will still fit after a meal here. *Open M-Sa 11:45AM-3PM, 7PM-12:15AM. 15 Beauchamp Pl., 589-4252*

33 San Lorenzo ★★★$$/$$$ This first-class Italian restaurant attracts the kind of people who appreciate *carpaccio* prepared 3 ways, fresh game in season (pheasant with chestnuts) and sweetbreads with Parma ham. The staff seems to know all the glamorous hairdos and suits personally, but service to unknowns is just as attentive and courteous. *Open M-Sa 12-3PM, 7:30-11:30PM. 22 Beauchamp Pl., SW3. 584-1074 or 589-4633*

34 Bruce Oldfield. What do Joan Collins and Princess Diana have in common? A passion for Bruce Oldfield, who creates evening dresses which cling to the wearer and linger in the memories of everyone else. If you have what it takes to wear his creations (the figures in every sense) you are lucky indeed. *Open M-F 10AM-6PM, Sa 11AM-6PM. 41 Beauchamp Pl., SW3. 581-8934*

35 Deliss. If you do not have *neutral* feet—that is, if you suffer from chronic footache because you are impossible to fit—Deliss is where you should invest an airfare or 2 for made-to-measure shoes. Among the sizeable feet shod here are those belonging to **Keith Richards, Princess Michael of Kent, Jesse Norman** and **Marvin Mitchelson.** The shoes are beautiful and at prices

you can actually consider. The shop will also make shoes from your own design or copy a beloved pair of old favorites. *Open M-F 9:30AM-5:30PM, Sa 12-4PM (closed daily for lunch between 1-2PM). 41 Beauchamp Pl., SW3. 584-3321*

36 Bill Bentley's. ★★$$ Sit at the bar, order a dozen oysters and a half bottle of Muscadet, and thank your lucky stars you are in London. The proper restaurant upstairs serves British fish dishes such as Dover sole and salmon trout. *Open M-Sa 11:30AM-2:30PM, 6:30-10:30PM. 31 Beauchamp Pl., SW3. 589-5080*

37 Khun Akoran. ★★$$ The newest restaurant in the neighborhood serves a long and impressive list of classic Bangkok specialties. Try the *Toong ngern Yejyeung* (minced prawns and baby corn in a spicy sauce), and finish with the steamed whole banana with coconut cream. *Open daily 12-3PM, 7-11PM. 136 Brompton Rd., SW7 (1st floor). 225-2688*

38 Montpelier Street. This Regency village between Brompton Road and Knightsbridge boasts some of the most expensive real estate in London. Check out the oils and watercolors, carpets, clocks, porcelain, furniture, wine, silver and jewelry offered at **W & FC Bonham & Sons, Montpelier Galleries.** Find out the time of the sale for the treasures which interest you. (Painting sales are every Thursday at 11AM; silver is usually sold on Tuesdays; furniture usually goes on the block on Thursdays; and jewelry and ceramics on Fridays once a month.)

39 Montpeliano. ★★$$ A favorite of the art dealers and collectors who bid at the nearby galleries. The restaurant is noisy and wonderful and filled with the sunniness and warmth which characterize the Italians and their food. The pasta is delicious (*fettuccine Montpeliano* wins everytime), as is the fresh grilled fish, the tender and flavorful veal and the sweetbreads with wild mushrooms. The wine list is serious proof that the Italians deserve more honor than they often receive. Consider a bottle of *Brunello di Montalcino. Open M-Sa 12:30-3PM, 7-12PM. 13 Montpelier St., SW7. 589-0032*

40 Shezan ★★$$ This Indian restaurant in a quiet muse just off Montpelier Street steadfastly maintains its reputation for outstanding northern Punjabi *haute cuisine.* The decor is chic and minimal, allowing all attention to be focused on the delicately spiced food which can be magical. Try the *murgh tikka Lahory,* the *Khyberi* chicken or the butter *poussin.* A bottle of *Gewurztraminer* goes well with the food. *Open M-Sa 12-2:30PM, 7-11:30PM. 16-22 Cheval Pl., SW7. 589-0314*

41 Harrods. (1901-5, Stevens and Munt) In the past, man's desire for greatness led to the creation of cathedrals and palaces. Today, it leads to department stores, and Harrods is Notre Dame, the Taj Mahal and Blenheim. Even if the argument *Bloomingdales vs. Harrods* rages over dinner tables, and even if the silk-scarved ladies of England vow that Harrods has gone downhill, the fact remains that this cathedral of consumerism is hard to beat.

CROMWELL & BROMPTON ROADS

Behind the solid and elegant Edwardian facade, 4,000 employees in 214 departments stand ready to fulfill your every request. You can hire a chauffeur, organize a funeral, open a bank account, book a trip around the world, reserve all your theatre and concert tickets, take out books from the private circulating library or have your ancestry researched. And, of course, you can buy just about everything your heart desires, including a yellow lab from the pet department, a pair of Rayne pumps (preferred by the Queen and Mrs. Thatcher), a silk dress by Patricia Lester (only available here), a Waterford crystal carafe, a set of pale blue Egyptian cotton sheets and a bottle of Krug Grand Cuvee to be delivered to your hotel and drunk whilst adding up the bills. If you are afraid that this palace of temptation will make you lose sight of the exchange rate, plan your visit around the January sale, the most famous event of the year. It is a true test of consumer stamina, but if you are tenacious and strong, you will be rewarded with real bargains.

Above all, don't miss the **Food Halls,** with their stunning mosaic friezes and fabulous displays of food. (The **wet fish display** is a masterpiece!)

For a sociological study of one of the purest slices of English life, go up to the kennel where English ladies up from the country for the day leave their labradors and Jack Russells.

Harrods has 5 restaurants and 5 bars, including a health juice bar and a wine bar. The **Georgian Room** is always *full up for tea.* People start lining up outside the elegant double-banquet room around 3:15PM, hoping to sit on the green velvet furnishings and sip tea at the tables covered with pink linens and an array of buns, pastries, salads, butters, creams and jams.

Harrods open M, Tu, Th, F 9AM-5PM; W 9:30AM-6PM; Sa 9AM-6PM. Knightsbridge, SW1. 730-1234 (Theatre tickets: 589-1101)

42 **Richoux.** ★ ★ $$ These tea shops serve breakfast, morning coffee, lunch, afternoon tea, dinner, late supper—unique in London—and irresistable chocolates and pastries for dessert. Visit after 2PM, when the lunch crowd has come and gone, for a more restful meal. *Open M-F 8:30AM-7PM, Sa 9AM-7PM, Su 10AM-7PM. 86 Brompton Rd., SW3. 584-8300. (Also 172 Piccadilly, W1. 493-2204 and 41A South Audley St., W1, 629-5228)*

43 **Le Metro.** ★ ★ ★ $$ The only drawback to this wine bar is its popularity; if dozens popped up all over London, the quality of life would be immeasurably improved. The restaurant serves the best of things French—*salad frisseé aux foies de volailles,* cheeses that are fresh and ripe, good soups, casseroles and tarts, and a choice of first-rate, carefully chosen wines, with a special selection of important *crus* by the glass, made possible by the cruover machine. The place closes in the afternoon, when one would dearly love a cup of good coffee. But it opens early in the morning for genuine espresso or frothy café crème and croissants. *Open M-F 7:30AM-3PM, 5:30-11PM; Sa 7:30AM-3PM; Su 7:30-11AM. 28 Basil St., SW3. 589-6286*

44 **L'Hotel.** *Moderate/Expensive.* A small country inn—the kind you never seem to find—located right in the heart of Knightsbridge. There are only 12 rooms, so you have to book well in advance in order to have pine furniture, Laura Ashley fabrics, twin beds, color TV and clock radios, all at a reasonable price. This is the step-child of the elegant Capital Hotel, 2 doors down. (Phone calls go through to the Capital switchboard.) It is extremely popular with discriminating Americans who aren't on expense accounts. The front door is locked at 10PM during the week and 6PM on weekends, but you are given your own key, which makes you feel like you actually live here. And then there is **Le Metro** wine bar next door, which can be entered from L'Hotel. For women traveling alone, this is one of the best places in London to stay and feel at home. A continental breakfast, brought to your room each morning, is included in the price. *28 Basil St., SW3. 589-6286*

45 **Capital Hotel.** *Deluxe.* David Levin is a first-class hotelier, and when he decided to open his own hotel, he purposefully went about creating the very best. The Capital is small, modern, sophisticated, personal, attractive and one minute from **Harrods.** The 62 rooms are packed with as many of the creature comforts as could fit into their rather small dimensions, including bathrobes, toothbrushes and roses for every lady. If you consider the elegant surroundings, perfect location and standard of service, even the price seems reasonable. *Basil St., SW3. 589-5171*

Within the hotel is:

Capital Hotel Restaurant. ★ ★ ★ $$ More than anything, it is the restaurant which has put the Capital Hotel on the map. *The Good Food Guide* singled out the Capital as the best place for an executive lunch (1985) and accolades for the chef, **Brian Turner,** appear with delicious regularity in the British press. This is a luxury restaurant without the asphyxiating atmosphere of deluxe, and although the menu is in relentless French, the food and the kitchen are English at its best. Inventive but never precious, the best choices are langoustines from Scotland in a memorable salad with baby turnips, sea urchines and scallop mousse, and a sweetbread terrine with a morels sauce. The chocolate *marquise* is justly famous, and the wine list draws serious winelovers from far and wide. *Open M-Sa 12:30-2:30PM, 6:30-10:30PM; Su 12-2PM, 7-10PM. 589-5171*

46 **Basil Street Hotel.** *Moderate.* Traditional English charm abounds at *Basil Street,* which has been owned by the same family since it was built in 1910. The hotel has a loyal clientele of English country folk who make twice-yearly trips to London to shop and see plays. The prices appeal to the British sense of economy, the location is ideal, and the service is proper. Afternoon tea is an institution, served in a drawing room that looks like a setting for an Agatha Christie novel, with the characters and the tea seemingly untouched by the passage of time. Also popular with the frugal English is the restaurant **Upstairs.** The salad bar, buffet and selection of hot dishes are almost in the category of English school food, but a cut above. *Tea 4-5:30PM; coffee 10:30AM-12PM; lunch 12-3PM. 8 Basil St., SW3. 581-3311*

47 Scotch House. Believe it or not, if you want a cashmere sweater or scarf, you will do better here, in terms of quality and price, than at Harrods. The shop has a huge choice of the best Scottish woolens and a good children's department, with kilts and jumpers and even those unfortunate, tiny Burberry's that make kids look like dwarfs. The French, astute shoppers that they are, come here as soon as they arrive in London. *Open M, Tu, Th 9AM-5:30PM, W 9AM-6:30PM, F&Sa 9AM-6PM. 2 Brompton Rd., SW1 581-2151*

48 Mr. Chow. ★ ★ ★ $$ The restaurant's popularity goes back to the 60s, when the owner decided to combine the style and exuberance of an Italian restaurant, complete with Italian waiters, with the innate *nouvelle cuisine* of the finest Chinese cooking. The decor is chrome and dimmed glass with the chic of another era, and the inventive menu is explained in down-to-earth language. (Dragon's Eye: *Don't be frightened by the title. It's only quail's egg with prawn on toast.*) Have lemon sole cooked in Chinese wine and mushrooms (Drunken Fish), Gambler's Duck (like Peking Duck but better) and the green noodles with pork and prawns. The perfect choice from the wine list is a bottle of Gewurztraminer, which goes well with the subtly spiced food. *Open daily 12:30-2:45PM, 7-11:45PM. 151 Knightsbridge, SW1. 589-7347 or 589-8656*

49 Hyde Park Hotel. *Deluxe.* More a stately home than a hotel, the Hyde Park is as much a Knightsbridge institution as the Horse Guards who trot past it each day. The Edwardian splendor of the magnificent marble entrance hall, gilded molded ceilings and Persian carpets the size of cricket fields leave you wondering how Buckingham Palace can hold a candle to it, and one suspects that the service is far better here. Guests who have delighted in the pampering include Winston Churchill and Mahatma Gandhi, for whom a goat was milked each day. In the last few years, the hotel has been completely refurbished with no expense spared. Although you no longer see the Maharajahs and sultans who occupied whole floors in the days before WWI, you do see the *soignée* jet set who are impossible to tie to a nationality. The rooms and suites are country house size and furnished with silk curtains, brass beds and good antiques, recalling the tranquility of a country chateau. *Knightsbridge, SW1. 235-2000*

Within the hotel are:

Park Room. ★ ★ $$ The grandly proportioned Hyde Park restaurant overlooks the greenery of Hyde Park's Rotten Row. At midday, a sumptuous, self-service luncheon is laid out in the center of the room, with layers of tender, cold roast beef, chicken liver pâté and salads amidst the silver and fine china. It is just enough delicious nourishment for an afternoon of shopping at Harrods. The Park Room is also open for breakfast, morning coffee, afternoon tea and dinner. *Open M-Sa 7:30AM-11PM, Su 8AM-11PM. 235-2000*

Grill Room. ★ ★ $$$ The very good wine list, with a large selection of first grove clarets, compliments the fine Scottish beef, all served in an intimate, oak-paneled room with wonderful views over Hyde Park. *Open M-F 12:30-2:30PM, 7-11PM; Su 12:30-2:30PM, 7-10PM. 235-2000*

50 Sheraton Park Tower. *Deluxe.* The modern exterior looks like a brick ear of corn, and it hasn't improved with age. But this luxury hotel offers rooms with a view (the higher up the 17 stories you go, the better the room and the view), and you can absolutely count on spacious comfort and reliable service. *101 Knightsbridge, SW1. 235-8050*

Within the hotel is:

The Restaurant. ★ $$ Service is as simple as the name, with a useful range of buffets and prix fxe pre-theatre menus. The honest, fresh food is refreshingly priced. *Open daily 12PM-12AM.*

51 The Berkeley. *Deluxe.* It is pronounced the *Barkly*, and despite the overall theme of rich elegance, it has a personality of its own. The hotel is known for providing service to suit every whim, including a rooftop indoor-outdoor swimming pool where Jesse Norman takes an occasional plunge, a sauna, a small, exclusive cinema (the Minema) and a florist. Such distinguished luxury is usually associated with things of the past. But this Berkeley is new, built in 1972. The old Berkeley, which sat on the corner of Berkeley and Piccadilly Street, wasn't left behind: the charming reception room, complete with paneling, designed by a young and unknown architect named Sir Edwin Lutyens, was re-erected here. It is this obsessive attention to detail that makes the hotel one of the most popular in London. *Wilton Pl., SW1. 235-6000* With in the hotel are:

Berkeley Restaurant. ★ ★ $$$ Mauve dominates the very English room furnished in Colefax and Fowler chintzes and lime oaked paneling, with a portrait of Sir Thomas More observing the elegant surroundings. The food is English and Continental and very good indeed, with skillful handling of baby spring lamb, game in season and the best fish from the oceans nearby. *Open M-F&Su 1-2:30PM, 7-11PM. Closed Sa. 235-6000*

Buttery. ★ $$ Named after the restaurant which stood for 60 years on the corner of Berkeley Street and Piccadilly, the new Buttery doesn't quite attract the *beau monde* of its namesake, but it has other merits. Chief among them is the magnificent fresh fish display which allows you to choose the fish of your choice from the menu. At lunchtime, there is a tempting hot and cold buffet, as well as *à la carte*. In the evening, there are excellent steaks, pasta dishes and more seafood. *Open M-Sa 12:30-2:45PM, 7:30-11:15PM. Closed Su. 235-6000*

Minema. The unique cinema has regular film showings (well-chosen foreign films in particular) and is also available for private showings. It is comfortable, small (68 seats) and much-loved by cinema buffs. *235-6000*

52 Grenadier. ★ ★ ★ $ The atmosphere of this pub is as old and military as in the days when it was the Officer's Mess of the Duke of Wellington's soldiers, complete with a ghost of an officer who was flogged to death for cheating at cards. The excellent Officer's fare in the finest British tradition is highly thought of, so if you want to have lunch or dinner, it helps to book. But if at the end of a long day spent in South Kensington and Knightsbridge, all you want is a bitter, you can count on the best, and a warm welcome as well. *Open daily 11AM-3PM, 5:30-11PM. 18 Wilton Row, SW1. 235-3074*

CROMWELL & BROMPTON ROADS

Portobello Road Market

London has nearly 60 street markets, and **Portobello Road Market** in Kensington is among the most intriguing. Each Saturday, thousands of bargain-hunting tourists and collectors converge on the narrow, mile long stretch of road in search of that one-of-a-kind souvenir or long-lost silver teapot. You can find a little of everything in the 2,000 stalls lining Portobello Road, from antiques and silver (for which the market is especially well known) to coins, kitchenware, rugs, bicycles, records and second-hand clothes. Real treasures—and bargains—are rare, and there is a lot of junk, but the fun is in the search, and if you are dedicated, you will find dealers with interesting things at reasonable prices. You can lunch on delicious savory and sweet crepes at **Obelix**, located in the middle of the market, or stop for a snack at the food stalls at the north end of the road. *Sa antique market 8:30AM-5PM; some shops open M-F 9AM-5PM. Take the underground to Notting Hill Gate and walk up Pembridge Rd., W11.*

BESTS

David Kingsley
Advertising Executive, London

Ja's Chinese Restaurant on Penton Street has the best Peking Duck in London, outside of the Golden Duck, of course, but cheaper. All the dishes are excellent, with a bias towards the piquant Schezuan on the menu. The restaurant is moderately priced for London and informal. *Open daily 12-2PM, 6pm-12AM. 22 Penton St., N1. 837-4503*

Sharon Lee Ryder
Writer, New York

Chiang Mai is a must for afficianados of Oriental food. The menu offers items not found in more typical Thai restaurants, most of it flown in fresh from Bangkok. This is no hole in the wall ethnic establishment, as its prices will attest. Its decor is well-designed and understated, and the prices are moderate by established standards. Although it is tempting to overeat, save room for fresh litchis and other exotic fruits. *Open daily 12-3PM, 6-11PM. 48 Frith St., W1. 437-7444*

Aspects features jewelry for sale and frequent exhibitions of one-of-a-kind clothing and *art* furniture in its gallery space. Forget the furniture (and perhaps most of the older exhibitions, although the clothing on view is quite exceptional). Instead go for the jewelry, some by British designers, some by Dutch and perhaps a few other nationalities. All of it is innovative in the use of unusual materials and concepts of how jewelry is worn on the body. It is the first jewelry that is *well-designed* by any standards and is also very affordable. *3-5 Whitfield St. 580-7563*

Henry Steiner
Designer, Hong Kong

Buy *Time Out* magazine as soon as you arrive at Heathrow. It is a weekly guide to London with a lively, inquiring editorial style and a permissive, poor-but-honest layout. Along with dependable listings and critiques of cinemas, theatres, abortion clinics and protest rallies is a short roster, constantly reviewed and amended, of good, inexpensive restaurants of varying cuisines.

You can buy picture postcards from all over at the **Postcard Gallery** on Neal Street. Owner and designer Derek Birdsall has colored the small space black and covered the walls with cards in floor to ceiling racks. Horror movies stills, kitsch landscapes, etc. suitable for collecting, framing, trading or even mailing are available here. *32 Neal St., WC2. 379-6177*

Lou Klein
Designer, Alexandria, Virginia

Go to the **Food Hall** in **Harrods Department Store** to look at the amazing fish sculpture which could be an enormous lobster with a trout in each claw and millions of anchovy around it, a cluster of huge Dover soles surrounded by prawns and kippers, or a manta ray formed in the shape of a tulip surrounded by countless sardines and shrimps, all constantly being cooled with a fine spray of water from a tiny fountain that is hidden in the middle. *Knightsbridge, SW1. 730-1234*

Jim Dine
Artist

South Kensington. The tube station and the beautiful early 19th century streets and squares around my studio.

Victoria and Albert Museum. I have spent many, many years learning there. I go to see the ceramics in the Shriber Collection. I have a big collection of 18th century English pottery called Wheildon, and they have marvelous examples of 19th century English pottery and ceramics. You never can miss at the V&A—there is always something great.

Ponte Nuovo near where I live off Fulham Road. A man called Mr. Masquali is the owner or head waiter or whatever he is; but I have known him for many years at other restaurants too. *126 Fulham Rd., SW3. 370-6656*

Bagatelle. A fine, fine restaurant run by a young Frenchman and a Japanese chef. *5 Langton St., SW10. 351-4185*

Wilton's. It never changes, and it is always great. *27 Bury St., SW1. 930-8391*

British Museum. I always go to see the antiquities in the Egyptian room, which is just grand. I don't always see the Elgin Marbles—they are too much for me sometimes, so I save them for every 2 or 3 years. I always hit the room with just Etruscan bronzes in the cases that are endless, and I sit there and draw a little drawing.

Poons. A Chinese restaurant in Covent Garden. *4 Leicester St., WC2. 437-1528*

National Gallery. It is fabulous, but I don't go there all the time, partly because of how you get there. To me Trafalgar Square is inaccessible—you can't park, and I drive or take my bicycle almost everywhere.

Harrods to get my hair cut.

David Levin
Director, Capital Hotel

Any of the suites with a view on the park side of the **Hyde Park Hotel.**

The restaurant on the fourth floor of **Fortnum and Mason** for the tea, tranquility and touch of yesteryear.

Robert Gould, the head Hall Porter at the Capital Hotel. He is the kindest and most considerate of men. In 15 years, no one has ever had an adverse comment about him.

The **Connaught Hotel** is my favorite deluxe hotel.

Attending auctions at all the very fine sale rooms in town: **Sothebys, Christies, Bonham-Phillips.** No other city in the world can offer such enjoyment.

The **Capital Hotel** is my favorite small hotel because of the very high standards of food, wine and service.

Barbaralee Diamonstein
Writer, Television Interviewer, Producer and the longest term commissioner of the New York City Landmark Preservation Commission

Reading Room and **Egyptian Gallery** at the **British Museum.** *Great Russell St., WC1. 636-1555*

Anything at **Claridges**, including the bathrooms. *Brook St., W1. 629-8860*

Liberty fabrics and foulards. *210 Regent St. W1. 734.1234*

Swaine, Adeney and Brigg's umbrellas. *185 Piccadilly, W1. 734-4277*

Gate entrance to the **Victoria and Albert Museum.** *Cromwell Rd., Sw1. 589-6371*

Tea room and food department at **Fortnum and Mason.** *181 Piccadilly, W1. 734-8040*

Antique shops on **Bond Street,** from **Mallet,** to **Partridge's** to **Christopher Gibbs.**

Superb ham and 200 varieties of excellent cheeses at **Paxton and Whitfield.** *93 Jermyn St., SW1. 930-0259*

Sac Freres, dealers in amber for more than 80 years. *45 Old Bond St., W1. 493-2333*

F. Sangorski and G. Sutcliffe, the most famous bookbinders in England (a by-product of the Arts and Crafts Movement). *1 Poland St., W1. 437-2252*

Culpeper Ltd., named after the 17th century herbalist Nicholas Culpeper. Soups, dried herbs, herbal cosmetics and medicine. *21 Bruton St., W1. 839-2400*

---

10 Best Restaurants
The Good Food Guide, 1986

The Good Food Guide is the Anglo-Saxon answer to *Michelin.* But whereas the *Michelin* uses the logic of symbols, the *Good Food Guide* reveals with a love of language. Alert and learned palates, under the direction of **Drew Smith,** rank the best according to number. The top London 10 in 1986 are:

Le Gavroche. (17/20) *...no tricks, just an honest attempt to serve the finest food in the finest restaurant.* Open M-F 12:30-2PM, 7-11PM. 43 Upper Brook St., W1. 730-2820

La Tante Claire. (16/20) *It can hold its place beside the present great French restaurants by being consistently excellent.* Open M-F 12:30-2PM, 7-11PM. 68 Royal Hospital Rd., SW3. 352-6045/351-0227

Connaught Hotel. (15/20) *It is above all reliably good throughout the length of the menu.* Open daily 12:30-2PM, 6:30-10PM. 16 Carlos Pl., W1. 499-7070

Inigo Jones. (15/20) *The food is refined...everything is served filleted, out of its shell, off the bone.* Open M-F 12:30-2:30PM, 6-11PM; Sa 6-11PM. Garrick St., WC2. 836-6456

Rue St. Jacques. (15/20) *...Gunther Schlender ...manages to do the set-piece modern dishes with more elan than others.* Open M-FSa 12:30-2:30PM, 6:30-10:30PM; Su 12-2PM, 7-10PM. 5 Charlotte St., W1. 637-0222

Capital Hotel. (14/20) *The food is very good but does not scream of there being a big ego in the kitchen.* 22 Basil St., SW3. 589-5171

Dorchester Hotel. (Terrace Restaurant and Grill Room). (14/20) *Anton Mosimann's reputation precedes his restaurants...but his dining rooms lag behind.* Grill Room open M-Sa 12:30-2PM, 6-11PM; Su 12:30-2:30PM, 7-11PM. Restaurant open M-Sa 6-11:30PM. Closed Su. Park Ln., W1. 629-8888

Hilaire. (14/20) *...a set price menu that changes almost daily with the markets...the diversity is remarkable.* Open M-F 12-2:30PM, 7-11:30PM; Sa 7-11:30PM. 68 Old Brompton Rd., SW7. 589-8993

Interlude de Tabaillau. (14/20) *Jean-Luis Tailleband's cooking seems to have caught a new breath...all the signs of a kitchen in creative overdrive.* Open M-F 12-2PM, 7-11:30PM; Sa 7-11:30PM. 7-8 Bow St.,WC2.379-6473/836-9864

Litchfield's. (14/20) *The menus continue to excite...novel combinations are artfully achieved.* Litchfield Terrace, Sheen Rd., Richmond, TW9. 940-5236

The Good Food Guide 1986, edited by Drew Smith. Published by the Consumers' Association and Hodder & Stoughton Ltd.

The King's Road romantic, free and fitful,

runs the entire length of a territory known as **Chelsea** synonym for swinging London in the 60s, now a chiaroscuro stage-set for punks and Sloane Rangers. Chelsea is the most authentic village left in London. The neighborhood nestles against the River Thames, south of Westminster and Hyde Park, and more than any other part of London, it has a riverside personality. King's Road, parallel to but out of sight of the river, is Chelsea's main street, a long, straight and irresistable thoroughfare which flows through—and animates—the ancient and modern neighborhood.

Spending a day in Chelsea, strolling down the King's Road and wandering down the side streets, is one of the best ways to feel like you are on a first name basis with London. The streets, the architecture and the history have a sympathetic and humane dimension, crowned by Christopher Wren's magnificent **Royal Hospital.** For many Londoners, this is the most beautiful building in London, and it still provides shelter to war veterans whose distinguished scarlet and blue uniforms are part of the iconography of Chelsea life. It is here, in Chelsea, in houses that have become grand in our inflationary age, that Oscar Wilde, Whistler, Sargent, Thomas Carlyle and Turner lived, in an atmosphere of all-pervasive coziness. History feels oddly personal here, as though the ghosts of Henry James, Augustus John and Oscar Wilde walk the streets in their dressing gowns. The atmosphere of Bohemian nonchalance survives in spite of the high cost of property and the cruel clog of cars.

The King's Road, however, has a personality all its own. This vital highway created by Charles II as his *Route de Roi* to Hampton Court is the backbone of Chelsea, and it is *avant-garde,* unpredictable, ever-changing, transient, anarchic, life-loving, decadent, visual and overtly self-conscious. Chelsea, in schizophrenic contrast, is profoundly residential, a village of prosperous residents who pay dearly to live in desirable houses in a maze of narrow, well-kept streets. Chelsea dwellers are stylish Londoners who appreciate the potent legacy of their *quartier's* past: riverside town, royal suburb and artists' colony of London. They enjoy the domestic, relaxed scale of the streets lined with trees and privilege and family houses (there are relatively few apartments in this area), and they endure with confident humor the King's Road, confining their regrets to the little fishmonger, the greengrocer, and the local baker, long ago replaced by boutiques and antique markets.

Even if the area no longer vibrates with the fashions of Mary Quant or provides domiciles for Mick Jagger and Co., it has an innate vitality and a tantalizing variety of styles and beliefs. Until last year, this was Margaret Thatcher's private London address; it is where punk began and survives; and it is the original home of the

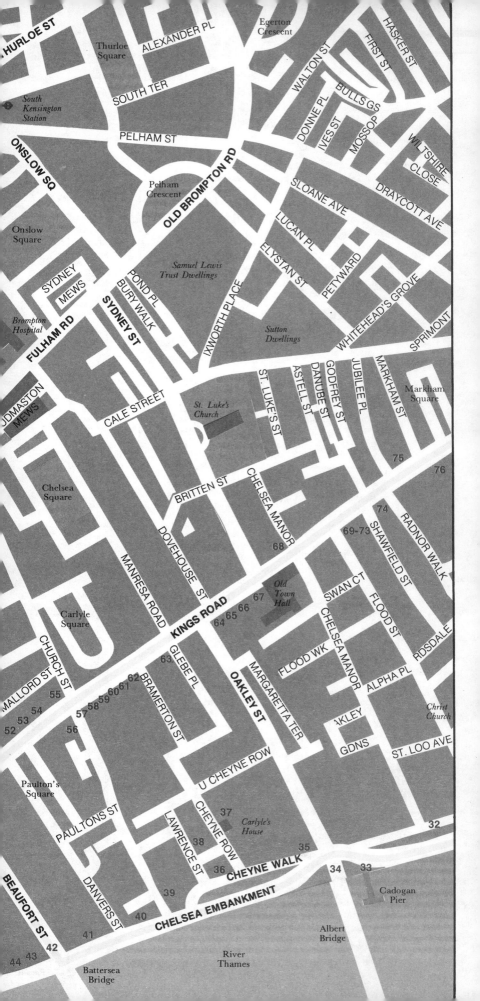

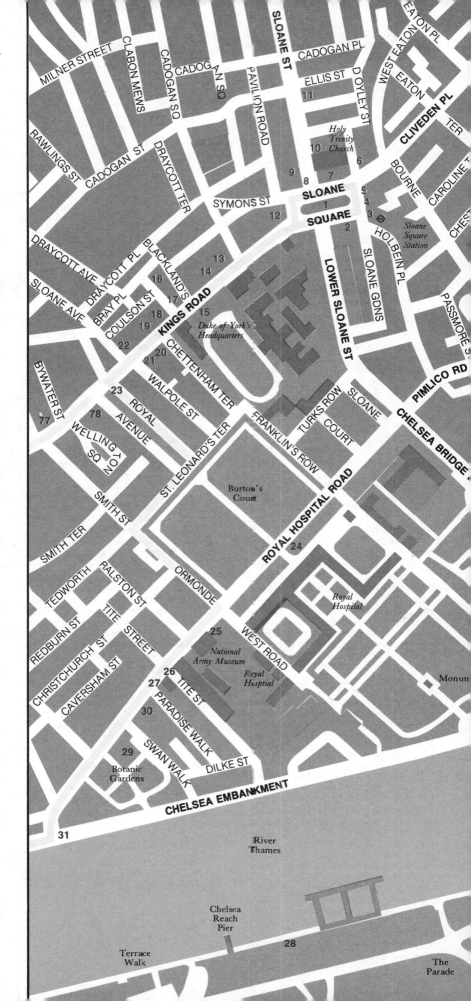

Designer's Guild. Currents of illustrious history flow like clear streams in the little side streets. The King's Road may seem tame and peaceful now, but dotted along the way, in shops no wider than a king-size bed, the fashions of the future, for better or for worse, are being scissored today.

This walk features a long thoroughfare, but ideally it should be explored in a circular manner, leaving the King's Road at **Royal Avenue** to enjoy the dense history, neighborhood pubs and riverside easiness of Chelsea, then returning to the King's Road at **Beaufort Street** and going back in the direction of **Sloane Square.** The ideal day to be here is on a Saturday, when the King's Road is in full bloom, complete with punks and weddings, residents and visitors.

1 **Sloane Square** (c. 1780, Henry Holland) Chelsea begins here, under a tent of young plane trees and with a soundtrack of cars and taxis that drowns out the watery music of one of London's rare fountains (by Gilbert Ledward, presented to Chelsea by the Royal Academy in 1953). Nothing grows in the Square, save the trees, but color is provided by the flower seller who is here, day in and day out, year round. The Square was named after one of Chelsea's most distinguished residents, **Sir Hans Sloane,** a wealthy physician at the beginning of the 18th century, president of the Royal Society, and at one time, owner of practically all of the village of Chelsea. Sloane lived in Henry VIII's former manor house, and his vast collection of plant specimens, fossils, rocks, minerals and books was the foundation of the British Museum.

2 **WH Smiths.** This ubiquitous bookseller—76 in London—located on the east side of Sloane Square is a good place to acquire maps, guides, writing paper, pens, magazines, newspapers or paperbacks. There is also a large selection of international periodicals. *Open M-Sa 8:30AM (for newspapers) and 9AM (for everything else) to 6:30PM; W to 7PM; Sa to 6PM. Sloane Sq., SW1. 730-0351*

3 **Sloane Square Tube Station.** The underground station was built over one of London's streams (the Westbourne) which is carried in a cast-iron conduit above the trains. In 1940, a German bomb hit the station, fracturing a gas main and injuring and killing scores of staff and passengers. *Sloane Sq., SW1.*

4 **Royal Court Theatre.** (1888, Walter Emden and WR Crewe; remodeled in 1965 and 1985) *Look Back in Anger* put the 1950s, Chelsea, playwright John Osbourne and the Royal Court Theatre on the map. After the dramatic explosion of the angry young men, things were never quite the same. Postwar England had to make way for a new aristocracy of bitter talent, relinquishing the stronghold of the duller, safer aristocracy based on class. In fact, the message had been preached at the Royal Court for decades, when Harley Granville-Barker was producing (1904-7) the early plays of George Bernard Shaw. Now this is the resident theatre for the **English Stage Company,** and productions are invariably first-rate, original, controversial and well worth taking a chance on if you want to see the best in London theatre. *Sloane Sq., SW1. 730-1745*

5 **Oriel Grande Brasserie de la Place.** ★ ★ ★ $$ One of the most welcome newcomers to Sloane Square is this French cafe, with most of the advantages of a French cafe—good coffee and croissants served early in the morning, *croque-monsieurs* served all day, good wine by the glass, newspapers on sticks, attractive cane chairs and marble-top tables. But you will long for the speed and professionalism of French waiters, sadly lacking in their English counterparts. It is the best place in the area for breakfast, and good for lunch and dinner as well. Fits in perfectly with an evening at the Royal Court Theatre. (Dickensian warning: it gets crowded at lunch and late afternoon—watch your handbag, etc.) *Open daily 9AM-1AM. 50-51 Sloane Sq., SW1. 730-2804*

6 **David Mellor.** Outstanding contemporary design for the kitchen and dining room. Handmade wooden salad bowls and pottery bowls and glassware—the best from British craftsmen—along with a superb choice from France. Very good cutlery. *Open M-F 10AM-6:30PM; Sa 10AM-6PM. 4 Sloane Sq., SW1. 730-4259*

7 **Royal Court Hotel.** *Moderate.* No matter how much they fix this place up, it still has the atmosphere of a provincial English hotel located near the train station. The 101 rooms have all the modern comforts, including 24-hour service. *Sloane Sq., SW1. 730-9191*

Within the hotel is:

Old Poodle Dog Restaurant. ★ $$ The hotel restaurant attempts to be a cut above provincial and is especially good for an early English breakfast. The newly redecorated pink dining room is more ambitious than the rest of the hotel. *Open for breakfast M-Sa 7-10AM, Su 7:30-10:30AM; lunch daily 12-2:30; dinner daily 6:30-10:30PM. 730-1499*

Sloanedom

You don't have to be in London long before you hear the word **Sloane,** referring not only to the Square but to a group of people identified by the name and its appendage, **Sloane Ranger.** It all began when 2 clever journalists,

Peter York and Ann Barr, decided to call a certain class of Englishmen *Sloanes*, and their girlfriends, sisters, mothers and wives, *Sloane Rangers*. Sloane Ranger-land is briefly defined as the postal districts SW 3, 5, 7 and 10, known to the public as Knightsbridge, South Kensington and Chelsea, although in these inflationary times the Sloanes extend as far as Battersea, Wadsworth, Clapham and Putney (but always south of the river). Sloane is not the English equivalent of preppy because the layers of class and tradition are too deep and inimitable. You can identify Sloanes by their speech (eavesdrop at the **General Trading Company**) and by their dress (silk headscarves tied under the chin, strings of pearls, even with sweat shirts from Benetton, gold signet rings on the little finger, quilted green coats, Labradors never far behind). The best Sloane of all is the **Princess of Wales**, but to really understand Sloanedom you have to remember those pictures of her when she first got engaged: ruffled shirt with ribbons at the neck, round cheeks and flat shoes. She had a Sloane job (working in a kindergarten—Sloanes have the minimum of formal education, and the Princess of Wales does not even have the English equivalent of a high school diploma) and Sloane instincts (a love of home, animals, the countryside and children). The

Sloane world is the English world of nannies, private schools, Church weddings, Ascot, the Chelsea Flower Show, pheasants (which they raise, shoot and eat), Christmas and dogs. And if this all sounds incomprehensibly vague, buy the *Sloane Ranger Handbook*, a thorough and amusing sociological survey of a single class which became a bestseller, available at the General Trading Company.

---

8 **Sloane Street.** What Bond Street was 30 years ago. Sloane Street has quietly become one of the smartest streets in London, taking its lead from **Harvey Nichols**, by far the most stylish department store in London, **Valentino, Ungaro, Bruno Magli** and such fashion innovators as **Joseph Brown**. The recent opening of the **Chanel** boutique is the final mark of Sloane Street's importance. The fashion world can be found sipping cappuccino at **L'Express** in the basement of and run by **Joseph**.

9 **General Trading Company.** The GTC is just off Sloane Square, but it is the personification of everything Sloane—and if you aren't sure what that means, come here and look around. It is a Sloane-size country house of a store, with irresistible objects that fit into English country life, from Chatsworth to Battersea. Check out the

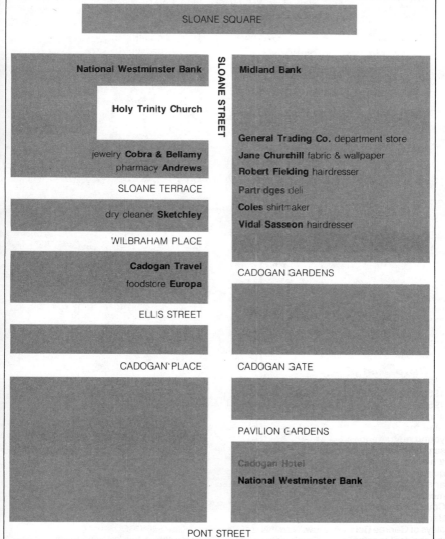

SLOANE SQUARE

SLOANE STREET

National Westminster Bank

Holy Trinity Church

jewelry **Cobra & Bellamy**
pharmacy **Andrews**

SLOANE TERRACE

dry cleaner **Sketchley**

WILBRAHAM PLACE

Cadogan Travel
foodstore **Europa**

ELLIS STREET

CADOGAN PLACE

Midland Bank

General Trading Co. department store
Jane Churchill fabric & wallpaper
Robert Fielding hairdresser
Partridges deli
Coles shirtmaker
Vidal Sassoon hairdresser

CADOGAN GARDENS

CADOGAN GATE

PAVILION GARDENS

Cadogan Hotel
National Westminster Bank

PONT STREET

PONT STREET

HANS STREET

CADOGAN PLACE

Coutts & Co.
restaurant **Rib Room**
clothing **Jaeger**
women's clothing **Nicholas of London**
decorations **Charles Hammond**

Ivor Gordon fine jewelry
Stephanie Kehin shoes
De Havilland antiques
Vidal Sassoon hairdresser
Harabel women's clothing
Konrad Furs
New Art Center
Bleyle German women's clothing
Ungara jewelry
Ebel jewelry
Fendi leather goods
Walter Steiger shoes

COTTAGE WALK

sweaters **Joseph Bis**
chemist **Moore**
women's clothing **Frederick Fox**
dry cleaner **Sketchley**
gallery **Crane Folk Art**
clothing **Valentino**
hairdresser **Neville Daniel**

clothing **Gordon Lowes**
florist **Pulbrook & Gould**
hairdresser **Cadogan Club**

clothing **Laura Ashley**
National Westminster Bank
public house **The Gloucester**

lingerie **Courtenay**
silversmith **Dibdin**

HANS CRESCENT

Aston Martin Ltd.
Coutts & Co.
Chanel clothing
National Bank of Pakistan
Bank of Credit and Commerce
London Bedding Center
Please Mum children's clothing
Issey Miyake women's clothing
Holiday Inn
Joseph tricot/woolens
Kenzo women's clothing
Joseph clothing & interiors
L'Express cafe/restaurant
Erreuno women's clothing
Pied a Terre shoes
Garners restaurant
Andre Bogaert jewelry
Bally shoes
Woodhouse men's clothing
Bertie shoes
New Man clothing
Brown's women's clothing
La Cicogna maternity & children's clothing
Joseph women's clothing

SLOANE STREET

HARRIET STREET

women's clothing **Cecil Gee**

women's clothing **Friends**

clothing **Elegance Maternelle**
chocolates/cafe **Bendicks**
linens **Descamps**

luggage **Louis Vuitton**

Midland Bank
clothing **Leather Rat**
books **Truslove & Hanson**
shoes **Bruno Magli**

department store **Harvey Nicols**

BASIL STREET

Cobb butcher

Atkinson silver/goldsmith

Banco de Bilbao

Barclay's Bank

Knightsbridge Tube Station

KNIGHTSBRIDGE

KNIGHTSBRIDGE

china department, the antiques upstairs, the garden department and the children's toy department. This is where **Princess Diana** had her wedding list, a fact uncovered by the brilliant sleuthing of reporter Maria Brenner (everyday china—Royal Worcester's Eversham; glass pattern—Apollo by Royal Brierly). Fledgling Lady Dianas work here as sales assistants, but most of them are waiting for their princes, so the service is rather uninvolved. The cafe downstairs serves Sloanish foods like zucchini quiche, lemon syllabub and chocolate cake. Expect long lines at lunch time (excellent for observing Sloane accents and sartorial habits and Sloanedom in general). *Open M-F 9AM-5:30PM, Sa 9AM-2PM (Sloanes spend their weekends in the country with family and friends). 144 Sloane St., SW1. 730-0411*

10 **Holy Trinity.** (1888-90, JD Sedding) This church is a euphoric ecclesiastical *homage* to the Arts and Crafts Movement, in spite of the destructive effects of German bombs in WWII which destroyed the vault over the nave. The stunning east window was made by **William Morris and Company** to the designs of **Burne Jones;** the grill behind the altar is by **Henry Wilson;** and many other pre-Raphaelite artists contributed to the Gothic glorification which abounds. Check notices on the church door for lunchtime concerts. *Sloane Sq., SW1.*

11 **Hotel Wilbraham.** *Moderate.* One of the rare hotels which offers the atmosphere of shabby-genteel country England in the heart of London, and at refreshingly fair prices. Ask for a largish room with your own bath and you will be extremely pleased. Book well in advance. *1 Wilbraham Pl., Sloane St., SW1. 730-8296*

12 **Peter Jones Department Store.** (1936-38, W. Crabtree with Slater, Moberly and CH Reilly, consultants) A much-acclaimed piece of modern design which still succeeds 50 years after it was built. The architects followed the curve of the King's Road and created a building that has the grace and shapeliness of an ocean liner. Duchesses and secretaries shop here, and Sloanedom buys school uniforms here (great stuff to take back for the kids: well-made, classic English children's clothes at very reasonable prices). The china and glass department has a superb selection of English patterns, and the linen department offers beautiful Egyptian cotton sheets, Scottish woolen blankets, Irish linen tablecloths and napkins. On the first floor, you will find ladies' leather gloves lined in cashmere, Sloanish leather picture frames and sensible country shoes, all at a lot less than you would pay anywhere else. Members of the sales staff are all called *partners* (at the end of the year they get a share of the profits), and they are some of the most helpful salespeople in London. *Open M, Tu, Th-Sa 9AM-5:30PM, W 9:30AM-7PM. Sloane Sq., SW1. 730-3434*

13 **Body Shop.** You might easily get hooked on these beauty products, made from natural ingredients that stimulate the appetite—rosemary, jojoba, cocoa butter, honey, orange blossom. They are sold in refillable plastic bottles at the lowest prices possible and tested without cruelty to animals. The shop now offers a range of perfumes that have a remarkable resemblance to the big names, but they are offered here at everywoman prices. *Open M-Sa 10AM-6PM. 54 King's Rd., SW3. 225-2568*

14 **Blushes.** ★ $ Popular bistro-wine bar with a few tables on the sidewalk year-round. It is an agreeable place to have a salad, a slice of game pie and a glass of wine and to watch a rarefied bit of the world go by. *Open M-Sa 12PM-12AM, Su 12-11:30PM. 52 King's Rd., SW3. 589-6640*

15 **Duke of York's Headquarters.** (1801, John Saunders) Behind the iron railings are the barracks for several London regiments of the Territorial Army. The handsome Georgian brick building with its central Tuscan portico (best viewed from Cheltenham Terrace) was originally built in 1801 as a school for children of soldiers. The bright red and blue uniforms of the children were present in Chelsea until 1909, when the school was moved to Dover. *King's Road., SW3*

16 **John Sandoe Books.** Just off the King's Road on a little street called Blackland's Terrace is the best literary bookshop in London, beloved by readers and writers. John Sandoe, handsome, silver-haired and pink-cheeked, has a knowledge of books that would put many an Oxford don to shame. He gives patient credit to writers, has a devoted clientele of literate aristocrats and will send your books anywhere in the world. The best bookshop in London today. *Open M-Sa 9AM-6PM. 10 Blackland's Terrace, SW3. 589-9473*

17 **Next.** These started out 4 years ago as shops for women's clothes, with emphasis on workable and matching clothes at approachable prices arranged in an attractive setting. Then came a men's Next, with a look for the jazzier executive. Next but probably not last is a home furnishings shop with clean, attractive and affordable linens, fabrics and furniture designed by Tricia Guild. It is all so imaginative, liveable and reasonable, that it is bound to be the success story of the 80s. *Open Tu, Th, F, Sa 10AM-6PM; M 10:30AM-6PM; W 9:30AM-7PM. 76-78 King's Rd., SW3. 584-5269. (Also on the King's Road: No. 69, Shoes and Accessories; No. 72, Interiors; No. 76, men's clothing; No. 102, women's clothing.*

18 **G&D Boulangerie.** ★★ $ A quick coffee and croissant, standing or sitting on a stool. Always good to know. *Open M-Sa 8AM-6PM, Su 9AM-4PM. 74 King's Rd., SW3. 584-1873*

19 **Hobbs.** Shoes that look comfortable, with great style and a look definitely all their own. They are designed by Marilyn Anselm, are made in Italy and are wonderfully affordable. If you like them, this will be your shoe store. The clothes are interesting but less reliable. *Open M-Sa 10AM-6PM. 84 King's Rd., SW3. 581-2914*

20 **Wheelers.** ★★ $$ This chain of English fish restaurants dates back to Victorian days, and only recently has the cooking made the transition to the 1980s. Instead of Dover Sole prepared 50 ways, they wisely prepare this aristocrat of the sea in fewer and better ways. Attractive room, excellent set-menu lunch and succulent, fresh native oysters in season from Wheeler's own beds. The wine list is far better than in the old Wheeler days. *Open M-Sa 12:30-2:30PM, 6-11PM; Su 6:30-10:30PM. 33C King's Rd., SW3. 730-3023*

21 **Pied a Terre.** High-fashion French and Italian-made shoes in great colors and first-rate designs which allow you to foot the bill without serious mishap. In winter, the boots are handsome indeed. One of 4 shops. The Bond Street shop has handmade shoes a cut—and price—above. *Open M-Sa 10AM-6PM, Th until 7:30PM. 33D King's Rd., SW3. 730-9240*

22 **Chelsea Kitchen.** ★ $ Cheap and honest, and after 2 decades, a King's Road institution. Everything is fresh and homemade, including the bread, scones and pastries. Popular for breakfast. *Open M-Sa 8AM-11:45PM, Su 12-11:30PM. 98 King's Rd., SW3. 589-1330*

23 **Royal Avenue.** A triumphal route intended to connect **Sir Christopher Wren's** Royal Hospital with Kensington Palace. The ambitious design, conceived by Wren for William III, never got beyond the King's Road. But the majesty of the 4 rows of plane trees, lined by 18th and 19th century houses, makes a magnificent impression. The avenue is also James Bond's London address. You can see Chelsea Hospital in the distance as it leads to **St. Leonard's Terrace** on the north of **Burton's Court**, a large playing field with an 18th century gate which was the original entrance to the Hospital.

24 **Royal Hospital.** (1682, Sir Christopher Wren) Guidebooks perpetuate the emotional myth that Nell Gwynn, mistress of Charles II, was so moved when a wounded soldier begged for alms, that she persuaded the King to build the Royal Hospital. The more likely truth is that Charles was impressed and inspired by reports of Louis XIV's Hotel de Invalide. In 1682, the diarist Sir John Evelyn and the Army Paymaster General Sir Stephen Fox drew up plans for a hospital and residence for pensioners of the army, and Charles II commissioned Wren, who chose the magnificent river site. After St. Paul's, this is Wren's masterpiece of beauty. The buildings still provide shelter to 400 war veterans known as the **Chelsea Pensioners.** (The original brief was to provide shelter for 476 men.)

Each year on the birthday of Charles II, 29 May 1660, the pensioners celebrate Charles's escape from Cromwell's troops—he hid in an oak apple tree after the Battle of Worcester—by placing a wreath of oak leaves around the neck of the bronze statue of Charles II in the **Figure Court** (carved by **Grinling Gibbons**). On this day, the pensioners change from their blue winter uniforms, designed in the time of the Duke of Marlborough, to their scarlet tunics for summer, and receive double rations!

The Hospital consists of a central block, which houses the chapel and the main mall, connected by an octagonal vestibule. The pensioners live in the twin galleries or wings which run at right angles to the river. The small **museum** in the **Secretary's Office Block** on the east side of the Hospital contains prints, uniforms, medals and photographs associated with the Hospital and its history, including 2 large paintings in the **Wellington Hall**—the *Battle of Waterloo* by **George Jones**, and **Haydon's** *Wellington Describing the Field of Waterloo to George IV.*

The pensioners have their meals in the **Great Hall** under the *Triumph of Charles II,* a huge wall painting of the King on horseback, trampling over serpents, with the Royal Hospital in the background. Around the Hall are portraits of British kings and queens from Charles II to Victoria. When Wellington was laid in state here in 1852, several mourners were trampled to death by the crowds.

The **Chapel** is pure Wren, with his signature black and white marble floor, fine carved paneling and altar rail. The glass case beside the altar contains a prayer book placed there in 1690, opened to a prayer of thanksgiving for the Restoration, without which there would be no Royal Hospital. Visitors are welcome to attend services on Sundays. The best way to see the Royal Hospital is with a Chelsea Pensioner as your guide, and there is almost always one around who is willing to provide this service. (A gratuity is usually welcome.)

In the 18th century, the **Ranelagh Gardens** of the Royal Hospital were a vast pleasure garden open to the public, complete with a gilt amphitheatre and a site for eating, drinking, music, masquerades, fireworks and balloon flights. Canaletto painted it, Mozart played in it, the Royal Family enjoyed it and all levels of London society loved it—all before 1803 when it closed its doors. Now this part of the Royal Hospital grounds is the site of the **Chelsea Flower Show**, and for 4 days in May, some of the exuberance and pleasure of those early times is relived. *No admission fee to Royal Hospital. Open M-Sa 10AM-12PM, 2-5PM; Su 2-4PM. Chapel services Su at 8:30AM, 11AM, 12PM. Royal Hospital Rd., SW3. 730-0161*

To General Sir S. Dundas, K.B. Governor of the Royal Hospital &c.&c.&c. this plate is respectfully inscribed by his humble Servant—Thos Faulkner.

Chelsea Flower Show

The English are not considered a passionate race, but when it comes to their gardens, they show all the fanatical emotionalism and commitment that the human spirit is capable of. One of the great events on the English calendar, guaranteed to cause English hearts to beat quicker, is the Chelsea Flower Show, the largest, most popular and most prestigious flower show in the world. For 4 days during the third week in May, a flower lovers paradise covers 22 acres of the **Royal Hospital** grounds in Chelsea. Inevitably the rain falls, and a gallant attempt to protect the glorious flowers is made by the great marquee which provides protection for 3½ acres of blooms and bloom lovers.

For 40 days and 40 nights—21 to put up the show, 4 days for the show and 15 to take it down—the **Royal Horticultural Society** concentrates on this immense and important event. Amateurs and professionals as well as the non-horticultural come to look, learn, judge and buy everything from Georgian roses to Gothic garden benches.

The English class structure is evident at this most English event, beginning with a special preview for the flower loving Royal Family, then Opening Day for members of the Royal Horticultural Society. Up to 70,000 people a day come to see the show. The cost of admission goes down each subsequent day as the flowers begin to feel the affect of so many breathless oohs and ahhs. On the last day, and many say the best day, the plants are sold off at closing.

Large marquees reflect English class and taste, and you can have champagne and strawberries, beer and sausages or tea and scones.

There is wonderful shopping too, with stands selling everything from handmade wicker baskets and English wellies to priceless botanical prints, floral tea towels, bowls of *pot pourri* and rare gardening books. But the great attraction is the gardens planted for the occasion. There are magnificent creations of flowers, shrubs, garden seats, stone paths, arbors, sunken ponds and gazebos, with the emphasis on flowers. Every inch is jam-packed with pink and white lupins, blue flax, pale green bells of Ireland, white and pink poppies, pale green tobacco plants, pink foxgloves, white artirrhinums, greeny-cream mignonette, pale blue Canterbury bells, lavender, intoxicating pink stocks, an honor guard of delphiniums, and increasingly, sentimental statuary—stone-colored epoxy resin foxes, nymphs and Neptunes. The genius of these gardens is that, in spite of the unreliable and unpredictable nature of plants, they all look perfect and as though they have been in existence for ever and ever. **Treasures,** the clematis grower, has won the coveted **Williams Memorial Medal**—the show's top award—for the last 3 years. It exhibits around 2,000 plants each year. The *tour de force* in 1986 was an exhibit of 4,000 cacti and succulents from Aberdeen.

Unless your heart's desire is to go on opening day, in which case you must become a member of the Royal Horticultural Society, you can attend the show by standing in line and buying a ticket. The lines themselves are fascinating and well worth the time spent eavesdropping on the conversations—*Are you acid or lime?* Acid. *Oh, hard luck.* To avoid the worst crowds, go in the late afternoon, when the people who have come down for the day have left but the 9-to-5 workers have not arrived.

25 **National Army Museum.** The Royal Hospital doesn't feel like a hospital, nor does it exude an atmosphere of military history, in spite of the fact that many of the pensioners are important war heroes. Just next door, however, is this museum which covers the history of the British Army from 1485 to the present day, including the Falkland's War. The museum houses 3 galleries—the **weapons gallery, uniform gallery** and **art gallery**, plus the history of the army, beginning with the Yeoman of the Guard in 1485. There are lots of models and dioramas of battles and a fascinating skeleton of Napoleon's horse Marengo. Originally founded at Sandhurst in 1960 and opened here in 1971, the museum is a must for students of military history and little boys who stare transfixed at the longbow retrieved from Henry VIII's ship, the *Mary Rose*, and who don't mind the sound of rifle fire that ricochets around the gallery. Artists represented in the **art gallery** include Reynolds, Romeny, Lawrence and Raeburn. *No admission fee. Open M-Sa 10AM-5:30PM, Su 2-5:30PM. Royal Hospital Rd., SW3. 730-0717*

26 **Tite Street.** A kind of distilled essence of Chelsea life can be found in this little triangle of streets—Tite Street, Dilke Street and Swans Walk—connecting the Royal Hospital Road with Chelsea Embankment. The brilliant and eccentric **Oscar Wilde** lived at **No. 34** Tite Street with his wife from 1884 until 1895. The study where he wrote *Lady Windemere's Fan, An Ideal Husband* and *The Importance of Being Earnest* was painted buttercup yellow with accents of red lacquer. The dining room, in shades of ivory and pearl, symbolized tranquility, the one quality which eluded Wilde permanently and fatally. Wilde was arrested and imprisoned for homosexual offenses, declared bankrupt and his house was sold while he was in Reading Jail. When he was released, he

KING'S ROAD & CHELSEA

moved to France, where he died in 1900. The plaque on Wilde's house was unveiled in 1954 on the centenary of his birth by Sir Compton MacKensie and an audience of Chelsea artists and writers.

The American artist **John Singer Sargent** lived at **No. 31** Tite Street in one of those studio houses that are pure Cheslea. Here he painted his portraits of the rich and famous and often beautiful, including the actress Ellen Terry and the American writer who lived around the corner on Cheyne Walk, Henry James. He died here in 1925.

The Bohemian portrait painter **Augustus John** had his studio at **No. 33**. Just next door at **No. 35**, a house which is now cruelly modernized and out of place, is the former home of one of America's greatest painters, **James McNeill Whistler.** The house was cursed long before Colin Tennant (now Lord Glenconner) transformed it into *Monte Carlo modern.* Whistler built the house, using white brick and green slate, to the designs of EW Godwin in the 1870s, intending it to be his home, studio and school. A libel suit he brought against the critic John Ruskin left Whistler with huge and unpayable legal costs, and he was forced to sell the house in 1879.

27 **Foxtrot Oscar.** ★ ★ ★$ A rather silly name and great popularity are the only drawbacks to this restaurant owned by an Etonian. Grilled steaks, terrific salads (seafood and smoked goose), imaginative and tasty versions of English classics like kedgeree and steak and kidney pie, and a creative wine list. Full of Sloanes wearing bright colors, with suntans and loud voices. So inexpensive, clever and relaxed that it is well worth a meal. *Open daily 12:30-2:30PM; 7:30-11PM. 79 Royal Hospital Rd., SW3. 352-7179*

28 **Japanese Peace Pagoda.** If you walk to the end of Tite Street on the Embankment and look across the River Thames, you can see the newest addition to the London riverside: the Japanese Peace Pagoda. The 100 foot bronze-gold leaf Buddha looking out over the river was inaugurated in May 1985. This temple of peace was built in 11 months by 50 monks and nuns, mainly from Japan. It is the last great work of the Most Venerable **Nichidatsu Fugii,** the Buddhist leader, who died at the age of 100, one month before his temple was completed. The temple sits majestically, nobly and peacefully in Battersea Park and is a great gift to Londoners and visitors alike. *Open 7:30AM-dusk. Battersea Park. 874-6464*

29 **Chelsea Physic Garden.** Walk through Dilke Street into **Swan Walk,** with its row of 18th century houses, and you will reach the handsome iron gates of the oldest surviving botanical garden in England, founded by the Worshipful Society of Apothecaries in 1673 (100 years before Kew) on 4 acres of land belonging to **Charles Cheyne.** In 1722, **Sir Hans Sloane,** botanist and physician to George II, became Lord of the Manor and granted a continuous lease, requiring the Apothecaries to present 50 items a year to the Royal Society (of which Sloane succeeded Isaac Newton as president) until some 2,000 had been acquired. In 1732, the first cotton seed was exported to the United States from the South Seas via the Physic Garden. India got its tea from China via the Physic Garden, and Malaya

got its rubber from South America via the Garden. In 1983, the Physic Garden opened its doors to the public for the first time in 300 years. Now, on 2 afternoons a week from spring until fall and under the watchful eye of Sir Hans Sloane himself (statue by John Rysbrack), you can examine some of the 7,000 specimens of plants which still grow here, including the famous cotton seed. The magnificent trees include the 30 foot olive tree which bears fruit each year, the Willow Patter tree and the exotic cork oak. Plants and seeds are for sale. *Admission fee. Open W and Su 2-5PM (mid-Apr to mid-Oct). 66 Royal Hospital Rd., SW3. 352-5646*

30 **La Tante Claire.** ★ ★ ★ $$$ If you have to choose between the Tower of London, Westminster Abbey and the British Museum or a meal at Tante Claire, strongly consider going for the latter. French, yes, but it is an outstanding treasure in London's considerable firmament and a perfect place for lunch (with a very generously priced fixed luncheon menu) while strolling through Chelsea. Recently expanded into the premises next door, the decor is now as chic and impressive as the cooking has always been. **Pierre Koffman** is that rare thing: a modest genius. A meal here combines deceptive simplicity with astounding imagination. The ingredients are treated with great respect, so you can choose from first-class game, beef, fish, lamb and vegetables in season, knowing that you will experience a revelation. The leek terrine is a good example: leeks, steamed until tender and placed in a mold, then sliced and served with slivers of truffle, surrounded by a *coulis de tomates*—unforgettable. The *foie gras,* in its various guises, is equally memorable; the cheeses are from Olivier and are perfection; and the desserts, even though you may feel that it simply isn't possible, are a *tour de force* and must be had. The set menu at lunch is an outstanding value. Reserve your table when you book your flight. *Open M-F 12:30-2PM, 7-11PM. Closed Sa and Su. 68 Royal Hospital Rd., SW3. 351-0227*

Henry VIII is indelibly engraved on the memory as a robust man who had 6 wives and went to excessive lengths in order to do so. A truer picture is of a brilliant, gifted, scholarly, athletic, musical and devout man who was handsome in youth—over 6 feet tall with blonde hair—and who had a great appetite for life. Sir Thomas More described him as a man *nourished on philosophy and the nine muses.* He is also the monarch who, more than any other, created the look of central London, even more than George IV and his architect John Nash.

31 **Chelsea Embankment**. This unbeatably beautiful walk along the river suffers from the noise and anxiety of relentless traffic. Still, it is worth making every effort to transcend the motorized roar to see this miraculously unchanged patch of Bohemian London. Chelsea Embankment begins at **Chelsea Bridge** (1934, Forrest and Wheeler), a graceful suspension bridge which edges up to the massive, dramatic **Battersea Power Station**. The station's 4 chimneys are a vital part of London's industrial archeology as well as the Thames riverline and have successfully resisted all attempts at demolition, even when they ceased to function. (In fact only 2 ever functioned: the front 2 were added purely for aesthetic reasons, to provide a sense of balance.)

32 **Cheyne Walk**. Where the **Royal Hospital Road** and **Chelsea Embankment** converge, the elegant Cheyne Walk begins. The embankment protects the single row of houses from traffic (somewhat), and through a row of trees, the lucky residents have a view of the Thames. Some of the happy few who have lived in these priceless Georgian brick houses include Rolling Stones guitarist **Keith Richards**, the illustrious publisher **Lord Weidenfeld** (still a resident), the recently knighted **Paul Getty, Jr.** and **Mick Jagger (No. 48)**. But it is the past residents who haunt the high windows. **George Eliot** lived at **No. 4** for 19 days after her late-in-life wedding to Johnny Cross, and died here. The pre-Raphael painter and poet **Dante Gabriel Rossetti** lived at **No. 16**, the finest house on the street. He led an eccentric *vie boheme* here, beginning in mourning with the loss of his wife Elizabeth Siddal (the model for Millais' painting of the dying Ophelia and deadly beauty in *Beata Beatrix* by Rossetti—both in the Tate Gallery). Rossetti's Chelsea *menage* included a kangaroo, peacocks, armadillos, a marmot, a zebu and frequent visits from fellow pre-Raphaelites William Morris and his wife Janey, who inspired great passion in Rossetti. No 16 is known as **Queen's House,** the name inspired by the initials *RC* on the top of the iron gateway, long assumed to be *CR,* standing for Catherine of Braganza, queen of Charles II. In fact, the initials stand for Richard Chapman, who built the house in 1717. Opposite the house in the Embankment Gardens is the **Rossetti Fountain**, a memorial to the artist from his friends, including John Everett Millais and GF Watts, and unveiled in 1887 by William Holman Hunt. The fountain is by **JP Seddon,** and the bust of Rossetti is by **Ford Madox Brown.** Unfortunately, the original bronze bust was stolen and replaced by this fiberglass copy. The plaque on **No. 23** Cheyne Walk commemorates the site of **Henry VIII's Manor House** which stood where **Nos. 19 to 26** Cheyne Walk are now. Henry VIII became fond of the Chelsea riverside during his many visits to his friend **Thomas More**, and the year after More's death he built a palace along the Embankment. Before he died, he gave the house to Catherine Parr, his last wife. 100 years later, the house was bought by Lady Jane Cheyne and in 1737, Sir Hans Sloane bought Henry VIII's old manor. More's own house was demolished a few years later. The gateway by **Inigo Jones** was given to the Earl of Burlington, who erected it in the gardens of Chiswick House, where it still stands.

33 **Cadogan Pier**. Each July, the pier just east of Albert Bridge is the scene of one of England's oldest contests, the **Dogget's Coat and Badge Race**. The race was begun in 1715 to celebrate the accession of George I to the throne and was sponsored by Thomas Doggett, who awarded a coat and badge to the winner. A moving ceremony re-enacting the final journey of Sir Thomas More from his home here on the river to the Tower of London where he was executed also takes place at the pier in July. *Cheyne Walk, SW3.*

34 **Albert Bridge.** (1873, RM Ordish) The bridge Londoners love the most. The lattice-work suspension bridge was recently repainted, and at night it is illuminated with strings of lights. *Cheyne Walk, SW3.*

35 **Pier 31.** ★ ★ $$$ Directly opposite the Albert Bridge is a smart new restaurant, Art Deco chic, with a menu which is 70% Japanese and 30% French, all prepared with the freshest, finest English ingredients by a team of Japanese chefs who are as skilled as brain surgeons. Sushi, tempura, a *teppanyaki* bar as well as grilled Dover sole, spring lamb and Scotch salmon. *Open daily 12-2:30PM, 7-11:30PM. 31 Cheyne Walk SW3 352-4989*

36 **King's Head and Eight Bells.** ★ ★ $ Worth coming in for a drink just to raise your glass to a pub which is 400 years old. The pub has been modernized a bit—18th century decor with engravings of Chelsea in those days. Gaze out at the river, enjoy the permanent buffet and try the Wethered's or Tusker bitter. *Open daily 11AM-3PM, 5:30-11PM. 50 Cheyne Walk, SW3. 352-1820*

37 **Carlyle's House.** A short walk up Cheyne Row to **No. 5** is one of the most fascinating houses in Chelsea and one of the few which is open to the public. The house was the family home of the writer **Thomas Carlyle** and his wife Jane. The rooms are almost exactly as they were 150 years ago when *The French Revolution* made its author famous, and Dickens, Tennyson and Chopin were visitors. Go down into the kitchen and see the pump, the stone trough and the wide grate where kettles boiled. Examine the rooms upstairs, with their four-poster beds, piles of books, mahogany cupboards, dark Victorian wallpaper (which covers up 18th century pine paneling) and attic, carefully designed to keep out the noise of the house and the street (not a success) with the horsehair chair and reading shelf. The painting *A Chelsea Interior* (1857) hangs in the ground floor sitting room and shows how little the house has changed. The tombstone in the small garden behind the house marks where a dog lies buried. Carlyle was a famous Chelsea figure, and all his long life *the sage of Chelsea* took solitary walks along these streets. A bronze statue of Carlyle (by **Boehm** and erected in 1882) in the **Embankment Gardens** of Cheyne Row, is said to look very much like him. Here the essayist and historian sits, surrounded by a pile of books, and gazes sadly at the river through an invasion of juggernauts. *Admission fee. Open Apr-Oct W-Sa 11AM-5PM; Su 2-5PM. 24 Cheyne Row, SW3. 352-7087*

38 **Cross Keys.** ★ ★ $ This small, friendly and popular pub spills out onto the sidewalk in summer when the pretty walled garden in the back isn't big enough. The cold table —salads, meats, pates, cheeses—is always fresh and good. *Open daily 11AM-3PM, 5:30-11PM. 2 Lawrence St., SW3. 352-1893*

39 **Chelsea Old Church.** In spite of the heartless traffic outside, the German bombs which flattened it and the unfortunate wooden Indian-style statue that sits impassively in front, this old church is spiritually intact and a glorious monument to its former parishioner, **Sir Thomas More.** You feel his presence in the chapel, built while Holbein was living with the Mores in their home nearby and designed in part by the Dutch artist. And you feel the deep sadness of the story of the gentle man of conscience who could not recognize his friend Henry VIII as head of the Church of England and grant his blessing for divorce, and paid for his conscience with his life. More wrote his own epitaph (against the south wall to the right of the altar) 2 years before his death. The Gothic tomb doesn't contain the remains of the saint, which are believed to be buried in the Chapel of St. Peter ad Vincula within the Tower of London. But Chelsea legend holds that his daughter, Margaret Roper, made her way back here with her father's head.

The ornate tomb with the urn is the burial place of Chelsea's next best-known citizen, **Sir Hans Sloane.** The chained books, including the *Vinegar Bible,* a 1717 edition which contains a printer's error converting the parable of the vineyard into the parable of the vinegar, are the only chained books still found in a London church. The square tower, made famous by so many artists, was a casualty of a German air raid in 1941, but it was rebuilt, and the careful restoration of the church is impressive. The **Lawrence Chapel** is supposedly where **Henry VIII** secretly married **Jane Seymour** a few days before their official marriage in 1536, a year after Sir Thomas More had ceased to be a conscience to the King. On summer days, the church is the setting for happier weddings, and each July a sermon written by More is read from the pulpit. A memorial wall stone commemorates the American writer **Henry James,** who lived in Chelsea and died near here in 1916. *Open Su and Tu-F 11AM-1PM, 2-5PM; Sa 11AM-1PM. Old Church St., SW3.*

40 **Roper's Garden.** This new (1965) garden on the site of part of **Sir Thomas More's** estate is named after **Margaret Roper,** beloved eldest daughter of More. It replaced a garden destroyed in a German air raid. See the stone relief of a woman walking against the wind by **Jacob Epstein,** who lived in Chelsea from 1909 until 1914. *Cheyne Walk, SW3.*

41 **Crosby Hall.** (1466) 300 years after **Sir Thomas More** was executed, this splendid mansion was transported, stone by stone, from Bishopsgate in the City to Chelsea. The Hall was originally built in 1407, then made into a royal palace by **Richard III,** and finally purchased in 1516 by More himself, so it is mere coincidence that in 1910 it made its way into More's Chelsea garden. It is now the dining room of the British Federation of University Women. The superb hammerbeam roof, the stunning oriel window, the long Jacobean table (a gift from Nancy Astor) and the Holbein painting of the More family, one of the 3 copies made by the painter for the 3 More daughters, are all worth seeing. The architecturally sensitive lament the post-war annex and neo-Tudor building of 1925 next door. *Open M-F 10AM-12PM, 2:30-5:30PM; Sa 10AM-12PM; Su 2:30-5PM. Cheyne Walk, SW3. 352-9663*

42 **Beaufort Street.** One of the busiest crossroads in Chelsea, connecting the King's Road to Battersea Bridge.

43 **Lindsey House.** (c. 1640-70) Remarkable for its beauty and its survival against all odds, this large country house is the only one of its date and size in Chelsea. It was built on the site of a farmhouse by the Swiss physician to James I and Charles I, **Theodore Mayerne.** In 1750, the house became the headquarters of the Moravian brethren, whose ideas of Utopia were rather grand and resulted in the house being sold and divided into separate dwellings. The remarkable cast of residents included painter **John Martin, Sir Mark Brunel,** who built the first tunnel under the Thames, and his son **Isambard,** who built many of England's suspension and railway bridges. (Brunel House, 105 Cheyne Walk, is named after the father and son engineers.) **Whistler** lived at **No. 96** from 1866-79 (one of 4 Chelsea addresses), and **Elizabeth Gaskell** was born here. The gardens to **No. 99** and **100** were designed by **Lutyens.** *Nos. 96-100 Cheyne Walk, SW3.*

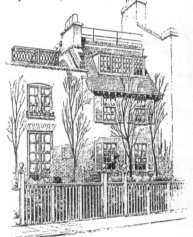

44 **Turner's House.** England's greatest painter, JMW Turner, lived in this tall narrow house during his last years and died here uttering his last words, *God is Light.* 119 Cheyne Walk, SW3.

45 **Man in the Moon.** ★ ★ $ This pub marks the beginning of World's End, that curve in the King's Road. It is a treasured institution—a first-rate theatre club presenting mostly modern plays, as well as a distinguished pub with beautiful engraved glass, a real fire in winter, real ale year round and lunchtime fare as well. *Theatre M-Sa. Open daily 11AM-3PM, 5:30-11PM. 392 King's Rd., SW3. 352-2876*

46 Astrix. ★ ★ ★ $ Formerly called Asterix after the French comic hero, this was London's first crêperie and the inspiration to its successors. The crêpes are made with buckwheat flour, and the winners include chicken liver and spinach ratatouille, with fruit and ice cream for dessert. The atmosphere is welcoming, the prices refreshing and the possibility of an informal meal served with French cider or *bouche*, very tempting. *Open daily 12PM-12AM. 329 King's Rd., SW3. 352-3891*

47 Natural Shoe Store. Started by an American, this might be your salvation if you are beginning to feel weary of foot. Sensible brogues and half-brogues, loafers, lace-up boots (beautiful but they do require wearing in), Frye boots and lots of clogs. *Open M-Sa 10AM-6PM. 325 King's Rd., SW3. 352-3721*

48 Darlajane Gilroy. Clever clothes which manage to be fun, fashionable and classic, a kind of Audrey Hepburn 50s look made new. Reasonable prices too. *Open M-F 11AM-7PM; Sa 10AM-7PM. 327 King's Rd., SW3. 352-2095*

49 Dome. ★ ★ $ A real brasserie, open all day, with French brasserie classics: *salade Niçoise, croque-monsieur, crudités, assiette de charcuterie, mousse au chocolat, espresso, citron pressé.* You can get coffee and a croissant or a full English breakfast. Crowded at lunchtime, but a welcome addition to the King's Road. *Open M-Sa 9AM-11PM; Su 9AM-10:30PM. 354 King's Rd., SW3. 352-7611*

50 Rococco Chocolates. Taste and imagination. This is the most eccentric chocolate shop in the world, and its owners, 2 pretty sisters not long out of art school, deserve a prize for their initiative and spirit as well as for their superb Belgian chocolates. The shop looks like an art gallery and the windows are always worth a perusal. You can have tea or coffee and a chocolate confection at one of the 3 tables designed by a sculptor and take away a selection of chocolates, ranging from sardines to *Venus's Nipples* (white chocolate topped with coffee beans which were enjoyed in *Amadeus*). *Open M-Sa 10AM-6:30PM. 321 King's Rd., SW3. 352-5857*

51 Chelsea Rare Books. Now a Chelsea institution, with an excellent section of secondhand and antiquarian books on Chelsea in particular and London in general. It is also the place to come for handsome, bound editions of Dickens, Scott and once in a blue moon, Jane Austen. By all means, go downstairs and have a look at the English prints and watercolors, which are usually well-mounted and reasonably priced. *Open M-Sa 10AM-6PM. 313 King's Rd., SW3. 351-0950*

52 Thierry's. ★ ★ $$ You have to ring the bell to enter this vintage Chelsea restaurant, which is a great favorite of Chelsea dwellers, who like the honest, carefully prepared and not overly original French dishes. The ambiance depends greatly on the warm and efficient **Di James,** who presides over the restaurant and charms newcomers and regulars alike with her interest in their meals and pleasure. *Open M-Sa 12:30-2:30PM, 7:30-11:30PM; closed 2 weeks in Aug/Sept. 342 King's Rd., SW3. 352-3365*

53 Liberty of London. A small and appealing outlet of the famous Regent Street department store, with its own line of tawny lawn cotton, William Morris fabrics and a few Liberty gifts like men's ties and silk scarves. *Open M, Tu, Th 9:30AM-5:30PM; W 9:30AM-6:30PM; Sa 9:30AM-5PM. 304A King's Rd., SW3. 352-6581*

54 Avoir du Pois. ★ ★ ★ $S Popular with Sloanes who otherwise play cricket when they aren't buying important English furniture at Christie's and Sotheby's. The menu is called *Private Pie*, a satiric gesture at the weekly *Private Eye*, and offers an eclectic choice of *nouvelle* (a seafood *pot au feu*), American (eggs benedict) and Japanese (sushi and teriyaki). The desserts are sublime. *Open daily 12-2:45PM, 7-11:45PM. Special brunch on Saturday and roast Scotch beef on Sunday. 334 King's Rd., SW3. 352-4071*

55 Osborne and Little. Conveniently just across the street from the Designer's Guild, because if you like one shop, you will probably like the other. The wallpaper and fabric in florals and clever *trompe l'oeil* marbles and stiples are all in very good taste. *Open M, Tu, Th, F 9:30AM-5:30PM; W 10AM-5:30PM; Sa 10AM-4PM. 304 King's Rd., SW3. 352-1456*

56 Manolo Blahnik. Just off the King's Road on quiet Old Church Street is this museum of a shoe shop, often with one priceless shoe in the window. These are the shoes that Sarah Ferguson wore down the aisle on her walk to becoming a princess and that Princess Diana has long worn, along with every genuinely glamorous lady in London. The shoes are beautifully designed and impeccably made in Italy in very limited numbers (12-15 pairs of each design), and they are worth every considerable pound you will pay. Particularly irresistible are the crocodile court pumps. *Open M-F 10AM-6PM; Sa 10:30AM-5:30PM. 49 Old Church St., SW3. 352-8622*

57 Designer's Guild. Outstanding design for the present and the future, with sofas, carpets and fabrics which are modern, timeless and country house comfortable all at the same time. **Tricia Guild** goes from strength to strength with her fabrics that look like Impressionist watercolors of English gardens. Stunning accessories, especially the pottery, baskets and lamps. *Open M-F 9:30AM-5:30PM; Sa 9:30AM-4PM. 271 & 177 King's Rd., SW3. 351-5755*

58 David Tron Antiques. 17th and 18th century English and Continental furniture. A very classy shop which, along with **Jeremy** 2 doors down, gives a certain tone to the King's Road. *Open M-Sa 9:30AM-5:30PM. 275 King's Rd., SW3. 352-5918*

59 Green and Stone. One of the few shops on the King's Road that has been here forever and still belongs to the original ethos of Chelsea. These dealers in art supplies carry beautiful sketch books and all you would ever want in oils and watercolors. For the unskilled, there is a tempting collection of old and new silver and leather frames and a very good framing service. *259 King's Rd., SW3.* 352-0837

60 **Jeremy Antiques.** Georgian and Continental 18th century furniture and works of art. If you have superb taste and can afford to indulge it, you will be quite happy here. *Open M-Sa 8:30AM-6PM. 255 King's Rd., SW3.* 353-0644

61 **Chelsea Antique Market.** The most *flea market* in style of the various antique markets on the King's Road, the most likely to yield a bargain and supposedly the first antique market in London. The stall owners still tend to be the friendliest. The strong point now is the books, and **Harrington Bros.** carries some of the best. Their emphasis is on travel books, atlases and maps, natural history and color plates and children's books. *Open M-Sa 10AM-6PM. 245-253 King's Rd., SW3.* 352-5689

62 **Johanna Booth.** One of the nicest shops on the King's Road and perhaps in all of London. Ms. Booth carries a careful collection of tapestries, Elizabethan and Jacobean furniture and wood carvings. She is patient, knowledgeable and nice, and her shop speaks of taste, simplicity and imagination. One whole wall is lined with antiquarian books, also for sale. *Open M-Sa 10AM-6PM. 247 King's Rd., SW3.* 352-8998

63 **Tiger, Tiger.** One of the best things about this toy shop is the price range. True, there are museum quality hand-carved Noah's Arks and stuffed seals and life-size (nearly) tigers that resemble the real thing on the price tag, but there are sheep hot-water bottles and those wonderful farm animals and terrific mobiles that any god-mother can afford. *Open M-Sa 9:30AM-6:30PM. 219 King's Rd., SW3.* 352-8080

64 **Givans.** A shop whose existence is a reminder that the King's Road was not always trendy. Irish linen sheets, luxurious towel bathrobes, damask table linens, all of the kind of quality that is well worth searching out and taking home. *Open M-F 9:30AM-5PM. 207 King's Rd., SW3.* 352-6352

65 **Henry J. Bean.** ★ $ Punks and ersatz punks join tourists and nuclear families in this Chelsea branch of yet another restaurant started by the industrious American Bob Payton (of Chicago Pizza Pie fame). He has figured out the formula for giving the English fast-food, American style, but better. Bean's is an English pub converted into an American saloon, starring potato skins, nachos, hamburgers, hot dogs, spicy chili, pecan pie, cheesecake, ice cream, brownies and during pub hours, cold American beer. The huge garden out back makes this a sunny day favorite on the King's Road. *Open daily 11:30AM-11:15PM. 195-197 King's Rd., SW3.* 352-9255

66 **Chenil Galleries.** This has a worthy tradition in Chelsea Bohemia, including the distinction of hosting the first public performance in 1923 of Edith Sitwell's eccentric and original *Facade* to William Walton's music and outraged reaction from the critics. Such high artistic legacy has not been maintained, although the galleries are still home to a few specialists in Art Nouveau and Art Deco. Picture dealers and furniture dealers come here. There is a garden restaurant as well. *Open M-Sa 10AM-6PM. 181-183 King's Road., SW3.* 351-5353

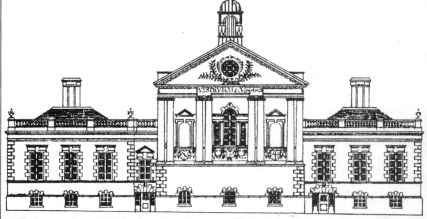

67 **Chelsea Town Hall.** On Saturdays, the punks parade outside on the steps, condescending to accept a small fee from photographers and camera-clicking tourists, and politely stepping aside for the optimistic stream of wedding parties. Young brides in long white dresses, youngish brides in pale pink suits, and various accomplices, ranging from 20 family members to 2 nervous witnesses, file in and out of the Chelsea Registry Office throughout the day. Formal photographs are usually taken on the steps outside, slowing traffic to a standstill and competing briefly with the spiked hairdos and mutilated fashions of a less optimistic ritual. Do feel at ease to stand and watch—it is an essential part of the *authentic experience. King's Rd., SW3.*

68 **Chelsea Farmer's Market.** Because so many of the foodshops in Chelsea have been replaced by fashion boutiques, antique markets and shops, this newish collection of small food shops, open-air cafes, delicatessens and restaurants is a welcome addition for the residents of Chelsea. You can get a good cappuccino, fresh and delicious sandwiches, hot and real pizzas, a cold beer or a glass of wine. Sit in the astroturfed piazza and enjoy your repast in the English sun. *Open daily 10AM-6PM. Sydney St., SW3.* 352-5600

69 **Edina Ronay.** The best fabrics—linens, silks, wools—with English *Brideshead Revisited* classicism, and French and Italian cut and *Je ne sais quoi.* Really, the prices seem expensive when you walk in because the shop is small and on the King's Road. But the quality is Rue St. Honoré, and you won't go wrong investing in an outfit. Ronay is famous above all for the handknit sweaters which established her name. *Open M, Tu, Th, F 10AM-6PM; W 10AM-7PM; Sa 11AM-6PM. 141 King's Rd., SW3. 352-1085*

70 **David Fielden.** The designs are for brides who have a sense of daring as well as the body for the long, figure-hugging, Hollywood-style dresses. *Open M-Sa 10AM-6PM. 137 King's Rd., SW3. 351-1745*

71 **Mr. Gubbins.** Dreamy wedding dresses and ball gowns made from antique and antique-looking silks and satins and lace, with a choice of Edwardian, Victorian and 1920s looks in dozens of designs which can be made for you in 2 weeks. Worth a trip to London for the dress of a lifetime. *Open M-Sa 10AM-6PM. 135 King's Rd., SW3. 351-1513*

72 **Antiquarius.** One of the earliest *antique hypermarkets,* and still one of the best. You will get agreeably lost in the maze of stalls, but you can find wonderful Georgian, Victorian, Edwardian and Art Nouveau jewelry, superb antique clocks, pictures, prints and tiles, and if you shop carefully, you can expect to pay less than in a proper shop. One of the longtime dealers at Antiquarius is **Trevor Allen,** who has irresistible antique jewelry and a good selection of Georgian and Victorian rings and earrings. There is also a cafe where you can renew your energies with coffee and a piece of chocolate cake. *Open M-Sa 10AM-6PM. 135-141 King's Rd., SW3. 351-5353*

73 **Quincy.** Owned by **Jones,** a few doors down, but more traditional, with very fine designs matched with quality fabrics. *Open M-F 10AM-6:30PM, Sa 9:30AM-6PM. 131-133 King's Rd., SW3. 351-5367*

74 **Chelsea Potter.** ★ $ A popular King's Road pub with an attractive interior, substantial lunches and sidewalk chairs in spring and summer. *Open daily 11AM-3PM, 5:30-11PM. 119 King's Rd., SW3. 352-9479*

75 **Chelsea Brasserie at the Pheasantry.** ★ $ This beautiful old building has been saved and restored and now serves as home to several restaurants, with the Brasserie having the best position. On sunny days, summer and winter, sit outside and have onion soup, B-L-T on toast, eggs benedict, or afternoon tea with scones, cream and jam. *Open daily 12PM-12AM. 152 King's Rd., SW3. 351-3084*

76 **Jones.** The window is worth a pause, and inside you will see *toute la rue du Roi* trying on the latest creations by Katherine Hammett, Body Map, Jean-Paul Galtier, Jones, of course, and other unknowns who must be pretty proud to have gained admittance into the most popular and possibly best unisex shop on the King's Road. (A new branch of Jones is, surprise, surprise, in Beverly Hills.) *Open M-F 10AM-6:30PM, Sa 10:30AM-6PM. 129 King's Rd., SW3. 352-5323*

77 **Beaton's.** Enter an era of England lost on the King's Road forever, except for the venerable Beaton's. Here the ovens still produce treacle tarts, granary bread, lemon curd pies and baps and scones, just as they have for over 80 years. You can even get a sausage roll and soup for lunch and watch equally ageless Chelsea neighbors come and collect birthday cakes, wedding cakes, Christmas cakes and of course, the 30 different breads baked here daily. *Open M-Sa 7:30AM-5:45PM. 134 King's Rd., SW3. 589-6263*

78 **Drummonds.** ★ $ A good old-fashioned cafe, open for breakfast, with a buffet lunch, afternoon tea and dinner. It is not easy to find these undemanding places with their easy hours. *Open daily 9:30AM-10PM. 49 King's Rd.,SW3. 730-8180*

Blue Plaques

More than 400 ceramic blue plaques decorate the houses, or sites of houses, where the *distinguished* once lived in London. The **Greater London Council** decides who is qualified for the honor, following certain guidelines: the person must have died at least 20 years ago, been born more than 100 years ago, and made some important contribution to human welfare or happiness. The first plaque was placed in 1867 on the house where **Lord Byron** was born on Holles Street in Westminster.

James Boswell lived and died on the site of 122 Gt. Portland St., W1.

Elizabeth Barrett Browning lived on the site of 50 Wimpole St., W1.

Charlie Chaplin lived at 287 Kensington Rd., SE1.

Sir Winston Churchill lived at 34 Eccleston Sq., SW1.

Samuel Taylor Coleridge lived at 7 Addison Bridge Place, W14 and at 71 Berners St., W1.

Charles Darwin lived on the site of 110 Gower St. WC1.

Charles Dickens lived at 48 Doughty St., WC1.

Benjamin Disraeli was born at 22 Theobalds Rd., WC1 and died at 19 Curzon St., W1.

Sir Edward Elgar lived at 51 Avonmore Rd., W14.

George Eliot (Mary Ann Evans) lived at Holly Lodge, 31 Wimbledon Park Rd., SW18 and died at 4 Cheyne Walk, SW3.

Benjamin Franklin lived at 36 Craven St., WC2.

Sigmund Freud lived at 20 Maresfield Gardens, NW3.

William Ewart Gladstone lived at 11 Carlton House Terrace, SW1, at 10 St. James's Square, SW1 and at 73 Harley St., SW1.

George Frederick Handel lived and died at 25 Brook St., W1.

Thomas Hardy lived at 172 Trinity Rd., SW17 and at Adelphi Terrace, WC2.

William Hazlitt lived on the site of 6 Bouverie St., EC4 and died at 6 Frith St., W1.

Henry James lived at 34 de Vere Gardens, W8.

Dr. Samuel Johnson lived at 17 Gough Square, Fleet St., EC4 and at Johnson's Court, Fleet St., EC4.

John Keats lived at Wentworth Place, Keats

Grove, NW3 and was born on the site of *The Swan and Hoop* public house at 85 Moorgate, EC2.

Rudyard Kipling lived at 43 Villiers St., WC2.

David Herbert Lawrence lived at 1 Byron Villas, Vale of Health, Hampstead Heath, NW3 in 1915.

TE Lawrence (Lawrence of Arabia) lived at 14 Barton St., SW1.

Katherine Mansfield lived at 17 East Heath Rd., NW3.

Karl Marx lived at 28 Dean St., W1.

W. Somerset Maugham lived at 6 Chesterfield St., W1.

Wolfgang Amadeus Mozart composed his first symphony at 180 Ebury St., SW1.

Napoleon III lived at 1c King St., W1.

Lord Horatio Nelson lived on the site of 147 New Bond St., W1 and at 103 New Bond St., W1.

Sir Isaac Newton lived on the site of 76 Jermyn St., SW1.

Florence Nightingale lived and died on the site of 10 South St., W1.

Samuel Pepys lived on the site of 12 and 14 Buckingham St., WC2.

Sylvia Plath lived and died at 23 Fitzroy Rd., NW1.

Captain Robert Falcon Scott lived at 56 Oakley St., SW3.

George Bernard Shaw lived at Adelphi Terrace, WC2.

Percy Bysshe Shelley lived at 15 Poland St., W1.

William Makepeace Thackeray lived at 16 Young St., W8, at 2 Palace Gardens, W8 and at 36 Onslow Square, SW7.

Anthony Trollope lived at 23 Queen Anne St., W1 and at 119 Cheyne Walk, SW3.

Joseph Mallord William Turner lived at 23 Queen Anne St., W1 and at 119 Cheyne Walk, SW3.

Mark Twain (Samuel L. Clemens) lived at 23 Tedworth Square, SW3.

HG Wells lived at 13 Hanover Terrace, NW1.

James Abbot McNeil Whistler lived at 96 Cheyne Walk, SW10.

Oscar Wilde lived at 34 Tite St., SW3.

Virginia Woolf lived at 29 Fitzroy Square, W1.

William Butler Yeats lived at 23 Fitzroy Rd., NW1.

BEST
Books of London

Peter Jackson
President, British Topographical Society

Ann Saunders, *The Art & Architecture of London* (Phaidon, 1984). A huge guide covering the whole GLC area in great detail.

Edward Jones & Christopher Woodward, *A Guide to the Architecture of London* (Weidenfeld & Nicholson, 1983). Exactly what it claims to be, in sections, with maps and a photograph of every building mentioned.

Malcolm Rogers, *Museums & Galleries of London* (Ernest Benn, 1983). Every museum and gallery, from huge to tiny, carefully described.

Weinreb & Hibbert, *The London Encyclopaedia* (Macmillan, 1983). Ideal for a quick reference, but not to be taken as the final word.

The Book of London (AA, 1979 & 1981). Every beautiful page in color covering every aspect of London, both topographical and human.

Felix Barker & Ralph Hyde, *London As It Might Have Been* (Murray, 1982). Amusing and amazing account of buildings that never were.

Hermoine Hobhouse, *Lost London* (Macmillan, 1971). Wonderful but sad illustrated survey of what has gone forever.

BESTS
Hercules Bellville
Film Producer

Marianne North Gallery, *Kew Gardens*

Leighton House Gallery, *12 Holland Park Rd., W14.*

The **London Library,** *12 St. James's Square*

The **Criterion Brasserie** (the walls and ceilings, not the food, alas), *Piccadilly Circus, W1.*

The **Whitechapel Gallery,** *80 Whitechapel High St.,E1.*

The **Michelin Building,** *Fulham Rd., Kensington, SW3.*

Glebe Place in Chelsea.

The view from **Spur Road** across **St. James's Park** to **Whitehall** in the evening. (View can be obscured by foliage in the summer).

BEST RESTAURANTS
George Lang
Owner, New York's Cafe des Artistes

Rue St. Jacques. The latest darling of London restaurant-goers, suprisingly located in Soho. The 2 owners, **Vincent Calcerano** and chef **Gunther Schlender,** have created one of the prettiest and most inventive restaurants in London. *Open M-F 12:30-2:30PM. Closed Sa & Su. 5 Charlotte St., W1.* 637-0222

Sweetings. Just about 150 years ago, when London's population reached the unheard of magnitude of 2 million, an oyster bar opened that was so small that the ceilings were higher than the length or width of its 3 little rooms. Sweetings hasn't changed much since: the Colchester oysters still have the briny taste of the nearby estuaries; the fried whitebait is brittle-crisp; the grilled plaice on the bone, the ubiquitous English flat fish, moist and firm at the same time (please don't spoil it with an automatic squeeze of lemon juice). All the nifty English standbys, such as potted shrimp, jellied eels and dressed crab, are on the daily menu (however, you should avoid the hot fish pies of the day). *Spotted dick* is the perfect get-off-the-diet dish, an English nursery dessert of a steamed pudding studded with raisins and covered with an irresistable golden sauce. Between 11:30AM and 3PM on weekdays, you can sit at one of the small marble-topped counters or join the crowd of blue-suited young bankers from London City proper who animatedly discuss the market while balancing a bottle of Muscadet and fried scampi without the assistance of a table or chair. *Open M-F 11:30AM-3PM. Closed Sa and Su. 39 Queen Victoria St., EC4. 248-3062*

The Ritz Restaurant. A wise editor once warned me that whenever I am inclined to use superlatives, I should play it safe by adding the qualifying phrase, *One of the…* Based on his advice, I am obliged to call the restaurant in the London Ritz Hotel *one* of the most beautiful restaurants in the world, but at least the reason for my caution can be made public at last. The oval dining room itself is an enchanting example of the French neo-classical Beaux-Arts school: the decor includes Louis XVI furnishings and fittings and a playful, garlanded bronze balustrade circling the ceiling, with its pinkish clouds drifting across a blue sky. One side of the restaurant overlooks the Green Park garden that is the property of the Queen, a privilege for which a *peppercorn rest* of a single pound is paid to Buckingham Palace every year. (I dare say it's even a better bargain than shopping with dollars in London.) The umbilical cord to the Escoffier-inspired, heavy classical cuisine has recently been cut, and the menu now features inventive dishes with considerable success. *Open M-Sa 7:30-10:30AM, 12:30-2:30PM, 6:30-11PM; Su 12:30-3PM, 7-10:30PM. Piccadilly. W1. 493-8181*

Inigo Jones. This restaurant was named after the great English architect who built the structure in which it is located. Jones wrote in 1614: *Ye outward ornaments oft to be sollid proportionalbe according to the rulles, masculine and unaffected.* The designers kept this in mind when they created this space, a complex interplay of old and new, velvet and rough stone, authentic period art and good contemporary furniture. *Open M-F 12:30-2:30PM, 5:30-11:30PM; Sa 5:30-11:30PM only. 14 Garrick St., Covent Garden, WC2. 836-6456*

Cafe Royale. If Whistler, Wilde and Beardsley considered it the most elegant restaurant in Europe, there must be something to it. *Open daily 12-3PM, 6-11PM. 68 Regent St., W1., Piccadilly. W1. 439-6320*

The Bombay Brasserie. We are so single-mindedly pursuing the authentic these days that soon we'll end up without flights of fancy, and diligent researchers will be our heroes, instead of the interpreters of dreams. But this restaurant is a refuge from that kind of dreary world. The talented designers and architects of this skylighted pavilion-style restaurant were chosen partly because they had never been to India, and therefore interpreted that world as they imagined it. The result is a place filled with wicker furniture, huge potted palms and cunningly romantic lighting that transports you from this high-ceilinged summer house to an exotic world that is neither London nor Bombay. The good ranges from irresistable *sev batata puri* (a crisp, paper-thin Indian bread topped with sweet-and-sour fruits, chili, boiled potatoes and quite a few other ingredients, making it a first cousin of the best Mexican junk foods) to a boned, stuffed and breaded quail in wine sauce. It doesn't really matter that some of this food can't possibly be Indian—you can have the real thing too. *Open daily 12:30-2:30PM, 7-11:45PM. 140 Courtfield Rd., SW7. 370-4040*

Lamb & Flag. I really don't care if Samuel Butler drank bitters at this 300-year-old pub or if one of Charles II's mistresses was a regular. The important matter at hand is that his pocket-size pub near Covent Garden serves an outstanding selection of English cheeses, from the snow-white *Welsh Caerphilly* to the orange-red *Leicester*. Young people spill out to the sidewalk in good weather. Inside they sit, stand or lean against the centuries old walls while enjoying a venison and claret pâté, or a sausage of ham sliced off the bone, accompanied by a pint of terrific ale. This is the place to meet, to date and to participate in a bit of contemporary London for 30 jolly minutes. *33 Rose St., WC2. 836-4108*

The Grill Room at the Dorchester. The art of giving pleasure is an antidote to the humdrum events in our lives, and the 38-year-old **Anton Mosimann,** the maitre-chef-orchestrator of the Dorchester, is a Leonardo da Vinci of this art form. His inventive games, the parade of refined and often witty renditions of basic dishes and ingredients, provide rare and delicious pleasures. The Grill Room of the Dorchester is distinct from other restaurants in that it serves lighter versions of the English classics without reducing the sensual pleasures of the old favorites. *Breakfast: M-Sa 7-11AM. Su 8-11AM. Lunch: daily 12:30-2:30PM. Dinner: M-Sa 6:30-11PM, Su 6:30-10:30PM. Park Lane, W1. 629-8888*

Tea at the Dorchester. Tea at the Dorchester's Promenade is so international that English is a second language. It is a nonstop tea party, dominated by haute gossip, and if you hear no evil, see no evil and speak no evil, you don't really belong. Cream tea, as it is called in England, is served with scones and golden-hued Devonshire clotted cream. It is not a question of whether you love it; it loves you by warming you inside and making you feel mellow. The flour-dusted scones, graced with a layer of butter, jam and cream, almost make you feel English. You take a little bite and all is well with the world. Even pouting expressions on the faces of the 4 gilded Saracens seem to change to tacit approval. *Tea served daily 3-6PM.*

It takes passionate pilgrims, vague aliens and other disinterested persons to appreciate the points of this admirable country, wrote the never disinterested Henry James in *English Hours.*

The Strand & Fleet Street

are for passionate pilgrims and vague aliens, those true and faithful lovers of London. Even though the walk includes an excursion into hugely popular **Covent Garden** and ends at the astonishing spectacle of **St. Paul's Cathedral,** the area has become rather less obvious in its display of treasures since the days when Boswell insisted that very little was *the equal of Fleet Street.* For the curious, the city lover, the history-minded and the Dickensian-spirited, the treasures of the Strand and Fleet Street are many, worthy and as Henry James himself said, *a tremendous chapter of accidents.*

This seamless thoroughfare echoing the path of the Thames has been the main route connecting Westminister to the City for more than 1,000 years. It has been a witness to 16 reigns, a sanctuary and university of English law and a *street of ink,* where events that transform—or settle into—history are written and printed for millions of readers all over the world. It is also the route from the world of government (Westminster) to the world of finance (the City), each deeply dependent on the other, each remarkably oblivious to the down-at-heel pathway which connects them.

Gone are the days when the mansions of the great bishops lined the Strand, entered by way of gardens which led down to the river. And gone also are the days when stupendous hotels, posh restaurants and elegant theatres were constructed here to reflect in the glory of the newly opened **Charing Cross Station.** The Strand survived the Reformation, when aristocrats replaced the bishops in their great houses, but it failed to triumph over another kind of reformation, the building of the **Victoria Embankment** in 1867, which reclaimed land from the Thames but isolated the street from the river, removing the Thames from view and slowly wringing the life from the thoroughfare. Too many massive office blocks have since devitalized stretches of the long street, paving the way for humdrumness by day and desertion by night. Yet, only two minutes to the north is the liveliest neighborhood in town, Covent Garden, which was a medieval vegetable garden of the monks of Westminister Abbey, and a vegetable market for all of London until 1977, when it was subsequently saved, resusitated and rejuvenated. Now conspicuously popular, Covent Garden is *the* neighborhood of the arts, restaurants, *la jeunesse,* the young at heart and of those inclined to combine walking with shopping, as this is now one of the shopping meccas of the capital.

This walk also includes the oldest wine bar in London (Gordon's Wine Cellar) where you can fortify yourself with a glass of madeira, and one of the oldest pubs (George Public House) where you can drink where that old London-lover Johnson drank after examining the house where he wrote the first English dictionary (**Dr. Johnson's House**), an endeavor only partially inspired by his need to earn the money to pay for the drink. You can have a look at the **Law Courts**, and the criminally inclined can sit in on a case. You will see where the news of the world is being printed (at least until every Fleet Street proprietor has relocated in pursuit of highly technologized facilities). But you will have to content yourself with the impressive facades, as tours usually require booking months in advance.

As you walk down the Strand and Fleet Street, you are following in the footsteps of an impressive list of walkers and talkers: Sir Walter Raleigh, William Congreve, Sheridan, Johnson and Boswell, Coleridge and Lamb, Fielding, Thackeray and Dickens. Nowadays, the singular figure of JP Donleavy (see his list of Bests on page 40) can be seen striding along this ancient route. Along the way, you will be guided and amazed by glimpses of St. Paul's, masterpiece and monument to **Sir Christopher Wren** and beacon of hope and guardian angel for Londoners during the bombing of the Second World War.

This is a fair weather weekday walk. The Strand and Fleet Street hibernate on weekends; Covent Garden can be frantically crowded on Saturdays; and on Sundays much of St. Paul's is closed to passing visitors.

1 **Charing Cross Station.** With the arrival of the railway at Charing Cross Station in 1863, the Strand became the busiest street in Europe, lined with enormous hotels, restaurants and theatres built in the euphoria of the age. Charing Cross is the mainline station closest to the heart of London—and one of the busiest. More than 110,000 people use the station each weekday, and if you are here in the morning during rush hour, you will come face-to-face with nearly half of them. *Strand, WC2.*

2 **Charing Cross Hotel.** *Moderate.* The hotel, designed by **EM Barry** in 1863-64, sits over the train tracks of Charing Cross Station and houses its waiting room. Railway hotels have a certain mystique, appealing to writers with vagabond souls and melancholy hearts. Trouble is, they always look better from the outside. Inside, you have to face hideous attempts at modernization, unmanageable legions of tour groups and a tired, unhappy staff. The Charing Cross Hotel is no different, but it does have a few redeeming features: appealing Renaissance motifs on the facade, a surprisingly old-fashioned and tranquil room on the first floor for morning coffee and afternoon tea, an immense staircase which the insensitive converters of this hotel have not yet managed to demolish and one of the better carveries in town. *Strand, WC2. 839-7282*

Within the hotel is:

Charing Cross Hotel Carvery. ★ ★ $ If you are traveling on a shoestring with a large family, this could be the answer to a few prayers: a set 3 course meal including coffee, dessert and service. Children under 5 eat for free, and those from 5 to 10 are only charged half price. The cafeteria-style service features all you can eat helpings of roast beef, lamb and pork. The vegetables tend to be overcooked and the desserts are lacking in taste. But the place is full of foreigners enjoying English roast beef. *Reservations recommended. Open M-Sa 12-10:30PM, Su 12-10PM. 839-7282*

3 **Charing Cross Monument.** In 1290, a sad and devoted **King Edward I** placed 12 *Eleanor Crosses* along the route of the funeral cortege of his beloved consort **Queen Eleanor** from the north of England near Lincoln to Westminster Abbey. The final stopping place was a few yards from here, where the statue of Charles I now stands looking down Whitehall. But the marble and Caen stone octagonal Eleanor Cross placed here was torn down by the Puritans in 1647. The Charing Cross in the forecourt of Charing Cross Station which you see today was designed by **EM Barry** in 1865, a year after he designed the Charing Cross Hotel. It's a memorial, not a replica, of the original Charing Cross. *Strand, WC2*

4 **Coutt's Bank.** The bank of the Royal family, established in 1692, has occupied this site of **John Nash** buildings since 1904. In a daring and skillful act of restoration in 1979, **Sir Frederick Gibberd** created an ultra-modern building behind Nash's neo-classical stucco facade and pepper-pot corner cupolas. *440 Strand, WC2.*

The old **Charing Cross Hospital** at 28 Villiers Street was moved to Fulham in 1973, but confusingly kept its original name, even though it is now nowhere near Charing Cross.

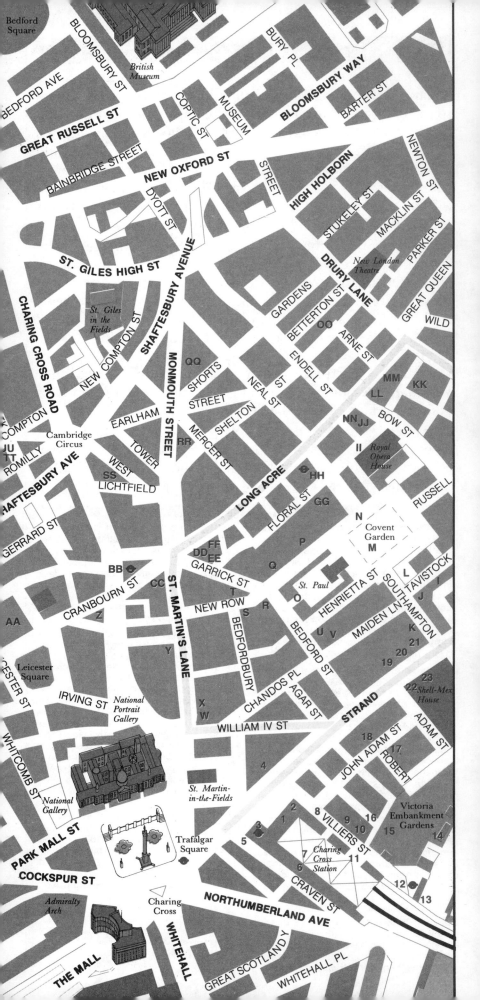

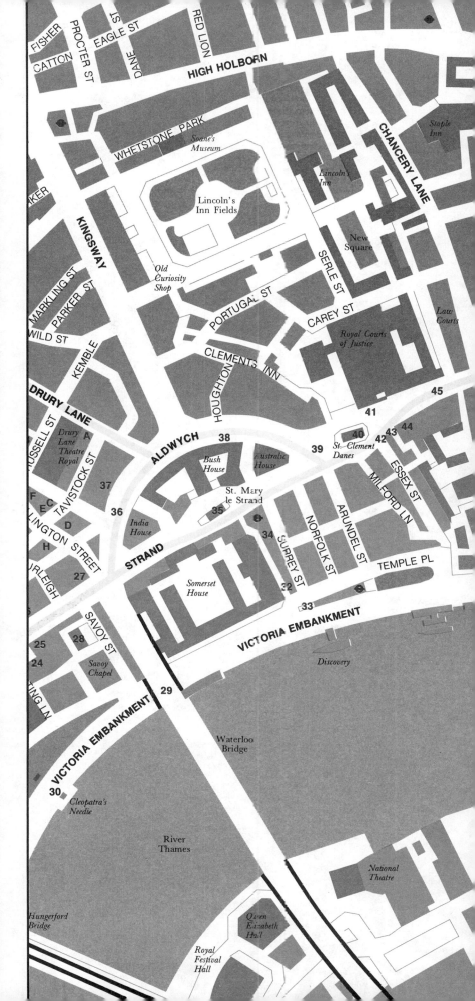

FISHER
CATTON
PROCTER ST
EAGLE ST
DANE ST
RED LION ST
HIGH HOLBORN

WHETSTONE PARK

Soane's Museum

CHANCERY LANE

Staple Inn

Lincoln's Inn

KINGSWAY

Lincoln's Inn Fields

New Square

Old Curiosity Shop

SERLE ST

PARKER ST
MARKLING ST
WILD ST
KEMBLE ST

PORTUGAL ST

CAREY ST

Law Courts

Royal Courts of Justice

DRURY LANE

CLEMENTS INN

HOUGHTON

45

RUSSELL ST
Drury Lane Theatre Royal
TAVISTOCK ST

ALDWYCH

38

39

41

St. Clement Danes

40

42 43 44

ESSEX ST

MILFORD LN

37

Bush House

Australia House

36

St. Mary le Strand

35

34

NORFOLK ST

ARUNDEL ST

TEMPLE PL

WELLINGTON STREET
F E C
D
H

India House

STRAND

SURREY ST

BURLEIGH ST

27

Somerset House

32

33

VICTORIA EMBANKMENT

25

SAVOY ST

28

24

Savoy Chapel

VICTORIA EMBANKMENT

29

Discovery

KING LN

30

Cleopatra's Needle

Waterloo Bridge

River Thames

National Theatre

Hungerford Bridge

Queen Elizabeth Hall

Royal Festival Hall

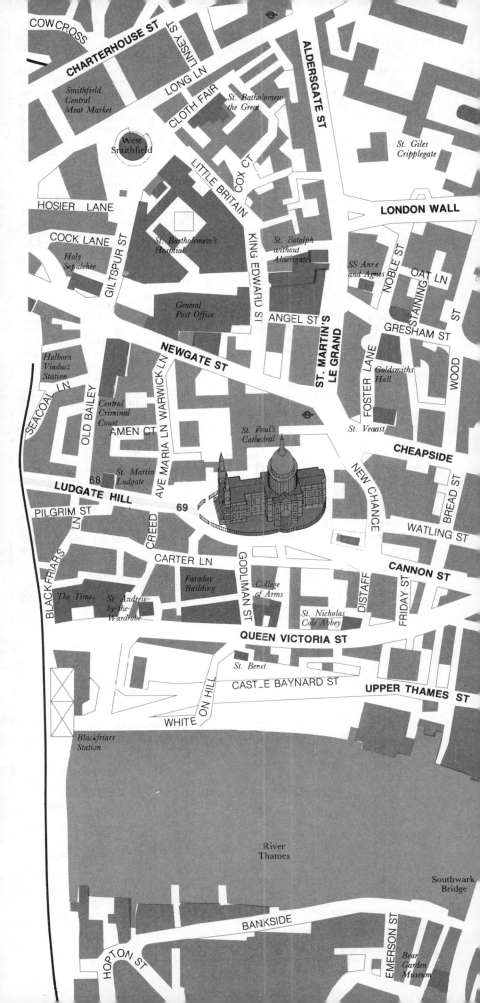

COWCROSS

CHARTERHOUSE ST

LINSEY ST

LONG LN

Smithfield
Central
Meat Market

CLOTH FAIR

St. Bartholomew
the Great

West
Smithfield

COX CT

LITTLE BRITAIN

ALDERSGATE ST

St. Giles
Cripplegate

HOSIER LANE

LONDON WALL

COCK LANE

GILTSPUR ST

St. Bartholomew's
Hospital

KING EDWARD ST

St. Botolph
without
Aldersgate

Holy
Sepulchre

SS Anne
and Agnes

NOBLE ST

OAT LN

STAINING

General
Post Office

ANGEL ST

GRESHAM ST

WOOD

NEWGATE ST

ST. MARTIN'S LE GRAND

FOSTER LANE

Goldsmiths
Hall

Holborn
Viaduct
Station

SEACOAL LN

OLD BAILEY

Central
Criminal
Court

AMEN CT

AVE MARIA LN

WARWICK LN

St. Vedast

St. Paul's
Cathedral

CHEAPSIDE

68

St. Martin
Ludgate

NEW CHANCE

BREAD ST

LUDGATE HILL

69

PILGRIM ST

WATLING ST

BLACKFRIARS LN

CREED

CARTER LN

GODLIMAN ST

CANNON ST

The Times

Faraday
Building

College
of Arms

DISTAFF

FRIDAY ST

St Andrew-
by-the-
Wardrobe

St. Nicholas
Cole Abbey

QUEEN VICTORIA ST

St. Benet

UPPER THAMES ST

CASTLE BAYNARD ST

WHITE LION HILL

Blackfriars
Station

River
Thames

Southwark
Bridge

BANKSIDE

HOPTON ST

EMERSON ST

Bear
Garden
Museum

THE STRAND & FLEET STREET

5 **Craven Street.** The street forms the west border of Charing Cross Station with Villiers Street on the east, and reaches down to the Embankment. **Benjamin Franklin** lived at No. 36 (1757-62, 1764-72).

6 **Craven Passage.** The passage leads under the arches of the railway station, and was made famous by the Flanagan and Allen song *Underneath the Arches.* It has a kind of accidental quality that seems more 1930s than 1980s. On Mondays through Saturdays, dealers operating out of minute stalls trade in coins, medals, militaria, model cars and trains, books and old records. At night, the passage becomes a shelter for London's derelict and homeless, solemnly watched over by policemen who appear tolerant if not sympathetic, unchanged since the 1930s, when **George Orwell** slept here and described it in *Down and Out in Paris and London.*

7 **Ship and Shovel Pub.** ★ ★ $ Before the Embankment reclaimed a slice of the Thames, the river flowed past this pub, then popular with dockers who left their shovels outside. The ship theme has survived, although the shovels and dockers are a thing of the past. Excellent bitters and ales, including Ruddles and Younges. *Open M-Sa 11AM-3PM, 5:30-11PM; Su 12-2PM, 7-10:30PM. Often closed on winter weekends, so check. 2 Craven Passage, WC2. 930-7670*

8 **Villiers Street.** Craven Passage connects to Villiers Street, named for **George Villiers,** Duke of Buckingham (also see **Buckingham Street**), whose fabulous York House covered the street. Villiers Street has a feeling of the past, with flower, fruit and newspaper sellers and 2 very special and very different attractions: the **Players Theatre Club** and Gordon's **Wine Cellar.**

9 **Grand Indian II.** ★ ★ $ Indian restaurants are one of the few culinary advantages that London has over other cities, and even if you are convinced you don't like curry, you have to try at least one Indian meal. This small, fresh restaurant is the sequel to the Grand Indian on New Row in Covent Garden and part of a new wave of Indian restaurants which prove that the days of flocked wallpaper and Eurocurry are numbered. *Tandoori* and *aachar gosht* or sour dishes are the specialty here. Their *niramish* (mixed vegetables fried with spices and herbs) are also excellent. *Open daily 12-3PM, 5:30-11:30PM. 31 Villiers St., WC2. 240-0785*

10 **Gordon's Wine Cellar.** ★ ★ ★ $ Even though Gordon's looks every bit its 300 years, it feels very 1940s, like a film set of London during the War, comraderie, warmth and safety below. The bottles are stored behind a locked grill; the tables and chairs don't match; the food is exceptionally good and laid out the way it must have always been, with homemade terrines, smoked hams, roasted birds, first-class English cheeses (Stilton, Red Windsor) and a large choice of fresh salads. Hot meals are served in the winter. The sherries, ports and madeiras from the cask are impressive, as are the German hocks. Once discovered, this could be your favorite London haunt. *Open M-F 12:15-2:45PM, 5:45-8PM. 47 Villiers St., WC2. 930-1408*

11 **Players Theatre Club.** Victorian music hall at its best, with the same high-spirited sense of humor and fun that delighted audiences in the days before radio, television and canned laughter. The only snag is that you must join, and even temporary membership must be taken out in person 48 hours before the show. But it is well worth it and makes for a terrific evening. There are 2 bars and a supper room, and drinks and snacks are served during the performances. *Theatre open Tu-Sa 6PM, Su 6:45PM; closed M. Performances Tu-Sa 8:30PM, Su 8PM. Villiers St., WC2. 839-1134*

12 **Embankment Underground Station.** The best route to **Hungerford Bridge.** Walk into the station from Villiers Street, out the other side and up the flight of stairs to the bridge.

13 **Hungerford Bridge.** (1863, John Hawkshaw) This bridge replaced one by **Brunel** of the 1840s, and the recent paint job makes it a handsome red tapestry of trussed iron across the Thames. It is the only bridge in central London for trains and people and is a useful pedestrian walkway to the concert hall and theatres on the South Bank, with stunning views towards the City and Waterloo Bridge. *Charing Cross, WC2.*

14 **Victoria Embankment Gardens.** During the summer, office workers and tired tourists relax in deck chairs, children sprint along the grassy slopes and bands play in the secluded and charming riverside garden. This is excellent picnic territory, with a considerable population of 19th century statues amongst the dolphin lamp standards and camel and sphinx benches. One of the best statues is of **Arthur Sullivan,** who wrote the Savoy operas with Gilbert. The inscription *Is life a boon?* is from *Yeoman of the Guard.* Another favorite is the World War I memorial to the **Imperial Camel Corps,** complete with a very fine miniature camel and rider. *Victoria Embankment, WC2.*

15 **York Water Gate.** A fairly ironic monument for the corrupt Duke of Buckingham. Built in 1626 in the Italian style with Buckingham's motto in Latin, *Fidel Coticula Crux* (the Cross is the Touchstone of Faith), and the Duke's coronet, the Gate marks where the Thames reached before the Embankment was built. *Victoria Embankment, WC2.*

16 **Buckingham Street.** Parallel to Villiers Street and named after the same Duke of Buckingham whose mansion was built here in 1626 on land formerly occupied by the Bishops of Norwich and York. The street's most famous resident, philosopher **Francis Bacon,** was evicted by Buckingham during his expansionist building program. In place of the Duke's mansion stands **Canova House,** an 1860s Italian Gothic structure with red-brick arches built by **Nicholas Barbon.** The Duke of Buckingham's entrance to his gardens from the Thames at the bottom of the street is marked with the **York Water Gate.**

George Villiers, Duke of Buckingham, was a clever opportunist, but not quite clever enough. A favorite of James I and his son Charles I, the Duke progressed from plain George Villiers to viscount, marquis and finally Duke of Buckingham in less than 10 years. His own ruthless behavior led to his assassination in 1628 and probably set the stage for Charles I's estrangement from Parliament and the Civil War—and the King's own execution.

17 **The Adelphi.** Parallel with the Strand is John Adam Street, the site of the late, lamented Adelphi, a stunning architectural and engineering achievement and London's first grand speculative housing development. It was built between 1768 and 1774 by the **Adam brothers,** William, James, and Robert, with John as economic advisor. (Adelphos is Greek for brother.) The scheme was a testament to fraternal genius, but it proved a disaster financially. With brilliant vision and dreamy optimism, the brothers leased the land between the Strand and the Thames and built a quay above the river, with 4 stories of arched brick vaults for warehousing. On top of this structure they created 4 streets (Adelphi Terrace, John Adam Street, Robert Street and Adam Street) and a terrace of 11 four-story brick houses which faced the Thames, inspired by the 4th century Palace of Diocletian at Spalato as well as Pompeii and Athens. The project almost ruined the Adam brothers, and the houses were eventually occupied by a lottery sponsored by Parliament in 1773. In the 19th century, the Adelphi became greatly popular with artists and writers and home for such literary celebrities as Thomas Rowlandson, Charles Dickens, John Galsworthy, Thomas Hardy, Sir James Barrie, HG Wells and George Bernard Shaw. Richard d'Oyly Carte lived at 4 Adelphi Terrace while producing the comic operas of Gilbert and Sullivan. In 1936, most of the Adelphi was demolished, a wanton act still lamented by architects and lovers of fine buildings. The legacy of the visionary speculation consists of the streets which the Adam brothers named after themselves and a few fragments: 1-3 Robert Street, with the honeysuckle pilasters which were the trademark of the Adelphi; the offices of *The Lancet* at 7 Adam Street, which are pure Adam; and 4-6 John Adam Street, which contain excellent elements of the scheme. The Adam brothers remained sufficiently undaunted to go on to speculate and build Portland Place north of Oxford Street.

18 **Royal Society of Art.** The most interesting building in the maze of once-Adelphi streets. Built by **Robert Adam,** it has all the noble tranquility, purity and order that epitomize Adam architecture, complete with a Venetian window with a scalloped stone arch and acanthus leaf capitals. The Society was founded in 1754 with the aim of encouraging art, science and manufacturing, and it employed talented artists and craftsmen of the day. The fine hall is decorated with 6 vast paintings by **James Barry** depicting the progress of civilization. *Paintings can be seen by applying to the Society after 9:30AM; closed Su. 8 John Adam St., WC2.*

19 **Adelphi Theatre.** Paternal devotion created the Adelphi, built in 1806 by John Scott to help launch his daughter's acting career. From 1837 to 1845, many of Charles Dickens' novels were performed here. But a real drama took place out front in 1897, when leading actor William Terris was shot by a lunatic. The theatre's simple interior, with its straight lines and angles and deep orange paneling, dates from extensive remodeling in 1930. Today the Adelphi is the home of popular musicals. *Strand, WC2. 836-7611*

20 **Vaudeville Theatre.** (1870, CJ Phipps) Completely refurbished in 1969, this is one of the most delightful theatres in London, with an elegant gold and cream decor, plum covered seats and a beautiful chandelier in the foyer. The Vaudeville has many long runs to its credit, including the first performances of Ibsen's *Hedda Gabler,* Barrie's *Quality Street,* and between 1954 and 1960, a record run of Julian Slade's *Salad Days. Strand, WC2. 836-9987*

21 **Stanley Gibbons International.** The largest stamp shop in the world and naturally the shop for British and Commonwealth stamps. There are 2 huge floors of stamps, albums, hinges, magnifying glasses and Stanley Gibbons stamp catalogues, and stamp auctions are held regularly. *Open M 10AM-5:30PM, Tu-F 9AM-5:30PM, Sa 10AM-1PM. 399 Strand, WC2. 836-8444*

22 **Strand Stamps.** Three stamp companies in one building, all nice to young collectors as well as those looking for the finest and the rarest. *Open M-F 10AM-5PM, Sa 10AM-2PM. 79 Strand, WC2. 836-2579*

23 **Shell-Mex House.** (1931, Messrs Joseph) Beyond Adam Street, the vista changes dramatically to the cold white bulk of Shell-Mex House and its mantelpiece clock larger than Big Ben, ticking away the time. The immense building stretches from the Strand all the way to the Embankment. The Strand front of red brick and stone is all that remains of the Hotel Cecil, once the largest hotel in Europe (800 rooms). It was built in 1886 and demolished in 1930 to make way for this fortress of offices. The front is best seen from the other side of the river on the South Bank, a favorite view for theatregoers during intermissions at the National Theatre. *Strand, WC2.*

THE SAVOY

24 **Savoy Hotel.** *Deluxe.* In 1246, Henry II presented Peter, Earl of Richmond with a splendid piece of land overlooking the Thames. Here the Earl, who was also the Count of Savoy, built a magnificent palace where he entertained beautiful French women, organized politically advantageous marriages into the Anglo-Norman aristocracy and created a feudal center of considerable power. The grand manor later came into the hands of **Simon de Montfort,** founder of the House of Commons, and the man who led the barons in their revolt against Henry III. The illustrious past of this palatial site reached a fiery climax when a mob of angry peasants under the leadership of **Wat Tyler** stormed the Palace, destroying everything of value, ripping tapestries into shreds, flattening the silver and gold, and finally burning the Palace to the ground. The flames were watched in the Tower of London by fourteen-year-old Richard II, who was planning a swift and ruthless repression of the peasant revolt. But the site seems to have been ripe for palaces, and in 1889 a luxurious hotel was built by entrepreneur **Richard d'Oyly Carte,** discoverer of Gilbert and Sullivan for whom he had built the still-existing Savoy Theatre on the same piece of land. The 7 story building took 5 years to complete and combined American technology with European luxury—the concrete walls electric lights and 24 hour elevators

THE STRAND & FLEET STREET

were all new to hotel construction in England. Tiny, bearded d'Oyly Carte outdid Peter of Savoy: he persuaded **Cesar Ritz** to be his manager and **Escoffier** his chef (his pots and pans are still at the hotel). Johann Strauss played waltzes in the restaurant and Caruso sang. After having tea here, Arnold Bennet wrote his *Grand Babylon Hotel.* Whistler stayed here with his dying wife, sketching her and the river from his room. The first martini in the world was mixed in the **American Bar**, which has long been a favorite meeting place of Americans in London. The Savoy has now fully recovered from its decline in the 1950s and 1960s, and now wins hearts with its Art Deco marble bathrooms and their dazzling chrome fixtures, afternoon tea in the Thames Foyer, and Edwardian riverside suites, which are filled with antiques, arched mirrors, fine plasterwork, Irish linen sheets and a gracious atmosphere which even kings and queens cannot resist. These days, the restaurants at the Savoy serve more American tourists and English merchant bankers than dukes and duchesses, but the food is no doubt better for it. *Strand, WC2. 836-4343*

Within the Hotel are:

Savoy River Room. ★★/★★★ $$$ With fine views through the trees to the Thames, this spacious salmon-pink room rates as one of the prettiest places in London to dine. The elegant setting is now matched with worthy cuisine, and if you have the set lunch Sundays through Thursdays, you can expect to eat well, feel rather grand and survive the arrival of the bill. Regulars recommend the house specialty of creamed *finnan haddie* garnished with a poached egg and the ribs of beef. One way to feel truly right with the world is to have breakfast in this sumptuous setting: freshly squeezed fruit juices, eggs, bacon, kippers, toast and marmalade and the famous Savoy coffee, surrounded by cabinet ministers, opera singers, tycoons and movie stars who have made this the place for the business breakfast in London, a city where that workaholic institution has been slow to get established. *Open for breakfast M-Sa 7-10:30AM, Su 8-10:30AM; lunch daily 12:30-2:30PM; dinner M-Sa 7:30-11:30PM, Su 7-10:30PM. 836-4343*

Savoy Grill Room. ★★★ $$$ Certain French food critics give the Grill Room a thumbs down, a mistake hard to understand. Under the talented guidance of young chef **Keith Stanley,** this very English paneled room offers English classics prepared with a delicate touch and rare imagination. The daily specialties are good indeed—Tuesday is steak, kidney and oyster pudding, Friday is cassoulet of lamb and haricot beans or smoked haddock and sea bass pie—and you can get turbot, clam and leek pie, Dover sole, grilled salmon trout or roast saddle of lamb all week. More sophisticated palates may prefer the *nouvelle* dishes like pheasant filled with a puree of morilles, cooked with red, green and yellow peppers in a pastry case, or strips of sole steamed with horseradish cream and lobster essence.

This is first-rate cooking from a thoughtful chef, served immaculately. There are some excellent wines at the lower end of the price scale and special pre- and after-theatre dinner menus which are a good value here in theatreland. *Open M-F 12:30-2:30PM, 6-11:15PM; Sa 6-11:15PM. 836-4343, ext. 2149, 2150*

24 **Savoy Theatre.** (1881, CJ Phipps) Built by **Richard d'Oyly Carte** for the staging of Gilbert and Sullivan operas and financed in part from the proceeds of *HMS Pinafore,* the *Sorcer* and *Pirates of Penzance.* D'Oyly Carte wisely purchased a derelict plot of land on the site of the old Savoy Manor and built the first theatre (and first public building) in the world to be lit by electricity, providing his audiences with opulence and comfort as well as wonderful comic operas. Today the theatre seems less prominent on the scale of comfort, but the productions are almost always long-running successes. Tickets usually cost slightly more than at other West End theatres, but if you are in the mood for a small and worthwhile splurge, book a pre- or after-theatre table in the Grill Room and tickets at the Savoy Theatre. The theatre is located on Savoy Court, adjacent to the Strand entrance to the Savoy Hotel. The court is the only road in England with driving on the right, allowed by a special Act of Parliament to provide easier access for carriages delivering their passengers to the theatre. *Savoy Ct., Strand, WC2. 836-8888*

Disheartening as it is to discover that hotels which endear themselves with their unique histories and strong characters are part of a **Hotel Group,** that is the way of the world. One can only hope that the Groups are run with proper respect for the history, location, originality and personality of each hotel within them. The most prestigious in the world is the **Savoy Group,** which in the capital alone owns the **Savoy Hotel** in the heart of theatreland and overlooking the Thames; **Claridge's** in Mayfair, which is a favorite of royalty and was acquired and rebuilt by Richard d'Oyly Carte in 1896; the **Connaught,** located on residential Carlos Place in Mayfair between Grosvenor and Berkeley Squares, which was conceived as a London home for the landed gentry and has long been considered one of the world's most desirable hotels; and the **Berkeley** off Piccadilly, acquired by d'Oyly Carte in order to tempt the brilliant hotelier George Reeves-Smith into his company, and now the only hotel in London to boast its own rooftop swimming pool and cinema. In 1970, the Savoy Group acquired the Paris jewel **L'hotel Lancaster** in the rue de Berri just off the Champs Elysees, a charming country chateau in the heart of Paris. Other members of the Group include 2 quintessentially English restaurants: **Wilton's** on Jermyn Street (see **St. James's**), managed by the Savoy since 1983, and famous for oysters, fish,

lobsters and game; and **Simpson's-in-the-Strand**, a bustling restaurant which has been serving Scotch beef and English lamb for 150 years (described below). And if seductive hotel living leaves you with signs of *mal du foie*, there is a health hydro, **Forest Mere**, an hour from London by train or car, which is an oasis of country scenery, swimming, tennis and treatments located in an Edwardian mansion.

SIMPSON'S
IN-THE-STRAND

25 **Simpson's-in-the-Strand.** ★ ★ ★ (Ambiance) ★ $$ (Food) Only a meal at Eton or Harrow could be more English than this, with tables arranged in long rows, dark wood paneling, and, at lunchtime during the week, a sea of dark-suited men watching as joints of beef and lamb are wheeled to their tables on elaborate silver-domed trolleys and carved to their specifications. The quality of the beef is praiseworthy, but the vegetables are limp and rank somewhere between school and prison food, and the only way to avoid feeling rushed is to order one course at a time. Approach a meal here as an authentic English experience, and enjoy the Stilton, treacle tart and house claret. *Open M-Sa 12-2:45PM, 6-9:45PM. 100 Strand, WC2. 836-9112*

26 **Strand Palace Hotel.** *Inexpensive.* Opposite the Savoy, this hotel is more hotel than palace, but the location is hard to beat, the price makes it one of the best values in London, and with the money you save, you can walk across the street and have an elegant lunch in the Savoy River Room overlooking the Thames. The Strand Palace doesn't have room service, but does have those very English electric kettles in all 775 rooms, a 24 hour coffee shop (rare in London), a pizzeria and a cocktail bar. *369 Strand, WC2. 836-8080*

27 **Lyceum.** ★ ★ ★ $ The tap room downstairs serves real ale and tranquility; the ground floor serves good salads, terrines and tarts; and the bar upstairs has views over the Strand. A passage leads from the pub to a disco and club, which was once the Lyceum Theatre, where theatre history was furthered in great performances by Henry Irving and Ellen Terry. *Open M-Sa 11AM-3PM, 5:30-11PM. 354 Strand, WC2. 836-7155*

28 **Queen's Chapel of the Savoy.** (1820, Sir Robert Smirke) A haven of tranquility belonging to the Duke of Lancaster, who is in fact the Queen. (The reigning monarch keeps this title, which goes back to Henry IV, who was Duke of Lancaster before he usurped the throne from Richard II.) Erected in the late perpendicular style in 1505 on the grounds of the Savoy Palace, the chapel has been used by royalty since the reign of Henry VII. The present building is almost entirely Victorian, rebuilt by **Sir Robert Smirke** in 1820 and restored by his brother **Sydney Smirke** after a fire in 1864. The original chapel was once part of the Order of St. John (1510-16), and since 1937, it has been part of the Order of Chivalry, the Royal Victorian Order. The heraldic plaque in the vestibule is made of gilded marrow seeds crushed into the seductive forms of the leopards of England. The stained glass window commemorates **Richard d'Oyly Carte (1844-1901)**, and another window is in memory of **Queen Mary**. The window with heraldic designs of the Royal Victorian Order was designed in part by King George VI. *Open Tu-F 11:30AM-3:30PM; closed Aug and Sept. Savoy Hill, WC2.*

29 **Waterloo Bridge.** Designed by **Sir Giles Scott**, completed in 1939 and opened in 1945. The Regency bridge it replaced was opened by the Prince Regent on the second anniversary of the Battle of Waterloo, and the name of the bridge was changed in honor of the great battle. On the right of the bridge is the only floating police station in London, manned by the Thames Division, which patrols the 54 mile precinct of river in police duty boats 24 hours a day and deals with ship accidents, flood warnings, aimless barges and bodies which make their way into the river. *Victoria Embankment, WC2.*

30 **Cleopatra's Needle.** The pink granite obelisk, rising 68 feet high and weighing 180 tons, was created around 1500BC by **Thotmes III** in Egypt on the edge of the Nile. Cleopatra had nothing to do with the obelisk, but it was named after the Queen when it was moved to Alexandria, the royal city of Cleopatra, during the Greek dynasty in 12BC. The Viceroy of Egypt gave the obelisk to Britain in 1819, and it was placed here by the river in 1878. The pedestal contains treasures the Victorians believed worthy of saving for posterity, including Bradshaw's *Railway Guide*, photographs of 12 pretty Victorian girls (and a photo of Queen Victoria), coins, china, bibles and a case of cigars. The sphinx at the base, still scarred by bomb damage suffered during World War II, faces in the wrong direction for sphinxes, according to sphinx experts. The obelisk is the companion to the one in Central Park in New York. *Victoria Embankment, WC2.*

Cruft's Dog Show, the world's most famous dog show, is held annually at Earl's Court in London. Its founder, **Charles Cruft,** entered the canine business in 1876, selling *dog cakes* in Holborn. In 1878, he was asked to run a dog stand at the Paris Exhibition. The first Cruft's Show opened in 1891 at the Royal Agricultural Hall in Islington. Now more than 90 shows later, 13,000 dogs enter the 3 day long competition. The winner receives a *dogly* £ 250, *Chum* dog chow for life and world-wide fame. The 1986 winner was *Ginger Christmas Carol*, an Airedale Terrier owned by Mrs. Alexandra Livraghi.

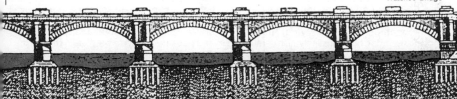

Waterloo Bridge

31 Somerset House. (1776-86, Sir William Chambers; 1830-35, Sir Robert Smirke; 1854, Sir James Pennethorne) One of London's premier neo-classical buildings stands facing the Thames east of Waterloo Bridge. Beloved by Londoners, the stately Somerset is one of the few Georgian buildings still gracing the riverside. Like the old Adelphi, Chambers' Somerset House rose out of the Thames before the construction of the Embankment. The great palace of the Protector Somerset (1547-72), with its magnificent chapel by **Inigo Jones** and riverside gallery by **John Webb,** stood on this site, and was at one time lived in by Elizabeth I when she was a princess and the queens of James I, Charles I and Charles II. The present building has enjoyed a less illustrious existence, housing administrative offices and institutions and the Registry of Births, Deaths and Marriages. The **State Rooms** in the north wing are being leased to the **Courtauld Institute,** and in 1988, the world famous Courtauld collection on Woburn Square (see **High Holborn**) will be brought here. From the other side of the river, Somerset House has a dignified magnificence more worthy of the outstanding paintings of the Courtauld than wills and testaments. *Strand, WC2. 438-6622*

32 King's College. Founded in 1829 by the Duke of Wellington, Archbishops and 30 bishops of the Church of England, and part of the University of London since 1898. Adjoins the east wing of Somerset House. *Strand, WC2.*

33 Statue of Isambard King Brunel. (1877, Baron Marochetti) Son of the equally famous Marc Isambard Brunel, he was the brilliant engineer who designed the Great Western Railway and built the *Great Western,* the first steamship to make regular voyages between Britain and America. *Victoria Embankment and Temple Place, WC2.*

34 Roman Bath. Tucked away down Strand Lane along the east side of Somerset House under a dark archway, this 15 foot enigma is certainly not Roman, possibly Tudor, but more likely 17th century. Built over a tributary of the River Fleet, it fills each day with 2,000 gallons of icy water which flow into a pipe and down into the Thames. David Copperfield used to take cold plunges here, but now the bath belongs to the National Trust and can be seen by appointment, although it is partially visible through a window. *5 Strand Ln., WC2. 633-5868*

35 St. Mary-le-Strand. (1718, James Gibbs) St. Mary-le-*Stranded* is the sadder, more apt name for this jewel of a church built on an island site and increasingly isolated by the widening of roads. The first major work by Scottish architect **James Gibbs** (St. Martin-in-the-Fields, the Redcliffe Camera at Oxford, the Senate House at Cambridge), St. Mary's dramatically combines styles—Ionic and Corinthian outside, Corinthian and Composite inside. As though in a self-fulfilling prophesy, the upper order contains the windows while the lower order is solid to keep out the noise from the street. In an act of continuing faith, the church is being restored. The splendid five-stage steeple, weakened by wartime bombing, pollution, traffic vibration and rusting iron clamps which bind the Portland stone, is being dismantled stone by stone. The hours are erratic because of the restoration, but if you get in, the barrel vault has ornate gilded and colored plasterwork. Thomas Becket was lay rector of the medieval church which stood here originally. The parents of Charles Dickens were married here. *Strand, WC2.*

36 Aldwych. The crescent, identified mainly by the name on the street wall, sweeps around an immense stone fortress occupied by **Australia House, India House** and **Bush House.** The word *Aldwych* is Danish and means *an outlying farm.* Its familiarity in London is enhanced by being the name of a Tube station and a theatre, the Aldwych, home of the Royal Shakespeare Company until 1982. *Between the Strand and Kingsway, WC2.*

37 Waldorf Hotel. *Expensive.* Old world charm, excellent service and a newly refurbished interior, with marble floors, crystal chandeliers, coral and white walls and palm trees and ferns. Tea in the **Palm Court Room** is one of London's greatest treats. You have a choice of Balijen India,

Lapsang Souchong China or the Waldorf's own blend of India Darjeeling, followed by an endless sequence of sandwiches, muffins, scones and clotted cream, pastries and cakes, accompanied all the while by a small combo playing *Sweet Georgia Brown* and *The Sunny Side of the Street*. *No reservations accepted, but jacket and tie are required. Aldwych, WC2. 836-2400*

38 **Bush House.** (1925-35, Helme and Corbett) *To the Friendship of English Speaking Peoples* is carved into the stonework of this vital building, which is the base of the **BBC External Services,** one of the most important broadcasting institutions in the western world. *Aldwych, WC2.*

COVENT GARDEN

A **Theatre Royal, Drury Lane.** (Seats 2,245) The present theatre is the fourth to stand on the site since 1662, twice destroyed by fire and once demolished. *What sir,* said owner Sheridan as his life's work went up in flames, *may a man not warm his hands at his own fireside?* Few London theatres have so illustrious or lengthy a past as Drury Lane. Nell Gwynn made her debut in *Indian Queen* in 1665 with King Charles II in the audience. King George II was shot at in the theatre in 1716, and his grandson George III was shot at here in 1800. One of Gainsborough's favorite models, Mary Robinson, was discovered here by the Prince of Wales while playing Perdita in *A Winter's Tale* in 1779, and this is where the Duke of Clarence, later William IV, first saw Mrs. Jordan, the Irish actress who became his mistress and mother of his children. Drury Lane was also the scene of riots over higher admission prices and impromptu duels that spilled from the pit onto the stage. Today, it is the safer home of musicals, most recently *A Chorus Line, Sweeney Todd* and Joe Papp's *Pirates of Penzance.* Benjamin Wyatt modelled the present theatre after the

great theatre at Bordeaux in 1811. The portico was added in 1820 and the pillars came from Nash's Quadrant on Regent Street. The interior is a patchwork of grand Continental, heavy Victorian, Baroque and Edwardian styles. *Catherine St., WC2. 836-8108*

B **Brahms & Liszt.** ★ $ A close neighbor to the Royal Opera House, but the name is cockney slang for having had a few too many. Popular, crowded and lively, generous first courses and salads, 5 copious dishes of the day and a reasonable selection of wines. *Reservations suggested for lunch. Open M-Sa 11:30AM-2:45PM, 5:30-11PM. 19 Russell St., WC2. 240-3661*

C **Luigi's.** ★ ★ $$ Crowded Italian bistro much loved by actors and singers, whose signed photographs line the walls. The food is authentic and mostly very good, especially the cannelloni. *Open M-Sa 12:15-3PM, 6-11:30PM. 15 Tavistock St., WC2. 240-1795*

D **Thomas De Quincey's.** ★ ★ $$$ French cuisine served in the original 19th century house where De Quincey wrote

Confessions of an Opium Eater. The imaginative food is prepared by Mitterand's former chef; the wine list is extensive, if a bit overpriced. *Open M-F 12:30-3PM, 6-11:15PM; Sa 6-11:30PM. 36 Tavistock St., WC2. 240-3773*

E **Cafe du Jardin** ★ ★ $$ This busy, unpretentious restaurant serves ambitious French regional specialties in an indoor garden. The food is an admirable mix of classic and *nouvelle,* with fish and game prepared with imagination and generosity. The cheeseboard with Brie, chaume and bleu d'Auvergne is the best of France, and the two-course pre-theatre menu is the best in the area. *Open M-Sa 12-2:30PM, 6-11:30PM. 28 Wellington St., WC2. 836-3796*

F **Blake's** ★ $$ It can get too crowded for comfort, but the self-service buffet and live music have devoted followings among the PR and advertising *beau monde.* Avoid Friday evenings unless your main interest is meeting someone. *Open M-Sa 11:30AM-3PM, 5:30-11PM. Wellington St., WC2. 836-5298*

G **Penhaligons.** A dreamy shop filled with silver mirrors and dressing table treasures The perfume is from the world of *Brideshead Revisited,* with bottles as beautiful as the scents, and for the moment at least, not available in every drug store and airport in the world. *Bluebell* and *Jubilee* are especially delicious. *Open M-F 10AM-6PM, Sa 10AM-5PM. 41 Wellington Street, WC2. 836-2150.*

H **Orso's.** ★ ★ $$ A flourishing first-class Italian restaurant with fried zucchini flowers and paper-thin garlic bread surrounded by actors and actresses, opera singers and the dress circle crowd. *Open daily 12PM-12AM. 27 Wellington St., WC2. 240-5269*

I **Joe Allen's.** ★ ★ $$ The doyen of American restaurants in London and still so popular that you can wait for a table even if you have made reservations. Convenient for Covent Garden and West End theatres. Good burgers, salads, chili, brownies. *Open M-Sa 12PM-1AM, Su 12PM-12AM. 13 Exeter St., WC2. 836-0651*

J **Youth Hostel Association Shop.** Great equipment for skiing, climbing and walking. *Open M-Sa 9:30AM-5:30PM. 14 Southampton St., WC2. 240-1358*

K **Virago Bookshop.** All the outstanding books which Virago has reissued in the last 5 years and a considerable selection of excellent history, biography, poetry and second-hand books. One of the most attractive bookshops in London. *Open M-F 10AM-7PM, Sa 10AM-6PM. 34 Southampton St., WC2. 240-6638*

COVENT GARDEN

L **Jubilee Market.** 180 stalls where you can find homemade silk lingerie for a fraction of the price you would pay in a regular shop, handknit sweaters, pottery, handcarved wooden salad bowls, etc. Poke around and the cream will rise to the top. The prices seem particularly good after shopping at the smart boutiques in the area. There are even a few fruit and vegetable stalls for old time's sake. *Antiques M 9AM-5PM; general Tu-Sa 9AM-5PM.*

M **Covent Garden Market.** Immortalized by a cockney flower girl named Eliza Doolittle who sold violets to rich opera goers here. Today the market has more in common with the luxury tastes of Henry Higgins than with the cockney vendors who can carry a tune. A brilliant example of urban survival, the restored central market is a tantalizing structure of iron and glass roofs covering a large square. It has dramatically revitalized this part of London, providing shops, restaurants, cafes and pubs. At the same time, it has freed the area of the wholesale fruit and flower market which for all its sentimental charm clogged this part of London mercilessly. The shops are mainly boutique-size branches of existing shops, but the selection is often *créme de la créme.* There is an antiques market within the piazza on Mondays, and a crafts market on Tuesdays through Saturdays.

Within the Market are:

Edwina Carroll. Unique clothes in a unique shop specializing in collector's quality and hand knit sweaters. *Open M-Sa 10AM-6PM. Unit 16. 836-9873*

Hobb's. Terrific shoes at affordable prices. *Open M-Sa 10:30AM-6:30PM. Unit 17.*

S. Fisher's. Classy cashmere and shetland sweaters, fine leather shoes and Barbour raincoats. The best of British design and as tweedy as Henry Higgins himself. *Open M-W 10:30AM-6:30PM, Th-Sa 11AM-7PM, Su 12-5PM. Unit 18. 836-2576*

Strangeways. Remember the cow in the bathtub butter dish? It was from Strangeways, who has also given legs to egg cups and humor to pottery. The teapots are funny and wonderful and worth lugging back home. *Open M-Sa 10AM-7PM. Unit 19. 379-7675*

Crusting Pipe ★ ★ $$. Candlelight, sawdust floor and a limited menu. Treat yourself to the smoked salmon and salad, or if you are really hungry, the game pie and potatoes. Excellent English cheeses and good wines. *Open M-Sa 11:30AM-3PM, 5:30-11PM. Unit 27. 836-1415*

Doll's House. The kind of dolls you dream about and see in Kate Greenwood books. Some look like museum pieces and some are. *Open M-Sa 10AM-8PM. Unit 29. 379-7243*

Pollock's Toy Theatres. Full of old toys and fascinating cardboard toy theatres. Also some pricey antique toys. *Open M-Sa 10AM-7PM. Unit 44. 379-7866*

N **Cafe Deli.** ★ $ Pastrami sandwiches served under the beautiful wrought iron canopy in the Piazza of Covent Garden. Light and inexpensive. The coffee should be better. *Open daily 9AM-7:15PM. Covent Garden Piazza, WC2.*

N **Creperie.** ★ $ Sweet and savory pancakes served at tables on the cobblestones around St. Paul's, Covent Garden. *Open daily 10AM-11:30PM. Covent Garden Piazza, WC2. 836-2137*

O **St. Paul's, Covent Garden.** (1633, Inigo Jones) When the thrifty 4th Earl of Bedford was developing Covent Garden, he asked Inigo Jones to design an economical church *not much better than a barn.* Jones complied, creating what he called the *handsomest barn in Europe.* The red brick church with a pitched roof, overhanging eaves and the famous Tuscan portico was the setting for the opening scene in Shaw's *Pygmalion.* It was gutted by fire in 1795 and carefully restored by Philip Hardwick. Known as the *actor's* church because of its close association with the theatre, there are numerous plaques commemorating actors, actresses and playwrights inside. *The Piazza, Covent Garden, WC2.*

P **Palms Pasta on the Piazza.** ★ ★ $ Light, airy and vastly superior to the pasta restaurants proliferating all over London. Everything is fresh and delicious. Start with the *bagna cauda* (raw vegetables served with a warm anchovy and walnut sauce). *Open M-Sa 12-11:30PM. 39 King St., WC2. 240-2939*

Q **Calabash.** ★ ★ $$ Exotic and delicious African food, with a laid back atmosphere that is distinctly appealing after the fashionable race of most of Covent Garden. Masks, head dresses and batik cloths decorate the walls and tables. Ghanaian chicken ground nut stew, Tanzanian beef stew with green bananas and coconut cream, Senegalese fish and excellent Morrocan and Algerian wines. *Open M-F 12:30-2:15PM, 6:30-10:30PM; Sa 6:30-10:30PM. 38 King St., WC2. 836-1976*

R **Moss Bros.** Known as Boss Bros. If you are invited to Ascot or a royal wedding, you will have to stop off here first for a morning coat and a top hat. Even the grandest gentlemen in town have been known to rent their dress wear here. Worth a look around. *Open M-Sa 9-5:30PM, Th until 7PM. Bedford St., WC2. 240-4567*

S **Naturally British.** Hard to resist creations by British designers and craftsmen, including clothes, furniture, pottery, table linens, pewter, baskets, toys and food. If you are looking for presents which are not available in department stores the world over, this is worth a visit. *Open M-Sa 10:30-7PM. 13 New Row, WC2. 240-0551*

T **Tourment d'Amour.** ★ ★ ★ $$ Sophisticated cooking has put the restaurant on the serious food-lover's list of important London restaurants. This is *nouvelle cuisine* at its best, and there is nothing which does not fall into the category of *beautiful to look at and difficult to execute,* including pastry boats filled with Toulouse sausage or chicken liver and port, grilled veal in a wonderful madeira sauce, and for dessert, an almond tart with cream and rum or a delicious white chocolate mousse. Eating here is an event which should not be rushed. *Open M-F 12:30-2PM, 6:30-11:30PM; Sa 6:30-11:30PM. 19 New Row, WC2. 240-5348*

U **Porters.** ★ ★ S$ This deservedly successful restaurant serves traditional English fare—pies and delicious nursery puddings like jam roly-poly and sherry trifle. High quality, honest prices and welcoming and fun for babies and toddlers. *Open M-Sa 12-3PM, 5:30-10:30PM. 17 Henrietta St., WC2. 836-6466*

V **Rules.** ★ ★ $$$ Nearly 200 years old, it is a museum of London's literary and theatrical *beaumonde.* The Prince of Wales, later Edward VII, and Lillie Langtry drank champagne behind a special door on the first floor, and Dickens had a regular table across the room. Today, Rules is a compulsory stop for visitors to London. The secret to a good meal here is selective ordering. Stick to the very English: Scotch beef with Yorkshire pudding, pheasant and grouse in season and weekday specials. A pre-theatre dinner is served from 6-11:30PM. *Open M-F 12:15-2:30PM, 6-11:30PM; Sa 6:15-10:45PM. 35 Maiden Ln., WC2. 836-5314*

W **Peppermint Park.** ★ $$ Bright decor—shocking pinks and greens with a lot of chrome—and an American menu—huge salads, burgers, omelettes, tacos and cakes and ice cream. Dancing from 12-2AM. It helps to be young. *Open M-Sa 12PM-1:30AM; bar and dancing until 2AM. 13 Upper St. Martin's Ln., WC2. 836-5234*

X **Cafe Pelican.** ★ ★ $$ Except for the stupidity of the licensing laws over which the cafe has no power, this is the best—and closest to authentic—brasserie in London. It opens early, closes late and seats 250, so reservations usually are not necessary. The menu meets just about any need, be it a *cafe complet* or sea bass cooked in seaweed and served with a fabulous *beurre blanc.* The set menu, the service and the setting may make you reluctant to try elsewhere during your stay in London. *Open daily 11AM-12:30AM. 45 St. Martin's Ln., WC2. 379-0309*

Y **Sheekey's.** ★ ★ $$ One of London's oldest and best loved fish restaurants, tucked away on St. Martin's Court alongside Wyndham's and the Albery Theatre. Immaculate lobster, salmon, turbot, Dover sole, skate in black butter, mussels in cream sauce, oysters in season, fish cakes and first-class vegetables. Have a dozen oysters with a bottle of house wine or a full meal at the long oyster bar. *Open M-Sa 12:30-2:30PM, 6-11:30PM. 28-32 St. Martin's Ln., WC2. 240-2565*

Z **Cork and Bottle** ★ ★ $ The best wine bar for wine, with more than 140 different kinds, including precious and rare and a staff intelligent enough to appreciate as well as decant the ones which require it. This is also one of the best wine bars for food, with mainly cold dishes that taste beautifully fresh. *Open M-Sa 11AM-2:45PM, 5:30-10:45PM. 44-46 Cranbourne St., WC2. 734-7807*

AA **Poons.** ★ ★ $ Rightly if frantically popular Cantonese restaurant specializing in wind-dried (salted) meats, especially duck and sausage. The endless menu also includes fish dishes—steamed scallops mussels in black bean sauce, stewed eel with garlic. *Open M-Sa 12-11:30PM 4 Leicester St., WC2. 437-1528*

BB **Chez Solange.** ★ ★ $ Popular with dedicated music lovers fortifying themselves for an evening in the Gods—the cheapest and highest tickets at the Royal Opera House and English National Opera. The bar backs onto the restaurant and offers great wedges of pâté and cheese. *Open M-Sa 11AM-3PM, 5:30-11PM. 11 St. Martin's Ct., WC2. 240-0245*

CC **Beotys** ★ ★ $ An old Covent Garden favorite and one of the oldest Greek restaurants in town (it opened the year World War II ended). Charming, competent waiters, delicious dolmades and succulent lamb. *Open M-Sa 12-2:30PM, 5:30-11:30PM. 79 St. Martin's Ln., WC2. 836-8768*

DD **Grimes.** ★ ★ $$ Offbeat and modest *Cold Fish Cafe* with some excellent seafood dishes. Try the fish soup or the smoked fish platter with a half-pint tankard of champagne. *Open M-Sa 12-3PM, 5:30-11:30PM 6 Garrick St., WC2. 836-7008*

EE **Inigo Jones.** ★ ★ ★ $$$ Chef **Paul Gayler** is one of the stars of the London culinary firmament, creating first-class French cuisine in this converted stained-glass workshop. Gayler's touch is in the sauces, with hints of curry, orange, mint and nutmeg adding just the right *nouvelle* to the cuisine. The portions are smallish but seductively arranged, and the minor details are given major attention—4 kinds of bread, vegtables to suit each entree and excellent cheeses The set lunch and pre-theatre menu (served between 5:30 and 7PM) are an exceptional value. *Open M-F 12:30-2:30PM, 5:30-11:30PM, Sa 5:30-11:30PM. 14 Garrick St., WC2. 836-6465*

FF **Stanfords.** The world's largest collection of maps, guides, charts, atlases and travel books. Your trip to the British Isles should begin here, and if maps are your thing, you will have difficulty getting any further. David Livingston had his maps drawn here, and world-class mountain climbers buy theirs here. *Open M-F 9AM-6PM, Sa 10AM-5PM. 12-14 Long Acre, WC2. 836-1321*

GG **Sanctuary.** One of the few drawbacks to traveling is the feeling that you are getting increasingly lumpish and unhealthy from all the extra meals and lack of exercise. Some dedicated travelers continue to jog or swim, but for a woman in London, the Sanctuary is one of the most idyllic and essential indulgences. For less than $25 a day you can restore your spirits and your health in this exotic haven, which includes a sauna, a Turkish steamroom, a fabulous swimming pool, a jacuzzi and a sun bed. Shampoo, conditioner, towels, soap, body lotion and cologne are provided free of charge. Indulge further with *Top to Toe* beauty treatments, including a massage, a facial and a healthy and delicious lunch in the food bar. *Open M-F 10AM-10PM, Sa 10AM-6PM, Su 12-8PM. 11 Floral St., WC2. 240-9635*

HH **Paul Smith.** Two shops next door to each other run by the classiest designer in Britain for the English gentleman with a stately home on the horizon. Shop No. 1 is tweedy and Ralph Laurenish; shop No. 2 is several shades more daring. *44 Floral Street. 379-7133*

II **Royal Opera House.** (Seats 2,154) Three different theatres have stood on this site since 1732. The great dome and regal red, gold and cream auditorium you see today is **Sir Edward Barry's** 1858 design. The frieze, *Tragedy and Comedy* by **Flaxman,** under the portico was salvaged from a fire at the theatre on the site in 1855. In 1946, Covent Garden became the national home of the Royal Opera and Ballet Companies. Some of the greatest names in opera have played in this lavish setting, including Patti, Nellie Melba, Caruso, Gobbi and Maria Callas. *Covent Garden, WC2. 240-1066; 24 hour recorded information, 240-1911*

JJ **Interlude de Tabaillau.** ★ ★ $$$ Closer to the Royal Opera House than its new dressing rooms, this sophisticated French restaurant is packed by day with publishers and media folk and by night with music lovers accustomed to the best seats in the house. The food can be uneven, but when it is good, it is very good. *Open M-F 12-2PM, 7-11:30PM; Sa 7-11:30PM. 7-8 Bow St., WC2. 379-6473*

KK **Fielding.** *Inexpensive.* A rare hotel in London: small, inexpensive, quiet and family run. It attracts performers from the Royal Opera House a stone's throw away and private celebrities like Graham Greene who are drawn by the discreet charm and perfect location. The rooms are pretty modest—most have showers instead of baths—but the pedestrianized street spares you from the sounds of cars during the night. Ideal if you are a music-lover or theatregoer. The hotel is named after **Henry Fielding,** the author of *Tom Jones* and a magistrate at Bow Street Court nearby. *4 Broad Ct., Bow St., WC2. 836-8305*

LL **Glasshouse.** Objects of art made in glass. The small pitchers with wings are exquisite. *Open M-F 10AM-5:30PM; Sa 11AM-4:30PM. 65 Long Acre, WC2. 836-9785*

MM **Magno's Brasserie.** ★ ★ $$ Not a brasserie at all, but a popular, well-run restaurant which has a highly original menu and a legion of faithful followers. Set menu at lunch and a highly recommended pre-theatre menu served between 6-7:30PM. *Open M-F 12-2:30PM, 6-11:30PM; Sa 6-11:30PM. 65A Long Acre, WC2. 836-6077*

NN **Cafe des Amis du Vin** ★ ★ $ A welcome and popular bistro tucked away in a narrow alley behind the Royal Opera House. The basement bar feels *vrais Pari-sianne* and offers *Boudin noir,* a *plat du jour* and a good selection of French and German wines. *Open M-Sa 11:30AM-11:30PM. 11-14 Hanover Pl., WC2. 379-3444*

OO **Ajimura.** ★ $$ A versatile and relaxed Japanese restaurant that prepares *sashimi* (raw fish), *sushi* (raw fish with rice), *tempura, sukiyaki, shabu-shabu* and an endless variety of set meals and menu specials. *Reservations suggested for lunch and dinner. Open M-F 12-3PM, 6-11PM; Sa 6-11PM. 51-53 Shelton St., WC2. 240-0178*

PP **Neal Street Restaurant.** ★ ★ $$ Owned by design visionary **Sir Terence Conran** and managed by his ebullient brother-in-law **Antonio Carlucci,** this sleek and tasteful restaurant features an eclectic menu of fine English, French and Italian food and occasional treasures—white truffles from Piedmont, wild mushrooms from autumnal forests. The pictures on loan from Conran's friend and gallery owner Kasmin are for sale, which puts the truffle prices in a new perspective. *Open M-F 12:30-2:30PM, 7:30-11PM. 26 Neal St., WC2. 836-8368*

QQ **Neal's Yard.** A mouthwatering little utopia tucked in between Monmouth Street and Short's Garden, with a bakery, grocery store, fruit seller and coffee shop. You can buy English farm cheeses in the dairy and dried nuts and fruit, spices and teas in the grocery store, and you can choose between quiches, pizzas and cakes, to take home or to eat upstairs in the informal and attractive tea room in the bakery. The atmosphere in Neal's Yard is relaxed, studentish and appealing, a nice change from the tourist and *nouveau* glamor of other parts of Covent Garden. *Neal's Yard, WC2.*

RR **Mon Plaisir.** ★ ★ ★ $$ Few restaurants in France are as authentic as this beloved place which looks like a set from a Pagnol film and serves the classics—*steak-frites, boeuf bourguinion,* perfect salads, cheeses and fresh French bread. Daily specialties are chalked up on a blackboard. The crowds at lunchtime keep returning for good reason—the food, the exceptional value and the spirited service. *Open M-F 12-2:15PM, 6-11:15PM; Sa 6-11:15PM. 21 Monmouth St., WC2. 836-7243*

SS **The Ivy.** ★ $$ Long established and popular with the theatre crowd; with classic and simple Italian and French cuisine. The special three-course lunch or dinner is a good value. *Open M-F 12-3PM, 6:15-11PM; Sa 6:15-11PM. 1 West St., WC2. 836-4751*

TT **Kettner's.** ★ ★ $ Three dining rooms: one modern and jazzy, with glass, chrome and futurist prints; the others elegant and Edwardian, with beautiful gilded ceilings and crisp white linen. This is the most attractive restaurant in Soho, with more than a touch of class. The champagne bar has 25 kinds of bubbly. Steaks, burgers, chili, salads and pizzas. *Open daily 11-12AM. 29 Romilly St., W1. 437-6437*

UU **Wheelers.** ★ ★ $$ Sit at the oyster bar in the busy downstairs saloon and have delicious fresh oysters from Wheeler's own beds, or climb the rickety staircase to the small upstairs rooms for Scotch lobster or Dover sole, all meeting newly impeccably high standards. *Open M-Sa 12:30-2:30PM, 6-10:45PM. 19 Old Compton Rd., W1. 437-2706*

39 **Statue of WE Gladstone** (1905, Sir Hamo Thronycroft) The grand old man (1809-1998) looks out bravely onto the sea of uncaring traffic from the middle of the roadway where the Strand is rejoined by the Aldwych. Gladstone, a liberal statesman, was prime minister 4 times. He introduced educational reform (1870), the secret ballot (1872) and succeeded in carrying out the Reform Act of 1884. But he failed to gain support for a home rule for Ireland which would no doubt have made the history of the 20th century in these islands more tranquil. *Strand, WC2.*

40 **St. Clement Danes.** (1680-82, Sir Christopher Wren) Now the church of the Royal Air Force. Wren's oranges-and-lemons church (so called because the church's bells play the tune from the nursery rhyme *Oranges and Lemons*), with its **James Gibbs** steeple (1719), was blitzed during the Second World War and was skillfully rebuilt by **WAS Lloyd** in 1955. The floor is inlaid with slabs of Welsh slate carved with the 735 units of the RAF, and the rolls of honors contain the 125,000 men and women of the RAF who died in World War I and II. The original pulpit by **Grinling Gibbons** was shattered in the bombing and painstakingly pieced together from the fragments. The organ was a gift from members of the U.S. Air Force and there is a shrine to the USAF under the west gallery. Each March, oranges and lemons (*Say the Bells of St. Clements*) are distributed to the children of the parish in a special service. **Samuel Johnson** worshipped here and is now silenced in bronze behind the church, where he gazes nostalgically down the street he believed to be unequaled: Fleet Street. *Strand, WC2.*

41 **Royal Courts of Justice** (1874-82, GE Street) Better known as the **Law Courts**, this dramatic Gothic ramble of buildings, with a 514 foot frontage along the Strand, was built in a period of Victorian reorganization of the legal system and opened by Queen Victoria in 1882, with the power and glory of the law architecturally proclaimed. The main entrance is flanked by twin towers and slate roofs. Above the entrance on the left, **Solomon** holds his Temple and on the right is the founder of English law, **Alfred the Great.** The lofty **Great Hall** (23 feet long and 80 feet high) contains a monument to the architect **GE Street,** who, in the Victorian tradition of tutelage, was a pupil of George Gilbert Scott and teacher of Philip Webb and William Morris. There are 64 courts spreading over 7 miles of corridors and 1,000 rooms. They are reached by way of the hall, and when the courts are sitting (M-F 10:30AM-1PM, 2-4PM during legal terms), the public is admitted to the back 2 rows. The courts are worth a visit if you are interested in seeing the English justice system at work, visually enhanced by the wigged presence of judges and barristers and undisguised solicitors. Read the *Daily Lists* in the central hall to decide what appeals to you in the still faintly Dickensian world of probate, bankruptcy and divorce. You are free to enter any court except those marked *court in camera* or *chambers. Strand, WC2.*

42 **George Public House.** ★ ★ $ Named after George III (1760-1820) and once frequented by Dr. Johnson and Oliver Goldsmith, the author of the *Vicar of Wakefield.* The famous timbered tavern has one long beamed and cozy room which serves buffet lunches, salads, tarts and puddings. The excellent lunchtime restaurant upstairs is frequented by journalists, lawyers, the innocent, the guilty and the tourist. *Open M-Sa 11:30AM-3PM, 5:30-11PM; restaurant M-F 12-3PM. 213 Strand, WC2. 352-9238*

43 **Twinings.** Chinese mandarins guard the Georgian entrance to the narrowest shop in London, which is the oldest business still on its original site and the longest taxpayer in Westminster. The shop also contains the widest teapot in the world. **Thomas Twining** opened the shop in 1716 as Tom's Coffee House, and the shop has been selling tea ever since it became the national drink. Alas, you cannot drink a cup of tea here; you can only buy it. Small museum in the back of the shop. *Open M-F 9AM-5PM and Lord Mayor's Saturday (second Sa in Nov). 216 Strand, EC4.*

44 **Wig and Pen Club.** ★ ★ $$ As the name indicates, this is a private club for lawyers and journalists, located in a modest 17th century house which is the only building on the Strand that survived the Great Fire of 1666. You can have a look around before noon, and amazingly, if you

Royal Courts of Justice

produce your passport, you can obtain a free temporary membership, which is especially nice for visiting lawyers and journalists. The club has an all-day alcohol license. *229-230 Strand, EC4. 583-7255*

Summer in England means Wimbledon, the races at Ascot, the regatta at Henley and **Pimm's Cup,** a favorite drink at all these events since James Pimm concocted the famous **Pimm's No. 1** in the 1840s. His confection of gin, fruit liquers, herbs, spices and bitters is more popular than ever today. Pimm's Cup is simple to make: take one part Pimm's No. 1 and add 2 to 3 parts mixer, plenty of ice, a thin slice of lemon or lime and a swirl of cucumber ring. You can alter the sweetness of the drink by using soda water, tonic, ginger ale, lemonade—even champagne. And to be perfectly proper, serve it in a frosted pewter or silver mug, as it's done in clubland.

45 **Temple Bar Monument.** (1880, Horace Jones) The spiky griffin stands on the site of Sir Christopher Wren's fine 3 arched gateway, which was here from 1672 to 1878. Sadly, it was dismantled because it was obstructing traffic and was moved to Theobald's Park in Hertfordshire. The griffin is a mythical beast famous for its voracious appetite, and appropriately, it marks the boundary between the City of Westminster, impelled by restraint, and the City of London, inspired by acquisition. The Temple Bar's griffin also marks the end of the broad, dozy Strand and the beginning of the congested and lively Fleet Street. The figures on either side of the griffin are **Queen Victoria** and **Edward VIII,** Prince of Wales. Periodic and welcome rumors that the gate by Sir Christopher Wren will return persist. *Fleet St./Strand, EC4.*

46 **Fleet Street.** The medieval main street, which echoed the curve of the Thames before its embankment, was named after the River Fleet, which is now a covered stream conveyed through a sewer under Farringdon Street and New Bridge Street. Since 1500, Fleet Street has been a *street of ink*— Caxton's assistant set up his press on *Fletestrete* around 1500, and until the spring of 1986, when Rupert Murdoch moved *The Times* to the high-tech and highly fortified Wapping, it looked as if it would continue for a few hundred more years. This lively, crowded street has a glorious and eclectic mix of styles and levels and a tremendous skyline defined by the tower and pinnacles of the Law Courts, the tower of St. Dunstan-in-the-West and the dome of St. Paul's Cathedral. One hopes that the editorial offices of the nation's newspapers will remain here. There could be no greater shame than the famous and infamous *street of shame* becoming a ghost town.

Most British **newspapers** are still printed on the streets and courts around Fleet Street. Traffic in the area is always heavy, with large lorries delivering gargantuan rolls of paper by day, and smaller vans and trucks driving at life threatening speed between 11PM and midnight, carrying the first editions of daily newspapers to train stations and airports. Late London editions are printed until 3AM. The first evening papers—the main one is the *Evening Standard*—begin appearing on the newsstands by lunchtime.

47 **Child's Bank.** The oldest bank in London (1671) and the inspiration for Tellson's Bank in Dicken's *A Tale of Two Cities.* The nonfictional list of early customers includes Charles II, the Duke of Marlborough, Nell Gwynn, Samuel Pepys, Oliver Cromwell and John Dryden. The bank is now part of Williams and Glyn's Bank. *Open M-F 10AM-3PM. 1 Fleet St., EC4.*

48 **The Temple.** An oasis of calm between the traffic of the Embankment and the bustle of Fleet Street. The Temple was originally the headquarters of the Knights Templars, a monastic order founded in 1119 to regain Palestine from the Saracens for Christianity. They settled at the Temple in 1160, but were suppressed by the Pope, and all that remains of their monastery is the Temple Church and the Buttery. Since the 14th century, the buildings have been leased to lawyers and today house 2 of England's 4 **Inns of Court (Inner Temple** and **Middle Temple),** the voluntary legal society which has the exclusive privilege of calling candidates to the bar. Visitors are free to stroll through the warren of lanes, courtyards and gardens and to admire the confidence of the buildings, each composed like an Oxford or Cambridge college, with chambers built around steep stairways, communal dining halls, libraries, common rooms and chapels. The tranquility of the setting is accentuated by the speed with which the lawyers, either wearing their gowns or carrying them over their arms loaded down with books and papers, race between their chambers and the Law Courts, the vast Gothic world which stretches from Temple Bar to the Aldwych.

The **Temple Church,** located within the precincts of the Inner Temple, was badly damaged during the Blitz, but has been skillfully repaired. The beautiful round nave, completed in 1185, is modeled after the Church of the Holy Sepulchre in Jerusalem. It is the only circular nave in London, and one of only five in England, all connected with the Knights Templars. The chancel was added in 1240. The rib vaulting within the Gothic porch is original.

The **Middle Temple Hall,** also painstakingly restored after the Blitz, is a handsome Elizabethan building with a splendid double hammerbeam roof and carved oak screen. Here, aspiring barristers are called to the bar upon passing their examinations. Lunch and dinner are served in the hall, and though residence at the Inns has become vestigial, the students must eat 3 dinners during each term here. Shakespeare's *Twelfth Night* is said to have been performed in the Hall in 1602. The round pond amidst the mulberry trees outside in **Fountain Court** was featured in Dickens's novel *Martin Chuzzlewit.*

The **Inner Temple Gateway,** leading back to the Strand, is a half-timbered three-story house which looks suspiciously stage set, but it is the real 17th century thing, with **Prince Henry's Room** on the top floor. *Temple, EC4.*

49 **Prince Henry's Rooms.** Above the archway leading to the Temple, the timbered house containing Prince Henry's Room was built in 1610 as a tavern with a projecting upper story. The great treasure inside is the Jacobean **ceiling,** one of the finest remaining enriched plaster ceilings of its date in London, with an equally enriched set of stories to go with it. The most persistant tale claims that the initials *PH* and the Prince of Wales' Feathers which decorate the ceiling commemorate the 1610 investiture of Henry, eldest son of James I and elder brother of the future and luckless King Charles I. The Prince died 2 years after his investiture from a chill caught after playing tennis, a game which can be said to have changed the entire course of British history. The Room also contains mementos of one of London's most important figures, the diarist **Samuel Pepys**. Pepys was born in 1633 on nearby Salisbury Court, Fleet Street, baptized in nearby St. Bride's Church, educated at St. Paul's Cathedral and lived most of his life close by Tower Hill. His remarkable shorthand diary fills many volumes, recording just over 9 years (1660-1669), but it is the liveliest and fullest account of London life ever written, and includes the Plague (1665) and the Great Fire (1666). The wide oriel windows looking down over Fleet Street and across to Chancery Lane manage to frame London's timelessness in a prism of light—the way one longs to see it. *Very small admission fee. Open M-F 1:45-5PM, Sa 1:45-4:30PM. 17 Fleet St., EC4.*

50 **Cock Tavern.** ★★$$ Another illustrious role call of former regulars: Nell Gwynn, Pepys, Goldsmith, Sheridan and Garrick, a theatrical lot of drinkers and thinkers who thoughtfully drank in this small tavern which still serves tradition, an excellent bar lunch and delicious roasts and puddings in the dining room. The original sign carved by **Grinling Gibbons** is happily preserved behind the bar upstairs, and the clientele is a civilized mix of journalists and barristers. *Reservations recommended for lunch in the restaurant. Open M-F 11:30AM-3PM, 5:30-8:30PM. 22 Fleet St., EC4. 353-8570*

51 **St. Dunstan-in-the-West** (1831-33, John Shaw) An architectural gem, beautifully situated on the north side at the curve in Fleet Street. Shaw's Victorian church with its octagonal tower, open work lantern and pinnacles, was built at the beginning of the Gothic Revival on the site of an earlier church whose great treasures were saved when it was demolished to widen Fleet Street. The church is unusually placed, with the tower and entrance on the south and the brick octagon of the sanctuary and altar on the north. Treasures from the earlier church include the communion rail carved by **Grinling Gibbons** and the old wooden clock (1671) with 2 wooden giants which strike each hour. In 1830, the Marquis of Hertford bought the clock for his house in Regent's Park. Viscount Rothermere, a British newspaper proprietor, later bought the clock and returned it to the church in 1935 to commemorate King George V's Silver Jubilee. The statue of **Elizabeth I** over the door (believed to be the oldest outdoor statue in London) and the statues of **King Lud** and his sons came from the Ludgate when it was torn down in 1760. The bronze bust of **Lord Northcliffe** (1865-1922), newspaper proprietor and founder of the *Daily Mail*, was sculpted by **Lady Scott** in 1930. *Open Tu and Th. Fleet St., EC4.*

52 **Hoare's Bank.** The only private bank left in London and still as old-fashioned, discreet and attractive as when it was founded in 1672. Well worth a peek inside. *37 Fleet St., EC4.*

53 **Printer's Devil.** ★★$ A museum of the printing trade with 2 working models of famous printing presses. The wine bar upstairs serves lunch on weekdays. *Open M-F 11:30AM-3PM, 5:30-11PM; Sa 5:30-11PM. 98 Fetter Ln., EC4. 242-2239*

54 **White Horse.** ★★$ An old coaching inn with 2 bars and a dining room upstairs which serves seafood pancakes, lobster and daily specials. *Open M-F 11:30AM-3PM, 5:30-11PM. 90 Fetter Ln., EC4. 242-7846*

55 **El Vino's.** ★$ A lot of history has been written over bottles of wine in this haunt of boozy journalists. What starts as a piece of gossip, idle speculation or a mischievous rumor and becomes an item in the *Standard Diary* or an article in *Private Eye* progresses to *something worth checking on* in more serious papers. Whoever said *in vino veritas* did not hang out at El Vino's on Fleet Street. This masculine institution is packed daily with journalists, lawyers and City businessmen; women weren't allowed to drink at the bar until 1982, and few do it today. A long wine list and simple foods like Scotch salmon and Smithfield beef. *Bar open M-F 11:30AM-3PM, 5-8PM; Sa 11:30AM-3PM. Restaurant open M-F 12:30-2:45PM, 5-8PM; Sa 5-8PM. 47 Fleet St., EC4. 353-6786*

56 **Wine Press.** ★★$ One of the few places on Fleet Street where women can feel at home. The light and airy wine bar serves snacks and has a large choice of wines, and the restaurant is good. *Open M-F 11:30AM-3PM, 5:30-11PM. 161 Fleet St., EC4. 353-9550*

57 **Printer's Pie.** ★$ Famous for the Queen Victoria mixed grill and the traditional English fare like shepherd's pie, sausages, mash and onions. *Open M-F 12-3PM, 5:30-10PM; Sa 12-3PM. 60 Fleet St., EC4. 353-8861*

58 **Dr. Johnson's House.** London is full of great men's houses, lovingly bought and preserved, restored, rearranged and revitalized in the spirit of the departed. True, they usually possess an orderliness that the former inhabitants would find astonishing, especially in the houses of writers. But if the absence of chaos requires us to slightly suspend belief, we are ever grateful to the foresight of individuals and charitable trusts which preserve these houses for us, allowing us to snoop and speculate on those whose lives and letters add so richly to our own. One of the most tempting for the London-lover is the house of **Samuel Johnson** one of 3 of his London residences and the one where he produced the first complete dictionary of the English language, published in 1755. Until he came to Gough Square, Johnson had lived in miserable lodgings, taking whatever literary hackwork he could find. But with the advance he was given to write the *Dictionary*, he leased 4 Gough Square in 1748. On the day he signed the contract to write the *Dictionary*, he composed the following prayer: *Oh God, who hast hitherto supported me, enabled me to proceed in this labour, and in the whole task of my present state; that when I shall render up, at the last day, an account of the* talent committed to me, I may receive pardon. For the sake of Jesus Christ, amen. Johnson installed his assistants in the huge attic, and for the next 11 years, they worked at their task. In March 1759, when his beloved wife, Tetty, 15 years his senior, died, he left this house, melancholy and impoverished, and went to live in Staple Inn. *Small admission fee. Open May-Sept M-Sa 11AM-5:30PM, Oct-April M-Sa 11AM-5PM. Now 17 Gough Sq., EC4. 353-3745*

59 **Ye Olde Cheshire Cheese** ★ ★ ★ $$ Probably the most profitable institution on Fleet Street. This dark, cozy, firelit pub is one of the few remaining 17th century chophouses in London, witnessing 16 reigns and hardly changing since it was rebuilt after the Great Fire of 1666. The 14th century crypt from Whitefriars monastery is beneath the cellar bar, and private parties can be held in it. The sawdust on the floor (changed twice daily) and the oak tables in *boxes* with benches on either side enchant foreigners, who long to have their England frozen in time. Considering the unrivaled popularity of the place, the food is pretty good, although the famous pudding of steak, kidney, mushroom and game which celebrated its bicentenary in 1972 no longer feeds 90 people or requires 16 hours to cook. Nor does it contain oysters and lark, but it is sustaining and flavorful. There are rich game puddings in autumn and winter, with a celebrity invited to dig into the first pudding of the season each October. Follow the pudding with Stilton or lemon pancakes and relish the Englishness of it all. *Open M-F 11:30AM-3PM, 5:30-11PM. 145 Fleet St., EC4. 353-6170*

Fleet Street is one of the best areas in London for a *pub crawl* and for eavesdropping on the world of print. Normal London **pub hours** are Monday through Saturday 11:30AM-3PM and 5:30-11PM (some close earlier), and Sunday 12-2PM and 7-10:30PM, although some are closed for all or part of the weekend. Pubs on Fleet Street (often called *the Street*) and the Strand which cater to the *wigs and pens*—barristers and journalists in the area—often shut by about 9PM when their clientele has departed. Some pubs in the area stay open for printers on the night shift who have their lunch around 10PM. Pubs with good food are popular with lawyers, editors and writers, so reserve for lunch.

60 **Daily Telegraph Building.** 1928, Elcock and Sutcliffe, with Tait) This massive, modernish neo-Greek building houses London's most sensible, conservative paper. The *Telegraph* was the capital's first daily penny paper, founded in 1855. *135 Fleet St., EC4.*

61 **Spatz.** ★ $ If you are feeling homesick for hamburgers, salad bars, steaks and martinis, this American-style restaurant will be a welcome find. There is even a *Happy House* from 5-7PM, when all drinks are the same price. *Open M-F 12-2:30PM, 5-11:30PM. Hill House, Shoe Ln., EC4. 583-2441*

A View from the Top: The Best Places to Look Down on London

St. Paul's Cathedral. 360 degree vista from the Golden Gallery at the top of the dome. 560 steps to this 280 foot vantage point. *Admission charge. Winter: M-F 10AM-3:15PM, Sa 11AM-3:15PM. Summer: until 4:15PM. Ludgate Hill, EC4. 248-2705*

National Westminster Tower. At 600 feet, Britain's tallest building. Not generally open to the public, but call and see if they will organize a private viewing. *25 Old Broad St., EC2. 920-5555*

Tower Bridge. Fabulous views over the Tower of London and of the river-life on the Thames. Ascend by the North Tower and traverse the river protected from the breeze in an enclosed 140 foot high walkway before descending by the South Tower. *Admission charge. Open Oct-Mar 10AM-4:30PM, Apr-Sept 10AM-6:30PM. Tower Bridge, SE1. 407-0922*

The Monument. Stone column built by Sir Christopher Wren between 1671-1677 to commemorate the Great Fire of London in 1666. It is 202 feet high and 202 feet west of the baker's shop on Pudding Lane where the fire started. The steep spiral staircase with 311 steps offers stunning views of the City. *Admission charge. Open Oct-Mar M-Sa 9AM-4PM; Apr-Sept M-Sa 9AM-6PM; May-Sept Su 2-6PM. Monument St., EC3. 626-2717*

Kenwood House. The beautiful landscaped gardens of this 17th century house offer panoramic 180 degree views of London. *Open daily Oct-Mar 10AM-5PM; Apr-Sept 10AM-7PM. Hampstead Ln., NW3. 348-1286*

New Zealand House. The view from the 18th floor is especially spectacular at night. It is used for private receptions and parties, so unless you are planning a party, it's not always possible to get in. *Haymarket, SW1. 930-8422*

Westminster Cathedral. The 352-and-a-half-foot-high St. Edwards Tower allows a general 360 degree panorama over London. *Admission charge. Open daily Apr-Oct 10AM-4PM. Ashley Pl., SW1. 834-7452*

Royal Observatory. In the Royal Park of Greenwich, the Royal Observatory looks over the Thames to London's east end and the Isle of the Dogs, with the National Maritime Museum and 17th century Queen's House in the foreground. Unbeatable. *Admission charge. Open Nov-Mar M-F 10AM-5PM, Sa 10AM-6PM, Su 2-5PM; Apr-Oct M-Sa 10AM-6PM, Su 2-5:30PM. Greenwich Park, SE10. 858-1167*

---

62 **Cartoonist.** ★ ★ $ A Fleet Street *local* and headquarters of the Cartoonist Club of Great Britain, with every square inch of wall space covered in framed original cartoons. The telephones are used by the pressmen, who are the regulars here. *Open M-Sa 11:30AM-3PM, 5-11PM. 76 Shoe Ln., EC4. 353-2828*

63 **Daily Express Building.** (1932, Ellis Clarke and Atkinson with Sir Owen Williams) Black glass tiles and chrome and one of the finest examples—inside and out—of Art Deco in London. *121-128 Fleet St., EC4.*

64 **Poppinjay.** ★ $ Next door to the *Daily Express* building and full of journalists at lunchtime and printers in the evening. *Open M-Sa 11:30AM-3PM, 5-11PM. 119 Fleet St., EC4. 353-5356*

65 **Old Bell Tavern.** ★ ★ $ An intimate and warm pub built by **Sir Christopher Wren** in 1670 to house and serve the workmen rebuilding St. Bride's nearby after it was destroyed in the Great Fire. *Open M-Sa 11:30AM-3PM, 5:30-11PM; Sa 11:30AM-3PM. 95 Fleet St., EC4 583-0070*

66 **St. Brides.** (1670-84, Sir Christopher Wren; 1701-3, tower) Wedged in between ponderous newspaper offices is Wren's *madrigal in stone,* one of his grander creations, with the tallest of his steeples (226 feet), the origin and inspiration of the wedding cake, resting on a plain, squarish nave. The church was damaged in the Blitz and beautifully restored in the 1950s. Optimistic journalists marry and attend memorial services for fellow journalists here, the latter ceremony inevitably continued up *the Street* at El Vino's in a boozy haze of memories about the departed. The crypt is now a museum, established in memory of Lord Beaverbrook. *Open daily 9AM-5PM. Fleet St., EC4. 353-1301*

67 **Reuter's and Press Association.** (1935, Sir Edwin Lutyens, with Smee and Houchin) Headquarters of 2 famous international news agencies. The genius of Lutyens comes through as always in this his last commercial building in London. Located next door to Wren's beautiful St. Bride's, the Edwardian architect was wisely inspired by and respectful of the wedding cake church, conceiving his L-shaped plan as a backdrop and linking the building to the west door of the church by a high-vaulted passage. *85 Fleet St., EC4.*

S.ᵗ Brides: Church.

The City's Redevelopment

The controversy surrounding the wanton disregard of perspective, scale and skyline in the City's redevelopment, at its most stupefyingly insensitive during the 1960s and 1970s, prompted a letter to the *London Times* from one of the firemen who kept watch over St. Paul's Cathedral during World War II: *The climax of the Nazi fire raids on the City came on December 29, 1940. Churchill sent a message to the firemen—Save St. Paul's. The New Year dawned with most of the area north of the Cathedral as far as Moorgate a smoking ruin: 8 Wren churches gone; 2 City Livery Halls gutted; Paternoster Row, with its millions of books, in ashes. The Cathedral Chapter House was burnt, but the Cathedral stood scarred but safe. Now you tell us that, 600 feet high,* a Seifert slab will overtop the Cross. The war memorial of the Fire Brigade Union carries lines from William Morris:

There in the world new builded
Shall our earthly deeds abide
Though our names be all forgotten
And the tale of how we died.

Newbuilded? *Those of us with the fire service in the City on those winter nights of 1940-41 thought it would be so. Reading the* Times *(1 March 1975) I felt we might as well have let it burn. It would have saved the grabbers and developers a lot of trouble and money and made it much easier for their architects. Certainly many a good fireman we lost in the City those nights might now be drawing his well-earned fire brigade pension.*

spired his religious architecture: he liked clear glass; lots of light; pale, beautiful colors; patterned black and white floors; decorative touches of gold; space which allowed worshipper to see and hear what was going on; and above, all, churches which emphasized man's power of reason as the foundation of faith. Wren was a deeply religious and humane man, son of a dean and nephew of a bishop. One of his great gifts was assembling and inspiring great craftsmen to work with him: **Grinling Gibbons, Jean Tijou** (ironwork), mastermasons like **Francis Bird,** and his clerk of works, **Nicholas Hawksmoor,** an architect who was a genius in his own right.

After the Great Fire of 1666, Wren submitted his plan for rebuilding the City, but it was rejected (his 18 foot long Great Model for St. Paul's is preserved in the library of the Cathedral). But eventually he did build 52 City churches and St. Paul's Cathedral, a contribution unparalleled in architectural history. During the Second World War, over a third of the City was destroyed and nearly all of Wren's churches were severely damaged. But because elaborate plans still existed, many have been beautifully rebuilt and today 23 remain. Wren is buried in the crypt of the Cathedral. His famous epitaph, written in Latin in a vast compass design under the dome, translates: *Beneath lies the founder of this church and city, Christopher Wren, who lived more than ninety years not for himself but for the public good. Reader, if you seek his monument, look around you.*

68 **St. Martin Ludgate.** (1677-87, Sir Christopher Wren) The sharp, dark obelisk spire is accent and prelude to St. Paul's Cathedral, a city prayer away. Wren's design centers around a cross inside a square, which is defined by 2 sets of stairs in the vestibule and 4 tall Corinthian columns which support 2 intersecting tunnel vaults. A magnificent brass candelabra hangs in the center of the crossing, and there is a pale, concerned pelican above the font. *Open May-Oct daily 10AM-4PM, Nov-Apr 11AM-3PM. Ludgate Hill, EC4.*

Sir Christopher Wren—he was knighted in 1672—was a remarkable polymath: brilliant Latinist, anatomist, astronomer, mathematician, engineer and architect. His training as a mathematician and astronomer may have in-

69 **St. Paul's Cathedral.** (1675-1711, Sir Christopher Wren) Walking up Ludgate Hill, the glimpses of St. Paul's are inspiring, reassuring and awesome. But just when you are within a few yards, the Cathedral grows smaller, the road veres too close and the statue of Queen Anne seems dumpy and distracting. It pays to step back a moment just when you realize you have reached Wren's greatest masterpiece to try and see what the architect himself intended: the slight curve of the road; the scale, monumental in the context of the medieval perspective; the magnificent dome, second only in Christendom to St. Peter's; and the skyline, uncluttered and harmonious. Even as late as 1939, before the German's chose St. Paul's as a main bombing site, the Cathedral stood in a tapestry of streets, courts, squares and alleys, and medieval London, which had spread far beyond the City's wall before the Plague of 1665 and the Great Fire of 1666, was still recognizable.

Three cathedrals have stood on this site. The first, founded by Bishop Mellitus in 604, was destroyed by fire in 1087, and was replaced by gigantic and Gothic Old St. Paul's. But the magnificent cathedral, with one of the tallest spires in Europe, fell into desperate decay, and after the Great Fire of 1666, lay in ruins. Six days after the fire, Wren, then 31, submitted his plan for rebuilding the City and the cathedral. It was rejected, but Wren remained undaunted, and finally, in May 1675, his design was approved. He laid the first stone on 21 June 1675, and the last was set by his son 33 years later. Wren managed to get an important concession attached to the design which gave him the freedom to make *ornamental rather than essential* changes during construction. He took full advantage of the clause, modifying his design considerably—including deleting a tall spire—during the 3 decades spent building the church. But before Wren's masterpiece was finished, a kind of persecution began; his salary was withheld because progress was said to be too slow, and 8 years after his triumph was completed, he was dismissed from his post as Surveyor of Works. Another insult came a year later, when a balustrade was added around the top of the Cathedral. Wren, retired and living in Hampton Court, would still come and sit under the dome of his monument: *If I glory, it is in the singular mercy of God, who has enabled me to finish a great work so conformable to the ancient model.*

St. Paul's was the first building in London to have an exterior of Portland stone, and when it was cleaned in the 1960s, Londoners were astonished to discover a dazzling building of golden honey-colored stone. In front of the Cathedral stands a statue of **Queen Anne** (1886) looking down Ludgate Hill. The original statue, carved in 1712 by **Francis Bird**, suffered from decay and occasional attacks, losing her nose, orb and sceptor, and was removed to the grounds of a girls' school in East Sussex in 1884. The Queen and the forecourt were originally inside a railing, which was sold at auction in 1874. At the same time, the road was expanded, bringing St. Paul's closer to the hellish stream of traffic *en route* to the City.

Something of the splendor of St. Paul's lies simply in its vast size, in its colorless serenity. Mind and body seem both to widen in this enclosure, to expand under this huge canopy where the light is neither daylight nor lamplight, but an ambiguous element something between the two...Very large, very square, hollow-sounding, echoing with a perpetual shuffle and booming, the Cathedral is august in the extreme, but not in the least mysterious. **Virgina Woolf** in *The London Scene*, a collection of 5 essays.

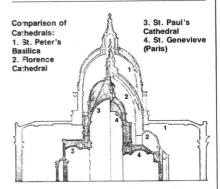

Comparison of Cathedrals:
1. St. Peter's Basilica
2. Florence Cathedral
3. St. Paul's Cathedral
4. St. Genevieve (Paris)

The spacious 78,000 square foot interior incorporates tourist groups more readily than Westminster Abbey, and in spite of its 300 years and large population of statues and monuments, there is a lack of clutter, unique in cathedral design. The focal point is the

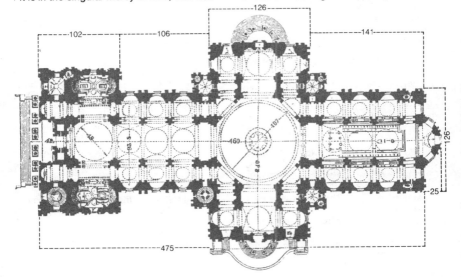

THE STRAND & FLEET STREET

huge dome-space at the crossing. The **dome** rises 218 feet above the floor and is supported by 8 massive double piers with Corinthian capitals. In a piece of mathematical genius, Wren actually created 2 domes, an inner dome covered in brickwork which supports the outer dome and the lantern. The spandrels contain 19th century mosaics executed by **Antonio Salviati.** *Matthew* and *John* were designed by **GF Watts;** *Mark* and *Luke* by **WEF Britten;** and *Isiaih, Jeremiah, Ezekial* and *Daniel* by **Alfred Stevens.** The surface of the dome is decorated with 8 large grisailles by **Sir James Thornhill** (1716-19) depicting scenes from the life of St. Paul. The epitaph to **Wren,** who is buried in the crpyt, is written in Latin on the pavement under the dome, and the plaque to **Winston Churchill,** also on the floor beneath the dome, was unveiled in 1974. If you are sound of wind and limb, it is well worth inspecting the dome more closely. For a small fee, you can climb the 259 steps to the **Whispering Gallery,** so-called because if you stand at the entrance, you can hear what is being said in a normal voice on the other side 107 feet away. The gallery offers spectacular views of the concourse, choir, arches, clerestory and the interior of the dome. If you are still feeling fit, climb the steeper spiral to the **Stone Gallery,** which surrounds the top of the drum outside. From here you can see all over London. For the heartiest, the **Golden Gallery** at the top of the dome takes you to the lantern and the golden ball.

The best place to start a tour of the monuments in the Cathedral is at the west entrance in the small **Chapel of All Souls,** a 1925 memorial to **Lord Kitchener** (1850-1916) and *all others who fell in 1914-18.* Behind the splendid ornamented wooden screen—carved by **Jonathan Maine,** one of Wren's great craftsmen, in 1698—is **St. Dunstan's Chapel,** reserved for private prayer. Beyond the chapel in the main aisle are various monuments, though Wren did not want memorials in the Cathedral and none were added until 1790. Most impressive is the monument to the **Duke of Wellington** which fills the central bay. Painter and sculptor **Alfred Stevens** spent 20 years creating the huge equestrian statue of the duke on top of a canopy, and it wasn't completed until 1912, nearly 40 years after Stevens' death. The third bay in the aisle contains an eery Victorian monument to **Viscount Melbourne** (1779-1848), Queen Victoria's first prime minister. The inscription above the double doors guarded by 2 angels reads: *Through the gate of death we pass to our joyful resurrection.* The **North Transept,** also called the **Middlesex Chapel,** is reserved for private prayer and contains a large marble font carved by **Francis Bird.** Beyond the crossing is the **North Chancel,** with a memorial screen which lists the names of former St. Paul's choristers who died in the two World Wars. The carved paneling on the right is the work of **Grinling Gibbons.** The marble statue, *Mother and Child,* by **Henry Moore** was presented to St. Paul's by the artist in 1984. The aisle terminates in the **Altar of the Modern Martyrs,** where the names of all known Anglican martyrs since 1850 are recorded in a book kept in a glass-topped casket. Pass through the fine ironwork gate by **Jean Tijou** and enter the **American Memorial Chapel,** paid for

entirely by contributions of people all over Britain as a tribute to the 28,000 members of the American forces who lost their lives in Britain or on active service from Britain during World War II. The names fill 500 pages of illuminated manuscript, bound in a red leather volume and presented to St. Paul's by General Eisenhower on 4 July 1951.

The **Choir** is enclosed by a low screen made from the original altar rail by **Jean Tijou** and contains the exquisite carved choir stalls made in the 1690s by **Grinling Gibbons.** The carved oak **baldacchino** (canopy) above the High Altar was created from some of Wren's unused drawings by **Godfrey Allen** and **SE Dykes Bower.** It replaced the rereredos damaged in 1941 and serves as Britian's memorial to the more than 324,000 men and women of the Commonwealth who died in the two World Wars.

The **Lady Chapel** in the eastern end of the south choir aisle contains the Cathedral's original High Altar. A life-size terra cotta figure of *Our Lady with Infant Jesus* sculpted by **Josephine de Vasconcellos** stands in the south aisle. Nearby is a statue of **John Donne,** the poet who became one of the finest preachers the Anglican church has ever produced and the most famous dean of St. Paul's (1621-31). When Donne believed he was about to die, he called for sculptor **Nicholas Stone** to come and draw him in his shroud. It is the only effigy which survived the Great Fire intact.

On the second pillar in the south aisle hangs a version of **William Holman Hunt's** most famous painting, *The Light of the World,* depicting a pre-Raphaelite Christ knocking at a humble door, overgrown with weeds. The door has no handle and can only be opened from the inside; this is the door of the heart. Nearly life size, it is the third and largest version of the painting Hunt produced and was presented to the Cathedral by wealthy shipowner Charles Booth in 1908.

The **Chapel of the Order of St. Michael and St. George,** with its beautiful woodwork by **Jonathan Maine** and colorful banners, can only be entered on a Supertour. The Order was instituted in 1818 for those who had given distinguished service to the Commonwealth. The chapel was dedicated in 1906 by Bishop Henry Montgomery, with the stirring words: *You who represent the best of the Anglo-Saxon race at work beyond the seas are now made the guardians of the west door of the Cathedral.*

If you leave the chapel and continue westward along the aisle, you will reach the **Geometrical** or **Dean's Staircase,** designed by Wren and built by **William Kempster.** Each stone step is set into the wall only a few inches, the weight at each level carried by the step below. The ironwork is by **Jean Tijou.**

The **Crypt,** entered from the South Transept and covering the whole length of the Cathedral, is probably the largest in Europe. Many famous people are buried here, including **Nelson** in the elegant black tomb Cardinal Wolsey had built for himself before he fell out of royal favor, **Wellington,** and **Wren** and his family. A black marble slab is inscribed with the famous Latin phrase composed by Wren's son: *Lector, si monumen-*

tun requiris, circumspice (Reader, if you seek his monument, look around you), also repeated on the pavement under the dome. The artists' corner commemorates **Van Dyke, Blacke, Turner, Reynolds, Constable** and many others. Noteworthy is the memorial to **John Singer Sargent** (1856-1925), designed by the artist himself, and the memorial to **George Frampton**, which includes a small replica of the statue of Peter Pan he sculpted for Kensington Gardens.

Small admission fee to each section. Visiting hours M-F 10AM-4:15PM, Sa 11AM-4:15PM. Nave opens at 8:45AM. Said matins M-F 7:30AM; holy communion daily 8AM and M-Th 12:30PM; choral matins Sa 10AM, Su 10:30AM; choral evensong M-Sa 5PM, Su 3:15PM; choral communion Su 11:30AM (July only choral communion Su 11AM replaces Su 10:30AM and 11:30AM services.) Supertours are conducted from the Friends' Table near the west door M-Sa at 11AM, 11:30AM, 2PM and 2:30PM. 248-2705

BESTS

Lord Weidenfeld
Publisher

The **library** of the **House of Lords.**

The **walk** from the top of **Bond St. down to Piccadilly** and St. James's Park and through Jermyn St.

Wilton's, the quintessentially English fish restaurant.

The **National Gallery** on Saturday mornings, especially the Italian Renaissance rooms.

Royal Opera House, Covent Garden on a Gala night.

Annabel's, the enduring conventional/unconventional dinner and after dinner meeting place.

The **Garrick Club** during the busy mid-week lunch hour.

Alan Fletcher
Designer, London

Anything Left Handed, whose motto is *our customers are never right,* carries scissors, pens, rulers, corkscrews and other practical items for lefties. *65 Beak St., W1. 437-3910*

Paintings of London
Helen McCabe
Art Historian and Writer

Claude Monet, *The Thames Below Westminster* (National Gallery)

Andre Derain, *The Pool of London* (Tate Gallery)

James McNeill Whistler, *Nocturne In Blue and Gold: Battersea Bridge* (Tate Gallery)

Antonio Canaletto, *View of the City of London from Richmond House* (Duke of Richmond & Gordon Collection)

Oskar Kokoschka, *View of Thames* (Tate Gallery)

Ginner, *London Bridge* (Museum of London)

Drummond, *St. James's Park* (Southampton Art Gallery)

Saul Bass
Designer, Los Angeles

Blakes Hotel, between Fulham and Old Brompton Roads on a quite residential street in the middle of the Chelsea area, is within shouting distance of good, small restaurants, interesting shops, galleries and people. *33 Roland Gardens, SW7. 370-6701*

Dr. Alan Kay
Apple Fellow, Computer Specialist

Portobello Hotel. All the rooms are handsomely furnished, and some are beautifully decorated around different themes: the *Round Room* has a round bed, the *Bath Room* is full of antique mirrors and the *Four-Poster Room* has 18th century mahogany. *North Kensington, 22 Stanley Gardens, W11. 727-2777*

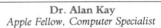

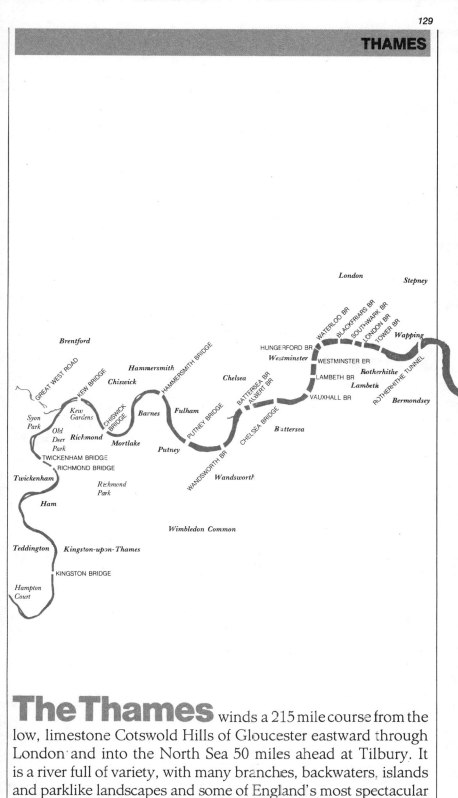

London   Stepney

Brentford

WATERLOO BR
BLACKFRIARS BR
SOUTHWARK BR
LONDON BR
TOWER BR
Wapping

HUNGERFORD BR
Westminster   WESTMINSTER BR

Hammersmith
Chiswick

GREAT WEST ROAD
KEW BRIDGE

Chelsea
Rotherhithe
LAMBETH BR   *Lambeth*

BATTERSEA BR
ALBERT BR
VAUXHALL BR   ROTHERHITHE TUNNEL
Bermondsey

Kew Gardens
Syon Park
Old Deer Park Richmond
Barnes Fulham
PUTNEY BRIDGE
CHISWICK BRIDGE
Mortlake
Putney
Battersea

TWICKENHAM BRIDGE
RICHMOND BRIDGE
WANDSWORTH BR
Wandsworth
CHELSEA BRIDGE

Twickenham

Ham
Richmond Park

Wimbledon Common

Teddington   Kingston-upon-Thames

KINGSTON BRIDGE

Hampton Court

The Thames winds a 215 mile course from the
low, limestone Cotswold Hills of Gloucester eastward through
London and into the North Sea 50 miles ahead at Tilbury. It
is a river full of variety, with many branches, backwaters, islands
and parklike landscapes and some of England's most spectacular
monuments along its banks. The upper reaches meander
through a broad, flat basin, flowing past **Windsor Castle**,
beautifully situated on the south bank, then around the 16th
century **Hampton Court**, and on to **Kingston Bridge** and
Teddington Lock, which marks the end of the tideway. It continues north to **Twickenham**, where **Ham House** and **Marble Hill House** face each other along its shores, through **Richmond, Old Deer Park** and the banks of **Kew Gardens** and
finally reaching the stone embankments which mark the start

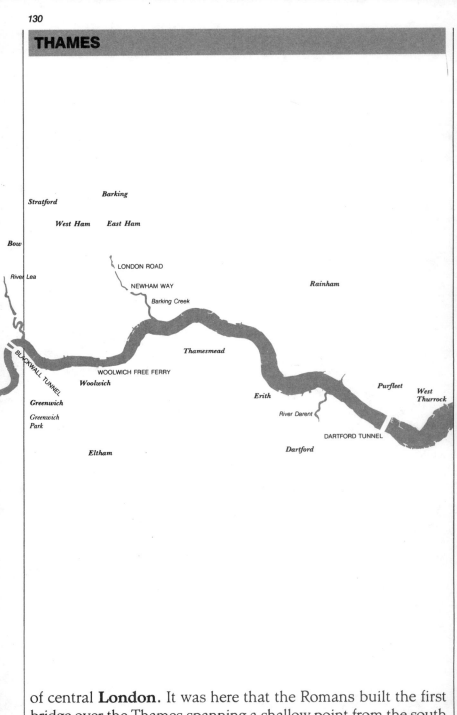

of central **London.** It was here that the Romans built the first bridge over the Thames spanning a shallow point from the south bank at Southwark to the north bank where the City now stands. Around this wooden bridge the settlement of *Londinium* grew up, quickly becoming a hub of communications and one of Europe's greatest ports. Many of London's historic landmarks reflect in the waters of the Thames: the **Houses of Parliament**, the **Embankment, St. Paul's Cathedral** and the **Tower.** Downstream from the Tower, one can still feel the Dickensian spirit in the deserted warehouses of dockland. (Abel Magwitch tried to escape along these shores in Dickens' *Great Expectations.*) But some of the best scenery is yet to come, as the river rounds the bend between **Wapping** and **Rotherhithe**, passes beneath the **Old Thames Tunnel** (the first tunnel to be built beneath the river, completed in 1843), and loops around the

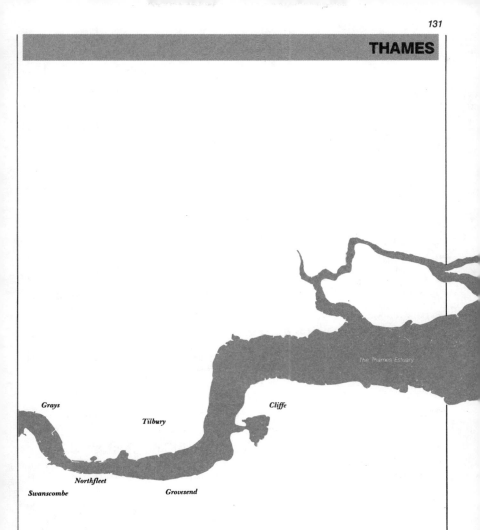

Grays

Tilbury

Cliffe

The Thames Estuary

Northfleet

Swanscombe

Grovesend

Isle of Dogs, where the tall masts of the *Cutty Sark* and Sir Christopher Wren's **Royal Naval College** dominate the skyline. Further downstream is the massive **Thames Barrier** at Woolwich Reach, designed to stop the surging tides which threatened to flood London (completed in 1982).

28 bridges cross the Thames, from the Tower Bridge in London to Teddington Lock: there is one footbridge (Richmond), 9 rail bridges and 18 road bridges. The oldest and the newest is London Bridge. The Thames is navigable from the North Sea upsteam to Lechlade, after which are a series of locks. Passenger steam ships travel daily during the summer between Oxford and Kingston, and from London upstream to Kew, Richmond and Hampton Court and downstream to Greenwich, Putney, Tilbury, Southend-on-Sea and Margate. (See the **Essentials** section at the end of the book for complete details on boat trips.)

High Holborn

has the grimmest associations of any walk in the book, beginning with the largest meat market in the world (**Smithfield Market**), brilliantly juxtaposed with London's oldest hospital (**St. Bartholomew's**). It includes two sites where most London executions have taken place (Smithfield and Newgate) and the courthouse (**Old Bailey**) where many major British murderers of this century, including the Yorkshire Ripper, have been held. The road divides at the green oasis of **Lincoln's Inn,** and then moves on to the irresistible and eccentric **Sir John Soane's Museum,** a small-scale rehearsal for the grand finale, the **British Museum.** You can see where Karl Marx wrote *Das Kapital* (**British Library**), enjoy more great paintings at the **Courtauld Institute,** founded by Sam Courtauld, who had a more imaginative understanding of the value of *das kapital*, and end the day in the company of London's greatest writer (**Dickens House**).

Somewhere between the hanging geese of Smithfield, the inspired vision of Thomas Rahere (who built St. Bartholomew's in 1123), the secluded beauty of Lincoln's Inn and the grandeur of the Elgin Marbles, you will see *real* London: scholars, butchers, doctors, lawyers, writers, the innocent and the guilty, all drinking in the same pubs, all part of a London, ancient and ageless.

This authentic and Dickensian slice of London must be explored on a weekday, beginning at the crack of dawn at Smithfield Market and followed by the ideal breakfast at the Fox and Anchor. The courts at the Old Bailey are only in session during the week, and Sir John Soane's Museum and Dickens House are closed on Sundays, though the British Museum and the Courtauld Galleries are open on Sunday afternoons.

1 Smithfield Market. At midnight, the vans begin arriving at the oldest and largest dead meat and poultry market in Europe, covering 10 acres and 2 miles of shop frontages. Unloading, weighing, cutting, marking and displaying all take place before selling begins at 5AM. Starting the day at dawn amidst the bustle and ordered vivacity of early city life makes you feel like an honorary and ordinary citizen, wherever you are. When you start a London day at Smithfield Meat Market, surrounded by white-coated butchers and bummarees (meat carriers), effortlessly carrying carcasses in imperious shades of pink, red, purple and brown—calves by Georgia O'Keefe, piglets by Mother Goose, anonymous rib cages by Francis Bacon—the surrealist

artistry takes over. Feathered friends—chickens, geese, turkeys—smooth, sweet and bloodless, hang alongside furry creatures—rabbits. The medieval feeling, all pervasive, allows guilt and nausea to recede: life depends on death, markets depend on life. Signs announcing beef from Australia, New Zealand and Scotland hang between the shining hooks, the hooks no competition for the arches, pillars, ornaments and swirls of ironwork that are worthy of a City church. The animated atmosphere is pure medieval, but the building is mid-Victorian, designed by **Horace Jones** and opened in November 1868 with a meaty banquet for 1,200 people. With typical Victorian high-mindedness, a small park was built in the center of Smithfield where the bummarees can rest, but predictably, they choose now as they chose then the Smithfield pubs in the area, which have special licenses to open in the early morning market hours.

The site has far more sinister associations than the slaughter of today. Originally a *smooth field* and hence the name (a corruption of Smoothfield), executions were held here as early as 1305, when **William Wallace**, the Scottish patriot, was executed on St. Bartholomew's Day. **Roger Mortimer**, who murdered Edward II and loved his Queen, was executed here on the orders of Edward III, and it was here that the confrontation between **Wat Tyler** and his band of revolutionaries and the 14 year old **Richard II** took place. The young King calmed the angry mob and promised them mercy and justice. The crowd took him at his word and peacefully dispersed, but the King delivered neither justice nor mercy, and Wat Tyler, stabbed by the Lord Mayor during the confrontation, died a few hundred yards away at St. Bartholomew's Hospital. From the 15th century onwards, Smithfield was the execution place for all who were convicted of heresy, including most of the 277 martyrs who died for their faith during the cruel and tragic reign of Mary I.

Smithfield was not totally grim. Once a year from Henry II's time until 1855, the great **St. Bartholomew's Fair** was held here. The 3 day event was the most important cloth fair in England, expanding as the export of wool and cloth grew. The days of great fairs and exports have passed, but the area has been kept alive by the remarkable and ironic juxtaposition of its 2 principle institutions: the meat market and the hospital. *Open M-Th 5AM-12PM; F 5AM-7PM. (If 5AM seems too early, the market remains animated until 9AM.) Smithfield, EC1.*

2 **Fox and Anchor.** ★★$ Full of bleary eyed medical students, young doctors and nurses and bummarees from the meat market eating huge platters of mixed grills: eggs, bacon, sausage, black pudding, kidneys, potatoes, tomatoes. Best appreciated after working up a greedy appetite. The special early morning market license which allows alcohol to be served between 6AM and 9AM is for *bonafide* market workers. Visitors get coffee. The decor is not much, but the ambiance is the attraction. *Open M-F 6AM-3PM. 115 Charterhouse St., EC1.* 253-4838

3 **Cloth Fair.** Leaving Smithfield Market *en route* to St. Bartholomew's Church, this narrow street on the north side of the church dates back to the days of the Bartholomew Fair. **Nos. 41** and **42** are 2 charming Jacobean (1640), pre-Great Fire houses, both well-preserved with 2 story wooden window bays that project over the sidewalk. *EC1.*

4 **St. Bartholomew the Great.** For lovers of antiquity and lovers of London, St. Bartholomew's is a kind of shrine, the oldest parish church in London (only the chapel of St. John in the Tower of London exceeds it in age). It was built, along with St. Bartholomew's Hospital, as an act of gratitude by **Thomas Rahere** in 1123 after he had a vision during a fever in which St. Bartholomew saved him from a monster. This Norman church quickens the heart of all who enter by its simple majesty and ancient beauty and by the inexplicable power that comes from the stones, the strong pillars, the pointed windows, the tomb of Rahere and the miracle of survival the church is witness to. You do not see it quite as Rahere, first canon and first prior, saw it. The massive nave was the choir of the original church; the original nave is part of the courtyard; and the 13th century entrance gate was originally the west entrance to the south aisle. But the choir and vaulted ambulatories, crossing, apsed chancel, 2 transepts and at least one bay of the nave are little changed since Rahere's time. The music sung during the choral service on Sundays seems to reach back in time, a heavenly complicity between stones, time, saints and angels. The seats and pews face towards each other in the formation of collegiate churches.

The restored **Lady Chapel** dates from the 14th century. The font is the only medieval font in the City and the 5 bells in the tower are pre-Reformation, with the oldest peal left in London, rung before Evensong on Sundays. The crypt and cloister have been restored, and the large chamber is dedicated to the City of London Squadron of the RAF, who have a memorial service here each year.

During the Reformation, the church was sold and fell onto hard times. The cloisters became a stable, the crypt was used for storing coal and wine, and the Lady Chapel became a printer's office, where a young printer named Benjamin Franklin worked. In the 1860s, architect **Sir Aston Webb** began the parliamentary restoration of the church. Along with his colleague **FL Dove**, he saved the reality and the spirit of St. Bartholomew's. The gateway was restored in memory of the 2 architects—notice the design of their coats-of-arms. The wooden figure of Rahere was carved from a beam taken from the church and placed here in memory of Sir Aston's son Philip, who was killed in action in France in 1916. *Open M, W-Su 9AM-5PM, Tu 11AM-5PM. West Smithfield, EC1.*

5 **St. Bartholomew's Hospital.** When Wat Tyler was stabbed by the Lord Mayor during his peasants' confrontation with the King, he was brought to Bart's and died in the emergency room. That was in 1331, and Bart's is still going strong, the oldest hospital in London and the only one of London's medieval foundations to continue on its original site to the present day. Like the church of **St. Bartholomew the Great**, the hospital was founded in 1123 by

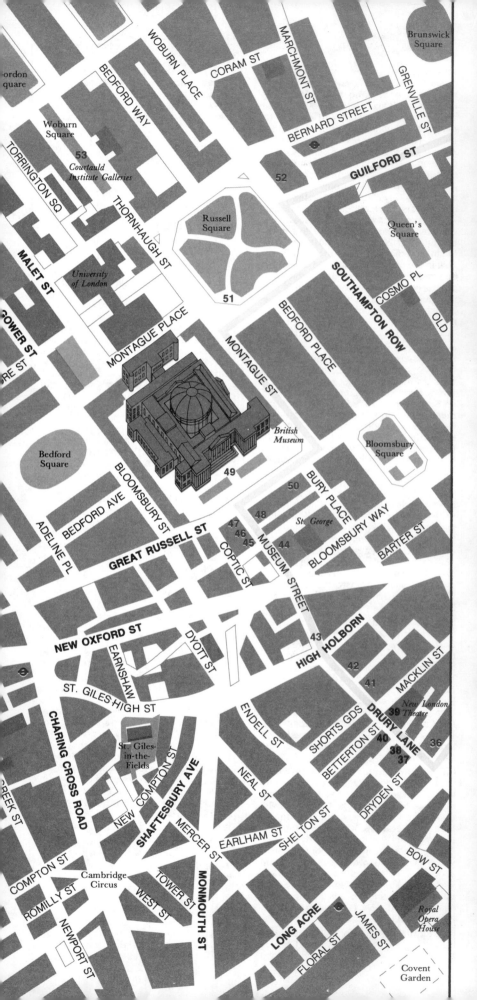

Brunswick
Square

WOBURN PLACE

CORAM ST

MARCHMONT ST

GRENVILLE ST

BEDFORD WAY

BERNARD STREET

ordon
quare

Woburn
Square

53
*Courtauld
Institute Galleries*

52

GUILFORD ST

TORRINGTON SQ

THORNHAUGH ST

Russell
Square

Queen's
Square

COSMO PL

MALET ST

*University
of London*

51

MONTAGUE PLACE

MONTAGUE ST

BEDFORD PLACE

SOUTHAMPTON ROW

OLD

GOWER ST

RE ST

*British
Museum*

Bloomsbury
Square

Bedford
Square

BLOOMSBURY ST

49

50

BURY PLACE

BLOOMSBURY WAY

BARTER ST

ADELINE PL

BEDFORD AVE

48

St. George

47
46
45

44

GREAT RUSSELL ST

COPTIC ST

MUSEUM STREET

NEW OXFORD ST

DYOTT ST

43

HIGH HOLBORN

42

41

MACKLIN ST

EARNSHAW

ST. GILES HIGH ST

*New London
Theatre*

39

CHARING CROSS ROAD

St. Giles-
in-the-
Fields

COMPTON ST

ENDELL ST

SHORTS GDS

BETTERTON ST

DRURY LANE

40

38
37

36

NEW

SHAFTESBURY AVE

NEAL ST

SHELTON ST

DRYDEN ST

REEK ST

MERCER ST

EARLHAM ST

BOW ST

COMPTON ST

Cambridge
Circus

TOWER ST

MONMOUTH ST

ROMILLY ST

WEST ST

LONG ACRE

FLORAL ST

JAMES ST

*Royal
Opera
House*

NEWPORT ST

Covent
Garden

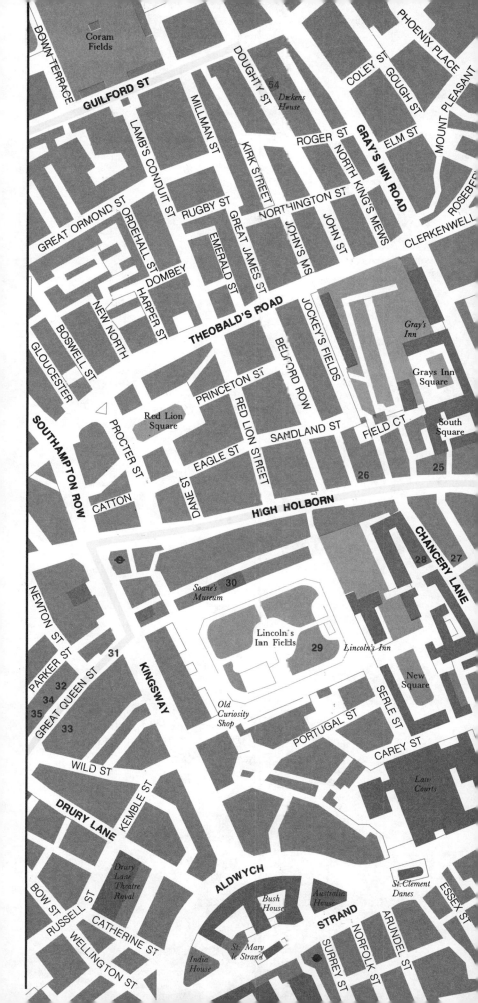

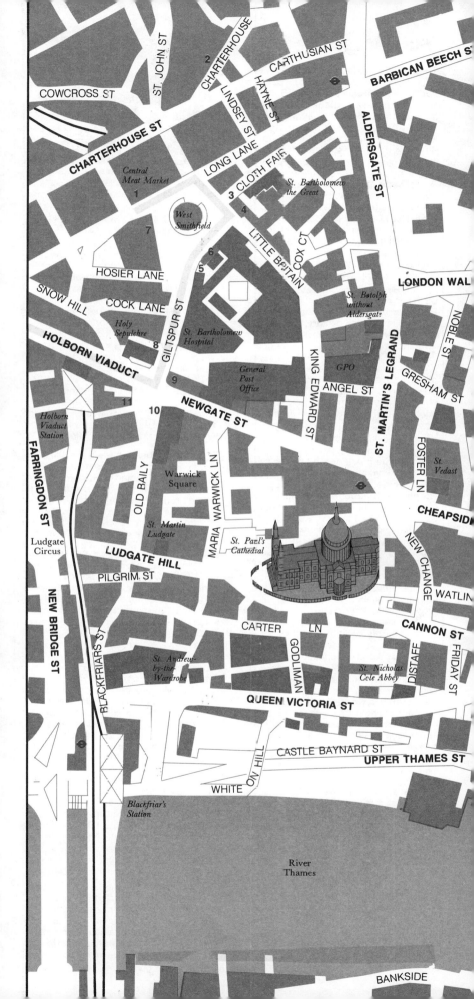

HIGH HOLBORN

Thomas Rahere, although **Henry VIII** is regarded as a kind of second founder after he dissolved the priory during the Reformation and granted a royal charter refounding the hospital in 1546. The gateway, built in 1702 by **Edward Strong the Younger,** is topped by a statue of Henry VIII by **Francis Bird.** The collegiate style buildings inside the great quadrangle were added by **James Gibbs** in 1730-70. Two large murals, *The Pool of Bethesda* and *The Good Samaritan* (1737) by **William Hogarth,** a governor of the hospital, line the staircase which leads to the **Great Hall.** The Medical School, which is a vital part of the hospital, is the oldest in London (1662). Known as Bart's and now part of the University of London, it has expanded in recent years into a new building in nearby Charterhouse. *West Smithfield, EC1.*

6 **St. Bartholomew the Less.** A small octagonal church whose parish is St. Bartholomew's Hospital. The chapel was founded in the 12th century, rebuilt in the 15th century (two 15th century arches survive under the tower), again in 1789 and 1820, and restored in 1951 following damage suffered during World War II. The register dates back to 1547 and records that **Inigo Jones** was baptized here in 1573. *Open 24 hours for friends and family of patients in the hospital. West Smithfield, EC1.*

7 **Bishop's Finger** (The Rutland) ★ ★ $ A good pub with 2 names and several devoted followings. Always called the Rutland, the name printed on the front, Bishop's Finger, is the name of one of the beers made by the brewery Shepherd Neame, which the pub is tied to. Bummarees from the meat market, doctors and medical students from Bart's, lawyers and reporters from the Old Bailey and money-makers from the City all drink together in the 2 bars, expanding into the park opposite on sunny days. *Open M-F 11:30AM-3PM, 5-11PM. 9-10 West Smithfield, EC1. 248-2341*

8 **St. Sepulchre.** The spacious church was orginally dedicated in 1137 to East Anglican **King St. Edmund.** It was rebuilt in the 15th century, restored after the Great Fire, possibly but not certainly by Sir Christopher Wren, heavily Victorianized in 1878, and sensitively repaired after the war in 1950. Known as the *Musicians Church,* St. Sepulchre has a long tradition of memorial services honoring composers and singers; a **Musician's Chapel** with windows in memory of singer **Dame Nellie Mella** and composer **John Ireland**; and exquisite kneelers with names of great musicians, bars of music and musical instruments worked in fine needlepoint. **Sir Henry Wood,** the founder of the Promenade Concerts, was baptized here, became assistant organist when he was 14 and is remembered in the central window of the north chapel, which is dedicated to **St. Cecilia,** patron saint of music. Every year on St. Cecilia's Day, 2 November, a festival is held in her honor, with the choirs of Westminster Abbey and St. Paul's.

American associations with the church inspired the window in the south wall of **Captain John Smith,** who led the expedition to Virginia in 1606-7. Taken prisoner by the Indians, he was saved by the chief's daughter **Pocahontas** just as he was about to be killed. The English captain became Governor of Virginia and Admiral of New England.

His savior Pocahontas married another settler, **John Rolfe** who brought her to England, the first in a long tradition of Englishmen marrying American women. Sadly, she suffered from the damp English winter and died.

Not all the associations of the church are as life-enhancing as the musical ones. To the right of the altar in a small glass case sits a handbell which was tolled outside the cell of a condemned man at midnight on the eve of his hanging. The bellman recited the following verses: *All you that in the condemned hole to lie; Prepare you, for tomorrow you shall die; Watch all and pray; The hour is drawing near. That you before the Almighty must appear; Examine well yourselves; in time repent. That you may not to enternal flames be sent. And when St. Sepulchre's Bell in the morning tolls. Lord have mercy on your souls.* All this, including the tolling of the great bell of St. Sepulchre on the morning of the execution, was arranged and paid for by a request or endowment of £50 made by Robert Dowe in 1605. *West Smithfield, EC1.*

9 **Viaduct Tavern.** ★ ★ $ A fascinating pub built over cells from the old Newgate Prison and named for Holborn Viaduct, the world's first flyover. Lavish interior with gold mirrors, an ornate metal ceiling and large paintings. Light lunches. *Open M-Sa 11:30AM-3PM, 5:30-11PM; Su 12-2PM, 7-10:30PM. 126 Newgate St., EC1. 606-8476*

10 **Old Bailey.** (1900-1907, Edward Mountford; extension 1972, McMorron and Whitby) The figure of *Justice,* neither blind nor blindfolded, stands on top of the dome, gilded in bronze and prelude to endless TV and film thrillers. The carved inscription *Defend the Children of the Poor and Punish the Wrongdoer* over the main entrance proves as difficult a combination today as it was when Fagin went to the gallows on this very site in Chapter LII of *Oliver Twist.* The Old Bailey is the **Central Criminal Court,** serving Greater London and parts of Surrey, Kent and Essex. It was originally a medieval gatehouse used as a prison for murderers and thieves. **Newgate Prison,** as it was known, played an important and dreadful role in London life. The conditions, despite numerous extensions and the installation of a windmill on the roof to improve ventilation, were notoriously barbaric. **Wat Tyler** led a successful assault and released all the prisoners in 1381. In 1750, a plague of jail fever swept through the prison, killing over 60 people, including the Lord Mayor, members of the jury and 3 judges, the origin of a tradition still honored whereby judges carry nosegays on the first day of each session to ward off vile smells and diseases.

The first Old Bailey (or Sessions House) was built in 1539 as a hall for trials of the accused. The men who condemned **Charles I** were tried here in 1660; **Oscar Wilde** was tried here in 1895; and famous 20th century murderers—**Dr. Crippen, Christie** and **Peter Sutcliffe** (the *Yorkshire Ripper*) were also tried here. In 1973, a terrorist bomb went off in the building during a trial of members of the IRA, which lead to fortress-like security during IRA trials. Public executions were held outside the Old Bailey from 1783 until 1868, replacing Tyburn as the site of the gallows. The road was widened to accommodate the large number of spectators.

The present building (1907) and extension (1972) accommodate 23 courts. Ten of them are in the old building entered on Newgate Street, which has a very unassuming door with the words *Ring bell hard* written above a doorbell, and the other 13 courts are in the new building entered from Old Bailey. Few experiences can be more fascinating than seeing the English judiciary at work during a trial here, with the judge and barristers in their white wigs and the accused in the *dock*. *Public admitted when court is in session 10:30AM-1PM, 2-4:15PM. Major trials in courts 1-4 attract large numbers, so you may have to wait in line. No children under 14, cameras or tape recorders. Old Bailey, EC4.*

11 **Magpie and Stump.** ★ ★ $ Famous old pub with an illustrious reputation. The secret passage between the pub and the jail has now been bricked up and the windows upstairs are no longer hired out for viewing public hangings, but friends and family of the innocent and the guilty gather here to fortify themselves during the trials and to toast or console each other following commutations and acquittals. In the quiet bar in the back, crime reporters and barristers drink after a day's work at the Old Bailey, though presumably any conversation between the 2 professions is off the record. *Pub lunch served. Open M-F 11.30AM-3PM, 5-11PM. 18 Old Bailey, EC4. 248-3819*

12 **Holborn Viaduct.** (1863-69, William Haywood) The world's first flyover, 1,400 feet long and 80 feet wide, built to bridge the valley of the Fleet and to connect Holborn with Newgate Street at a cost of 4,000 dwellings. Its elaborate cast-iron work is best seen from Farringdon Street. Four statues representing agriculture, commerce, science and fine art grace the north and south sides. Before the viaduct was built, the steep banks of this part of the river were very difficult to negotiate. Steps lead down to Farringdon Street and a small railway station (**Holborn Viaduct Station**), which serves commuters to the southern counties. *EC1.*

13 **City Temple.** A congregational church opened by the famous preacher **Dr. Joseph Parker** in 1874. The church was totally gutted in an air raid in 1941, and rebuilt incorporating the old facade in 1950 by **Lord Mottistone** and **Paul Paget**. *Holborn Viaduct, EC1.*

14 **St. Andrew Holborn.** (1684-90, Sir Christopher Wren) Wren's largest parish church, built on the site of a church founded in the 13th century. In 1704, Wren refaced the medieval tower of the original church which miraculously survived the 5 bombs which destroyed the interior of the church during World War II. The furnishings were replaced with treasures from the Foundling Hospital Chapel in Berhampstead, including the gilded 18th century organ which Handel gave to the hospital and the 18th century font and altar rails. The church records show the burial of **Thomas Chatterton** in 1770, the young poet who

committed suicide over the twin despair of poverty and nonrecognition and became a symbol of the Romantic movement. Essayist **William Hazlett** was married here, with Charles Lamb as his best man and Mary Lamb as a bridesmaid. The tomb of **Captain Coram**, founder of the Foundling Hospital, survived the bombs of World War II, and a weeping cherub watches over the great, good man. *EC1*

15 **Holborn Circus.** The statue of **Prince Albert** (1874) on a horse in the middle of a traffic island is sadly unworthy of the Prince who worked tirelessly for his adopted country, left a legacy of great museums and introduced the Christmas tree. *EC1.*

16 **Ely Place.** A fascinating cul-de-sac of 18th century houses still guarded by a watchman in a small gatehouse. Built on land belonging to the Bishops of Ely and officially owned by Ely Cathedral in Cambridgeshire, it remains legally under their jurisdiction, meaning London police cannot automatically enter, perhaps a more useful edict now that the lovely Adams doorways lead to offices of lawyers and accountants than when they lead to private houses. *EC1.*

17 **St. Etheldreda.** (Ely Chapel) When this church was built in 1290, it was, of course, a Catholic church, and like all churches in England during the Reformation, it became Protestant or Anglican. In 1874 the Roman Catholics bought it back, the first pre-Reformation church to return to the fold. A masterpiece of 13th century Gothic architecture (restored in 1935 by **Giles Scott**), the mood is one of great antiquity and warm everydayness. You enter to the smell of soup (from a small cafe in the adjoining house run by the church which provides morning coffee, lunch and tea to nearby residents) and incense (mass is said daily at 12PM). The windows at the east and west ends are noted for their superb tracery; the west window (c. 1300) is one of the largest in London. Modern stained glass windows by **Charles** and **May Blakeman** depict English martyrs. Very much a *living* church, St. Etheldreda's is active in Amnesty International and in the community. The vaulted crypt (1252) serves as a meeting room-Sunday school-storage area, irreverently and nicely chaotic. *Open 24 hours daily. Ely Pl., EC1.*

18 **Ye Olde Mitre Tavern** ★ ★ ★ $ Tucked away in the narrow alleyways of Ely Place, this 18th century pub was originally built in 1546 as lodgings for the servants of the Bishops of Ely. It is a perfect place for a *half-bitter* to quench your thirst after a salty breakfast at the Fox and Anchor. *Open M-F 11:30AM-3PM, 5:30-11PM. 1 Ely Pl., EC1. 405-4751*

19 **Hatton Garden.** The center of the diamond trade isn't what it used to be: office blocks have descended and ascended and most of the shops look so vulgar or so impenetrable that you have to be pretty expert to shop confidently. The impressive building housing the **London Diamond Club** is not open to the public. But **R. Holt** at No. 98 and **Andrew Ullman** at No. 10 are open. **Mineral Stones** at No. 111 cuts and mounts stones and minerals. Far more interesting value-wise are the Hatton Garden silver and jewelry auctions held every Thursday. Jewelry sales are at 1:30PM and silver sales are at 3PM on alternate weeks. Viewing is Friday from 9AM-4:30PM following each sale. *Call 242-6452 for more information. All shops and dealers open M-F 9:30AM-5:30PM. Hatton Garden, EC1.*

20 **Daily Mirror Building.** (1957-60, Sir Owen Williams & Partners; Anderson, Forster and Wilcox) An aggressive, vulgar newspaper has been translated into its architectural equivalent. Bad luck for Holborn. *New Fetter Ln., EC1.*

21 **Prudential Assurance.** (1879-1906, Alfred Waterhouse) This is what the late Sir John Betjeman, poet laureate and long time resident of the neighborhood (Cloth Fair behind St. Bartholomew's) admired, defended and fought hard to save: High Victorian architecture, massively confident. The Gothic red brick immensity no doubt inspires confidence in those who pass by the large insurance company. *142 Holborn Bars, EC1.*

22 **Leather Lane Market.** A lunchtime street market reached by a passage down the east side of the Prudential Assurance Building. New clothes at bargain prices—lambswool sweaters (called *jumpers*), shoes, jeans—some plants, fruit and vegetables are all sold here. The only leather can be found at a stall which sometimes sells genuine chamois. Inexpensive **Colin's Nest** serves *pie and mash*—steak pies, mashed potatoes, etc. *Open M-F 12-3PM. Leather Ln., EC1.*

23 **Barnard Inn.** The oldest surviving secular building in the City, incorporating remains of the Inn of Chancery where Pip and Herbert Pocket shared rooms in *Great Expectations*. The 14th century hall has 16th century paneling and fine heraldic glass. From 1894 to 1958, this was the hall of Mercer's School. Now it is occupied by a restaurant called **School Dinners,** which features typical English public school fare. *Admission to Barnard's Inn by appointment only. Holborn, EC1.*

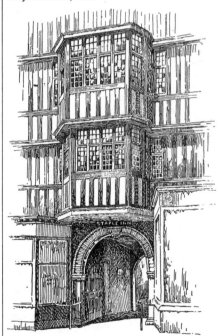

24 **Staple Inn.** The pair of gabled and timbered houses, dating from 1586, is the only survivor of pure, domestic Elizabethan London. Badly damaged in

1944 by a bomb and carefully restored, the Inn now houses offices and shops, including the **Institute of Actuaries. Dr. Johnson** lived at No. 2 in 1759-60 following his wife's death and his departure from Gough Square. *Holborn, EC1.*

25 **Cittie of Yorke.** ★ ★ ★ $ One of the largest pubs in London with the largest bar, this 17th century establishment must have served most of Holborn in days gone by. The large three-sided fireplace and little cubicles keep the place warm and intimate. The bar lunches are excellent and the real ales much appreciated by the legal clientele. *Open M-Sa 11:30AM-3PM, 5:30-11PM. 22-23 High Holborn, WC1. 242-7670*

26 **Her Majesty's Stationery Office. HMSO,** as it is known to Londoners, carries a remarkable collection of maps, charts, guides and travel books covering every inch of the British Isles. The shop also has the latest copies of laws passed in Parliament, museum replicas from the British Museum and attractive copies of English country maps. *Open M-F 8:15AM-5:15PM. 49 High Holborn, WC1. 211-5656*

27 **London Silver Vaults.** English silver has a richly deserved reputation: the silver content in silver marked with the hallmark of the British lion is the highest in the world and the tradition of design has been consistently strong. Unless you are familiar with hallmarks, makers and dealers, buying silver is bound to be an unnerving experience, and coming to this underground prison with over 100 cells containing the highest concentration of silver dealers in London is not reassuring. You have to make your way through a lot of junk in the beginning and encounter diffident dealers once the silver becomes desirable. If you can persevere and have a good idea of what you want, you will find lower prices than elsewhere. Study a simple hallmark card before you make a major silver purchase. *Open M-F 9AM-5:30PM, Sa 9AM-12:30PM. Chancery House, 53-65 Chancery Ln., WC2. 242-3844*

28 **Lincoln's Inn.** Of the four great Inns of Court (Lincoln's Inn, Inner Temple, Middle Temple and Gray's Inn), this is the most unspoiled, the only Inn to have escaped the Second World War without major damage. (The Inns were formed in the Middles Ages and were called *Inns* because they provided lodgings for lawyers and students of law.) Lincoln's Inn was established on the site of the Knights Templars' tilting ground after the dissolution of the Order in the early 14th century. The rolls of the Inn contain many famous names—Sir Thomas More, John Donne, Oliver Cromwell, William Penn, Horace Walpole, William Pitt, Disraeli, Gladstone—reflecting the times when most people of education became lawyers. The brick and stone buildings, arranged on a collegiate plan, date from the 15th century. Enter through the **gatehouse** (1518) facing Chancery Lane, which bears the arms of Sir Thomas Lovell. The Tudor red brick **Old Buildings** date from the early 16th century, and the **Old Hall** (1491) through the archway and small courtyard has a superb wooden roof and **Hogarth's** serious painting, *St. Paul Before Felix* (1748). The hall was the Court of Chancery from 1737 to 1883, and the case of Jarndyce vs. Jarndyce in *Bleak House* took place here. The red-brick **New Hall** and

Library (1845, Hardwick) contain the vast mural by **GF Watts**, *Justice, a Hemicycle of Lawgivers*, and the oldest and most complete law library in England, with nearly 100,000 volumes. **New Square** (1697, Serle) towards Lincoln's Inn Fields is on a tranquil and pretty courtyard of solicitor's offices, where 14-year-old Charles Dickens was once employed as a solicitor's clerk. The Gothic **chapel** was rebuilt in 1619-23. **John Donne** laid the foundation stone and gave the first sermon. *WC2.*

Nos. 57, 58. Circular porch added by Sir John Soane.

29 **Lincoln's Inn Fields.** Adjacent to Lincoln's Inn, the *field* was left open only after angry lawyers appealed to the House of Commons when property developers won the right to develop the space in 1620. The fine rectangular square is the largest in central London and is surrounded by many distinguished houses, including **Lindsey House** (Nos. 59-60) by **Inigo Jones** and its similar neighbor (Nos. 57-58) by **Henry Joynes**. *WC2.*

Drawing courtesy of David Gentleman

30 **Sir John Soane's Museum.** Sir John Soane (1753-1837), architect of the Bank of England, chose the largest square in central London for the site of his house. He required an appropriate setting for his enormous collection of antiquities and art, and the result is a house unlike any other in London. In rooms of unusual proportions built on varying levels in the manner of a labryinth, you can easily feel that time has been suspended and that you have entered the mind of a brilliant and eccentric master builder. Incorporated within the house are a **Monument Court**, an **Egyptian Crypt** and a mock-medieval ruin of a **Monk's Cloister**. In the **Picture Room** you can see **William**

Hogarth's paintings of *The Rake's Progress* (1732-33), ingeniously mounted by Soane so that they pull away from the wall, revealing hidden panels with subsequent paintings in the same series. A well known highlight of the collection, found in the **Sepulchral Chamber**, is the magnificent decorated *Sarcophagus of Seit I* (c.1300BC), discovered at Thebes in 1815 and snapped up by Soane when it was passed over by the British Museum. The collection contains many treasures and unpredictable juxtapositions of architectural fragments salvaged from buildings, such as the old House of Lords, which were destroyed during Soane's lifetime. Glancing through a window into the court known as the **Monk's Yard,** it is possible to catch a glimpse of a melancholy tomb inscribed *Alas, Poor Fanny,* a monument to Mrs. Soane's favorite dog. *Donations welcome. Open Tu-Sa 10AM-5PM. 13 Lincoln's Inn Fields, WC2. 405-2106*

31 **Great Queen Street.** Named in honor of Henrietta Maria, the devoted wife of Charles I. This once fashionable street is now lined with restaurants, including the private *media* club **Zanzibar**. *WC2*

32 **L. Cornelissen.** An old-fashioned shop with old-fashioned and very special art supplies: cobalt blues, British and French gold leaf, their own brand of violin varnish (Dragon's Blood—a transparent red coloring from the Middle East), pure squirrel mop brushes and quill brushes. *Open M-F 9:30AM-5:30PM, Sa 9:30AM-4:30PM. 22 Great Queen St., WC2. 405-3304*

33 **Freemason's Hall.** (1933, HV Ashley and F. Winton Smith) Heavyweight headquarters of the **United Grand Lodge of England,** with a central tower rising 200 feet above the street. The building was conceived as a war memorial to masons who died in the First World War. *Not open to the public. Great Queen St., WC2.*

34 **L'Opera.** ★ $$ Popular with singers, designers, musicians and opera lovers who flock here after Covent Garden and English National Opera performances. The predominantly French menu includes *bouillabaisse, moules mariniere* and salmon trout with tarragon. *Open M-F 12:15-3PM, 6-12PM, Sa 6-12PM. 32 Great Queen St., WC2. 405-9020*

35 **Alfredo's Sandwich Bar.** ★★$ One of the best places in town for that simple sandwich, with granary *baps* (brown rolls) and everything from cheese and pickle to smoked salmon. Order a sandwich and coffee to go (or *take away* as the English say) and eat in a Bloomsbury Square. *Open M-F 7:30AM-5PM. 35 Great Queen St., WC2.*

36 **Bhatti.** ★ $ Small, nearly new Indian restaurant with a classic but well prepared menu. Try the *prawn tandoori* (shrimp barbequed in clay ovens and served with onion and mint sauce); *chicken makhani* and the freshly baked Indian breads, especially *peshawari nan* (leavened bread filled with dried fruit). *Open daily 12-3PM, 6-11:30PM. 37 Great Queen St., WC2. 831-0817*

37 **Anello & Davide.** The best ballet and tap shoes and very appealing slightly period boots and shoes. Though the women's shoes never look made to last more than the average run of a West End show, the men's brogues look permanent. The Victorian-style button boots in soft

HIGH HOLBORN

leather are a great buy. *Open M-F 10AM-5:30PM, Sa 10AM-3:30PM. 35 Drury Ln., WC2. 836-1983*

38 Mansfield. A very chic shop specializing in antique luggage, mainly made from endangered species like crocodile and alligator. Ring the bell. *Open M-F 10AM-6PM, Sa 10AM-4PM. 30-35 Drury Ln., WC2. 240-7780*

39 New London Theatre. (1973, Michael Percival) The West End's newest theatre sits on one of the oldest foundations—the site has held a place of entertainment since Elizabethan times. The new London is ultra-modern, with moveable seats, lights, walls and stage surrounded by lots of glass. The seating was expanded from 952 to 1,102 to make room for the crowds for the feline phenomenon *Cats. 167 Drury Ln., WC2. 405-0072*

40 Last Days of the Raj. ★★$$ It looks more like Upper East Side New York than India, with its gleaming chrome and cocktail bar. But this Indian restaurant, run by a cooperative of first-rate chefs—6 Bangladeshis, an Indian and a Nepali— has an imaginative menu as well as favorites like *nam lamb tikka* and *prawn masala*. The restaurant provided all the food for the premiere parties of the *Jewel in the Crown. Open M-Sa 12-2:15PM, 6-11:15PM; Su 6-11:15PM. 22 Drury Ln., WC2. 836-1628*

41 His Nibs, Philip Poole. And it is his shop. Poole runs the finest shop on the street and one of the finest in Covent Garden. If this old and beautiful shop is replaced by a smart boutique, it will be a sad day indeed. Every make and age of fountain pen, every kind of ink, as well as beautiful pencils, paper, and objects related to fine writing can be found here. The white-haired Mr. Poole is the oldest resident on the street and an aristocrat among merchants. *182 Drury Ln., WC2. 405-7097*

42 Crumbs for Comfort. ★$ Sandwiches, hot pasta and pizza to go in this Italian takeaway. *Open M-F 9AM-6PM; closed mid-Aug to early Sept. 184 Drury Ln., WC2. 831-0138*

43 Museum Street. Once you cross the broad intersection of New Oxford, High Holborn and Bloomsbury Way, this narrow, friendly street is lined with some of the best antique print dealers in London.

44 SJ Shrubsole. Distinguished dealer in old English silver, with prices which look worthy of its neighbor, the British Museum. You will also find outstanding pieces of old silver plate and honest prices which reflect the integrity of the shop. *Open M-F 9AM-5:30PM. 43 Museum St., WC1. 403-2712*

45 Plough. ★$ A literary pub with Bloomsbury affections, popular with publishers and writers who appreciate the coziness in winter and the outdoor tables in summer. Bar lunch. *Open M-Sa 11:30AM-3PM, 5:30-11PM; Su 12-2PM, 7-10:30PM. 27 Museum St., W1. 636-7964*

46 Craddock and Barnard. A lovely small shop with etchings and engravings. You might find a Delacroix or Goya etching you can actually afford. *Open M-F 9:30AM-5:30PM (generally closed 2-3PM for lunch). 32 Museum St., WC1. 636-3937*

47 Weinreb Architectural Gallery. An outstanding collection of architectural prints as well as David Roberts' original hand-colored lithographs, special exhibitions of 18th and 19th century artists and themes. Pleasant staff. *Open M-F 10AM-6PM, Sa 10AM-1PM. 34 Museum St., WC1. 636-4895*

48 Print Room. Specializing in London and caricature prints c.18th and 19th century, with a large, tempting and reasonably priced collection of botanical prints. *Open M-F 10AM-6PM, Sa 10AM-4PM. 37 Museum St., WC1. 430-0159*

49 British Museum. Ennui, wrote the lyricist of an old song, was a day when the British Museum had lost its charm. It hasn't, as the hordes who head here daily will attest, and the only problem is managing to see the exhibits through the crowds.

When **Sir Hans Sloane,** physician, naturalist and collector, died in 1753, his will allowed the nation to buy his vast art, antiquities and natural history collection for £20,000, less than half of what it cost to assemble. The collection grew rapidly and magnificently—and right out of **Montagu House,** where it had been on display since 1759. In 1823, George III's huge library was given to the nation, and a decision was made to build new quarters for the burgeoning collection. The architect chosen was **Robert Smirke,** who designed a large quadrangle with an open courtyard behind Montagu House and replaced the house with a fine neo-classical facade with a portico decorated with figures representing the progress of civilization. The architect's brother **Sydney Smirke** converted the courtyard into the copper **Reading Room** in 1852-57. Problems with space were alleviated in the 1880s when the natural history exhibits moved to the **Natural History Museum** (see **Cromwell and Brompton Roads** walk) and in 1970 when the ethnographic exhibits were moved to the **Museum of Mankind** (see **Piccadilly** walk).

Start with the **Egyptian Sculpture Gallery** on the ground floor (Room 25). The massive granite figures can be seen over the heads of any number of people. At the door is the **Rosetta Stone,** fascinating not in itself (it is an irregularly shaped, closely inscribed piece of black basalt), but because of the way it changed our understanding of history. Written both in Greek and in 2 forms of ancient Egyptian script, the stone's Greek translation provided the key to deciphering hieroglyphics, unread for 1,400 years. Inside the gallery is an overwhelming introduction to the ancient Egyptians—massive sculptures, intricate pieces of jewelry and carvings. There is a haughty bronze cat, sacred to Bastet, from 600BC; a large reclining granite ram with a tiny figure from King Taharqa tucked beneath his chin; and from the Temple of Mut Thebes, carved in about 1,400BC, are 4 massive granite representations of the goddess Sakhmet, with the body of a woman and the head of a lion. The rest of the Egyptian exhibits are on the upper floors (Rooms 60 through 66).

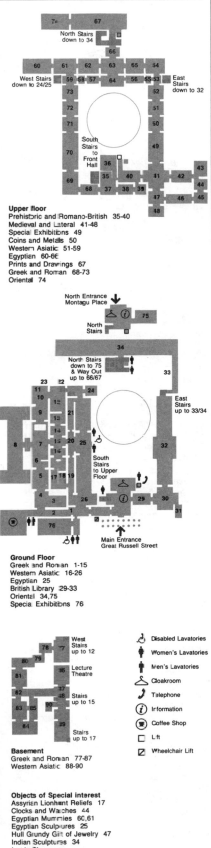

Upper floor
Prehistoric and Romano-British 35-40
Medieval and Lateral 41-48
Special Exhibitions 49
Coins and Metals 50
Western Asiatic 51-59
Egyptian 60-66
Prints and Drawings 67
Greek and Roman 68-73
Oriental 74

Ground Floor
Greek and Roman 1-15
Western Asiatic 16-26
Egyptian 25
British Library 29-33
Oriental 34,75
Special Exhibitions 76

Basement
Greek and Roman 77-87
Western Asiatic 88-90

Disabled Lavatories
Women's Lavatories
Men's Lavatories
Cloakroom
Telephone
Information
Coffee Shop
Lift
Wheelchair Lift

Objects of Special interest
Assyrian Lionhunt Reliefs 17
Clocks and Watches 44
Egyptian Mummies 60,61
Egyptian Sculptures 25
Hull Grundy Gift of Jewelry 47
Indian Sculptures 34
Lewis Chessmen
Lindisfarne Gospels 30
Magna Carta 30
Mildenhall Treasure 40
Parthenon Sculptures 8
Portland Vase 14
Rosetta Stone 25
Sutton Hoo Treasure 71

HIGH HOLBORN

Before climbing the stairs, visit Rooms 1 through 16, which hold the Museum's collection of **Greek and Roman Antiquities,** including the hotly contested **Elgin Marbles** (Room 8), sculptures from the Parthenon which were brought to England in 1816 by Lord Elgin and which the government of Greece is seeking to have returned. Mostly fragments, they are described in the diary of an attendant who helped move them into the Museum and who was assigned to the gallery where they were displayed. The diary of the attendant, John Conrath, can be seen in the British Library Galleries. *North side,* he wrote, describing the frieze which had been inside the great collonade, *a young man almost naked, putting a Crown on his head, another ready to mount, attended by his grooms, around the west corner a single person, a magistrate or director, two Chariots...South frieze, Seven more Bulls, a man Crowning himself...*Despite the disappointment of some early visitors at the eroded and broken state of the marbles, they have been an extremely popular exhibit since they were first installed, attracting such illustrious fans as the Grand Duke of Nicholas, later Czar Nicholas I of Russia, who spent 2 days looking at the marbles in 1817.

The upper floors hold **Medieval and Later Antiquities from Europe** (Rooms 41-47), with early examples of objects used in everyday life, including bronze weapons that look incapable of inflicting a mortal wound and the extraordinary **Lycurgus Cup,** a Roman goblet carved from a single block of green glass which shows the tortured face of the Thracian King Lycurgus as he is imprisoned by the tendrils of a vine. The rooms also contain remarkable displays of jewelry, and the **Gallery of Clocks and Watches** (Room 44) shows a range of time pieces from the Middle Ages to the beginning of this century.

On the ground floor, to the right of the entrance, are the **British Library Galleries,** where illuminated historical, musical and literary manuscripts and maps are displayed in glass cases. Also here is the large, firm signature of Elizabeth I as she signs the order sentencing her favorite, Essex, to death by beheading. On permanent display are 2 of the 4 surviving copies of the *Magna Carta* issued in 1215 by King John; the *Lindisfarne Gospels,* written and illuminated in 698; the *Gutenberg Bible;* and Shakespeare's *First Folio.*

The **British Library Reading Room,** with its domed ceiling and 30,000 reference books, is on view to visitors every hour on the hour from 11AM Monday through Friday. The Library has been used by readers as diverse as Karl Marx, Lenin, Gandhi, George Bernard Shaw and Thomas Carlyle, though the latter was so irked at the amount of time it took for him to receive his books that he went off in a pet and helped found the London Library. *No admission fee. Open M-Sa 10AM-5PM, Su 2:30-6PM. Coffee shop open M-Sa 10:30AM-4:15PM, Su 3-5:15PM. Great Russell St., WC1. 636-1555*

The British Museum, which backs on to **Montagu House,** occupies the site of the house built by the first **Duke of Montagu,** who, needing to repair a fortune sadly rent by the extravagances of erecting his mansion, set out to win the hand of the extremely rich and quite mad second **Duchess of Albermarle.** The Duchess, who insisted that she would only marry a crowned head of state, happily offered her hand when the Duke convinced her that he was the Emperor of China. The ghost of the erstwhile Empress must roam happily through the Museum's collection of Oriental antiquities, located in rooms 34, 74 and 75 on the ground floor and room 74 on the upper floor.

50 **Westaway and Westaway.** The largest and most affordable dealer in cashmere, lambswool, Shetlands, Arans, Icelandics, kitts, scarves, blankets, hats, suits and socks—anything warm in wool. Their Scottish cashmeres, woven in Scotland from the wool of cashmere goats in China, are considerably less expensive than anywhere else in London, with a far bigger choice than you are likely to find in Scotland. *Open M- Sa 9AM-5:30PM. Main shop 62-65 Great Russell St., WC1. 405-4479. Also 92-93 Great Russell St., 636-1718 (hand knits, designer knits and Shetlands).*

51 **Russell Square.** One of London's largest squares, lined with huge plane trees and houses once favored by lawyers and merchants. Readers of Thackeray's *Vanity Fair* may recognize this as the home of the Sedleys and Osbornes. The Square was laid out in 1800 by **Humphrey Repton** and named after the Russells, Dukes of Bedford, who owned the land. The elaborate statue of **Francis, 5th Duke of Bedford** (1809, Sir Richard Westmacott) shows the land-loving Duke leaning on a plow and holding corn. Some of the original houses by **James Burton** remain, including Nos. 25-29, which now contain the **Institutes of Commonwealth Studies** and **Germanic Studies,** branches of the Universithy of London. The great law reformer **Sir Samuel Romilly** lived and died by his own hand at No. 21. **Sir Thomas Lawrence** had his studio at No. 67 (later demolished) from 1805 until his death in 1830. Here he painted his series of portraits of princes, generals and statesmen who helped bring about Napoleon's downfall, which now hangs in the Waterloo Chamber at Windsor Castle. *WC1.*

52 **Hotel Russel.** *Moderate.* This rambling Bloomsbury monument looks and feels like it should be attached to the Great Western Railway. It was built by **Charles Fitzroy Doll** in 1898, with the Victorian appetite for size combined with modesty. The stairway is grand; the rooms are not. Still, there is a certain uncomplicated comfort and a loyal following. *Russell Square, WC1. 837-6470*

53 **Courtauld Institute Galleries.** Perhaps because it is hidden away on Woburn Square—accessible only by foot through a walkway off Russell Square or from Gordon Square, as Woburn is restricted to cars—the Courtauld Institute of Art is that rare and blessed experience in crowded London, a museum where, even on a Saturday in high summer, you can step back for a better look without stepping on a single toe.

The first 4 galleries contain 14th through 18th century art from Italy and the Netherlands given to the Institute in 1978 by **Count Antoine Seilern** and now known as the **Prince's Gate Collection.** The range of art is extraordinary, from **Palma Vecchio's** lush *Venus in a Landscape* to **Van Dyck's** *Portrait of a Man in an Armchair* to a tiny painting of the Madonna from the workshops of **Fra Angelico,** which dates from before 1440. Gallery III is given over entirely to the works of **Peter Paul Rubens,** from his vivid and violent allegorical paintings to his richly peaceful portraits like *The Family of Jan Brueghel the Elder.*

The last 3 galleries hold the brilliant Impressionist and Post-Impressionist paintings collected by **Samuel Courtauld,** who founded the Institute in 1931. The works are so familiar and frequently reproduced that they seem almost like icons of a world religion called 19th century art: **Modigliani's** *Female Nude,* which thousands of reproductions have failed to spoil; **Renoir's** *La Logue,* with a man staring at the stage through opera glasses while the viewer stares with equal intensity at his voluptuous partner, her neck wound round with crystal beads, her boldy striped opera cloak falling open to reveal the rose tucked between her breasts; a small enchanting **Rousseau** with 2 charmingly Chaplinesque policemen guarding *The Customs Post;* **Monet's** *Vase of Flowers,* full of pink and mauve mellows and so evocative of summer light that it cuts through the grayest London day; **Lautrec's** *Jane Avril in the Entrance of the Moulen Rouge;* and **Van Gogh's** *Self-Portrait with Bandaged Ear.* The Courtauld is scheduled to move from its present uninspired headquarters in 1988. The new rooms in Somerset House will be more easily accessible, and, alas, probably more crowded. *Admission fee. Open M-Sa 10AM-5PM, Su 2-5PM. Woburn Square, WC1. 580-1015*

DICKENS HOUSE
DOUGHTY STREET

54 **Dickens House.** A Victorian row house jammed with Dickensiana, made all the more amazing as it is one of 4 Dickens houses open to the public (the others are outside of London). This is where Dickens lived from 1837 to 1839 and wrote the latter parts of the *Pickwick Papers,* all of *Oliver Twist* and *Nicholas Nickleby* and the beginning of *Barnaby Rudge.* He also wrote some 550 letters here. It was in the sitting room that Dickens' 17-year-old sister-in-law Mary died in his arms, an emotional blow which he never got over. You can see the writer's desk, the china monkey he kept on it for good luck and the family bible. Only the first floor drawing room has been reconstructed to appear as it did in Dickens' time, but you can still feel the presence of London's greatest writer. *Open M-Sa 10AM-5PM. 48 Doughty St., WC1. 405-2127*

Nowhere in the world does **theatre** thrive as it does in London. Every night, between 40,000 and 50,000 people attend more than 50 theatres, with stages ranging from a platform in a pub in Islington to the plush grandeur of **Covent Garden**, from the comfort and advanced design of theatres in the **Barbican (Royal Shakespeare Company)** and the **South Bank (National Theatre)**, to revived and reverberating venues like the Palace. In 1985, nearly £100 million were spent on theatre tickets, with nearly half of that coming from tourists. Theatre has long been one of

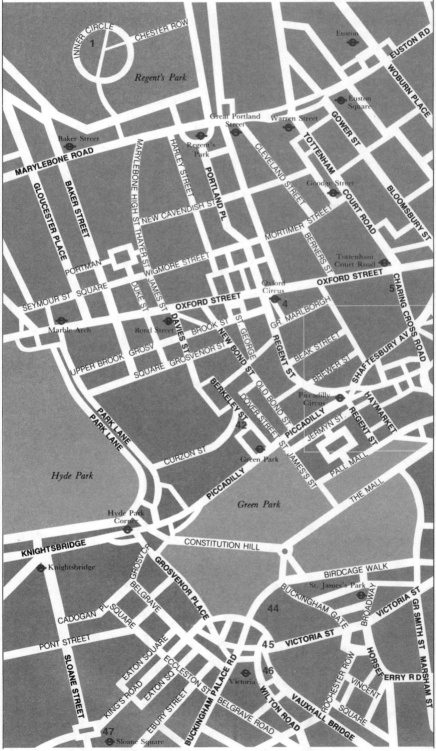

the London visitor's biggest attractions. The challenge in this inflationary age is to maintain the quality and daring of theatre while avoiding the obvious financial temptation of producing plays guaranteed to please the blander tastes of an international public. The spectre of Broadway looms large in London's West End, and the number of musicals (and the over-miking, which is a direct import from New York) suggests that it is an uphill battle.

Still, there is an impressive stable of outstanding playwrights—

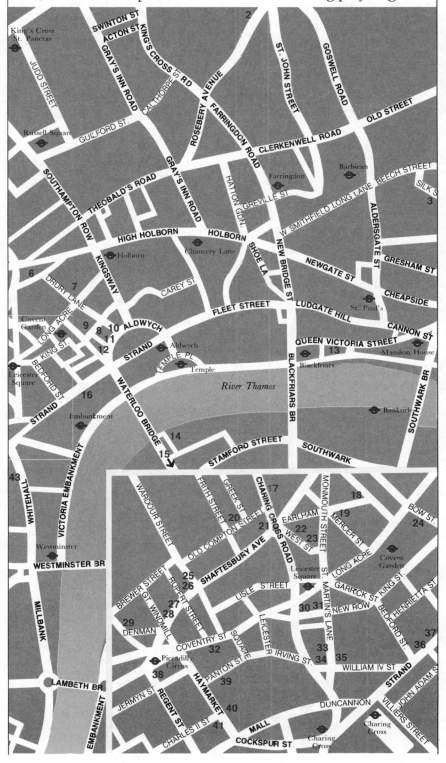

THEATRE

Harold Pinter, Tom Stoppard, Peter Shaffer, Alan Ayckbourn, David Hare, Caryl Churchill, Ronald Harwood—and a handfull of theatre geniuses—Sir Peter Hall, Trevor Nunn, Terry Hands—and of course the best actors and actresses in the world. Money is the only element that is not present here in quite the same amazing abundance.

Theatregoing is divided between the historic **West End** of **Shaftesbury Avenue, Charing Cross Road, Haymarket** and the **Strand**, and the subsidized modern powerhouses of British theatre on the South Bank and at the Barbican Center. There are restaurants to suit every appetite in theatrical London, whether you are looking for a drink, pub grub or French cuisine. Many have special pre- and after-theatre menus. The Covent Garden section on pages *115* to *118* is a helpful guide to dining in the area.

1 **Open Air.** (Seats 1,187) *Regent's Park, NW1.* 486-2431

2 **Sadler's Wells.** (Seats 1,500) Rosebery Ave., EC1. 278-8916

3 **Barbican Center.** When Queen Elizabeth II opened the Barbican in 1982, she called it *one of the wonders of the modern world,* and as usual, the Queen was not exaggerating. Designed by architects **Chamberlin, Powell** and **Bon** on a site which was heavily bombed during the Blitz, this walled city within the City covers 20 acres, rises 10 levels high descends 17 feet below sea level, and caps it all with the most extensive flat roof in Europe. The **Royal Shakespeare Company,** which is Britain's leading subsidized company and is based in Stratford-upon-Avon, moved to the Barbican Theatre from the Aldwych in 1982. The theatre, reached from levels 3 to 6, has 1,166 seats with raked stalls and 3 circles which project toward the stage, putting every guest within 65 feet of the action. The 109 foot double height flytower above the stage, used for scenery storage, is believed to be the tallest in the world. A remarkable stainless steel safety curtain descends during intermissions. Small productions of Shakespeare, revivals and new plays are performed in the **Pit,** which was originally a rehearsal space, but has been adapted to a flexible auditorium for 200 people. The **Concert Hall** (on levels 5 and 6) is the home of the **London Symphony Orchestra.** The area around the Barbican is slowly acquiring restaurants and cafes, but it is still a windy wasteland at night, and the catering in the Barbican is appalling. Getting to the Barbican can be a drag. One formula is to arrive by taxi and leave by the Tube, but the most practical way to to take the Tube both ways. It would help if the Barbican was better marked (*en route* and inside) and if tickets were sold in central London. Still, try and see at least one Shakespeare play by this brilliant company. *Recorded information, 628-9760; box office, 628-8795; credit card bookings, 638-8891*

4 **London Palladium.** (Seats 2,317) On Sunday nights during the 1950s, most of Britain tuned in to *Sunday Night At The London Palladium,* broadcast from this luxurious 1910 music hall. This is the home of great variety shows, Tommy Steele sopping in *Singin in the Rain,* a pantomime every Christmas and the Royal Command Performance. *Argyll St., W1.* 437-7373

5 **Astoria.** (Seats 820) Charing Cross Rd., WC2. 437-6565

6 **Shaftesbury.** (Seats 1,358) Shaftesbury Ave., WC2. 836-6596

7 **New London.** (Seats 1,102) The home of *Cats.* (See **High Holborn** for complete description). *167 Drury Ln., WC2.* 405-0072

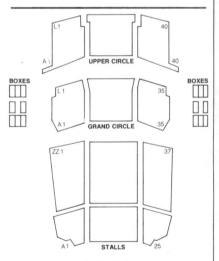

8 **Theatre Royal, Drury Lane.** (Seats 2,245) See the **Strand and Fleet Street** for complete description. *Catherine St., WC2.* 836-8108

9 **Fortune.** (Seats 432) Built after the First World War, its delightful little marble and copper foyer shows little evidence that money and materials were scarce. *Russell St., WC2.* 836-2238

10 **Aldwych.** (Seats 1,089) Slums between Drury Lane and Lincoln's Inn were razed to make room for Aldwych and Kingsway roads, and in 1905 the Aldwych became one of the first theatres to take up

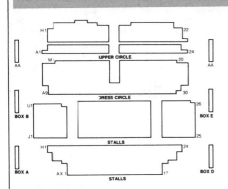

residence. Designed by **WGR Sprague** for Charles Frohmant, the Georgian theatre is handsome and ornate, uncomfortable and wonderful. This was the home of the Royal Shakespeare Company from 1930 to 1982, when it moved to the Barbican, and its absence is much lamented. Smash hits *Nicholas Nickleby* began here. Aldwych, WC2. 836-6404

11 **Strand.** (Seats 925). *Aldwych, WC2. 836-2660*

12 **Duchess.** (Seats 474) One of the best designed theatres in London, with excellent views from every seat. *Catherine St., WC2. 836-8243*

13 **Mermaid.** (Seats 610) Puddledock, Blackfriars, EC4. 236-5568

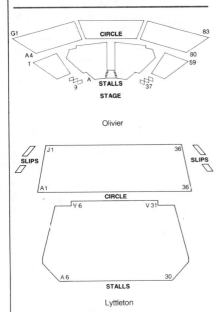

Olivier

Lyttleton

14 **National Theatre.** The world famous National Theatre Company was set up in 1962 under **Sir Laurence Olivier** and opened with Peter O'Toole in *Hamlet* in the **Old Vic** theatre. In 1951, construction of a new concrete cultural paradise for the Company, designed by **Denys Lasden,** was started on the South Bank. In 1976, the curtain was finally raised, with Sir Peter Hall as artistic director and Olivier as proud papa of the great Company. Incorporated under one vast roof are 3 theatres, 8 bars, a restaurant, modern workshops, paint rooms, wardrobes, rehearsal rooms and advanced technical facilities. The 3 theatres within the complex differ in design, but all have first class acoustics and site lines, en-

suring good seats all around. The tickets are also reasonably priced, with the added bonus of magnificent views of the Thames, the Houses of Parliament and St. Paul's. The **Olivier,** named after Sir Laurence Olivier, the first director of the theatre during its years at the Old Vic, seats 1,160 people in its fan-shaped auditorium. The dark-walled, rectangular **Cottesloe** (named after Lord Cottesloe, the Chairman of the South Bank Board and Council) is the smalled and most flexible, with removable seating for 400. Experimental plays and fringe theatre are performed here. The **Lyttleton** is a proscenium theatre, with roughly finished shuttered concrete walls for better acoustics and seating for 890 people. *For a free tour of the building and backstage, call 633-0880. South Bank, SE1. 928-2252*

15 **Old Vic.** (Seats 1,037) From 1962 to 1976, the Old Vic was the temporary home of the **National Theatre Company,** under the direction of **Sir Laurence Olivier.** Though the foundation stone, taken from the demolished Savoy Palace, dates from the theatre's opening in 1818, the rest of the Old Vic has changed interiors and owners many times, most recently in 1982, when Canadian entrepreneur *Honest Ed* Mirvish took over and gave the theatre a £2.5 million facelift. Now that Renaissance man Jonathan Miller has become director of the Old Vic, its great days should return. *Waterloo Rd., SE1. 928-7616*

16 **Savoy.** (Seats 1,122) Built by Richard D'Oyly Carte as the permanent home of Gilbert and Sullivan's comic operas, and more recently of the ingenius farce *Noises Off* by London playwright Michael Frayn. The Savoy was the first public building in the world to have electric lights. (See the **Strand and Fleet Street** for more details). *Savoy Ct., Strand, WC2. 836-8888*

17 **Phoenix.** (Seats 1,000) The theatre of **Noel Coward** and his beloved **Gertrude Lawrence,** who starred here together in a number of shows, including Coward's own *Private Lives* on opening night. In 1969, Coward opened the bar which is named after him. *Charing Cross Rd., WC2. 836-2294*

18 **Donmar Warehouse.** (Seats 200) A non-profit theatre in the raw located literally in a warehouse, with seats informally arranged around the stage. The Donmar was once used by the Royal Shakespeare Company for experimental productions (it is more comfortable nowadays) and now provides a venue for touring companies and its own fringe productions. *41 Earlham St., Covent Garden, WC2. 836-1071*

19 **Cambridge.** (Seats 1,273) *Earlham St., WC2. 836-6056*

20 **Prince Edward.** (Seats 1,666) *Old Compton St., W1. 437-6877*

21 **Palace.** (Seats 1,480) A vast palace of a theatre filled since 1891 with hits like *The Sound of Music, Cabaret* and *Jesus Christ Superstar.* It is now owned by composer **Andrew Lloyd Webber,** the 20th century hero of the English musical. *Shaftesbury Ave., W1. 437-6834*

22 **Ambassadors.** (Seats 460) *West St., Cambridge Circus, WC2. 836-6111*

23 **St. Martin's.** (Seats 550) *West St., Cambridge Circus., WC2. 836-1443*

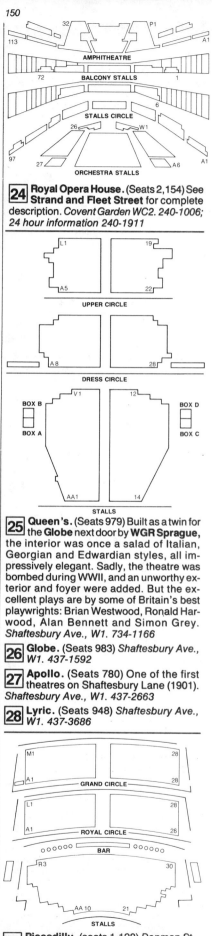

AMPHITHEATRE

BALCONY STALLS

STALLS CIRCLE

ORCHESTRA STALLS

24 **Royal Opera House.** (Seats 2,154) See **Strand and Fleet Street** for complete description. *Covent Garden WC2. 240-1006; 24 hour information 240-1911*

UPPER CIRCLE

DRESS CIRCLE

BOX B   BOX D
BOX A   BOX C

STALLS

25 **Queen's.** (Seats 979) Built as a twin for the **Globe** next door by **WGR Sprague,** the interior was once a salad of Italian, Georgian and Edwardian styles, all impressively elegant. Sadly, the theatre was bombed during WWII, and an unworthy exterior and foyer were added. But the excellent plays are by some of Britain's best playwrights: Brian Westwood, Ronald Harwood, Alan Bennett and Simon Grey. *Shaftesbury Ave., W1. 734-1166*

26 **Globe.** (Seats 983) *Shaftesbury Ave., W1. 437-1592*

27 **Apollo.** (Seats 780) One of the first theatres on Shaftesbury Lane (1901). *Shaftesbury Ave., W1. 437-2663*

28 **Lyric.** (Seats 948) *Shaftesbury Ave., W1. 437-3686*

GRAND CIRCLE

ROYAL CIRCLE

BAR

STALLS

29 **Piccadilly.** (seats 1,128) *Denman St., W1. 437-4506*

30 **Wyndhams.** (Seats 759) Built back to back with the Albery in 1903 by **WGR Sprague** for Sir Charles Wyndham. The 2 theatres are so close together that one spectator, invited onstage during *Godspell*, entered the wrong stage door and stumbled into a performance of *Pygmalion*. The bust over the proscenium is of actress Mary Moore, Wyndham's wife. *Charing Cross Rd., WC2. 836-3028*

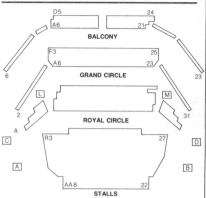

BALCONY

GRAND CIRCLE

ROYAL CIRCLE

A
C
A
AA 8   **STALLS**   22

31 **Albery.** (Seats 879) Built side by side with Wyndham's Theatre in 1903, this elegant Edwardian theatre moved effortlessly into the 1980s as the first theatre to use electrical flying scenery, a stunt that would have thrilled audiences in 1915, when *Peter Pan* was playing its boards. Sir John Gielgud made his first appearance here in *The Constant Nymph* in 1926, which ran for 587 performances. Lionel Bart's musical *Oliver* holds the record run of 2,618 shows between 1960 and 1966. The Albery was known as the **New Theatre** until 1973, when Sir Bronson Albery, a direct descendent of Charles Wyndham, became manager. *St. Martin's Ln., WC2. 836-3878*

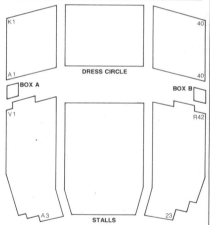

DRESS CIRCLE

BOX A   BOX B

STALLS

32 **Prince of Wales.** (Seats 1,122) Famous for its good family entertainment and television broadcasts. The Prince of Wales Theatre opened in 1884, and Charles Hawtrey's *The Private Secretary* was first produced here, with Beerbolm Tree in the lead. The sweeping curves and almost stark simplicity of the theatre date from 1936, when Robert Cromie redesigned it in the style of the era. *Coventry St., W1. 930-8681*

33 **Duke of York's.** (Seats 650) *St. Martin's Ln., WC2. 836-5122*

34 **Garrick.** (Seats 675) *Charing Cross Rd., WC2. 836-4601*

35 **Coliseum.** (Seats 2,558) London's largest theatre and home of the **National Opera Company**. The Coliseum, with its signature globe on top (which used to revolve), was built in 1902 for musical spectaculars, with luminaries Ellen Terry, Edith Evans, Lillie Langtry and Sarah Bernhardt appearing here in variety shows. Now many opera-goers claim that the finest opera productions in the world take place here. All are sung in English, and if opera is your thing, it is worth a trip to London during their season (August to May). *St. Martin's Ln., WC2. 836-3161*

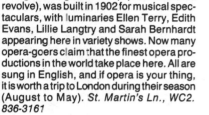

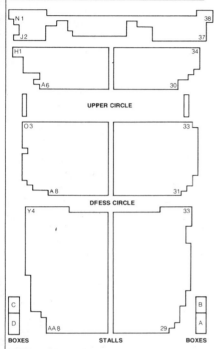

36 **Adelphi.** (Seats 1,500) Many Dickens novels were staged here in the last century and musicals have taken over in the 20th. (See the **Strand and Fleet Street** for complete description). *Strand, WC2. 836-7611*

37 **Vaudeville.** (Seats 694) The productions are mostly straight theatre, though the name suggests the music hall of earlier days. (See the **Strand and Fleet Street** for complete description). *Strand, WC2. 836-9988*

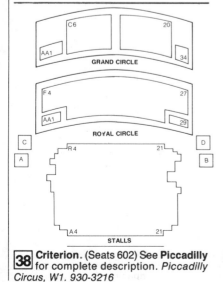

38 **Criterion.** (Seats 602) See **Piccadilly** for complete description. *Piccadilly Circus, W1. 930-3216*

39 **Comedy.** (Seats 780) Home of the American import *Little Shop of Horrors.* *Panton St., SW1. 930-2578*

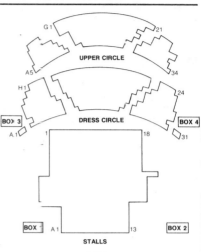

40 **Theatre Royal, Haymarket.** (Seats 906) Built in 1820 by **John Nash,** the grand portico of 8 Corinthian columns over the sidewalk is still in place, along with the 9 decorated circular windows above the portico. The interior has been much altered over the years. The theatre puts on excellent independent productions with big stars in quality plays. Bars in most of the West End theatres are pretty bad, with expensive drinks and undrinkable wine, and this theatre has one of the worst. Tuck a bottle of something delicious in your capacious handbag with 2 small hotel glasses, and spend the intermission on the sidewalk outside, enjoying the night air and toasting to your foresight. *Haymarket, W1. 930-9832*

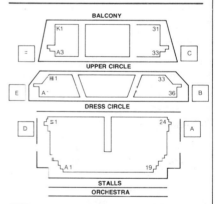

41 **Her Majesty's.** (Seats 1,209) The only theatre that changes its name to fit the monarch—Her Majesty for now. Popular Italian opera was performed here as early as 1705, when the first of 4 theatres was built on the site. After a fire in 1790, Michael Novosielski built the largest and most fashionable opera house in all of England, where evening dress was even required in the pit. The years that followed were the golden age of the opera house: Jenny Lind made her debut in 1841 and *Fidelio* had its English premiere here in 1851. Another fire, another rebuilding and competition from Covent Garden led to the demolition of the theatre. Only the royal opera arcade, added by John Nash in 1816, remains. The present French Renaissance theatre dates from

THEATRE

1897, built for Beerbohm Tree by **CJ Phipps** (of the Savoy Theatre). Smash hits such as the 2,238 run *Chu Chin Chow* in 1916, Noel Coward's *Bitter Sweet* in 1929 and more recently, a revival of *West Side Story* have kept the crown above the theatre through its third century. *Haymarket, SW1. 930-6606*

42 **Mayfair.** (Seats 310) *Stratton St., W1. 629-3036*

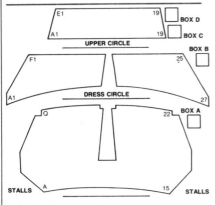

43 **Whitehall.** (Seats 662) Built in 1930 to the designs of **Edward Stone** on the site of the original Ye Old Ship Tavern. The clean, simple design led one newspaper to comment that the theatre made the government buildings in the area *look as if they need a shave.* The Whitehall has been the home of light comedies, reviews and farces, beginning with Walter Hackett's *The Way to Treat a Woman* in 1930 and moving on to Brian Rix's *Whitehall Farces* in the 1950s and 60s. *Whitehall, SW1. 930-7765*

44 **Westminster.** (Seats 585) *Palace St., SW1. 834-0283*

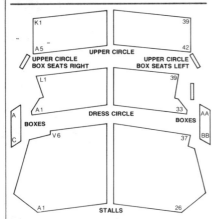

45 **Victoria Palace.** (Seats 1,565) Built as a music hall in 1910 by **Frank Matcham** for Alfred Butt, the theatre retains much of its original style: classical outside and rich and atmospheric inside, with grey marble walls, gold mosaics and white Sicilian marble pillars. A statue of ballerina Anna Pavlova, whom Butt introduced to London, stood atop the theatre until WWII, but the superstitious dancer pulled her car blinds down when she drove by. *Me and My Gal* played here until the outbreak of war in 1939. *Victoria St., SW1. 834-1317*

46 **Apollo Victoria.** (Seats 2,572) *17 Wilton Rd., SW1*

47 **Royal Court.** (Seats 401) See **St. James's Walk** for complete description. *Sloane Sq., SW1. 730-1745*

How to Buy Theatre Tickets

You can go directly to the Theatre Box Office, usually open from 10AM until the start of the evening performance, and choose from what is left. The earlier you go, the better the selection.

Or call the Box Office and reserve your tickets with a major credit card. You will need to show the card for identification purposes when you pick up the tickets. You can also reserve seats over the telephone, and pay for them by post or in person within 3 days.

Ticket agencies which sell West End theatre tickets are scattered throughout London and other large cities. Most charge an additional booking fee of 10-20%. Try *First Call*, a 24-hour, 7 day credit card service for London's top shows, concerts and movies. The service offers a wide range of tickets at all prices, and tries to provide a real choice of seat locations and numbers. Tickets are delivered by post or, if there isn't time, by courier to the box office for later collection. The booking fee is up to 70% cheaper than the fee charged by most other services. *Keith Prowse*, another ticket agency, doesn't charge a commission for certain theatres (theatre tickets, 636-8686; sports and music events, 631-3380).

For a real bargain, the Leicester Square Ticket Booth in the heart of the theatre district sells half-price tickets the day of the performance: 12-2PM for matinees; 2:30-6:30PM for evening shows. Obviously, tickets for hit shows may not be available. There is a small booking fee and a 4 seat maximum per person.

Most theatres are closed on Sundays.

London's Theatre Scene

Richard Pilbrow
Director, Theatre Projects, Ltd.

All the world's a stage. So wrote Shakespeare. Theatre in London is indeed a microcosm of Britain, a rich and varied scene where English and Broadway musicals compete with classical drama, boulevard comedy and the latest **Pinter, Ayckbourn** or **Stoppard.** Theatre from around the world has matured the London stage and now the whole world is drawn to taste its delights. Shakespeare would be pleased.

The success of the theatre is due to a very British mixture of compromise between commerce and art. The **Arts Council** (with state support) has helped to fertilize dozens of theatre companies around the country, which contribute a stream of new productions and talent to the *commercial* theatre of the West End. European theatre, from **Brecht** to **Ionesco,** American theatre, from **Tennessee Williams** to **David Mamet,** and the *musical* have all contributed to the theatre we find today. It is one area of life in Britain that can truly claim to be in the ascendancy, not the decline.

The **National Theatre** of Great Britain on

the south bank of the River Thames is a vast concrete edifice that houses 3 of the most advanced theatres in the world: the open stage **Olivier,** named after the company's founder, **Sir Laurence, Lord Olivier,** the **Proscenium,** the **Lyttleton** and the small, flexible courtyard space, the **Cottesloe.** Extensive workshops and backstage areas combine with foyers and cafes, bookshops, bars and restaurants, which are open to the public all day. Nearby is the first home of the National Theatre, the **Old Vic,** one of London's most famous theatres. It dates back to early Victorian times, but has been a center of excellence for over half a century.

North of the river, in the financial district of the City of London, is the ultra-modern **Barbican Arts Center.** This huge complex includes the London home of the **Royal Shakespeare Company,** as well as a major concert and conference hall, cinema, art gallery, library and exhibition spaces.

The West End theatres center around Covent Garden and Shaftesbury Avenue. The **Royal Opera House, Covent Garden,** houses both the **Royal Opera** and the **Royal Ballet** companies. This great theatre with a classical opera house and horse-shoe auditorium was built in 1858. London's other major opera company, the **English National Opera Company,** performs at the **Coliseum, St. Martin's Lane,** which was built in 1904 as a music hall, with encircling balconies and London's first revolving stage.

The **Theatre Royal, Drury Lane** was first built in 1662, and an early star to appear there was **Nell Gwynn.** The present interior was done in 1922. Since the war it has been the home of many Broadway musicals, from *Oklahoma, My Fair Lady* and *A Chorus Line* to *42nd Street.* Perhaps next in rank is the **Palace Theatre** at Cambridge Circus, now owned by **Andrew Lloyd-Webber,** but first built in 1891 as the **Royal English Opera House.** Such hits as *the Sound of Music, Cabaret* and *Jesus Christ Superstar* have played its boards.

Down Shaftesbury Avenue are the **Globe** (1906), the **Queen's** (1907, but bombed in 1940 and rebuilt in 1959), the **Apollo** (1901) and the **Lyric** (1888). South of Piccadilly Circus is the **Prince of Wales Theatre** (1937) and the **Theatre Royal, Haymarket** (1880). The first of 4 theatres behind the magnificent portico (1820) in Haymarket was built in 1720 on the site of an old tavern. In 1896, actor-manager **Beerholm Tree,** with the profits from his hit *Trilby,* built a new theatre over the road, **Her Majesty's.** It was later to house such successes as *Chin-Chin-Chow* (1916), *The Good Companions* (1931), *West Side Story* (1958 and 1984) and *Fiddler on the Roof* (1967).

To the south of Covent Garden on the Strand are the **Adelphi** (1806, rebuilt in 1930), home of popular musicals, the **Vaudeville** (1870, rebuilt in 1926); the **Strand** (built by the American impresarios, the **Shuberts** in 1905) and the **Aldwych** (1905). Nearby the Aldwych is the historic **Lyceum Theatre** (1765, rebuilt

1834), home of the first English actor to be knighted by Queen Victoria, **Sir Henry Irving.** With the interior remodeled again in 1904, the theatre closed in 1939, and has remained a dance hall ever since. It remains London's *sleeping beauty,* as it is a huge, fine, yet unused theatre.

Between Soho and Covent Garden stand the **Shaftesbury Theatre** on Shaftesbury Avenue (1911), the **Phoenix Theatre** (1930) and **Wyndhams** (1899) on Charing Cross Road, and the **Duke of Yorks** (1892) and **Albery** (1903) on St. Martin's Lane. The last 3 magnificently represent the best of the architectural qualities of intimacy and concentration, allied with a theatrical atmosphere that is found in so many London theatres.

Upon these stages many of the great English actors have played: **Olivier, Gielgud, Richardson, Schofield, Guiness** and many more. In the late fifties at the **Royal Court Theatre, Sloan Square,** **George Devine** began the **English Stage Company** which bred the *angry young men* of **John Osborne's** *Look Back in Anger,* and a new generation of playwrights, performers, and directors took the stage. London is the center of British theatre, film and television, and writers, directors, designers, actors and actresses are still drawn to the capital.

The theatre *boom* of the early 1980s has revitalized newer theatres (sometimes from existing cinemas), such as the **New London** (*Cats*), the **Prince Edward** (*Evita* and then *Chess*), the **Apollo Victoria** (*Starlight Express*) and the **Dominion** (*Time*).

There are over 50 *fringe* theatres around London that are less formal and less expensive than the West End. Some of these wax and wane with the years, but others, such as the **Warehouse, Covent Garden, Tricycle, Kilburn, Orange Tree, Richmond** and **King's Head, Islington** consistently create theatre of high quality. Some of the mainstream writers, including **Howard Barker, David Hare** and **Howard Brenton** owe their beginnings to the fertile fringe.

CAMDEN

ROYAL COLLEGE ST

CAMDEN STREET

BAYHAM STREET

HIGH STREET

EVERSHOLT

PRINCE ALBERT RD

OUTER CIRCLE

8 *London Zoo*

ALBANY STREET

HAMSTEAD ROAD

St. Pancras Station

7 *Regent's Park*

Euston Station

EUSTON

GOWER

SOUTHAM

Madame Tussaud's

6

PORTLAND PL

TOTTENHAM CT

EDGWARE ROAD

ROAD

MARYLEBONE ROAD

British Museum

HARROW ROAD

SEYMOUR PLACE

GLOUCESTER PLACE

BAKER STREET

5 *Wallace Collection*

MORTIMER ST

ROAD

BISHOP'S BRIDGE

Paddington Station

WIGMORE STREET

STREE

PRAED STREET

SUSSEX GARDENS

OXFORD

SHAFTS CR

BURY

BAYSWATER ROAD

N CARRIAGE DRIVE

CHARING CR

STREE

HAYM K T

REGENT

Trafalg Square

PICCADILLY

WHITE

SOUTH CARRIAGE DR

KENSINGTON ROAD

KNIGHTSBRIDGE

St. James's Palace

THE MALL

QUEENS GATE

Royal Albert Hall

BROMPTON ROAD

SLOANE STREET

GROSVENOR PL

BIRDCAGE

WK

Black Mus

3

Victoria and Albert Museum

VICTORIA ST

GREAT SMITH ST

W A

CROMWELL

Victoria Station

OLD BROMPTON ROAD

FULHAM ROAD

KINGS ROAD

Buckingham Palace

BUCKINGHAM PALACE RD

Tate Gall

VAUX

REDCLIFFE GARDENS

FINBOROUGH ROAD

BEAUFORT ST

CHEYNE WALK

ALBERT BRIDGE

CHELSEA EMBANKMENT

LUPUS ST

GROSVENOR ROAD

CHELSEA BRIDGE

BATTERSEA BRIDGE

BATTERSEA PARK ROAD

NINE ELMS ROAD

WANDSWORTH ROAD

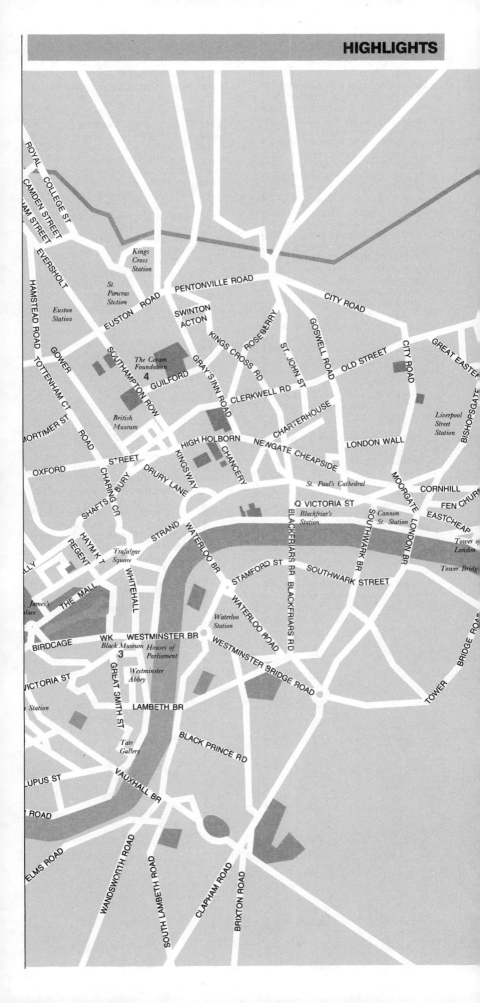

ROYAL COLLEGE STREET

CAMDEN STREET

HAM STREET

EVERSHOLT

HAMSTEAD ROAD

Kings Cross Station

St. Pancras Station

Euston Station

PENTONVILLE ROAD

CITY ROAD

EUSTON ROAD

SWINTON ACTON

GOWER

ROAD

TOTTENHAM CT

SOUTHAMPTON ROW

The Coram Foundation

4

GUILFORD

KINGS CROSS RD

ROSEBERRY

ST. JOHN ST

GOSWELL ROAD

OLD STREET

CITY ROAD

GREAT EASTE

British Museum

GRAY'S INN ROAD

CLERKWELL RD

Liverpool Street Station

BISHOPSGATE

MORTIMER ST

STREET

HIGH HOLBORN

CHARTERHOUSE

NEWGATE CHEAPSIDE

LONDON WALL

OXFORD

CHARING CR

BURY

DRURY LANE

KINGSWAY

CHANCERY

St. Paul's Cathedral

MOORGATE

CORNHILL

FEN CHUR

SHAFTS

Q VICTORIA ST

EASTCHEAP

HAYMKT

REGENT

STRAND

WATERLOO BR

Blackfriar's Station

Cannon St. Station

LONDON BR

Tower o London

LY

Trafalgar Square

STAMFORD ST

BLACKFRIARS BR

BLACKFRIARS RD

SOUTHWARK BR

SOUTHWARK STREET

Tower Bridg

James's lace

THE MALL

WHITEHALL

WATERLOO ROAD

BIRDCAGE

WK

WESTMINSTER BR

Black Museum

3

Houses of Parliament

Waterloo Station

TOWER

BRIDGE ROA

VICTORIA ST

GREAT SMITH ST

Westminster Abbey

WESTMINSTER BRIDGE ROAD

Station

LAMBETH BR

Tate Gallery

BLACK PRINCE RD

LUPUS ST

VAUXHALL BR

ROAD

ELMS ROAD

WANDSWORTH ROAD

SOUTH LAMBETH ROAD

CLAPHAM ROAD

BRIXTON ROAD

HIGHLIGHTS

1 **Tower Bridge.** London's best known bridge became a museum in 1982, and the original hydraulic machinery which operated the bridge is on display, along with exhibits which explain the Victorian genius behind the design. Built in 1894 by **Sir Horace Jones** and **John Wolfe-Barry,** the Gothic towered bridge represents Victorian architecture and engineering at its best. The twin towers of steel encased in stone support the 1,000 ton weight of the bascules which, until 1976, were raised and lowered by the original hydraulic machinery located in the piers of the towers. At the peak of London's river traffic and before steam replaced tall masts, the bascules rose as many as 650 times a month. Now they are operated by electricity and only open a few times a week. The glass-enclosed walkway, stretching majestically across the London sky 140 feet above the Thames, offers splendid views in every direction. From here you can step back and see the architectural variety of the City, from the Portland stone office buildings on Tower Hill to the brick and concrete of the post-war rebuilding and the glass and steel of the last 20 years. *Admission fee. Open Apr-Oct daily 10AM-6:30PM; Nov-Mar M-Sa 10AM-4:45PM. Last tickets sold 45 min. before closing. Tower Hill, EC3. Tube: Tower Hill*

2 **Tower of London.** Though the crowds can be as thick and forbidding as the gray-brown stone, this medieval monument, with its displays of armor and exquisite Crown Jewels, must be seen at least once in a lifetime. 900 years of fascinating though brutal history are embraced within these walls, and even though the Tower's violent years are long past, an atmosphere of impending doom still lingers. The Tower has been used as a royal palace, fortress, armory, treasury and menagerie, but it is best known as a merciless prison. Being locked up here, especially in Tudor times, was tantamount to almost certain death. Anne Boleyn, Catherine Howard, Lady Jane Grey,

Sir Thomas More and Sir Walter Raleigh are but a few who spent their final days, and in some cases years, in the Tower.

The buildings of the **Royal Palace and Fortress of the Tower of London,** as it is officially known, reflect almost every style of English architecture, as well as the different roles the Tower has played. William the Conqueror started the **White Tower** in 1078, and it was completed 20 years later by William Rufus. Richard the Lionheart strengthened the fortress in the 12th century by building a curtain wall with towers, of which only the Bell Tower remains. Henry III (1216-72) and his son Edward I (1272-1307) completed the transformation into the medieval castle of today. The 120 foot wide moat, now covered with grass, was kept flooded with water by a series of sluice gates until 1843. Prisoners and provisions were brought in through **Traitors Gate,** when the Thames was still London's main highway. A gate in the **Bloody Tower** leads to the inner precincts. Once known as the Garden Tower, the Bloody Tower acquired its unpleasant name after the Little Princes mysteriously disappeared from it in 1485. Controversy still rages over whether Richard III, their uncle and Protector, had them murdered so he could secure the throne. Sir Walter Raleigh was a prisoner in Bloody Tower from 1603 to 1615, and this is where he wrote *A History of the World.* In 1471, Henry VI was discovered murdered in **Wakefield Tower** next door. Almost every stone in **Beauchamp Tower** contains desperately scratched messages from prisoners, pathetic reminders of those who perished. Nearby is the **Chapel Royal of St. Peter ad Vincule,** built in the 12th century and restored by Henry VIII in 1512 after a fire. The chapel is the burial place of the Duke of Somerset, Duke of Northumberland, Anne Boleyn, Catherine Howard and Lady Jane Grey, all of whom were beheaded.

But glittering amidst the historical doom and gloom are the **Crown Jewels,** the Tower's

From a 1597 survey by W. Haiward and J. Gascoyne.

most popular attraction. Dazzling and brilliant, almost breathing with fire, the spectacular collection far exceeds its reputation. The jewels were housed in Martin Tower until 1671, when the audacious Colonel Blood came very close to making off with them. They are now heavily guarded by Yeoman Warders in an underground strongroom in the 19th century **Waterloo Building.** Here robes, swords, scepters and crowns adorned with some of the most precious stones in the world are displayed. Most of the royal regalia was sold or melted down after the execution of Charles I in 1649. Only 2 pieces escaped: the **Annointing Spoon,** probably used in the coronation of King John in 1199, and the 14th century **Ampulla.** The rest of the collection dates from the restoration of Charles II in 1660. **St. Edward's Crown** was made for Charles II and has been used by nearly all of his successors, including Queen Elizabeth II. It weighs almost 5 pounds and is adorned with more than 400 precious stones. The priceless **Imperial State Crown,** originally made for Queen Victoria, contains some of the most famous stones in the world, including the Second Star of Africa, the Stuart Sapphire and the Black Prince's balas ruby. Monarchs have worn this crown when leaving Westminster Abbey after coronation ceremonies, at the State Opening of Parliament and at other state occasions. The exquisite Koh-i-noor diamond adorns the **Queen Mother's Crown,** made especially for the coronation of Queen Elizabeth II in 1937. But even grander is the 530 carat Star of Africa, believed to be the largest cut diamond, which is on the **Sovereign's Orb and Sceptre.** Most spectacular of the many swords is the **State Sword,** decorated with diamonds, emeralds and rubies which form the national emblems of England, Scotland and Ireland.

The imposing Kentish and Caen stone walls of the **White Tower** dominate the Tower of London. Built in 1078 for William the Conqueror by a Norman monk, the walls are 15 feet thick at the base, 11 feet at the top and 90 feet above ground level. In 1241, Henry III, finding comfort within such dimensions, added a great hall and royal apartments and had the exterior whitewashed, hence the name White Tower. Today the tower houses the collection of **Tower Armories,** dating from the time it was the chief arsenal of the kingdom. The **Tudor Gallery** is the centerpiece of the collection. Here the personal armors of Henry VIII portray his massive presence more than any portrait ever could. On display are the armors made for foot combat when the King was young, slim and charming, the famous ram's horn helmet and King Henry's Walking Staff, a spiked club with 3 gun barrels in the head.

St. John's Chapel, on the second floor of the White Tower, is one of the finest examples of early Norman architecture, with its simple columns, round-headed arches and beautiful tunnel vaulting. Apart from the windows, which were enlarged by Sir Christopher Wren, the chapel remains much as it was in 1080 when it was completed. It was here in 1503 that Elizabeth of York, wife of Henry VII, lay in state surrounded by 800 candles and that Lady Jane Grey prayed before her execution in 1554.

The Tower's great sense of history and tradition lives on through ceremonies which have been performed virtually unchanged for centuries. Most famous is the **Ceremony of the Keys,** perhaps the oldest military ceremony in the world. Each evening at precisely 8 minutes to 10PM, the Chief Yeoman Warder, in a large scarlet coat and accompanied by 4 soldiers, secures the main gates of the Tower. As the clock strikes 10PM, a bugler sounds the Last Post. On 21 May of each year, representatives from Eton College and King's College, Cambridge place lilies and white roses in the oratory of Wakefield Tower where Henry VI was murdered in 1471, forever remembering him as the founder of these 2 great centers of academe. Tradition also continues with the daily feeding of the 6 ravens who live within the Tower's walls. Legend has it that if the ravens leave, the Tower will crumble.

To attend the Ceremony of the Keys, write (suggesting alternate dates) to the Resident Governor, Constable's Office, HM Tower of London, London EC 3N 4AB. Tower of London open Mar-Oct, M-Sa 9:30AM-5:45PM, Su 2-5:45PM; Nov-Feb, M-Sa 9:30AM-4PM. Tower Hill, EC3. 709-0765. Tube: Tower Hill.

3 **Black Museum.** Hidden behind the elaborate security of **New Scotland Yard** is perhaps the hardest museum to see in London. It is possible to telephone and, with permission, arrange a visit, but it is not a place for the squeamish. The Black museum is a teaching museum, and the sad lesson is that there are people who attempt to kill the Queen, who place bombs in crowded department stores and who send exploding letters through the mail. The exhibits contain the actual evidence removed from the scene of such crimes. The displays relate to famous murders, notorious prisoners, drugs, terrorism, murder of police officers, espionage, hijacking, bank robbery, counterfeiting and pornography. The first Black Museum opened in Old Scotland Yard in 1875, when it was still believed that the shape of the skull showed whether a person had a criminal nature. Crime detection is now a computerized science, but the words on the plaque by the door of the museum retain their truth: *Every object here has behind it a story of success or despair.* You can only visit by making an appointment, which is difficult. *Contact: Curator of Black Museum, Metropolitan Police, New Scotland Yard, Broadway, London, SW1. 230-4398 Tube: St James's.*

4 **Thomas Coram Foundation for Children.** Known as the **Foundling Hospital,** this is one of the most unusual small museums in London. It owes its origin to sea captain Thomas Coram (1668-1751), who made his name as a colonizer of America. Returning to London, Coram was shocked to see the number of abandoned infants. He enlisted *21 ladies of nobility and distinction, half a dozen dukes and one short of a dozen earls* to petition George II for help in establishing a home for the foundlings.

The painter **William Hogarth** was one of the original governors and with his wife served as a foster parent to the children. Hogarth's major work, the *March to Finchley* (1746) and a superb, robust portrait of *Captain Coram* (1740) are 2 treasures in the museum's picture collection, which includes works by **Gainsborough** and **Reynolds.** The composer **Handel** was also an early benefactor. He not only gave performances to aid the children, but also bequeathed his own copy of the *Messiah,* which is now on exhibit.

The collection which makes the museum unforgettable is found in a lovingly preserved 18th century room known as the **Courtroom.** Here you can inspect the mementos left by mothers in the baskets of their abandoned infants: coral beads, locks of hair, a black wooden hand, a section of a map of England, earrings, watch seals, coins, a crystal locket, a single delicate lace glove, the letter *A* cut in metal, and a message scratched on mother of pearl, *James, son of James Concannon, late or now of Jamaica, 1757.* These tokens were the foundlings' only clues to parentage, the only hope of being able to answer the question: who am I? *Admission fee. Open M-F 10AM-4PM. 40 Brunswick Square, WC1. 278-2424*

4 **Wallace Collection.** (Hertford House) One of the finest collections of French furniture, paintings and objects d'art in the world. Visiting this grand townhouse and seeing the owner's private art collection is much more intimate than going to a museum. The rich and varied collection was acquired by 4 generations of the **Hertford** family during the 18th and 19th centuries. The second Marquess, who added to the collection of English portraits with **Romney's** *Mrs. Robinson* and **Reynold's** *Nelly O'Brien,* bought Hertford House, then known as Manchester House, in 1797. But it was the fourth Marquess (1777-1842) who transformed the family's art collection into what you see today. An eccentric recluse in Paris who delcared *I only like pleasing paintings,* the fourth Marquess amassed works by **Fragonard, Boucher, Watteau** and **Lancret** for what can only be considered a paltry sum after the Revolution, when 18th century art was unfashionable. He also lavishly purchased 18th century French furniture by **Boulle, Cressent** and **Riesener,** including the chest of drawers made for Louis XV's bedroom at Versailles and pieces made for Queen Marie-Antoinette. Upon his death, the Marquess left his collection to his illegitimate son, **Sir Richard Wallace** (1818-1890) who had acted for him in all of his transactions. He added the European armor and the medieval and Renaissance works of art. Wallace brought the collection to Hertford House, and his widow left it to the nation. Don't miss the exquisite collection of gold boxes, mounted with Sevres porcelain and jewels, or the wrought-iron and bronze staircase balustrade which was made in c. 1735 for the Palais Mazarin (now the Bibliotheque Nationale). It was sold in 1855 as scrap iron, but rescued by the fourth Marquess. *No admission fee. Open M-Sa 10AM-5PM; Su 2-5PM. Hertford House, Manchester Square, W1. 935-0687. Tube: Bond St.*

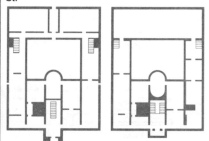

Ground floor   First floor

5 **Madame Tussaud's.** Forget whatever you may have against waxworks— there is nothing ordinary about Mme. Tussaud's. It has been a British institution since 1802, and once you see it, you will understand why it attracts more than 2 million visitors a year. Part of the fun is watching the British themselves, who love to visit this museum and can be observed speaking their minds to the wax images of the controversial trade union leaders or standing with hushed respect before the figures of the Royal Family. Mme. T. learned her trade making death masks during the French Revolution, and those of **Louis XVI** and **Marie Antoinette** are displayed on spikes beside the actual blade which beheaded them. The oldest surviving likeness (1765) is that of **Mme. du Barry** (known as *sleeping beauty*). A mechanism hidden in the bodice of her dress allows the figure to breathe. **Henry VIII** is surrounded by all 8 of his wives, and there is a full recreation of the wedding party of the **Prince and Princess of Wales.** The wax likenesses are most often modeled from life and are never behind glass. They stand in small tableaux as figures from history, politics, literature, sports and entertainment. There is a room devoted to contemporary heroes (**David Bowie's** hair moves and **Elvis** talks) and a chamber of horrors (**Hitler, Jack the Ripper, Charles Manson**). There are museum guards made of wax and an incredibly lifelike, exhausted tourist who dozes in a chair with guidebook in hand. *Admission fee. Open daily Oct-Mar 10AM-5:30PM; Apr-Sept 10AM-6PM. Marylebone Rd., NW1 (next to Baker Street Tube Station). 935-6861*

6 **Regent's Park.** London is a city of parks and squares, and nowhere do nature and the built environment meet more gloriously than at Regent's Park. The essence of **John Nash's** original plan of 1811 to turn 500 acres of farmland into a park survived through 8 years of government commissions. His spectacular terraces, iced with stucco and lined with columns, surround the park and make it look like a gigantic wedding-cake, and are named after the titles of some of George III's children. **Cumberland Terrace** (1826) with its magnificent pedi-

ment and 276 yard facade lined with Ionic columns, is the most splendid; **Chester Terrace** (1825) is the longest, stretching 313 yards with 52 Corinthian columns; and the elegant **Clarence Terrace** (designed by Decimus Burton in 1823) is the smallest. Many of the terraces were tenderly restored after suffering bomb damage during World War II. The neo-Georgian **Winfield House,** now the residence of the US ambassador, is located on the site of St. Dunstan's Lodge, designed in 1825 by Decimus Burton for the legendary 3rd Marquess of Hertford who, it is said, used it as a harem. The curiously shaped boating lake, reaching out in every direction and surrounded by ash groves, is undeniably romantic. The exquisite **Queen Mary's Garden** contains 40,000 rose bushes laid out in large beds, each with a different variety. **Regent's Canal** skirting the northern boundary of the park runs for 8 miles from Paddington to Limehouse and passes by the animals at the Zoo. *Regent's Park NW1. Tube: Regent's Park, Baker St.*

7 **London Zoo.** One of the oldest and most pleasant zoos in the world. The gardens of the Zoological Society of London were first laid out by **Decimus Burton** in 1828 and now spread over 36 enchanting acres of Regent's Park. Most of the 6,000 animals have been released from those depressing iron ages that make them look bored and lethargic and are free to roam in settings similar to their natural habitats, separated from the public by moats. One of the most spectacular settings is the **Mappin Terraces,** with pelicans, wild pigs, bears and mountain sheep and goats on separate levels of an artificial mountain. The **Children's Zoo and Farm** is always a thrill for kids, and a large crowd always turns up to watch the elephants take their baths at 11:30. *Admission fee. Open Apr-Oct M-Sa 9AM-6PM, Su 9AM-7PM; Nov-Mar open daily 10AM-4PM. Regent's Park, NW1. 722-3333. Tube: Regent's Park, Mornington Crescent, Camden Town.*

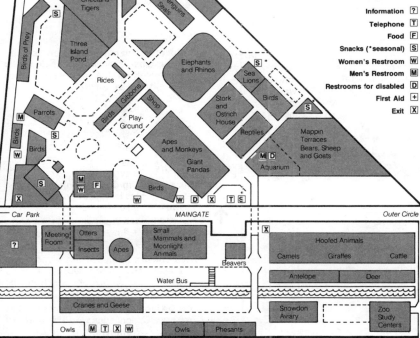

LONDON ZOO

Information	?
Telephone	T
Food	F
Snacks (*seasonal)	S
Women's Restroom	W
Men's Restroom	M
Restrooms for disabled	D
First Aid	+
Exit	X

CHILDREN'S LONDON

Main Attractions

Madame Tussaud's. Lifelike wax impressions of historical characters, famous people, pop singers and film stars. Sleeping Beauty actually breathes. *Open M-F 10AM-5:30PM, Sa-Su 9:30AM-5:30PM. Marylebone Rd., NW1. 935-6861*

Tower of London. Built during the reign of William the Conqueror, the Tower has been used as a prison, a mint and even a menagerie. Don't miss the magnificent Crown Jewels or the Green where 17-year-old Lady Jane Grey was beheaded. *Open Summer, M-Sa 9:30AM-5:45PM, Su 2-5:45PM; Winter, M-Sa 9:30AM-4:30PM. Closed Su. Tower Hill, EC3. 709-0765*

The London Toy and Model Museum. Toys down through the ages. See all the toys you could have bought for a penny at the turn of the century. There are plenty of knobs to push to set mechanical toys in motion. *Open Tu-Sa 10AM-5:30PM, Su 11AM-5:30PM. 23 Craven Hill, W2. 262-7905*

Science Museum. Head for the Children's Gallery and a den of working models. Try your hand at flying a plane on a simulator or peer through a periscope up to the floor above. *Open M-Sa 10AM-6PM, Su 2:30-6PM. Exhibition Rd., SW7. 589-3456*

Planetarium. Lose yourself in outer space watching films projected onto the vast copper dome. *Open M-F 11AM-4:15PM, Sa-Su 10:15AM-5PM. Marylebone Rd., NW1. 486-1121*

Bethnall Green Museum of Childhood. The country's largest collection of doll houses and hundreds of toys for all ages are exhibited. Artistic talent? Join an art workshop on Saturdays. *Open M-Th & Sa 10AM-6PM, Su 2:30-6PM. Closed Friday. Cambridge Heath Rd., E2. 980-2415*

Natural History Museum. Meet Diplodocus in the entrance hall—this enormous monster has been extinct for 135 million years! Or gaze at the 90-foot-long giant Blue Whale suspended from the ceiling. *Open M-Sa 10AM-6PM, Su 2:30-6PM. Cromwell Rd., SW7. 589-6323*

Pubs

In Britain it can be difficult to get a drink. Not only are there licensing laws which tell you when and what to drink, but if you have children in tow, you will have to leave them outside unless they are over the age of 14.

The following pubs have gardens where children are welcome—if the weather allows, of course:

Cross Keys. Popular Cheyne Walk pub with an exceedingly pretty patio boasting a long list of horticultural prizes. In spite of the Russian vine, there is seating for 30 to 40. *2 Lawrence St., SW3. 352-1893*

Admiral Codrington. Children are welcome in both the restaurant and the conservatory. Even if it is raining, the perspex roof allows you to sit in this bright and cheery room surrounded by hanging plants. *17 Mossop St., SW3. 589-4603*

Spaniard's Inn. Come rain or shine, Spaniard's Inn caters to kids, either in the large beer garden with a 100-bird budgerigar aviary or indoors in the Turpin's Bar on the second floor. *Hampstead Lane, NW3. 455-3276*

Earl of Lonsdale. After a morning at Portobello Market, you can sit in the shade of an Iolanthus tree in the flag-stoned garden. *277 Westbourne Grove, W11. 727-6335*

Scarsdale Arms. There is a very picturesque patio surrounded by flower boxes and hanging baskets suspended from the plane tree branches. Children are catered for indoors in the restaurant. *23a Edwardes Square, W8. 937-1811*

Duke of Somerset. Pretty paved patio—the only pub in the City of London with one. *Little Somerset St., Aldgate, E1. 481-0785*

Clothing

Scotch House. You can find boy's bermudas or girl's dresses in your own family tartan in the kid's department. Classic swing-back coats and a good range of knitwear. *Open M-F 9AM-5:30PM, Sa 9AM-4:30PM. 2 Brompton Rd., SW1. 581-2151*

Peter Jones. Wide range of children's clothes for all occasions at reasonable prices. *Open M-F 9AM-5:30PM. Sa 9AM-1PM. Sloane Square, SW1. 730-3434*

Marks and Spencer. With over 250 stores in the UK, their success lies in rigorous quality control and competitive prices. The knitwear and underwear are especially good. *Open M-W 9AM-5PM, Th 9:30AM-7:30PM, Sa 9AM-6PM. 458 Oxford St., W1. 486-6151*

Laura Ashley. Similar versions as the adult range. Floral cotton dresses for girls and sailor suits for boys. *Open M-Sa 10AM-6PM. 9 Harriet St., SW1. 235-9797*

Mothercare. For ages up to eleven-and-a-half. Fashion garmets as well as strollers and safety seats. *120 Kensington High St., W8. 937-9781*

The White House. Exquisite christening robes and traditional smocking, all embroidered in their own workshops. Silks and cashmere for those special occasions. *Open M-F 9AM-5:30PM, Sa 9AM-1PM. 51-52 New Bond St., W1. 629-3521*

Second-Hand Clothes

Children's Bazaar. Little trendies can swoop up *Sloan Ranger* hand-me-downs for approximately half the original price. *Open M-F 9:30AM-5PM, Sa 10AM-12PM. 162c Sloane St., SW1. 730-8901*

Children's Bookshops

Puffin Bookshop. *Open M-Sa 10AM-8PM. 1 The Piazza, Covent Garden, WC2. 379-6465*

Muswell Hill Children's Bookshop. *Open M-Sa 9:15AM-5:15PM. 29 Fortis Green Rd., Muswell Hill, N10. 444-5500*

The Children's Bookshop. *Open M-Sa 9AM-5:30PM. 66 High St., Wimbledon Village, SW19. 947-2038*

The Book Boat. Housed on a barge on the river next to *Gypsy Moth. Open M-W, F-Su 10AM-5PM. Closed Th. Cutty Sark Gardens, Greenwich, SE10. 853-4383*

Young World. Books in the basement of this toy shop. *Open M-Sa 9:30AM-6PM, Su 12-6PM. 229 Kensington High St., W8. 937-6314*

CHILDREN'S LONDON

The Lion and the Unicorn. *Open M-Sa 9:30AM-5:30PM. 19 King St., Richmond, Surrey. 940-0483*

Harrods. Second Floor. *Open M, Tu, Th, F 9AM-5PM; W 9:30AM-7PM; Sa 9AM-6PM. Knightsbridge, SW1. 730-1234*

Home Helps

Universal Aunts Ltd. This old and established company offers nannies, babysitters, cooks, companions, dog walkers, sightseeing guides, flat-letting and more. *250 Kings Rd., Chelsea, SW3. 351-5767*

Poppinjay Nannies Ltd. Nannies, nurses, housekeepers, cooks and mother's helpers. Their Children's Escort Service will escort unaccompanied children on journeys to, from and within the UK. *2a Hasker St., SW3. 581-3278. Children's Escort Service: 584-9572*

Childminders. Babysitters and staff for light domestic work. *67 Marylebone High St., W1. 935-2049, 935-9763*

The Nanny Service. Temporary nannies (5 months or less) or permanent staff. *Oldbury Place, W1. 935-6976, 935-3515*

Babysitters Unlimited. Babysitters, all with references, and cooks and party helps. *London House, 271-273 King St., W6. 741-5566, 741-5567*

Knightsbridge Nannies. Supplies nannies all over the world and caters to the home market with temporary staff, maternity nurses and babysitters. *5 Beauchamp Place, SW3. 584-9323*

Solve Your Problem Ltd. Mother's helps, babysitters, party helps, secretarial and clerical staff and even dressmakers. *1a Drayson Mews, W8. 937-0906, 937-0907*

Nannies (Kensington). Nannies supplied for either long or short-term appointments. *16 Stratford Rd., W8. 937-3299*

BEST
London Children's Books

A Bear Called Paddington by Michael Bond
Peter Pan by J M Barrie
The Finding by Nina Brown
Smith by Leon Garfield

Running Scared by Bernard Ashley
The Dark Behind the Curtain by Gillian Cross

BEST
English Toys

Hamley Vintage Vehicles (Rolls Royce, London taxi, Red double-decker bus)
Canterbury teddy bears
Hornby train sets
Peggy Nesbitt dolls (Princess Diana)
Lead soldiers (Changing of the Guard)
Goldenbear Snowman (book and video by Raymond Brigg)
Jigsaw puzzle of Big Ben

BEST
English Children's Books

Danny Champion of the World by Roald Dahl
Nature of the Best by Jenni Hawker
Summer of the Zeppelin by Elsie McTutcheon
Thunder and Lightnings by Jan Mark
Minnow on the Say by Philippa Pearce
Horse by Jane Gardem
Postman Pat's Foggy Day by John Cunliffe

Top 10 Toys
Hamley's
The largest toy store in the world

Trivial Pursuit
The Bandai Robo Machine Winchtruck
Lego Technic Car Classic
Fischer Price Roller Skates
Hamley Bear (with red waistcoat)
Cheer Bear Care Bear
Playmobile Children and Swing
Thomas the Tank Engine Sit and Ride
Little Tikes Cozy Coupe
Sindy's High Society Ball Gown (designed by the Emanuels, who created Princess Diana's wedding gown)

CALENDAR

January

January Sales. Cashmere and every other English luxury at civilized reductions. Harrods' sale is the most famous, but you pay the price.

Chinese New Year. January and February. Weave your way through the streets of Soho. Lion Dance and streamers on Gerrard Street.

International Boat Show. Europe's largest boat show. *Earl's Court, SW5.*

World Championship Tennis Doubles Tournament. *Albert Hall, SW7.*

Rugby Union Internationals. January to March at *Twickenham, Middlesex. 892-8161*

Benson & Hedges Masters Snooker Tournament. Snooker, a variety of pool, is played with 15 red balls and 6 balls of different colors. *Wembley Conference Center, Wembley, Middlesex. 902-1234*

Trafalgar Square. 30 January at 11AM. Service commemorating the execution of Charles I in 1649. Sponsored by the Royal Stuart Society.

February

Crufts Dog Show. 11,000 dogs compete for Supreme Champion. *Earls Court, SW5. 385-1200*

Valentine's Day. 14 February. The English send their Valentine's to *The Times.* The messages say more about their emotional capacity than all English literature.

Clown Service. Clowns International commemorates its founder, Joseph Grimaldi, with a clown show after the service. *Holy Trinity Church, Beechwood Rd., E8.*

CALENDAR

March

British Summertime. Clocks go forward.

Chelsea Antiques Fair. Creme de la creme English antiques show. *Chelsea Old Town Hall, SW3.*

Daily Mail Ideal Home Exhibition. Lasts for 3 weeks. *Earls Court, SW5.*

Oranges and Lemons Service. On or near 28 March. Service during which children receive an orange or lemon to commemorate the fruits arriving in London. *St. Clement Danes, WC2.*

Oxford and Cambridge Boat Race. Thousands watch the teams battle upstream from Putney to Mortlake. A classic since 1829.

Camden Festival. A chance to hear music, classical and contemporary, that is rarely performed. *Box office: 355-7727*

Easter Monday. Procession and Easter carols. *Westminster Abbey, SW1.*

London Harness Horse Parade. Easter Monday morning. A procession of London's working horses. *Inner Circle, Regent's Park, NW1.*

April

April Fool's Day. Inspires the British humor. Beware.

Grand National. The famous steeplechase: 4 and a half miles, 30 jumps. Watch in a pub or, better, go. Two special trains leave Euston Station at 8:10AM and 8:26AM. Eat your 4-course breakfast in the Pullman. *Reservations: 387-9400. Buses take you to Aintree.*

The Whitebread Badminton Horse Trials. Four-day trials held at Badminton, Avon. Show-jumping, cross country and the Royal Family.

Mars London Marathon. 20,000 runners take over 26 miles of London's streets.

HM Queen's Real Birthday. 21 April. 21 gun salute in Hyde Park and Tower Hill at noon.

Tyburn Walk. Last Sunday in April. A silent procession from the Old Bailey to Tyburn Convent in honor of Catholics hanged at the Tyburn gallows.

Shakespeare's Birthday. 23 April. Service at Southwark Cathedral.

Good Friday. Most stately homes open their season.

Cricket Season begins.

Polo Season begins. Charles plays and Diana watches. *Cowdray Park, Midhurst, West Sussex and Guards', Smiths Lawn, Windsor Great Park, Egham, Surrey.*

Covent Garden Proms. A week of sponsored opera and ballet at the Royal Opera House. A chance to see World Class performances at amateur prices. *Box office: 240-1066*

May

Chelsea Flower Show. A beautiful 4-day horticultural display. *Royal Hospital Grounds, Chelsea, SW3.*

Glyndebourne Festival Opera Season. Mid-May until August. Long dresses, dinner jackets, champagne picnics. Edwardian splendor in a setting by Mozart, and one of the finest small opera companies in the world. *For tickets: write in March for booking form to Glyndebourne, New Lewes, Sussex; Ringmer 812321 or call early on the day you want to go in case of cancellations.*

Summer Exhibition at the Royal Academy. May to mid-August. Large exhibition chosen from even larger number of applicants. British art today, all for sale. *Royal Academy, Burlington House, Piccadilly, W1.*

Oak Apple Day. 29 May. The Chelsea Pensioners in their red and blue uniforms decorate Charles IIs statue with oak leaves. Their founder escaped in the Battle of Worcester in 1651 by hiding in an oak tree (or so he said). *Royal Hospital, Chelsea, SW3*

Royal Windsor Horse Show. *Great Park, Windsor.*

American Memorial Day. 30 May. Wreaths placed at the Cenotaph in Whitehall, the grave of the Unknown Warrior in Westminster Abbey and Lincoln's statue in Parliament Square. A moving ceremony for homesick Americans.

June

Beating the Retreat. Household Division. Massed bands and marching at the Horse Guards Parade, SW1. One week later by the Royal Artillery.

Derby Day. Most prestigious flat race of all. The horse who wins is worth $20,000,000 in stud value the minute he crosses the finish line. Even the Queen bets. *Epson Racecourse, Surrey.*

Grosvenor House Antiques Fair. 10-day antique fair for the rich, the grand, the museum, the American Express. *Grosvenor House, Park Lane, W1.*

Trooping the Colour. 11 June or the nearest Sunday. The Queen's *official* birthday parade. She rides side-saddle from Buckingham Palace to Horse Guards to receive the Colour from her Foot Guards. Spectacular pomp. *Horse Guards Parade, Whitehall, SW1.*

Royal Ascot. Third week in June. It was known for its social significance and outrageous hats before *My Fair Lady* and nothing has changed. The Queen always goes. *Berkshire Racecourse.*

Antiquarian Book Fair. A book lovers dream: rare and second-hand books from all over the world. *Europa Hotel, Grosvenor Square, W1. 493-1232*

Open Air Shakespeare Season. Shakespeare as you like it: outdoors on summer nights in Regent's Park. June to August. *Box office: 486-2431*

First Test Match. 5-day international Cricket match. *Lord's Cricket Ground, St. John's Wood, NW8.*

Wimbledon Lawn Tennis Championships. 2 weeks from Monday in mid-June to first Sunday in July. Send for an application between 1 October and 31 January: *All England Lawn Tennis Club, Church Rd., Wimbledon, SW19.* Your application (and 100,000 others) will be put in a ballot box for Center and No. 1 courts.

July

Princess Diana's Birthday. 1 July (the Princess of Wales was born in 1961).

Henley Royal Regatta. Last Thursday in June to first Sunday in July. The Ascot and Wimbledon of rowing. Boats race 2-by-2 along the Thames. Strawberries and cream with champagne in the car park. Very pretty too. *Henley-on-Thames, Oxfordshire.*

Royal Tournament. Spectacular 2 week military exhibition by all branches of the Armed Forces. *Earls Court, SW5.*

Henry Wood Promenade Concerts. Mid-

July to mid-September. The *Proms*. Outstanding concerts every night. Go to Royal Albert Hall and choose a night. Tickets by ballot for the emotional last night. The *Prommers* buy the cheapest tickets and stand or sit on the floor. *Royal Albert Hall, SW7.*

Doggett's Coat and Badge Race. Late July/early August. Founded in 1714, it is the oldest rowing event in the world. Single sculls race from Tower Bridge to Chelsea.

City of London Festival. Concerts and plays held in historical buildings in the City.

Royal Garden Parties at Buckingham Palace. 3 successive weeks. 6,000 people tramp over the gardens to the strains of Gilbert and Sullivan. Not open to the public, but fun to watch the elegant invited masses arriving and leaving.

Parliament breaks for summer recess. You can now tour the Houses of Parliament.

August

Edinburgh Festival. The arts festival that started it all. Still the oldest and largest. It is now full of TV movie producers looking for talent.
Grouse shooting begins 12 August. Getting the first grouse on the table is the English equivalent of *Beaujolais Nouveau*. There is even a wool shirt named *August 12* in honor of the start of the season. Because of milder winters and later springs, the grouse are still babies in August and shouldn't be aimed at or eaten until September.

Bank Holiday Weekend. Last weekend in August. Traditional fairgrounds on Hampstead Heath. Notting Hill carnival, West Indian music, food, dancing.

September

Autumn Antiques Fair. 10-day antique fair. *Chelsea Town Hall, SW3.*

Battle of Britain Week. Thanksgiving service at Westminster Abbey.

Royal National Rose Society Show. A rose is a rose is a rose, but these are Victorian, Georgian, Edwardian, unforgettable. *Royal Horticultural Society Hall, Vincent Hall, SW1.*

October

Pheasant shooting begins on 1 October. This is what good English restaurants do best, but don't order it until 10 October, when the pheasants have been *hung* properly.

Trafalgar Day. Sunday nearest 21 October. The Battle of Trafalgar is remembered with a procession from Horse Guards Parade to Nelson's Column for wreath laying and hymns. *Trafalgar Square, W1.*

National Service for Seafarers. Wednesday nearest 21 October. Another service on the anniversary of the Battle of Trafalgar in the cathedral where Nelson is buried. *St. Paul's Cathedral, EC4.*

National Brass Band Festival. The land of the brass band with great trumpeting. *Royal Albert Hall, SW7.*

Motor Shows. Useful for tax-free Jaguars and Minis. *Birmingham and Earls Court.*

Halloween. October 31.

November

State Opening of Parliament. Watch the Queen leave Buckingham Palace in the Irish State Coach on her way to Parliament. Prince Charles and Princess Diana ride in the second coach. Go to the nearest pub and watch the speech on TV. *House of Lords, Westminster.*

Guy Fawkes Night. 5 November. Bonfires and fireworks light up the sky in memory of the Gunpowder Plot of 1605.

Lord Mayor's Procession and Show. Inauguration of the Lord Mayor for his year of office. Join the crowds en route from the Guildhall to the Royal Courts of Justice.

Le Nouveau Beaujolais. 15 November. More hysteria than in Paris.

Remembrance Sunday. Second Sunday in November. A moving ceremony remembering those who died in the 2 World Wars, attended by the Queen, members of the Royal Family and leading politicians. Music by Elgar and a 2 minute silence. *Cenotaph, Whitehall, SW1.*

December

Royal Smithfield Show. Cows, pigs, sheep and horses all looking sweet and clean. Go early and have a farmer's breakfast at **Fox and Anchor** (*115 Charterhouse St., EC1. 253-4838). Earls Court, SW5).*

World Doubles Tennis Championships. *Olympia, W14.*

Annual Ice Show. December to March. This is the land of **Torville and Dean.** *Wembley, Middlesex.*

Christmas Tree donated by Oslo, Norway is erected in Trafalgar Square. Carol singing every evening from about 14 December.

Royal Choral Society Carol Concerts. *Royal Albert Hall and Guildhall.*

Watchnight Service. 31 December. 22 to 24 hours remembering the night during the Blitz when St. Paul's was hit 29 times. *St. Paul's Cathedral, EC4.*

Big Ben chimes the big 12, *Auld Lang Syne*, on 31 December. Crowds gather in Trafalgar Square.

DAY TRIPS

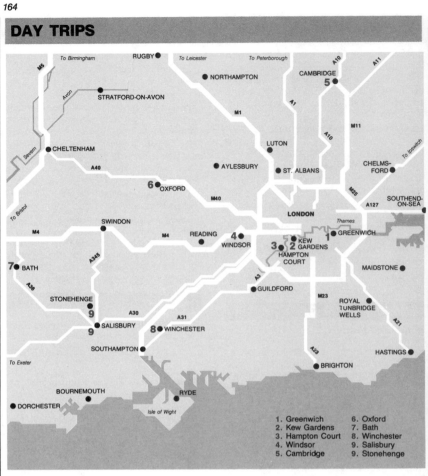

To Birmingham · RUGBY · To Leicester · To Peterborough · A10 · A11

M5 · Avon · STRATFORD-ON-AVON · NORTHAMPTON · CAMBRIDGE **5**

Severn · CHELTENHAM · A1 · M11

A40 · LUTON · A10

To Bristol · **6** OXFORD · M40 · AYLESBURY · ST. ALBANS · CHELMS-FORD · To Ipswich

M25 · SOUTHEND-ON-SEA · A127

LONDON · Thames

SWINDON · READING · **4** · KEW GARDENS **2** · GREENWICH **1**

M4 · M4 · WINDSOR · **3** HAMPTON COURT

To Exeter · A345 · **7** BATH · MAIDSTONE

A36 · STONEHENGE · A3 · GUILDFORD · M23 · ROYAL TUNBRIDGE WELLS

9 · A30 · A31 · SALISBURY **9** · **8** WINCHESTER · A21

SOUTHAMPTON · A23 · HASTINGS

BRIGHTON

BOURNEMOUTH · RYDE · DORCHESTER · Isle of Wight

1. Greenwich
2. Kew Gardens
3. Hampton Court
4. Windsor
5. Cambridge
6. Oxford
7. Bath
8. Winchester
9. Salisbury
9. Stonehenge

1 **Greenwich.** This Thames-side city was once the center of the world and it is still possessed with the confidence and grandeur befitting that position. Greenwich Meridian (zero degree longitude) and Greenwich Mean Time still reign in the world, and the vistas, elegant buldings and parklands make you long for the Empire, feelings increased by the tall masts of the *Cutty Sark* looming over the streets of the city. Now drydocked near Greenwich Pier, she is the last of the great tea-clippers which could sail 360 miles in a single day. This ship is now a museum *(open M-Sa 11AM-6PM),* as is the smaller *Gypsy Moth* nearby, which sailed around the world in 1966 with Sir Francis Chichester alone at the helm. *(Open M-Th, Sa 11AM-6PM: closed F-Sa).* The domes and collonades of the **Royal Naval College,** a feast of **Wren, Vanbrugh** and **Hawksmoor,** magnificently preside over the River Thames. Inside the Naval College, the walls of the **Painted Hall** aré lined with paintings by **Sir James Thornhill** (done in 1708-27). The **chapel,** opposite, was redone with fine intricate detailing after a fire in the late 18th century. *(Painted Hall and chapel are open M-W, F-Su 2:30-4:30PM; closed Th.)* The **National Maritime Museum,** farther back from the river, houses the finest collection of

Royal Naval College

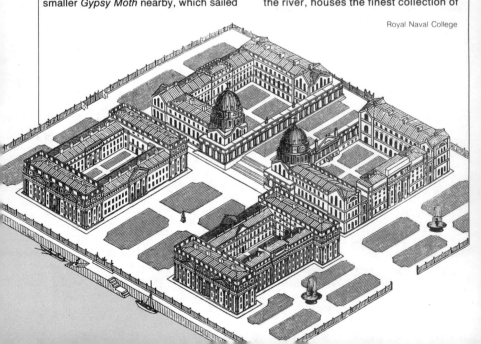

DAY TRIPS

Royal Observatory

globes in the world, along with marine paintings, navigational instruments, Nelson relics and model ships. The centerpiece of the Museum is the pure and classical **Queen's House,** designed by Inigo Jones in 1616-35. The great hall—a perfect cube—and the *tulip* staircase are both stunning. Henry VIII and his daughters Mary and Elizabeth were born here. *(Open Tu-Sa 10AM-6PM, Su 2-5:30PM.)* From the Queen's House, pass through **Greenwich Park,** with its delightful Flower Garden, to the buildings of the **Royal Observatory,** designed by Wren for Charles II in 1675-76. Inside is a fascinating collection of telescopes and astronomical instruments. *(Open M-Sa 10AM-6PM, Su 2:30-6PM.* A river walk from the Naval College takes you to the extraordinary **Thames Flood Barrier,** comprised of 10 enormous movable gates between river piers and abutments on either bank. *The best way to reach Greenwich is by river boat. Boats depart from Westminster Pier every 20 minutes from 10:30AM to 3PM for the 45 minute journey. The last boat leaves Greenwich at 3:45 PM in the winter and 5:45 in the summer. Trains run from Charing Cross to Maze Hill every half-hour and take 20 minutes. The bus route to Greenwich is dreary, but buses 177 and 188 run between Greenwich and Waterloo Station, making the journey in 35 minutes. If going by car, take A200.*

---

2 **Kew Gardens.** It began as a hobby for Princess Augusta, mother of George III, back in 1759 and blossomed into the most famous collection of flowers and plants in the world. Kew Gardens is a botanical paradise of more than 300,000 varieties, set in 300 lush acres along the east side of the Thames. Officially called the *Royal Botanic Gardens,* it was given to the nation by the Royal Family in 1841, and is, for all its pleasure-giving, a scientific institution where plants are studied, classified and cultivated. Kew Gardens offers a constantly changing display of flowers, as well as rock gardens, a stream with aquatic birds, a herbarium with more than 5 million varieties of dried plants, and stunning paths down to the river (with a sublime view of **Syon House** across the Thames). Amidst the greenery is an array of 18th century garden follies, designed by Sir William Chambers for Princess Augusta: classical temples, ruins of a Roman arch, a fanciful 10-story pagoda and an Orangery. The **Palm House,** with its sweeping curves of glass and iron, was built in 1844 by Decimus Buron and houses tropical plants from both hemispheres. All the greenhouses are architectural masterpieces, as are the grand entrance gates in the corner of Kew Green, also by Burton. Be sure to see **Queen Charlotte's Cottage,** the **Japanese Pagoda** and, if you are lucky enough to come in the spring, the **rhododendron dell.** *Small admission fee. Gardens open daily 10AM-sunset; greenhouses open daily 11AM-5PM. 940-1171. The best way to get to Kew Gardens is by river boat from Westminster Pier. Boats leave for the 75 minute journey every 30 minutes from 10:30AM to 3:30PM. You can also take a train or the underground to and from Kew. Trains leave from Waterloo Station for Kew Bridge, and the Tube to Kew Station is on the District Line. If driving, take A30.*

DAY TRIPS

3 **Hampton Court.** Not really out of town, but down the road 15 miles from London (and better still, down the river), Hampton Court is a *must* as far as day trips go. The palace was built in the 1500s by Cardinal Thomas Wolsey, minister to Henry VIII. Wolsey's wealth and lifestyle so exceeded the King's that, inevitably, the King pushed the Cardinal out of the Court and took up residence himself. Henry VIII added a moat, a drawbridge and a tennis court, amenities enjoyed by the 5 of his 6 wives who lived in the palace. Elizabeth I loved Hampton Court, and Charles I lived in it as king and as a prisoner of Cromwell. When William and Mary came to the thrown in 1689, they revamped the palace, with Christopher Wren and Grinling Gibbons in charge. The south front was severely damaged by fire in March of 1986, but luckily, most of the paintings and art treasures were saved. Signs marked with arrows are scattered throughout the palace to help you find your way to **Cardinal Wolsey's Apartments;** the **King's Dressing Room,** with works by Holbein and Mabuse; the **Great Hall,** which was the site of Henry VIII's famous banquets and performances of Shakespeare's plays by the playwright's company; and the lower **Orangery,** with the 9 tempera paintings *The Triumph of Julius Caesar* (1485-92) by Andrea Mantegn. The 50 acres of landscaped gardens are absolutely beautiful and the **Maze** is irresistible. *Admission fee. Open Apr to Sept M-Sa 9:30AM-6PM, Su 11AM-6PM; Oct-Mar M-Sa 9:30AM-5PM, Su 2-5PM, 977-8441. In summer, go by boat from Westminster Pier to Hampton Court. Boats leave at 10AM, 10:30AM, 11:30AM and 12PM. The train from Waterloo Station takes 35 minutes. You can also hop a frequent Green Line Bus—No. 715A, 716, 718 or 725.*

4 **Windsor.** Windsor lies on a pretty bend of the Thames 21 miles from London and is home to a magnificent park, a famous boy's school (Eton) and the largest castle in the world still lived in by royalty—Windsor Castle. The castle has been a royal residence for more than 900 years. William the Conquerer first built a round keep of timber in 1078 (now long gone), and over the centuries, monarchs have enlarged the castle and constructed new buildings. Edward IV began **St. George's Chapel** in the 1820s. It is one of the best examples of perpendicular architecture, with its elaborately carved stone vaulting. Henry VIII, his third wife Jane Seymour, Charles I and other monarchs are buried in the choir. The **State Apartments,** on the opposite side of the cas-

tle, are decorated with paintings by Van Dyck and Rubens. Within the same complex is Queen Mary's fabulous **Dolls' House,** designed by Sir Edwin Lutyens. The contents are a magical one-twelfth life size, with one inch books by Kipling in the library. The **Great Park** at Windsor is as fascinating as the castle, with 4,800 acres of lawns, trees, lakes, herds of deer, ancient ruins and Prince Charles—when he is playing polo on **Smith's Lawn.** *St. George's Chapel open daily 10:45AM-3:45PM, closed Jan.; State Apartments (when the Royal Family is not in residence) and Dolls' House open M-Sa 10:30AM-5PM, Su 1:30-5PM, closes at 3PM in winter. Call 075-35-65538 for more information.*

Across the cast iron foot-bridge is **Eton College,** the best known public school in Britain, founded in 1440 by Henry VI. It is best to visit the school when you can see the students in their Eton wing collars and tails. Etonians exude an air of confidence which is quite unrivalled, and it is no suprise that the alumni includes 20 British prime ministers. *Schoolyard and Cloisters are open daily from 2-5PM. Windsor can be reach by train in 23 minutes from Paddington Station (change at Slough for Windsor and Eton Central); or in 50 minutes direct from Waterloo Station to Windsor Riverside. The Green Line bus from Hyde Park Corner takes 90 minutes. Windsor is walking country, but if you want to drive, M4 and then A308 will get you their in an hour.*

King's College

5 **Cambridge.** If you can only manage one excursion to the *palaces of privilege and academe,* choose Cambridge. A few decades younger than Oxford, it is architecturally more cohesive, more beautiful and less interrupted by the city itself. Cambridge is located in a part of England called East Anglia on the edge of the Cam River, and the colleges back on to the River (hence the term *Backs).* The most interesting of the 29 schools at Cambridge are: St. John's, Trinity (founded by Henry VIII); Clare; King's (the chapel has beautiful stained-glass windows, fan vaulting and lofty spires); Corpus Christi; Queen's; Peterhouse and Jesus. The ideal time to visit is May Week, a 10 day period in June when graduating seniors receive their degrees. Festivities take place throughout the city, including a rowing competition on the Cam. Be sure to plan your day

to include evensong in King's College Chapel, and however touristy it may seem, allow yourself to be *punted* on the River Cam along the Backs—it rivals the gondola in Venice in terms of sheer tranquility and beauty. Cambridge is not known for culinary achievement, but you can get a good pub lunch at **Free Press,** which serves imaginative salads and excellent pies. *(7 Prospect Row, Cambridge, 0223-68337).* If you can't get back to London for dinner, take a taxi to **Panos,** which serves a mixture of French and English food and has good grills. Try to book in advance. *(154 Hills Rd., Cambridge, 0223-212958). Cambridge, 54 miles from London, can be reached by train direct from Liverpool Street Station in 75 minutes; by bus from Victoria Station in a little under 2 hours; or by car on M11 to Junction 10 in 90 minutes.*

6 **Oxford.** The Gothic turrets, towers and spires of famous colleges dominate the center of Oxford, which has been a university town since the 1200s. Oxford University (like Cambridge) is a collection of 30 colleges. St. Edmund Hall, Merton and Balliol, built in the 13th century, are the oldest of the colleges. Magadelen (pronounced *maudlen),* the most beautiful, was once home to

student notables from the likes of Wolsey to Wilde. A visit during the academic year (mid-October to mid-May) is most interesting; the colleges are deserted or filled with Americans on summer programs during summer holidays, although the buildings are open all day. Most of the colleges can only be visited in the afternoon during the school year. You won't eat better anywhere in

DAY TRIPS

Magadelen

Oxford—or perhaps in England—than at **Le Petit Blanc,** which serves regional French food with the finest English ingredients. Book now! *(272 Branbury Rd., Summertown, Oxford, 0865-53540). Oxford is 56 miles from* *London and can be reached by train from Paddington Station in 60 minutes (trains leave hourly), or by bus from Victoria Station in 1 hour and 45 minutes. If you are driving, take M40 and A40 (90 minutes).*

7 **Bath.** Elegantly proportioned Bath is as perfect as a novel by Jane Austen, who came here, sipped the water in the Pump Room and captured its grace, elegance and usefulness in *Persuasion.* This Georgian city of terraces, crescents and squares is the most famous spa in England, and worth a visit for its warm springs, Roman ruins, glorious architecture and gently Austenesque atmosphere. The Romans, nostalgic for the warm waters of home, founded Bath in 43AD and stayed for 4 centuries. But it wasn't until the 18th century, when luminaries such as Gainsborough, Queen Victoria and Lord Nelson were regular visitors, that Bath became the fashionable spa town that is remembered today. The Roman baths, among the most striking ruins in Europe, are still the city's major attraction. Excavations nearby have unearthed relics ranging from coins to a sacrificial altar. You can sample water from the fountain in the **Pump Room,** which Dickens said tastes like *warm flat-irons. (Open M-Sa 9AM-6PM, Su 11AM-5PM).* The Georgian perfection of the town is largely the work of two 18th century father and son architects, both named John Wood. The modern architecture, well, close your eyes. Today, smart Londoners come to Bath for the city's renewed cultural life as well as the waters. After its heyday in the 18th century, Bath's reputation went downhill. But the last 2 decades have brought new life to Bath. One of the greatest achievements is the renovation of the **Theatre Royal,** which until a few years ago was a third-circuit theatre. Now it hosts some of the country's top productions before they move on to London. The best place to eat in Bath is **Popjoys.** But you absolutely must book in advance for their fabulous English food, served in the sumptuous house where Richard *Beau* Nash lived with his girlfriend Juliana Popjoy. Everything is fresh and delicious. Be sure to save room for the syllabub, which is as exquisite and English as Bath itself. *(Sawclose, Bath, 0225-60494). 116 miles from London, Bath can be reached in 70 minutes by highspeed train from Paddington Station; by bus from Victoria Station in 3 hours; or by car on M40 to Junction 18, then A46, in 2 hours.*

8 **Winchester.** Ancient capital of England, graceful and unspoiled, and a perfect trip to combine with Salisbury and Stonehenge, only 20 miles away. Winchester was the capital of England for nearly 250 years, from 829 until the Norman Conquest, when the Normans gradually moved the capital to London. King Alfred and the Danes reigned here from 871 to 900, developing Winchester into a great center of learning. Picturesque **High Street,** the center of the city, is lined with a charming medley of buildings dating from the 13th century. Near the end of the street is the **Great Hall** (1235), all that remains of Winchester Castle, demolished in 1644-45. An early fake Round Table of the legendary King Arthur hangs in the hall, which was the scene of many medieval parliaments and notable trials, including that of Sir Walter Raleigh for conspiring against James I. The beautiful early Norman **Cathedral** set in a peaceful close is the longest medieval cathedral church in Europe (556 feet), made to seem longer by its height (78 feet). The best view is from Magdalen Hill, the approach road to Winchester from the east, which emphasizes its setting in the city. Begun in 1079, consecrated in 1093 and partially rebuilt in 1346-66, it contains of wealth of treasures, most striking of which are the 7 richly carved chantry chapels, especially **Bishop Wykeham's Chantry,** in the west end of the Nave, which contains an effigy of the great builder, statesman and founder of Winchester college and New College, Oxford. On the wall opposite are a brass tablet and window to **Jane Austen** (1775-1817) who is buried here. The bronze statues of **James I** and **Charles I** are by Hubet Le Sueur (1685). Under the organ loft in the north Transept is the **Chapel of the Holy Sepulchre** (12th century) with superb wall paintings (c.1170-1205) of the Life and Passion of Christ. The oak screen separating the Choir from the Nave is by **Sir Gilbert Scott,** and the magnificent stalls (1305-10), with their misericords carved with human, animal and monster motifs, are the oldest cathedral stalls in England, except for some fragments at Rochester. The **Library** over the passage between the south transept and the Norman arches of the old **Chapter House** was built in the 12th century and reconstructed in 1668. It contains 4,000 printed books and rare manuscripts, most important of which is the *Winchester Bible* (12th century), one of the finest medieval manuscripts.

If you walk about a miles south of the Cathedral, you will come upon the ancient **St. Cross Hospital**, where the Wayfarer's Dole of a horn of beer and a portion of bread—once a handout to the needy—is still offered to visitors.

Winchester, 65 miles from London, can be reached by train from Waterloo Station in 65 minutes (trains leave 45 minutes past the hours); or by buses leaving Victoria Coach Station every hour for the 2 hour and 10 minute journey. By car, take M3 and A33.

9 **Salisbury.** Wiltshire's country town of Salisbury, 83 miles from London, rests on a plain where the rivers Nadder and Bourne flow into the Avon, quietly expressing the calm beauty of this charming medieval town and its famous cathedral. Salisbury's other major attraction is its convenient location, just 10 miles from Stonehenge, one of the most important prehistoric monuments in Europe.

Classic Salisbury **Cathedral,** consecrated in 1258, is the perfection of English cathedral architecture, made even more beautiful by its majestic spire (c. 1320) rising above the water-meadows beside the Avon. At 404 feet high, it is the tallest spire in England, enchanting the eye with its deceptive lightness—the 6,400 tons of stonework put such a strain on the 4 bearing columns that they are slightly bent. The Avon marks the western side of the Cathedral's grounds, and a 14th century wall of stone from **Old Sarum,** a cathedral which was razed in 1331 to provide building materials for the cathedral close, bounds the other 3 sides. The interior of the cathedral is not as breathtaking as the exterior, due in part to the ruthlessness of Wyatt's renovations (1788-89) in which he removed the screens and chapels and rearranged the monuments in rows. Happily, the restoration by Sir Gilbert Scott in 1859 minimized some of the damage. The cathedral contains tombs of the Crusaders and those who died at Agincourt. Other treasures include exquisite lancet windows with patchworks of glass from the 13th and 15th centuries and a 14th century wrought iron clock which was restored to working order in 1956. The **Cloisters** and beautiful octagonal **Chapter House**, built from 1364 to 1380, were modeled after Westminster Abbey. Many of the cathedral's treasures are displayed in the Chapter House, including one of four exisiting copies of the *Magna Carta,* brought here for safe-keeping shortly after 1265.

A couple of miles west of Salisbury and easily reachable by bus or car is the splendid **Wilton House,** the home of the Earl of Pembroke for more than 400 years, with 17th century staterooms by Inigo Jones. The incomparible art collection includes 16 van Dyck's, hung in the famous double cube room (60 feet long by 30 feet high and 30 feet wide) where General Eisenhower planned the Normandy invasion. *Admission fee. Open Apr-Oct M-Sa 11AM-6PM, Su 1-6PM. Wilton House is 2 miles west of Salisbury, and can*

be reached by bus every half hour in 18 minutes or by car on A30.

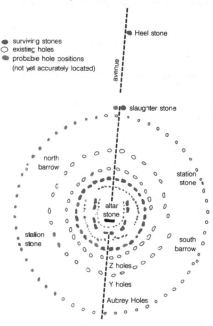

- ● surviving stones
- ○ existing holes
- ● probable hole positions (not yet accurately located)

Heel stone

avenue

slaughter stone

north barrow

station stone

altar stone

station stone

south barrow

Z holes

Y holes

Aubrey Holes

Stonehendge plan showing the solstitial alignment of the axis of symmetry.

Just 10 miles northwest of Salisbury is **Stonehenge,** a must for prehistoric remains buffs. The great, historic structure is one of the oldest and most important Megalithic monument in Europe, dating from between 1850BC and 1400BC. Though the fence around Stonehenge (added for its own protection) makes it look like a captive animal, taking away from the initial impact, the sight of the long, eerie collection of stones is still breathtaking and the way the monument interacts with the sun on certain days of the year is astounding. The stones are arranged in 4 series within a circular ditch 300 feet in diameter. The outer ring, with a diameter of 97 feet, is a circle of 17 sandstones connected on top by a series of lintel stones. The second ring is of bluestones; the third is horseshoe shaped; and the inner ring is ovoid. Within the ovoid lies the **Altar Stone**, made of micaceous sandstone. The great upright **Heelstone** is in the **Avenue**, the broad road leading to the monument. Some of the stones, weighing up to 4 tons each, have been shown to come from the preseli Hills in Wales, a distance of some 135 miles. Stonehenge was at one time believed to be a druid temple, a theory contradicted by the fact that the druids didn't arrive in Britain until c. 250BC. In 1963, British astronomer Gerald Hawkins theorized Stonehenge was a huge astronomical instrument used to accurately measure solar and lunar movements as well as eclipses. Stonehenge is 10 miles northwest of Salisbury on A345.

Salisbury is 83 miles from London, and can be reached by way of a picturesque railway journey, leaving from Waterloo Station 10 minutes past each hour and arriving in Salisbury 90 minutes later. There are 2 bus trips daily from Victoria Coach Station which takes 3 hours, but the bus service in the afternoon from Salisbury is often at awkward times—take the train! The station is a 10 minute walk from the center of Salisbury, If you are driving, take M3 and A30.

HISTORY

Event	Year	Monarch / Dynasty
(BC) Julius Caesar invades Britain.	55-54	
(AD) Roman Conquest of Britain by Emperor Claudius. First London bridge is built.	43	
London is destroyed by Queen Boadicea.	61	
Roman Army withdraws from Britain to defend Rome.	410	
The Vikings invade Britain and create havoc, sacking London as well.	851	
	871	Alfred the Great (871-901)
Alfred the Great occupies London.	886	
	925	Athelstan (925-40)
Canute captures London	1017	Canute (1017-35)
	1042	Edward the Confessor (1042-66)
Consecration of first Westminster Abbey.	1065	
	1066	House of Normandy / Harold (1066)
William the Conqueror crowned at Westminster Abbey.		William I (1066-87)
Fire destroys most of the City and St. Paul's.	1087	William II (1087-1100; probably murdered)
White Tower is completed. William Profus begins to build the Great Hall at Westminster.	1097	
	1100	Henry I (1100-35)
	1135	Stephen (1135-54)
	1154	House of Plantagenet / Henry II (1154-89)
Construction begins on London Bridge, the first stone bridge, completed in 1290.	1176	
	1189	Richard the Lionheart (1189-99; killed in battle)
London establishes rule by mayor.	1190	
	1199	John (1199-1216)
King John signs Magna Carta at Runnymede.	1215	
	1216	Henry III (1216-72)
First Parliament is summoned; English state begins.	1265	
Consecration of present Westminster Abbey.	1269	
	1272	Edward I (1272-1307)
Old St. Paul's Cathedral is completed, half as tall as the present building.	1280	
	1307	Edward II (1317-27; murdered)
	1327	Edward III (1327-77)
Edward III claims the French throne, and the Hundred Years War begins.	1337	
Westminster becomes regular meeting place of Parliament.	1338	
Black death strikes Europe; about half of London's 60,000 citizens die.	1348	
	1377	Richard II (1377-99; deposed and murdered)
Wat Tyler's Peasant Revolt.	1381	
	1399	Henry IV (1399-1413)
	1413	Henry V (1413-22)
Henry V's victory at Agincourt.	1415	
	1422	Henry VI (1422-61; deposed)
Joan of Arc is burned.	1431	
War of Roses begins.	1455	
	1461	House of York / Edward IV (1461-83)
Caxton's printing press is set up at Westminster Abbey.	1476	
Princes probably murdered in the Tower.	1483	Edward V (1483; probably murdered) / Richard III (1483-85)
Accession of Henry Tudor.	1485	House of Tudor / Henry VII (1485-1509)
Henry VIII builds St. James's Palace.	1509	Henry VIII (1509-47)
Fall of Wolsey. Henry VIII moves into York Place (renames it Whitehall) and takes over Hampton Court.	1529	
Henry VIII's Reformation; dissolution of the monasteries, including Westminster Abbey.	1533	
Henry VIII divorces Katherine of Aragon.	1534	
Anne Boleyn is executed at the Tower of London.	1536	
Jane Seymour dies while giving birth to Edward VI.	1537	
Henry VIII marries Anne of Ueres.	1540	
Katherine Howard is executed in Tower of London.	1542	
Henry VIII marries Katherine Parr.	1543	
	1547	Edward VI (1547-53)
	1553	Jane (1553-54; beheaded)
Mary marries Philip II of Spain and reinstates Catholicism. Citizens are martyred at Smithfield.	1554	Mary I
Elizabethan Age begins (45 years)	1558	Elizabeth I (1558-1603)
Mary, Queen of Scots, flees to England (executed 1587). Royal Exchange is set up.	1568	
Shakespeare arrives in London.	1585	
Spanish Armada tries and fails to invade Britain.	1588	
Wood from Theatre in Shoreditch is used to make the Globe of Bankside.	1598	
	1603	House of Stuart / James I (James VI of Scotland; 1603-25)
Guy Fawkes tries to blow up Parliament in Gunpowder Plot.	1605	

Event	Year	Monarch / Political
Pilgrims sail on Mayflower and settle in New England.	1620	
Inigo Jones' Banqueting House is completed.	1625	Charles I (1625-49; beheaded)
Covent Garden is laid out	1631	
Quarrels between Charles I and Parliament lead to Civil War between the Royalists and Parliament. King is forced to leave London.	1642-6	
Charles I is executed at Banqueting House.	1649	
	1653	Commonwealth: Oliver Cromwell, Protector (1653-59) House of Stuart (Restored)
	1660	Charles II (1660-85)
Great Plague; 100,000 die.	1665	
Great Fire destroys half of London; 7 die.	1666	
Christopher Wren designs and builds St. Paul's and 51 London churches.	1666-1723	
	1685	James II (1685-88; deposed and exiled)
Glorious Revolution. William and Mary come to the throne.	1688	William III and Mary I (joint monarchs; 1689-1702)
Bank of England founded	1694	
Whitehall Palace destroyed by fire.	1698	
	1702	Anne (1702-14)
	1714	House of Hanover George I (1714-27)
	1760	George III (1760-1820)
Dr. Johnson's Literary Club is founded.	1764	
Royal Academy of Arts is founded	1768	
Adelphi Theatre is built by Robert and John Adam.	1772	
America declares its independence from Britain	1776	
Lord Nelson dies at the Battle of Trafalgar and is buried in St. Paul's.	1805	
Gas lighting is installed on Piccadilly	1814	
Wellington defeats Napoleon at Waterloo. John Nash lays out Regent's Park, Portland Place, Regent Street and the Mall.	1815	
	1820	George IV (1820-30)
National Gallery is founded	1824	
First Police Force is founded. First London bus.	1829	
	1830	William VI (1830-37)
Barry and Pubin start the Houses of Parliament; completed in 1860.	1835	
London's first passenger railway opens, running from Southwark to Greenwich. London University receives Royal Charter.	1836	
Buckingham Palace becomes permanent residence of the Sovereign.	1837	Victoria (1837-1901)
Nelson's statue is erected in Trafalgar Square. Brunel's Rotherhithe Tunnel (the first under the Thames) is built.	1843	
British Museum is built on grounds of Montagu House.	1844	
Great Exhibition in the Crystal Palace at Hyde Park.	1851	
First mailbox on corner of Fleet Street and Farringdon Street.	1855	
Tooley St. fire, worst since 1666.	1861	
Opening of first underground railway.	1863	
Victoria proclaimed Empress of India.	1887	
Jack the Ripper strikes in Whitechapel.	1888	
Creation of London County Council, giving the city a comprehensive government for the first time.	1889	
First electric railway tube, from the City to Stockwell.	1890	
Tower Bridge, with double drawbridge, is built.	1894	
Queen Victoria's Diamond Jubilee.	1897	
	1901	House of Saxe-Coburg Edward VII (1901-10)
First fleet of horseless carriages. Harrods opens on Brompton Road.	1905	
World War I; London is damaged from Zeppelin air raids.	1914-18	
Women win right to vote.	1918	
General Strike.	1926	
	1936	Edward VIII (1936; abdicated) George VI (1936-52)
World War II; the Blitz; St. Paul's stands among ruins.	1939-45	
Rebuilding of London.	1945-55	
Festival of Britain. Southbank is built as cultural center (Royal Festival Hall).	1951	
	1952	Elizabeth II
Clean Air Act ends fog and smog in Central London.	1956	
Post Office Tower is built.	1965	
New London Bridge and New Stock Exchange completed.	1973	
National Theatre is built.	1976	
Silver Jubilee of Queen Elizabeth.	1977	
Royal Wedding of Prince Charles and Princess Diana. National Westminster Bank is built, at more than 600 feet, the tallest commercial building in London.	1981	
Lady Mary Donaldson becomes first female Lord Mayor.	1983	
Greater London Council abolished.	1986	

ESSENTIALS

Airports. Two airports serve London: **Heathrow** and **Gatwick.** You can get into London easily, inexpensively and relatively quickly from either one. Heathrow is a lot closer to London, but the train service from Gatwick to Victoria Station is fast and easy, so if you can get a cheaper flight that goes into Gatwick, you'd be wise to take it.

Heathrow is 14 miles from central London. You can reach Hyde Park (Knightsbridge Tube) by underground railway in about 40 minutes. If the prospect of taking public transportation seems too daunting, there is a helpful Tourist Information Center in the ticket hall of Heathrow Central Underground (open 9AM-6PM daily), and they will patiently tell you where to go and how to get there. Heathrow Central is on the Piccadilly line and is relatively new. Tubes leave Heathrow about every 8 minutes, and the fare is under £2. The first train to Heathrow leaves King's Cross at 5:30AM Monday to Saturday and at 7:28AM on Sunday. Departures start from Heathrow at 5:07AM Monday to Saturday and 6:49AM Sunday. The last train into London leaves Heathrow at 11:50PM Monday to Saturday and 10:51PM on Sunday. The **Airbus,** a bus service between Heathrow and London (Liverpool St. via Cromwell Road terminal in South Kensington, Piccadilly and Fleet Street), costs a little more (they take dollars and francs) and takes a little longer (50 minutes), but you can see the sky and English cars and buses along the route into London. If it is still too much, relax and take a black taxi into London, and be prepared to pay between £15 and £18 for the spacious tranquility. *For more information, call Heathrow Central Information Center, 730-3488.*

If you are booked on a charter flight, Virgin Airways or People Express, you will probably arrive at **Gatwick.** But no matter how tired you are from the journey, don't take a taxi into London. Fast trains run every 15 minutes from Gatwick and reach Victoria Station in 30 minutes. The trains are in the basement, and even though lifts (elevators) are being built, you will probably have to struggle with your luggage to and from the train, including a flight of steps. Free portering is supposedly available (part of Gatwick's attempt to be popular), but they are not always in evidence. There is also a Greenline bus service which runs every half hour from Gatwick Coach station and takes 70 minutes. *Information desk, 02-933-1299.*

Trains. The whole country is connected to London via British Rail, and there is a circular network of train stations which leads you into the English countryside, or just as far as the suburbs. You can buy tickets at the **British Rail Travel Center** (*4-12 Lower Regent St., SW1*) for all rail travel in Britain and rail and sea journeys to the continent and Ireland. Tickets are not inexpensive, so ask about cheap day returns, special fare tickets, etc. Children under 16 pay half-price and those under 5 ride free.

General Train Information: 246-8030

Paddington Station (for west of England — Oxfordshire, Cornwall — and South Wales): 262-6762

Liverpool Street Station (for East Anglia — Cambridgeshire, Suffolk, Norfolk — and Essex): 283-7171

King's Cross Station (for northeast England and east coast to Scotland): 278-2477

Waterloo, Charing Cross and Victoria Station (for southeast and southern England — Brighton, the coast): 928-5100

Euston Station (for midlands, north Wales, northwest and west coast of Scotland): 387-7070

Victoria Station (for the Continent, including the Venice Simplon Express train, Victoria to Venice; Gatwick Airport):928-5100

London Transport. The only way to become a citizen of a city, albeit a temporary one, is to use public transportation. Mastering the Tube or the bus puts the city at your feet, eases the pressure on the wallet and orients you in a way that taxi rides never will. Various passes are available which save time and money. Most are valid on buses and the underground, and can be bought from underground station ticket offices. The **Travelcard,** a combined bus/underground weekly, is the best value for central London. Travel and information centers are located in the underground stations at Heathrow Central, Euston, King's Cross, Piccadilly Circus, Charing Cross, Oxford Circus, Victoria and St. James's Park.

The Underground. The **Tube,** as it is better known, is fast clean (ish), safe and easy to use (though not as fast and easy as the Paris Metro, as it is older and has greater distances to cover). Tube stations are indicated by the round red and blue London Transport signs. Service starts at 5AM and ends around midnight. Buy your ticket before getting on the train, either from a vendor or machine. Keep your ticket, which you will present to the guard at the end of your journey. (Some exits are becoming automated, but you still must keep your ticket to put through the automatic barrier.) Large-scale maps of the underground network are in each station, and each compartment of the train has a map of the route the train follows. Maddeningly, trains going to various destinations use the same platform, so look at the lit-up sign above the platform as the train pulls in to verify the destination and route. Prices depend on the length of the journey from one zone to another, not from station to station. One ticket takes you to your destination, but there are cheaper fares, such as a cheap day return if you are making a round trip and can travel between certain hours.

The Big Red London Bus. If speed is not the priority, take a London bus. The view of London from the top of a bus is unbeatable, and the bus itself, fire engine red, double-decker, with its roller coaster movements and friendly atmosphere, is one of those essential authentic experiences. People waiting in the queue will help you, and when you get on the bus the conductor will advise you and even tell you when you reach your destination. Find a seat, tell the conductor your destination and he will sell you a ticket. Like on the Tube, the fare is tied to zones, but the bus is cheaper. A Red Bus Rover gives you unlimited bus travel for a day and costs about £2. Also check out the Travelcard. A few buses have been modernized and you pay as you enter, but happily most still have conductors. **Bus Etiquette** is as follows:

1. Only a wedding is more sacred than the bus queue in England. Respect it: find the end and go to it.

2. Bus stops have signs showing the numbers of the buses which stop there, outlines of the bus route, and sometimes a map of the route.

3. If the stop is marked *request,* wave the bus to stop.

4. Smoking is allowed on the upper deck, so the pleasure of being on top has its drawbacks. Legislation to prohibit smoking on buses is *en route.*

5. There is no standing on the upper deck or on the platform.

6. Even though the English do it, don't jump off—or onto—a moving bus.

7. The conductor will come and collect your fare and tell you when you reach your stop if you ask him to.

3 Scenic Bus Routes. The numbers refer to bus routes and are displayed on the front of each bus:

11—King's Road, Sloane Square, Victoria Coach Station, Victoria, Westminster Cathedral, Westminster Abbey, Westminster, Whitehall, Horse Guards, Trafalgar Square, National Gallery, Strand, Law Courts, Fleet Street, St. Paul's.

53—Regent's Park, the Zoo, Oxford Circus, Regent Street, Piccadilly Circus, National Gallery, Trafalgar Square, Whitehall, Horse Guards, Westminster, Westminster Bride, Imperial War Museum, Elephant and Castle.

88—Bayswater, Hyde Park, Marble Arch, Oxford Street, Oxford Circus, Regent Street, Piccadilly Circus, Trafalgar Square, National Gallery, Horse Guards, Whitehall, Westminster, Millbank, Tate Gallery, Vauxhall Bridge.

Taxis. Who has not been in love at one time with a black London taxi? Capacious, timeless and honorable, these shiny black taxis, (nearly all are Austins) are icons of English dependability and integrity. Great travelers consider London taxi drivers the best in the world, and rare is the experience of announcing your destination and getting a blank look. The drivers take tough exams to prove their knowledge of the streets, and have an honor code to take the shortest route, charging only what appears on the meter. A 10 minute journey will cost £3 and a 20 minute journey £5. There is a surcharge for large baggage after 8PM and on weekends and holidays. Tip between 10% and 15%. If you are suspicious beyond a doubt about route or price, take the driver's number and call the Carriage Office (278-1744). A taxi is for hire when the yellow *For Hire* sign is lit. The driver should stop if you flag him down, and if your destination is under 6 miles and within London borders, he must take you.

You can also call a 24-hour **radio cab,** pay for being picked up (the distance required to reach you) and avoid the pleading wait in the street.

Minicabs. These are not black taxis but ordinary cars, available by telephone only. Ask the price when you call and confirm it when the taxi arrives. Minicabs are the best value if you are going a long distance and can be a good value for getting to the airport when you are laden with packages and baggage. The rates for a trip to Heathrow are standard and reasonable. The drivers lack the incredible knowledge of London that black London taxi drivers have, so they do sometimes get lost. *Call Addison Lee, 720-2161; or Abbey Car Hire, 720-2161.*

Driving. Try very hard to avoid it, but if you are renting a car to drive into the English countryside, be prepared for a few nerve-wracking moments in London. One alternative is to call **European Chauffeurs Ltd.** *(580-7183,* who will drive you and your car to a site on your route, getting out of the worst of the city traffic. **Universal Aunts** *(351-5767,* will do the same or you can drive and follow one of their guides. The price for both of these services is around £25. Otherwise, drive slowly and keep saying to yourself *left, left, left* so you remember to drive on the left side of the road.

Renting a car in London is the same as renting a car anywhere in the world. Prices vary greatly, and insurance and VAT add considerably to the cost. A credit card is just about as indispensable as a valid driver's license. You must be over 21, sometimes over 23, and have had your license for over a year.

Expect to pay at least £100 a week. Companies like Hertz and Avis give discounts of up to 50% if you book your car when you buy your ticket. so if you are planning to tour the country, arrange for a car in advance.

Avis: Locations throughout London,
848-8733

Hertz: Locations throughout London,
679-1799

Europcar: Locations throughout London,
950-5050

Geoffrey Davis: Chauffeur driven and luxury cars. Davis House, 129 Wilton Rd., SW1.
834-8484

Camelot Barthropp: Exclusively chauffeur-driven cars. Headfort Place Garage, SW1.
235-0234; Heathrow Airport, 759-1305

Parking. Parking in central London is a nightmare, and police wheel clamps (the Denver Boot) are used with infuriating regularity, especially in Knightsbridge, Kensington and Chelsea. If you are clamped, it will cost you £25, a trip to Marble Arch to pay and a wait of about 2 hours to get unclamped. Be sure and carry an ample supply of 10p and 50p pieces for meters.

Bicycles. An enchanting way to get around London if you can remember to stay on the left side of the street, and if you lock your bike conscientiously. The bus and car fumes are a drag, so try and avoid the main routes. The **London Cycling Campaign** *(Tress House, 3 Stamford St., SE1, 928-7220)* is an excellent source of cycling information. You can rent bikes from:

Savile's Cycle Store. 97 Battersea Rise, SW11. 228-4279

Dial-a-Bike. 18 Gillingham St., SW1.
828-4040

Tours. Bus tours are a good way to get a sense of the lay of the land, but avoid those with recorded commentary. There are 2 basic types of tours: the **panorama,** which is a one-and-a-half to two hour, 18 to 20 mile, non-stop sightseeing tour; and the full and half-day guided tours, which cover Westminster Abbey and the Changing of the Guard in the morning and St. Paul's and the Tower of London in the afternoon.

ESSENTIALS

London Regional Transport is the best bet for the panorama. Tours depart every hour on the hour from Piccadilly Circus and Victoria, 9AM-8PM; Marble Arch (Speaker's Corner) and Baker St. Station, 10AM-5PM, every day except Christmas. There is no need to book; just get on the bus (222-1234). The **Culture Bus** is a terrific idea, even though it is not really a tour. This bus service runs a circular route around the capital and stops at 22 sights, including the British Museum, Madame Tussaud's, the Victoria and Albert Museum, the Tate Gallery, the Tower of London, HMS Belfast, and Harrods. One £4 ticket enables you to hop off and on the yellow Culture Bus all day long. Buses leave every 20 minutes *(834-6732 for more information)*.

The **Harrods** tour is not recommended for panoramas, but it is excellent for half- and whole-day tours, and it includes a civilized lunch at the English restaurant **Locket's** in the heart of Westminster. The tour is expensive (£43), but that includes all entrance tickets, lunch, a good guide, a small number of passengers (limited to 40) and sheer comfort. *Leaves from Harrods (581-3603).*

Boat Trips. The best way to see London, if you are blessed with a warmish, sunnyish day. You can cover the entire 28 snaking miles of the Thames from Hampton Court to Greenwich Palace on one of the passenger boats which spend their days cruising up and downstream from central London. Boats leave from Westminster Pier, opposite Big Ben, and travel upstream to Kew (a one-and-a-half hour journey) every 30 minutes, from 10:30AM-3:30PM. You can also go to Hampton Court via Richmond (a 3 to 5 hour journey) at 10AM, 10:30AM, 11:30AM and 12PM. Boats going downstream to Greenwich (a 45 minute journey) depart every 20 minutes. There is even a trip to the **Thames Flood Barrier,** the world's largest movable flood barrier, which incorporates historical views down river and crosses the Meridian Line. This boat has a licensed bar and hot and cold food and leaves at 10AM, 11:15AM, 1:30PM and 2:45PM. Another great boat trip, especially for children, is the **Zoo Waterbus.** These boats depart from Little Venice, at the end of Blomfield Road, W9, every hour on the hour, from 10AM-5PM, and travel to the zoo along Regents Park Canal. The trip takes 40 minutes, and tickets include a special rate for the zoo.

There is also a one-and-a-half hour cruise aboard the traditionally painted pair of canal boats, **Jason** and **Serpens,** which travel along Regent's Park Canal *(opposite 60 Blomfield Rd., W9, 286-3428).*

Walking. You only really know and love a city through your eyes and feet, and London offers stupendous rewards to the walker. Such distinguished feet as those of Daniel Defoe, Samuel Johnson, James Boswell, John Gay and Thomas Carlyle made walking the streets of London part of their life's work. Look both ways before crossing the street. Far more Americans in London are struck down by cars than by terrorists. Walking tours are listed in the back of the *Times* and in the weekly *Time Out* magazine.

Climate. Believe it or not, London's climate is moderate and mild. It does rain a lot, but the sun also shines a lot, and there hasn't been fog or smog in London for 20 years.

Whatever the season, bring sweaters and jackets for evenings, and raincoats, umbrellas and shoes that are kind to your feet and tolerate long distances and the odd puddle.

Money. Inflation has been sharply checked in the UK, but some things (hotels, gasoline, good restaurants) will always seem cruelly expensive, while others (theatre tickets, woolens, books, antiques) make you feel personally prosperous. The exchange rate varies daily and can be found in the *Times* each morning, but it is best to check with a bank because that is the rate you will actually get. Change your money and traveler's checks in one of the 4 main banks (Barclays, Midland, National Westminster and Lloyds) and not in shops and hotels, where the exchange rate will always punish you. Above all, avoid places such as Chequepoint Services, which invent exchange rates that suggest the dollar resembles the currency of Albania. Banking hours are M-F 9:30AM-3:30PM. National Westminster has a Bureau de Change at Platform 8 in Victoria Station, which is open from 8AM to 9PM daily. American Express *(6 Haymarket, SW1, 930-4411)* is open M-Sa 9AM-6PM and Su 10AM-6PM, and gives a fairly decent rate. You can cash a personal check with an AMEX card for up to $1,000. If you get seriously short of money, you can have money cabled to you at any post office, supposedly in less than 12 hours from the time it is sent. The post office will give you a Girobank check and cash it on the spot when you produce your passport. The English currency is pounds sterling (£). Check it out before you spend it. £1 is a small, thick goldish coin; 50 pence is a large hexagonal silver coin; 10p is large, silver and round; 20p is tiny and hexagonal, and there are 100 pence (p) in a pound. £5 notes are blue, £10 are brown, £20 are purple and £50 are greenish gold. Credit cards are as popular here as they are in America, with Access (the English Mastercard) and Barclaycard (Visa) being the most widely used. Markets and antique dealers give better prices for cash.

Pickpockets. The London that Dickens knew and wrote about has largely disappeared, but pickpockets remain. Watch your bag, keep cash tucked away in a pocket close to your body, and when sitting in cafes, don't put your handbag on the floor by your feet. Also, when trying on clothes, don't leave your bag in the dressing room if you go in search of a larger mirror or another size. Leave large amounts of cash and valuable jewelry in the hotel safe: you haven't thought of a hiding place that they haven't thought of. Still, it is not as bad as Paris or Rome.

Telephones. Red telephone booths are as fundamentally English as black taxis and red double-decker buses. The trouble is that the English think Americans are on the phone all the time. If you are planning to live up to the image, buy a **Phone Card** from a post office. These are particularly useful for international calls and come in units of 10, 20, 40, 100 or 200 at 10p a unit (£1 to £20). They can minimize frustration considerably as more and more phone booths (called phone boxes) are converting to this vandal-proof method. Notices inside the phone booths which accept phone cards only tell you the nearest place to obtain a card. Otherwise, find a phone which takes money (some take

5p, 10p and 50p; while others take only 10p). Payphones are twice as expensive as private phones; all phones in England cost about twice what those in America cost. You can call home collect by dialing the international operator at 152. Other useful phone numbers:

Police, Fire and Ambulance: 99 (no coins needed)

American Express Travel Service: 930-4411

American Embassy: 490-9000

London Directory: 142

US Directory: 155

International Telegrams: 193

America Direct: 0101-area code-number

Weather Forecast: 246-8091

Time: 123

Teletourist (daily events): 246-8041

Children's London (recorded info): 246-8007

Teledata (car trouble, lost keys, general help): 200-0200

Release (legal help): 603-8654

London Transport Lost Property: 486-2496

Taxi Lost Property: 278-1744

SportLine: 222-8000

Lost or Stolen Credit Cards: American Express: 0273-696-933, M-F 9AM-6PM; otherwise 222-9633. Diners' Club: 0252-516-261, 24 hours daily. Mastercard: toll-free 0101-314-275-6690, 24 hours daily. Visa (Barclaycard): 0604-21288, 24 hours daily.

Post Offices. There are main post offices, little news agents, candy shop post offices and enormous branch post offices. Usually the hours are M-F 9AM-5PM, Sa 9AM-12PM. A lot goes on in a post office, including the issuing of pension payments, TV licenses and dog licenses, so the queue to buy a stamp can be rather long. Buy a lot and save time. Rates are always going up. Ask for special issue stamps and you will probably get something pretty.

Telex. British Telecom now runs a walk in telex facility which is open M-F 9AM-5PM. You can send a telex to the States (£1.80 a minute) and receive messages. Messages can be sent and received at any time. *1A The Broadway, St. James's SW1. 222-6155. On weekends and after 8PM, call 836-5432.*

Health. Take out health insurance before you come. Gone are the days when you could get treated free in an emergency. Now you will be treated without questions, then charged at the private patient rate, which can be expensive. England and the US have no reciprocal health agreement. If you haven't arranged for medical coverage before arriving, do so as soon as you get here. Not all hospitals in London have emergency rooms, but the following do:

St. Stephen's Hospital, 369 Fulham Rd., SW10. 352-8161

Charing Cross Hospital, Fulham Palace Rd., W6. 748-2040

St. Thomas Hospital, Lambeth Palace Rd., SE1. 928-9292

Westminster Hospital, Dean Ryle St., Horseferry Rd., SW1. 828-9811

St. Bartholemew's Hospital, West Smithfield, EC1. 600-9000

Royal Free Hospital, Pond St., NW3. 794-0500

For emergency dental care service, call 677-6363 or 584-1008 for a 24-hour referral service.

Toilets. There are never enough public *loos* and they never seem to be nearby. All public buildings (museums, department stores, cinemas and theatres) have loos, and if you are discreet and unobtrusive, you can take advantage of those in large hotels. Pubs and restaurants generally expect you to be a customer. More and more automated loos in the French style are appearing on streets and in parks.

Shopping. Shopping is the single most popular activity with visitors to London, winning out over the theatre, the Changing of the Guard and the Elgin Marbles. Hours are generally Monday to Saturday from 9AM-5:30PM, but small boutiques and antique shops open later and are often closed on Saturday. Many stores close at noon or 1PM on Saturdays. The recent attempt to pass a law allowing Sunday trading failed, so there is almost no shopping on Sundays. Antique shops and shops outside the center of London sometimes close for lunch.

The price marked on an item is the price you pay—no additional taxes are added on at the cash register. Major credit cards are accepted in most shops, though not in all antique shops. It is better to cash your traveler's checks at a bank and pay cash than to use them in a shop unless they are in pounds sterling.

The main shopping shrines are the **West End**, which includes the famous **Oxford Street**, with its large department stores, John Lewis and Selfridges; and **Regent Street** with Liberty and Acquascutum. Just north of Oxford Sreet is **St. Christopher Place**, which has some of London's smartest shops (Margaret Howell, Mulberry) and **South Molton Street** (Browns, Kenzo and Joseph). **Bond Street, Burlington Arcade, Piccadilly, St. James's** and **Jermyn Street** are all in the West End shopping area as well (*see Piccadilly and St. James's sections*). **Covent Garden** is London's newest and liveliest shopping area (*see the Strand section*), while **Soho** is famous for its food shops and fruit and vegetable markets. **Charing Cross Road**, in the same area, has the densest concentration of bookshops. **Knightsbridge** is chic and expensive and ranges from the vast and palatial Harrods to the miniscule boutiques on **Beauchamp Place** (*see Brompton and Cromwell Roads section*). **Chelsea** shopping is wonderfully relaxed and getting better all the time. The area includes the **Fulham Road** and the **King's Road** (*see King's Road section*). **Pimlico** is the place to go for antiques, as are the many London markets.

VAT. The Value Added Tax, at 15% of the marked price, can be substantial. But if you are leaving the UK within 3 months, you can claim back the VAT on many of the items you buy. Make sure the shop operates the over-the-counter export scheme, which involves filling out a VAT707 form (the shop will give it to you along with a stamped, addressed envelope). You must carry the goods for which you intend to collect a VAT refund as hand luggage and present them to UK customs as you leave the country. Customs

ESSENTIALS

will stamp the forms, and then you mail them back to the shop before leaving the country. If you forget and pack the goods, or simply cannot carry them, then you have to show them to the officials when you arrive in the US, get the form stamped there, and mail it to the shop. The shop will send you a check in sterling, which can end up costing a lot to process through your bank. The bigger the purchases, the more sensible this process is.

Museums. Famous, fabulous and free. Spend as much time in them as you can. Most are open all day from Monday to Saturday and in the afternoon only on Sunday. Check to be sure. (Museum of London, Sir John Soanes and the Dulwich Art Gallery are all closed on Monday, for example.)

Pubs. They are as much a part of the English way of life as cafes in France. You have to have at least one drink, and preferably a meal as well, in a pub in order to complete the English experience. The word *pub* is short for *public house,* and if you look above the doors of most of them, you will find the proprietors listed as *landlords.* Pubs are cursed with two drawbacks: they are smoky and they have odd hours, generally daily from 11AM-3PM, 5:30PM-11PM. In the outskirts of London, they tend to open and close a half-hour earlier. Ten minutes before closing, the barman calls *last orders.* Don't expect to get very exotic drinks in a pub (don't even aim for a dry martini). The pub drink is beer, and if you want cold beer, ask for a lager. Ale should be served cellar temperature, like a red wine, and if you are in a *real ale* pub, ask for a *Best Bitter,* which is a not-really-bitter brew with a taste of malt and hops. Specify *half* or *pint.* There is no waitress service, even in pubs which serve food. You have to go to the bar and place your order, pay when you are served, and carry your drinks and food to a table. Pub food has a vocabulary all its own: *Bangers*

are tasty, cold sausages; *chips* are french fries; *crisps* are potato chips; *Cornish pasties* consist of chopped meat and potatoes wrapped in dough and baked; *pork pie,* chopped pork flavored with anchovies, seems to be designed to make you thirsty; and *sausage rolls* are delicious mealy sausages rolled in dough.

Afternoon Tea. Civilized, refreshing and much harder to come by than you would expect in the land of tea and sympathy. All the better hotels offer tea between 3:30-5:30PM, and trying to get a cup earlier or later can be difficult. In fact, trying to get a cup of a tea without the accompanying cakes and sandwiches is close to impossible. There is something to be said for skipping lunch or planning an after-theatre supper and treating yourself to a traditional tea, which will include sandwiches, scones, cakes and pastries.

Tipping. In hotels and restaurants, a 10% to 15% tip is customary. Irritatingly, the service is often included in the bill, and not clearly marked. Check, and if you aren't sure, ask. If the service has been very good, you may wish to leave something on top, which should be left in cash. Taxi drivers expect between 10% and 15%. Porters, cloakroom attendants and hairdressers also expect a small tip. If you are invited for a weekend in the country in a large house where there is a certain standard of grandeur (dressing for dinner) and evidence of a housekeeper or maid, you can leave money on your dressing table just before your depart. (A couple staying two nights usually leaves £5.)

Public Holidays. New Year's Day, Good Friday, Easter Monday, May Day (first Monday in May), Spring Bank Holiday (last Monday in May), August Bank Holiday (last Monday in August), Christmas Day and Boxing Day (Dec. 26). Holidays in England are referred to as Bank Holidays because the banks are shut on those days, and most other places as well.

INDEX

INDEX

INDEX

INDEX

INDEX

THE
SURVEY
OF
LONDON:

Contayning

The Originall, Increafe, Moderne
Eftate, and Government of that City,
Methodically fet downe.

*With a memoriall of thofe famoufer Acts of Charity, which for
Publicke and Pious Ufes have bene beftowed by many Worshipfull
Citizens and Benefactors.*

As alfo all the Ancient and Moderne Monuments erected in the
Churches, not onely of thofe two famous Cities, LONDON and
WESTMINSTER, but (now newly added)
Foure miles compaffe.

Begunne firft by the paines and induftry of IOHN STOVV,
in the yeere 1598.

And now completely finifhed by the ftudy and labour of A.M. H.
and others, this prefent yeere 1633.

Whereunto, befides many Additions (as appeares by the Contents
are annexed divers Alphabeticall Tables, efpecially two:
The firft, an Index of Things.
The fecond, a Concordance of Names.

To order **ACCESS**GUIDES:

1. Circle the price in the table on the other side of this page.
2. Circle the shipping and handling charge that applies to your order.
3. Add the circled prices:

$ _____ order(New York residents add applicable sales tax

$ _____ shipping and handling

$ _____ (total)

4. Write your mailing address below:

_____
Name

_____
Address

_____
City, State & Zip Code

5. Send a check or money order with this coupon to:

ACCESSPRESS Ltd.
59 Wooster Street, 5th floor
New York, NY 10012-4349

Please allow 4-6 weeks for delivery

CREDITS

courtesy Apple Computer

Richard Saul Wurman

Writing and Research
Carla Carlisle *Senior*
Marlene Hamilton *Research*
  Assistant
Pippa Hayes *Research Assistant*

Project Directors
Jean Linsteadt *Editor*
J. Abbott Miller *Art Director*

Production Coordinator
Michael Everitt

Production
Judy Cohen
Maria Giudice
Janice Hogan
Susan Pace
Naoto Sekiguchi
Lisa Victor
Daniel Wiley

Typesetting
Kenneth Ludacer

Word Processing
Immanuel Ness

Cover Photography
Reven T.C. Wurman

Proofreading
Mary Pfister *Index*
Esther Allen

Administration
Jane Rosch *Administrative Director*
Bruce McQueen
Richard Rosch
Steven Cohen

Printing
Ron Zebarth *Northwest Web*

Photocomposition
Walter Kellner *Tru-Colour of Ariz.*

Printing Supervision
Bill Dorich *Graphics Management*

Thanks
London Regional Transport
55 Broadway London SW1H OBD
(London Regional Transport
Underground Map, inside back
cover)

The Society of West End Theatres
Bedford Chambers, The Piazza
Covent Garden, London WC2E
8HQ

Special Thanks
Ken Brecher *Highlights*
Susan Dooley *Museum Bests*
Herbert Fry *London in 1889*
Faustino Galan *Technical Support*
David Gentleman *Illustrations*
Ken Linsteadt *Illustrations*
Colin Forbes *Pentagram Design*
Richard Pilbrow *Theatre Projects*
**James Stirling, Michael Wilford
  and Associates** *Illustrations*
John Weale *London in 1851*

We gratefully acknowledge **Alan
Siegel** and **Siegel & Gale** for
hosting the production of
LONDONACCESS and **Peter
Frishauf** of **SCP** *(Surgical Care
Publications)* for technical support
and workspace.

Richard Saul Wurman, FAIA, is an
architect, graphic designer, carto-
grapher and recipient of Guggenheim,
Graham, Chandler and NEA Fellow-
ships. He is President of Sui Dynasty,
Inc. and T.U.B. The Understanding
Business, Ltd. and has authored, co-
authored and designed more than 35
publications including *Urban Atlas,
Making the City Observable, Cities:
Comparison of Form and Scale,
Various Dwellings Described in a Com-
parative Manner, Yellow Pages of
Learning Resources, Yellow Pages
Career Library, The Nature of Recreation, Notebooks and Drawings of Louis
I. Kahn, Whole Pacific Catalog,* and
*What Will Be Has Always Been-The
Words of Louis I. Kahn.* Mr. Wurman
has been: a member of the policy
panel for the NEA; Chairman of the
1972 IDCA Conference; Co-Chairman
of the 1st Federal Design Assembly,
1973; Co-Chairman of T.E.D. Technology Entertainment Design Communications Conference, 1984; and has
had many university affiliations including Cambridge University, England, USC, UCLA, Cal Poly Pomona,
Yale University, et al. He is a
member of A.G.I. Alliance Graphique
Internationale and is a board member
of the AIGA.

ACCESSPRESS Ltd.
Co-owners
Richard Saul Wurman
Frank Stanton
  President Emeritus CBS, Inc.